An Offer We Can't Refuse

An Offer We Can't Refuse

THE MAFIA IN THE MIND
OF AMERICA

George De Stefano

FABER AND FABER, INC.

An affiliate of Farrar, Straus and Giroux

New York

Faber and Faber, Inc.
An affiliate of Farrar, Straus and Giroux
19 Union Square West, New York 10003

Distributed in Canada by Douglas & McIntyre Ltd.
Printed in the United States of America
First edition, 2006

Library of Congress Cataloging-in-Publication Data
De Stefano, George, 1955–
   An offer we can't refuse : the Mafia in the mind of America / by George
De Stefano. — 1st ed.
      p.   cm.
   Includes bibliographical references and index.
   ISBN-13: 978-0-571-21157-9 (hardcover : alk. paper)
   ISBN-10: 0-571-21157-7 (hardcover : alk. paper)
   1. Mafia—United States.   2. Italian Americans—Social conditions.   I. Title.

HV6446.D43 2005
364.1'06'0973—dc22

                                                          2005012667

Designed by Jonathan D. Lippincott

www.fsgbooks.com

1   3   5   7   9   10   8   6   4   2

To Rob Eisdorfer, *con amore e gratitudine*,
and to my parents:
George De Stefano, Sr., and Angela Di Pietro De Stefano

Contents

An Offer We Can't Refuse

Introduction

The Mafia is dead.

Long live the mafioso.

At the dawn of the new millennium, the Italian American mafia barely resembled its old fearsome self. Beginning in the 1980s, vigorous law enforcement drove gangsters out of many of their traditional rackets and put many of its leaders in prison. In early 2003, Joseph Massino, the Bonanno organization boss and the last purported head of New York's notorious "five families" of crime still at large, was arrested and a year later was convicted on murder and racketeering charges and sentenced to life imprisonment.

Then Massino did something unheard-of for an old-time mafia chief: he broke *omertà*, the venerable code of silence, and became a government witness.

John Gotti, the publicity-loving "Dapper Don," died of cancer in prison in 2002; a year later his brother Peter, his successor as boss, was tried, convicted, and imprisoned.

Vincent "the Chin" Gigante, the Genovese family chief who had eluded justice for years by feigning insanity—how could this mumbling old man shuffling through Greenwich Village in a tattered bathrobe be a cunning crime lord? his lawyers had argued—was also put behind bars. At his sentencing in March 2003, the Chin admitted, to the chagrin of his lawyers and the mental health professionals who had long attested to his impaired state of mind, that it had all been an act.

And among those mafiosi not yet dead or incarcerated, *omertà* further collapsed as wiseguys increasingly chose to do the unthinkable:

spill family secrets to prosecutors rather than stoically accept decades of imprisonment.

Chazz Palmintieri, the Bronx-born actor who has played gangsters in such films as *Analyze This* and *Bullets Over Broadway*, and who grew up in a mobbed-up neighborhood, explains why *omertà* no longer governs mafiosi in their dealings with law enforcement. "Once a DA says to a wiseguy, 'I wish you'd talk to me, 'cause if you don't you will never see the sun for the next fifty years,' whaddaya gonna do? The guy will talk. It's just that way. And by rights, he should talk. Let 'em put you away for forty years, fifty years? . . . People talk. So that's what broke that code of silence."

No wonder an Italian journalist has called the current chapter of the American mafia's history *"il declino del padrino"*—the decline of the Godfather.[1] But if the mob indeed is dying, American popular culture tells a different story, one in which Italian American organized crime— the mafia, La Cosa Nostra, the mob—remains a potent, if troubled and diminished force.

The spectacular success of the HBO series *The Sopranos* currently provides the most compelling testament to the gangster genre's enduring popularity. Created by veteran television writer David Chase (né De Cesare), the series, about a depressed New Jersey mobster whose two "families," his crime crew and his blood relatives, are giving him major *agità*, is the most successful program in the history of cable television. The show has consistently attracted more viewers than its competition on broadcast television, even though the networks reach three times as many homes as HBO.[2] In 2004 *The Sopranos* received an Emmy award for Best Drama Series, the first time a cable show won in that category.

The Sopranos has made stars of the actors who portray the two central characters, Tony and Carmela Soprano: James Gandolfini, previously a character actor with a solid but unspectacular career in movies, and Edie Falco, acclaimed for her roles onstage and in independent films. The show has also served as a virtual employment agency for dozens of Italian American actors and actresses, based in New York and New Jersey.

To cultural critics, *The Sopranos* is not simply an enormously popular and clever spin on gangster mythology. Academics and journalists have acclaimed the show as dramatic literature, reminiscent of Dickens and George Eliot, as a reflection of the concerns and struggles of the postmodern American middle class ("our gangsters, ourselves"),[3] and as a deconstruction of the male supremacy, racism, and fascism inherent in gangsters and gangsterism.

No, *The Sopranos* is no mere entertainment. The show is "so perfectly attuned to geographic details and cultural and social nuances that it just may be the greatest work of American popular culture of the last quarter century," according to *New York Times* critic Stephen Holden.[4] Critical adulation of *The Sopranos* inspired a *Saturday Night Live* spoof that led off with Holden's quote and followed it with ever-more-effusive pretend blurbs from other critics, reaching peak absurdity with "Someday *The Sopranos* will replace oxygen as the thing we use to breathe."

Plaudits for the show also come from psychiatrists enthralled by the portrayal of their profession in the scenes of Tony Soprano's therapy sessions. (There appears to be a general consensus among practitioners that these scenes constitute the most accurate depiction of the talking cure in the history of American popular culture.)[5] The Internet magazine *Slate* runs a feature every Monday in which a group of shrinks comment on the previous night's episode, paying particular attention to the performance of Dr. Jennifer Melfi, Tony's therapist.

The Sopranos also has spawned a growth industry in merchandising, including soundtrack CDs with titles like *Peppers and Eggs*, DVDs of each season's complete episodes, pricey coffee table books, a cookbook featuring recipes purportedly created by the chef in the show's fictional Nuovo Vesuvio restaurant, and even a line of men's clothing. Now male fans can actually dress like Tony S: HBO has signed a licensing pact calling for Zanzara International, a Florida apparel maker, to market dress and casual shirts and silk ties under the Sopranos brand to department stores.[6]

Tony Soprano may be the top dog in today's media mafia, but his arrival on the cultural landscape was preceded, and has been followed, by many other portrayals of mob life. From Rico "Little Caesar" Bandello and Tony "Scarface" Camonte in the 1930s to the Corleones in the 1970s to today's intrapsychically troubled New Jersey "waste management specialist," the mafia gangster has been established as a pop-culture archetype of enduring fascination to Americans of all ethnic backgrounds.

A very partial list of mob movies from the past twenty years includes John Huston's 1985 mafia satire *Prizzi's Honor*, Brian De Palma's *The Untouchables* (1987), David Mamet's *Things Change* (1988), Jonathan Demme's *Married to the Mob* (1988), Martin Scorsese's *Goodfellas* (1990) and *Casino* (1995), *My Blue Heaven* (1990), *The Freshman* (1990), *The Funeral* (1996), *The Don's Analyst* (a little-seen 1997 comedy made for television that was the first film to portray the mafia don as analysand), *Donnie Brasco* (1997), and *Babe: Pig in the City* (1998), featuring a gangster bulldog who speaks in the familiar raspy tones of Don Vito Corleone. These films were followed by *Jane Austen's Mafia!* (1998); the Robert De Niro–Billy Crystal wiseguy-in-therapy comedy *Analyze This* (1999) and its less successful sequel, *Analyze That* (2002); *Mickey Blue Eyes* (1999); *Ghost Dog: The Way of the Samurai* (indie director Jim Jarmusch's bizarrely recombinant mafia/martial-arts/blaxploitation film of 1999); *The Crew, Wannabes,* and *Dinner Rush*, all from 2000; *The Mexican* (2001), with James Gandolfini stretching his talent—here he plays a *gay* gangster; *See Spot Run* (2001); *Made* (2001); *Avenging Angelo* (the late Anthony Quinn's straight-to-video, final film); *Dr. Doolittle 2* (2001), with its animatronic raccoon and beaver mafiosi; and *This Thing of Ours*, from 2003. *Friends and Family* (2003) was a gay mafia farce about two male lovers "out" to their families about their relationship but closeted about their gangster "lifestyle" as mob enforcers.

Shark Tale, a 2005 animated feature from Steven Spielberg's DreamWorks SKG company, broke new ground. The hit film was set in an aquatic underworld, with Robert De Niro and his frequent director, Martin Scorsese, supplying the voices of shark gangsters with Italian names who say things like "fuhgeddaboudit" and "capeesh." Noting the target audience of *Shark Tale*, an Italian American antidefamation organization decried the film as "the first children's mafia movie."

Some of these films are outstanding, others mediocre, and a good number are sheer dreck. But the seemingly endless stream of mob movies attests to the continuing fascination of filmmakers and movie-goers with Italian American crime stories.

Film has been the medium most responsible for creating and perpetuating the Mafia myth. But on television, gangsters with Italian surnames have been a surefire audience draw, from *The Untouchables* in the 1950s to more recent shows like *Crime Story*, *Wiseguy*, *Bella Mafia*, *Oz*, *The Last Don*, and, of course, the *The Sopranos*.

Not surprisingly, mafiosi are a staple of such TV crime dramas as *NYPD Blue* and *Law and Order*. But they also turn up in the most unlikely places. Italian mobsters have invaded children's shows, albeit in a more cuddly form. *The Animaniacs*, a cartoon series, features a group of mafioso pigeons known as the Goodfeathers, and *Muppets Tonight* boasts a Muppet mafia don and his gorilla bodyguard.

Network television, spooked and challenged by *The Sopranos*, has tried to capitalize on its popularity by developing "family"-themed dramas. In 2002, NBC premiered *Kingpin*, focusing on a Latino drug dealer obviously modeled on Michael Corleone—the character's name is Miguel—with a soupçon of Tony Soprano. The show, too derivative of its Italian American forebears yet lacking their quality, didn't fare well with critics or viewers.

Publishing, too, thrives on the mob, with both fiction and nonfiction titles regularly muscling their way onto the bestseller charts. Recent mafia-themed books include Mario Puzo's final novel, *Omertà*; Peter Maas's *Underboss: Sammy "The Bull" Gravano's Story of Life in the Mafia*; *Donnie Brasco: My Undercover Life in the Mafia*, by former mob-busting FBI agent Joseph D. Pistone; *Goombata: The Improbable Rise and Fall of John Gotti and His Gang*, by John Cummings and Ernest Volkman; Stephen Fox's *Blood and Power*; and criminologist James B. Jacobs's *Gotham Unbound* and *Busting the Mob*.

Two of the most perennially popular gangland chronicles are Gay Talese's saga of the Bonanno family, *Honor Thy Father*, and his cousin Nick Pileggi's *Wiseguy*, which Pileggi and director Martin Scorsese adapted for the latter's film *Goodfellas*. Alexander Stille's *Excellent Cadavers* (1995) is a superb account of the Sicilian mafia in the 1980s and its dealings with Italian American organized crime groups.

The Sopranos has generated its own publishing miniboom, with academic and popular titles like *This Thing of Ours: Investigating "The Sopranos"*; *The Psychology of "The Sopranos"*; *"The Sopranos" on the Couch*; *Tony Soprano's America*; and *A Sitdown With "The Sopranos."*

Add to these books many far less distinguished titles—*Joey the Hitman* and *Fuhgeddaboutit: How to Badda Boom, Badda Bing and Find Your Inner Mobster*, to name just two—and you've got an entire genre: mob-lit.

Pop music has been another arena in which performers indulge their (and their audiences') fantasies of mafia outlawhood. Some African American rap performers positively revel in Italian gangster imagery. Snoop Dogg, a professed admirer of Al Pacino and his mobster roles, titled his 1996 hit CD *Tha Doggfather*. "Hip-hop got mad love for [Pacino] since 'The Godfather,' " Snoop Dogg enthused to *Newsweek*.[7]

Snoop isn't the only gangsta rapper to identify with Italian gangsters. Kiam Holley, a New Yorker known to hip-hop fans as "Capone," is, with his partner "Noreaga" (Victor Santiago), one of the music's most popular acts. Master P, a New Orleans–based rap producer, handles a solo artist called Lil' Italy, and a group he dubbed the Gambino Family. Irving Lorenzo, a Queens, New York–born Latino better known as Irv Gotti, is a successful "gangsta" rap impresario—his production company is called Murder Inc., after the notorious Brooklyn-based syndicate—and his pseudonym is an homage to the Dapper Don.[8] The raunchy rapper Lil' Kim released a CD in 2003 titled *La Bella Mafia*, with a track dedicated to John Gotti's novelist daughter Victoria and "the whole Gotti family."

The pervasiveness of mafia imagery extends even to advertising. A 2001 TV commercial from the U.S. Dairy Council depicted two stereotypical Italian thugs, one named "Vinnie," who couldn't break their victim's bones because the calcium in milk had made them too strong. Coca-Cola has exploited Chazz Palmintieri's tough guy image in television commercials for Vanilla Coke. A print advertisement in favor of arts education in schools placed by the Ad Council and Americans for the Arts claims that the great Italian Renaissance painter Caravaggio was "a guy" whose life "was filled with the turbulence and excess of more than a dozen Mario Puzo novels." The ad asks, "But does the average kid on the street even know who Caravaggio is? Fuhgedaboudit."

Beyond its origins as a Sicilian word denoting organized crime, "mafia" has become a general term for any semisecretive association, not necessarily criminal, that wields or is perceived to wield inordinate power. Homosexual producers, agents, and other film executives are said to make up a "gay mafia" or "lavender mafia." An episode of the popular NBC sitcom *Will and Grace* focused on the character Jack's fear of the gay mafia, whose Godfather turned out to be none other than Elton John.

It seems ironic that the mafia is flourishing in popular culture at a time when Italian American organized crime is on the decline. As criminologist James B. Jacobs reports in *Gotham Unbound*, vigorous law enforcement has purged La Cosa Nostra from many of the labor and industrial rackets that used to be its main source of wealth and power. Now, other ethnic crime syndicates, whether Russian, South American, or Asian, are commonly referred to as mafias. Not only must Italian gangsters share the name they once owned with Russian, Colombian, and Asian crime syndicates, but these non-Italian crime groups are challenging the remaining Italian American gangs for control of the illicit activities the latter used to dominate.

But perhaps it's not surprising that the Mafia myth seems so powerful while the real mafiosi are comparatively hamstrung. The cowboy became a figure of American mythology, celebrated in popular culture, after the West was "won" for white settlers. Although the American mafia is now a shadow of its former self, American popular culture tells a very different story. "The mystique of the Mafia exists even when the Mafia doesn't," observes novelist and journalist Anthony Mancini. "It's just too good a myth to abandon."[9]

The roots of the movie mobster lie in the social history of the late nineteenth and early twentieth centuries, when southern Italian immigration to America was at its height. Most of the immigrants came from Naples, Calabria, and Sicily, underdeveloped regions where poverty and weak civil authority had fostered organized criminal activity. Before and during the early years of immigration, the European and American press reported the Italian government's attempts to suppress southern Italian crime groups, the Neapolitan *camorre*, the Calabrian 'Ndrangheta, and the Sicilian *mafie*.

The first film image of the Italian immigrant, however, was the simple newcomer happy to be in "dis-a beeyootiful America," appearing in John Ford's 1924 silent film *The Iron Horse*. This new arrival might be a voluble barber, a pushcart vendor, or a good-natured waiter. But whatever his job (and it was always a "he"), he was a stock character with no life of his own.

The classic 1930s films *Scarface* and *Little Caesar* represented the birth of the mobster archetype—or stereotype, as many Italian Americans complain. Before those cinematic milestones, movie gangsters were generally Irish Americans, often played by James Cagney, in films like *Public Enemy*. The Celtics often had a cocky, roguish charm, but the Italians who replaced them as Hollywood's favorite bad boys were portrayed as sinister and utterly amoral. As critic John Mariani has observed, "The real creeps all had vowels at the end of their names."[10]

Ever since, southern Italian criminals have functioned in pop culture as the *echt*-gangsters, the ones who invented organized crime and who have given it a certain dark, old-world panache and mystique that audiences of diverse backgrounds find irresistible. The early Hollywood films set the standard that was further developed by gritty crime melodramas like *Kiss of Death*. In the 1970s the gifted directors Francis Ford Coppola and Martin Scorsese elevated the genre to new heights of artistry with *The Godfather* and *Mean Streets*. Their gangsters were not just vicious thugs; they had, in addition to a southern Italian cultural specificity lacking in earlier portrayals, greater psychological and behavioral complexity. Some even had moral conflicts about their criminality.

Why do stories about Italian American organized crime continue to fascinate so many Americans? Many explanations have been offered for their perennial popularity. Gangsters, noted critic Robert Warshow, are the " 'no' to the great 'yes' that is stamped so large over American culture."[11] They say that bourgeois society doesn't work, and that it's better—more fun, more rewarding—to be bad than be an upright citizen. Mafiosi act out the yearning of the law-abiding to flout society's conventions, to be an outlaw. But as *Sopranos* creator David Chase has said, gangsters, or at least the characters in his show, do want to be bourgeois. They've just taken an unorthodox route to upward mobility.

The western is considered by many to be the precursor to the gangster film. Like tales of the old West, mob movies are a modern story of America's transformation from a frontier society to an industrialized one in which new ethnic groups had to struggle, sometimes violently, to claim their share of the American pie. That explanation, however, doesn't address the enduring popularity of the genre in a postindustrial society where the conflicts of the early twentieth century immigrant era have been largely resolved.

It may simply be that mafia movies, when they are well done, appeal to audiences because they contain everything that concerns and excites us—family, sex and romance, power, betrayal, and violence. They epitomize what film critic Pauline Kael famously identified as the essential concerns of American movies: "kiss kiss bang bang." Add to the sex and violence *Mangia, mangia*, since food—the preparation and lusty enjoyment of southern Italian cuisine—is one of the essential tropes of the genre.

The figure of the mafia don may speak to a less salutary part of our nature, the psychological need to surrender one's personal autonomy to a powerful authority figure, whether a grand inquisitor, God, or Don Corleone. Some of us identify with powerful mobsters "not just because we have a wish to dominate and command but because we have a wish to attach ourselves to power through submissiveness and obedience."[12]

Whatever the Mafia myth signifies to Americans in general, it has particular meaning for Italian Americans. As sociologist Daniel Bell observed in his study *The End of Ideology*, crime has been a route to upward mobility for other ethnic minorities, particularly Jewish and Irish immigrants.[13] As Tony Soprano has said, "My father was in it, my uncle was in it. There was a time there when the Italian people didn't have a lot of options."[14]

But the association with criminality has clung to Italian Americans so tenaciously that many Americans, regardless of their ancestry, cannot see Italians through any other lens than that of La Cosa Nostra.

Like many Italian Americans, I've had firsthand experience of the tendency of *gli americani* to conflate "Italian" and "mafia." Some years ago I phoned a corporation located in a Southern city on business. The woman who answered asked me to repeat my name, and to spell it. "That's Eye-talian?" she asked. When I replied in the affirmative, she exclaimed, "Why, you must know the Godfather!" Even though I am a middle-class professional with a graduate degree who has never even met a gangster, the fact that I was an Italian American from New York signified only one thing to her: mafioso.

Italian Americans have a paradoxical status in American society. They constitute one of America's largest ethnic groups; nearly 16 million people identified themselves as being of Italian ancestry in the 2000 census. The figure represents an increase of roughly 9 percent over the 1990 census, making Italian Americans the only European ethnic group whose reported numbers actually grew. This defies the trend for individuals of European descent to identify themselves as American rather than belonging to a specific ethnic group or ancestral heritage.

Members of this large, apparently growing, and highly visible ethnic group have distinguished themselves in business, politics, medicine, sports, entertainment, and the arts. But in popular culture Italian Americans are depicted mainly via several related stereotypes: as vicious criminals (any mafia movie or TV show), boorish and bigoted lowlifes (see the films of Spike Lee), or lovable buffoons (studly and stupid Joey Tribianni on TV's *Friends* and its spin-off, *Joey*). These types are by no means mutually exclusive; Tony Soprano's character incorporates all three.

Other minorities have been invisible or grossly caricatured in popular media. African Americans were demeaned as "Toms, Coons, Mulattoes, Mammies, and Bucks," to borrow the title of Donald Bogle's famous study of black stereotypes in the movies. Native Americans were bloodthirsty savages, Asians were wily and inscrutable, and gays were simpering sissies or psycho killers. But in recent decades portrayals of these groups have become more diverse and true to life.

Italian Americans, however, continue to be defined mainly through the tiny minority of criminals known as gangsters, mobsters, mafiosi, goodfellas, and wiseguys, and through the related stereotype of the crude, sexist, and violence-prone "gavone." In the popular view, Italian culture equals mafia culture, not surprising when characters such as Tony Soprano, and Michael Corleone before him, are depicted in all their ethnic specificity.

Irish American author Terry Golway has observed, "No doubt there are some, perhaps even many, films and books with Italian-American themes that do not feature organized crime. No doubt there are many Italian-American film or television characters who are not made to sound like rejects from *Saturday Night Fever*. But it seems fair to say that *The Godfather* trilogy, *Goodfellas*, and now *The Sopranos* have inextricably linked Italian Americans with organized crime, at least in the mind of our pop-culture consumers."[15]

Italian Americans have an ambivalent relationship to the mafia image. Many protest these portrayals, claiming the gangster genre defames them. The National Italian American Foundation (NIAF) has denounced *The Sopranos* as a grotesque caricature. A Chicago Italian American organization filed a lawsuit against the show under an Illinois ethnic defamation statute. Another advocacy group, the New Jersey–based One Voice, gave its "Pasta-tute Award" to David Chase, the Italian American creator of *The Sopranos*. And any newspaper or magazine article that praises the artistry of Chase's show will inevitably elicit letters to the editor from outraged Italian Americans.

The antagonism toward *The Sopranos* sometimes verges on the hysterical. Organizers of New York City's annual Columbus Day Parade in 2002 refused to permit two cast members from the show to march in the parade. The actors, Lorraine ("Dr. Jennifer Melfi") Bracco and Dominic ("Uncle Junior") Chianese, were to be guests of Mayor Michael Bloomberg. When they were banned from the parade, Bloomberg declined to participate and instead took his spurned *Sopranos* stars to lunch at an Italian restaurant in the Bronx.

At a NIAF-sponsored forum on *The Sopranos* held in New York City in May 2001, Professor Joseph Scelsa, director of the Italian American Institute of the City University of New York (CUNY), described mafia stereotyping as a "holocaust" for young Italian Americans, while Camille Paglia, a pugnacious cultural critic known for her disdain for identity politics and what she perceives as a tendency of minorities to engage in "victimology," decreed that "they"—a purported anti-Italian liberal elite comprising media and academic figures—"would never do this [ethnic stereotyping] to Blacks or Jews."[16]

Many other Italian Americans, however, avidly consume mafia movies and TV shows. They often experience a thrill of recognition in the depictions of Italo-American life that are as central to the popularity of these entertainments as the conniving and killing, as when Carmela Soprano says, "Anyone want some of last night's *sfogliatella*?," pronouncing the pastry's name in the Neapolitan dialect that virtually all Italian Americans recognize, or when *Sopranos* mobster Paulie Walnuts, seething with resentment over the high-priced caffe latte and espresso at a Starbucks-like coffee bar, exclaims, "We created this stuff! How come we're not getting a piece of this action?"

In fact, substantial numbers of Italian Americans seem to fantasize about being members of the eponymous crime clan. Several thousand of them, done up in what they apparently regarded as mafia high fashion (shiny suits and pinky rings on the men, big hair and tight dresses on the women), auditioned for parts in the show during an open call held during the summer of 2000.

One of the most prominent of Italian Americans, former New York City mayor Rudolph Giuliani, demonstrates that this ambivalence isn't confined to the average paisan. Giuliani liked to boast that his administration had succeeded in driving the mob out of several of its key rackets in organized labor and industry. "We're sending the clear and unequivocal message," the prosecutor-turned-politician said in a 1996 speech, "that we do not tolerate organized crime in the Fulton Fish Market, the carting industry, the San Gennaro festival, or anywhere."[17]

But though the ex-mayor may deplore real gangsters, he is a *Godfather* devotee who reportedly does a dead-on Vito Corleone impression. A vocal fan of *The Sopranos*, he even attended the premiere of the show's third season at Radio City Music Hall. During his second term as mayor, Giuliani attempted to cut off city funding to the Brooklyn Museum because it had exhibited a painting he regarded as anti-Catholic. But he rejects any criticism that by proclaiming his enthusiasm for gangster stories he acquiesces in the defamation of people of his own ethnicity.

It's also no secret that it is often Italian Americans themselves who write, direct, and act in these films and TV shows, which makes Italian American stereotyping different from that of other groups. (It should be noted, however, that these artists function in an entertainment industry in which they usually are the hired hands, not the executives.) Some who have achieved considerable success portraying mobsters, whether as actors, writers, or directors, have had a hard time bank-rolling Italian American projects that were not gangland dramas. The actor and director John Turturro, noting that it took him five years to raise the money to make *Mac*, his film about his father and uncles, construction-workers-turned-homebuilders, said, "If the movie had been about three brothers who were criminals, I would've had the money like that."[18]

Are the Italian Americans who produce these works self-hating or deracinated? Or are they ethnic Americans secure enough in their as-similated status that they feel free to explore the darker side of their group's experience? Perhaps they are just astute artists who are catering to the marketplace and the seemingly insatiable appetite of movie audi-ences for gangster stories. But even if one allows that they are catering to market forces and a well-established audience, their work, with its emphasis on dehumanizing brutality, does promote a skewed vision of Italian American life and culture. Robert Viscusi, a New York author and professor who founded the Italian American Writers Association, an organization dedicated to nurturing and promoting the diversity of Italian American culture, argues that these artists waste their talent "giving new life to old nightmares."[19]

But mafia images of Italian Americans differ from most stereotypes in another way besides the fact that they are often perpetuated by their ostensible victims. The fascination of non-Italians with the mafia actu-ally contains an element of admiration for Italian Americans. For some *americani*, the effect of decades of gangster movies and TV shows may be a belief that people of Italian ancestry are more likely to be involved with criminal activity than other groups. But it often seems that fans of *The Godfather* or *The Sopranos* want to be Italian Americans, or what they believe Italian Americans to be like, based on the images fed them by the entertainment industry. They love the trappings of the mob genre: the colorful nicknames, the bawdy humor, the food fetishism, the adventure and romance of a secret society of males who flout soci-ety's conventions and follow their own code. Even the violence is titil-lating, because who hasn't felt the urge to "whack" an enemy?

The identification of Italian Americans with organized crime is so entrenched that even though more recent immigrant groups have established crime gangs, some can't imagine them ever displacing the Italians, in actual criminality or in popular culture. *New York Times* columnist Clyde Haberman observed, tongue-in-cheek: "Let's face it, more recent arrivals have simply not held their own. The Russians, sad to say, have been a keen disappointment. You keep reading how their mobsters are fearsome, how they can be brutal, how they have taken over entire New York neighborhoods from the old Mafia of Sicilian origin. That may be so. But seriously, can you name a single Russian gangster? Can you imagine, at this point, anyone proposing a television series called 'The Sopranoffs'?"

Haberman observed that "a logic-bending romanticism has attached to [gangsters]. All you have to do is write a screenplay or television script containing any or all of the following words—yo, 'ey, badda-bing, fuhgeddaboudit, capeesh—and the odds are good that you've got yourself a show. You don't think so? Geddoudaheah."[20] But Haberman's only half right. If all you do is mix and match the genre's clichés, you've got a lousy mob movie. The genre endures, despite fallow periods, because gifted artists—Coppola, Scorsese, Chase, and a few others—keep finding ways to reinvigorate it.

Once my initial indignation passed, I realized that the Southern woman who had said, "You must know the Godfather!" wasn't deliberately insulting me. "It was such a great movie!" she added. Captivated, like countless other Americans, by Coppola's film, she couldn't imagine that I would be offended by being associated with the world it depicted.

I began by declaring that Italian American organized crime is on the wane. Few experts dissent from this conclusion, but those who do point out the mafia's adaptability: run out of many of their traditional rackets, some gangsters have found new scams in stock market swindles and health care fraud. It seems, however, that law enforcement has kept up with this trend, tearing down these new profit centers almost as quickly as wiseguys set them up.

Pop-culture portrayals of the mob also have kept up with organized crime's shifting fortunes; *The Sopranos* cannily incorporates the *declino del padrino* as a recurring theme. The mafia's rise and fall, in fact, has been a leitmotif of some of the best-known and -loved mob films, including *The Godfather*. Regardless of how much life is left in real gangsterism, media mafiosi don't yet seem an endangered species.

Throughout this book, the word "mafia" appears in both capitalized and lowercase forms. As most experts now recognize that there is no single, centrally directed criminal conspiracy known as "the Mafia," I use the uppercase only in quotation, or when I refer to the pop-culture phenomenon I call the Mafia myth. My own preference is for the lowercase "mafia," as linguistic shorthand for Italian American criminal organizations, both here and in Italy.

This book will explore the mafia genre as an enduring pop-culture mythology that has a special significance for Italian Americans, as it is inextricable from the social history of Italian immigrants and their descendants. I have not written, however, a comprehensive history of Italian Americans, or of Italian American organized crime. But it is impossible to understand the mythology without some familiarity with the social terrain from which it emerged.

My treatments of both Italian American and mafia history are selective, interpretive, focusing on key events and issues, often from my particular perspective as a third-generation Italian American, the grandson of poor southern Italians who came to America during the mass migration of the early twentieth century. I grew up in an Italian American milieu, and for much of my adult life I have been thinking and writing about the complexities of my ethnic heritage. But I am also a gay man with left-of-center political beliefs, and I view the mafia, Italian American experience, and media representations of both from a point of view infrequently heard on these topics. For example, I acknowledge Italian traditions of progressive political activism, when much commentary about Italian American politics paints this ethnic group as uniformly conservative. And in my treatment of gangster entertainment, I consider gender, sexuality, and homosexuality, since movies like *The Godfather* and shows such as *The Sopranos* are about what it means to be a man or a woman perhaps as much as they are about violence, ethnic identity, and baked ziti.

Nor is this book meant to be an encyclopedic history of the enter-

tainment industry's depictions of Italian American organized crime, although I do trace the gangster genre's development and explore in
some depth the two key "texts" of mob entertainment, *The Godfather*
(both Mario Puzo's novel and Francis Ford Coppola's trilogy of films)
and that cable TV show that could have been called *Son of The Godfather* if its name wasn't *The Sopranos*.

My intent, then, is to explore a myth "too good to abandon," in
which a small piece of one group's historical experience has come to
overwhelm the larger picture, as in a family portrait in which the
gavone cousin Paulie bum-rushes the camera and blocks the other relatives in the viewfinder. The result is a skewed portrait to which the
family might object, but one from which outsiders can't avert their
eyes. And, truth be told, though the family might be touchy about others seeing that photo, they might look at it themselves from time to
time, enjoying Cousin Paulie and his antics as a guilty pleasure.

Vito Corleone's "I'm gonna make him an offer he can't refuse" long
ago became a cliché. (It's even an entry in *Bartlett's Familiar Quota-
tions*.) But the overfamiliar line from *The Godfather* expresses not only
mafia business philosophy but the relationship between the gangster
genre and generations of moviegoers, television viewers, readers, pop
music fans. For close to a century, we have been seduced by, and been
unable to refuse, the dangerous allure of Little Caesar, Don Corleone,
and Tony Soprano. Our attraction to them, and the longevity and pervasiveness of their presence on the cultural landscape, says a lot about
all of us, and about our fears, wishes, and desires.

3771290

1

Italians to Italian Americans: Escaping the "Southern Problem"

O Mafiosi,
Bad uncles of the barren
Cliffs of Sicily—was it only you
That they transported in barrels
Like pure olive oil
Across the Atlantic?
        —Sandra Mortola Gilbert[1]

From the late nineteenth century to the mid-1920s, southern peninsular Italy and Sicily lost so many of its sons and daughters to emigration that their departure has been likened to a hemorrhage. Among the millions of impoverished, landless, often illiterate emigrants were my grandparents, the De Stefanos from Avellino, near Naples, and the Di Pietros from eastern Sicily. They left—no, *escaped* —a world where they had been politically disenfranchised, oppressed by the *latifondisti* (big landowners), the central government in faraway Rome, and the Church, whose priests counseled humble acceptance of their plight, in the hopes of better times in *paradiso*. The lot of my forebears and of so many other Italian Americans was unemployment, famine, disease, and natural disasters like the earthquakes that could devastate entire towns of the Mezzogiorno, as the regions south of Rome are collectively called.

This mass migration was unparalleled in European history, and to this day no other nation, barring outright religious persecution or ethnic pogroms, has lost so many of its inhabitants to emigration as Italy.[2]

Mario Puzo, whose *Godfather* is perhaps the best-known fictional account of the southern Italian immigration experience, observed, "The main reason for this enormous flood of human beings from a country often called the cradle of Western civilization was a ruling class that for centuries had abused and exploited its southern citizens in the most incredible fashion. And so they fled from sunny Italy, these peasants, as children in fairy tales flee into the dark forest from cruel stepparents."[3]

The exodus of southern Italians began barely twenty years after the unification of Italy in 1861. Before the Risorgimento, Italy had been a patchwork of states ruled by the Vatican and by foreign powers. Southerners were hopeful at first that the new Italian state would end the political tyranny and economic exploitation that had been their lot for centuries. But it quickly became apparent that the new central government, dominated by men from the northern region of Piemonte (Piedmont), would be no more benevolent toward the impoverished peasants, artisans, and urban working poor of the southern regions than had been their foreign rulers.

The newborn Italian state, in fact, turned out to be even tougher on the southern poor than the Spanish and French Bourbons and the other foreigners who had ruled the Mezzogiorno. Giuseppe Garibaldi, who led the insurrection against the Bourbons, won the trust and support of southern Italians eager to throw off Bourbon rule. But Garibaldi was a military figure; he was not adept in either politics or constitutional law. Sicilian landowners pressured him to abandon the promises of land reform that had secured the support of southerners for his revolt. And once the Bourbon army was no longer a threat, Garibaldi's troops fired on peasant rebels, thereby sending the landowning class the clear message that his forces "were defenders of order, not of social revolution."[4]

Before the Risorgimento, southern Italy had low taxes, negligible debt, and inexpensive food. When the South lost its autonomy after 1861, taxes rose steeply. The new national government not only imposed a heavy tax burden on the South but also conscripted its sons into the Italian army. Landowners controlled local elections, since peasants were not allowed to vote. Even the appropriation of the Church's vast land holdings and its wealth by the government worsened the situation of the southern poor, as the new tenancy terms were more onerous and it became increasingly difficult to obtain credit. In the 1880s, when the government imposed new tariffs on imported goods, Italy's trading partners retaliated. The loss of export markets hit the Mezzogiorno particularly hard, as capital was diverted from southern agriculture and invested in northern industry.[5]

Southern Italians quickly discovered the falseness of the Risorgimento's promises of liberal democracy and respect for the human rights of the citizens of the entire Italian nation. The new government's attentions were focused on the interests of the North at the expense of the southern regions. (For example, the Italian government concentrated nearly all of its water control and irrigation projects in the North, even though such assistance was desperately needed in the South.)[6] And in the South, social relations remained oppressive, with landowners exerting near-total power over the landless, in what can only be likened to a master-slave relationship.

The callous injustice of the new order was compounded by the central government's practice of attributing the ills of the Mezzogiorno to a "southern problem." The Marxist theorist Antonio Gramsci, a Sardinian, described the Italian stereotypes of the North versus the South:

. . . the South is the ball and chain that prevents a more rapid progress in the civil development of Italy; Southerners are biologically inferior beings, either semi-barbarians or out and out barbarians by natural destiny; if the South is underdeveloped it is not the fault of the capitalist system, or any other historical cause, but of the nature that has made Southerners lazy, incapable, criminal and barbaric.[7]

The antipathy between northern and southern Italy had deep historical roots. The North

was proud of the glorious culture it had produced during the Renaissance. It had entered the industrial age and was dreaming the nineteenth century's dreams of Progress. The South had remained unchanged and clung to its family system and its me-

dieval codes of Byzantines, Normans, and Arabs. These were the
cultures that had influenced the *Mezzogiorno* . . . and not the
French and German cultures that had influenced the North.[8]

Social scientists elaborated the doctrine of innate southern Italian
inferiority in tracts such as Alfredo Niceforo's *Contemporary Barbarian
Italy* (1898), which portrayed the peoples of Sardinia, Sicily, and the
southern mainland as primitive, much less evolved than the peoples of
central and northern Italy. Niceforo and other "sociologists of posi-
tivism," as Gramsci called them,[9] reduced southerners to "alleged facts
of positivist sociology (rates of crime, education, birth rate, mortality,
suicide rate, and economy)," and grounded their putative scholarship in
racist biology—citing, for example, the allegedly different cranial sizes
of northerners and southerners.[10]

Given the failures of the new Italian constitutionalism to guarantee
the rights of southerners, and the northern racism toward the people of
the Mezzogiorno, it is hardly surprising that the main effect of the
Risorgimento on the South was to "mangle the life of the people of
Southern Italy, who at the time of national unification constituted at
least two-fifths of the population of Italy."[11]

There was armed resistance by southerners to the oppressive new
order. These rebellions were put down, often with horrific violence,
and their adherents invariably were described in the Italian press as
bandits and brigands. But, as legal historian David A. J. Richards observes, under the newly created national government,

> one aspect of the promises of Italian liberal nationalism was
> met, the extension to the people of the South of a right they had
> not enjoyed under previous governments, namely, the basic
> right of movement (including the right to emigrate). Respect for
> at least that basic human right enabled the people of the South
> reasonably to address and make a choice (namely, of political al-
> legiance) that they had not previously been able to make.[12]

That choice was to leave an inhospitable homeland, where they had
been abused and denigrated, and told it was their innate inferiority that

caused their suffering. Towns and villages were depopulated, as southern Italians fled the grinding poverty, hunger, and political oppression they called *la miseria*, to seek *pane e lavoro*—bread and work—in *Lamerica*. Throughout southern Italy, "Wherever people were leaving for America, there was the cacophony of families separating, crying, entreating, promising, and the din of children shouting and laughing, too young to comprehend the poignancy of the farewells."[13] The emigrants left in overcrowded ships where conditions were hardly fit for cattle, much less humans. Most could only afford to travel in steerage, the section of the ship far below decks and near the rudder. Passengers were packed into compartments holding at least three hundred people. "Women traveled without husbands, men traveled alone, and families were installed in small cubicles, each passenger allotted a berth that served both as bed and storage place."[14] There was only saltwater for washing, and the smell of human waste often permeated the area.

After having endured the hardships of their voyage across the Atlantic, the emigrants found themselves in New York, where they faced an uncertain reception. Being largely unskilled and of rural origin, they were poorly equipped to succeed in the industrializing American economy. Nearly half of those who arrived between 1900 and 1914 were illiterate, the highest rate of the eleven largest ethnic groups arriving at Ellis Island.[15] In addition, many suffered from contagious diseases, such as cholera and tuberculosis; these unfortunates were sent back to Europe. The southern Italian immigrant, then, had only one advantage upon arrival in the *strano paese* (strange land) of America: a fierce determination to work hard for his family.

Unscrupulous Italians who had already established themselves in America took advantage of the new arrivals' eagerness for work. Waiting on the docks for the emigrants to disembark, these newly minted *americani* recruited their *paesani* into packaged labor gangs, a form of contract labor known as the *padrone* or boss system. "The *padrone* then sold the gang as a labor package to an American business firm, collecting from both ends [from the workers and employers] for signing away the sweat of his countryman's brow below the market price."[16]

Late in the nineteenth century, the United States enacted legislation meant to eradicate the evils of the *padrone* system by forbidding the importation of foreign workers under any type of contract. But the law's complexity, and its failure to define what constituted a contract, made enforcement extremely difficult. A *padrone* could easily circumvent the law by substituting oral agreements for written ones. The *padrone* system lasted through the peak years of Italian immigration, waning only when the numbers of Italian immigrants in the United States were so high that any newcomer could find assistance in obtaining work, and a place to live, without having to rely on a *padrone*.[17]

The *padrone* system wasn't the only instance of Italian American *prominenti* acting against the interests of the impoverished newcomers. "Italian-language newspapers opposed the formation of labor unions and attacked social reforms that would have aided their less fortunate countrymen," observed Mario Puzo.[18] Puzo overlooks, however, the actual labor organizing and political radicalism of many southern Italian immigrants. The martyred anarchists Nicola Sacco and Bartolomeo Vanzetti and the labor activist Carlo Tresca—assassinated in 1944 by a mafioso—are some of the most famous of immigrant radicals. But thousands of men and women from the Mezzogiorno established a diverse, vibrant, and militant left-wing movement, comprising the full spectrum of radical ideologies, from anarchism and syndicalism to democratic socialism to communism. In virtually every substantial Italian immigrant community, leftists established Italian-language newspapers with names such as *Il Proletario* and *La Voce del Popolo*.

My grandfather, Giuseppe (Joe) Di Pietro, from Ragusa, Sicily, was part of this radical immigrant world. My first exposure to left-wing ideas, in fact, came in conversations we had in the mid-1960s about the Vietnam War and the exploitation of working people under capitalism. Three decades later, when I brought a friend from Sicily to dinner at my parents' home, my mother waxed nostalgic about her father. And the first thing she mentioned to our Sicilian guest was, "Well, Salvo, you know my father was a communist . . ."

Fear of foreign-born radicals fueled virulent anti-immigrant sentiment in the years immediately following World War I. Nativists, united under the slogan "America for Americans," demanded new laws to protect the nation from southern and eastern European immigrants, who purportedly would infect America with their dangerous radical ideas and engage in violent subversion. Immigrants were blamed for the labor unrest occurring in industrial America, even though native-born Americans dominated the ranks of labor militants.[19] In 1919 the Department of Justice arrested and deported hundreds of leftists, most of them eastern European Jews and southern Italians. The mass arrests—known as the Palmer raids because they were enacted through the office of Attorney General A. Mitchell Palmer—heightened the conviction that America was under attack by dangerous foreign radicals, and that more restrictive immigration policies were the answer to the threat.[20]

But for southern Italians, the main obstacle to their acceptance by native-born Americans was the association of people from the Mezzogiorno with organized crime. Americans had read newspaper accounts of brigandage in the South, as well as stories about the sanguinary doings of Neapolitan *camorre*, the Calabrian 'Ndrangheta, and the Sicilian *mafie*. Racist stereotypes of southern Italians as having a peculiar, possibly inborn tendency toward criminality followed the immigrants to the Americas, where such images were reinforced in both the popular press and in elite opinion journals. The headline of a *New York Times* editorial from 1876, "A Natural Inclination Toward Criminality," says it all. There was no question mark in the headline, nor did the editorial entertain any doubt regarding the veracity of this claim. The *Times* authoritatively informed its readers that the "natural inclination" stemmed from the fact that "the Italian is lazier, more gossiping, and fitter for intrigue than the American."[21]

But to the *Times* editorialists, "the Italian" did not represent all Italians. The previous year, when some of the first Neapolitan and Sicilian immigrants had begun to arrive in New York, the *Times*, in an editorial titled "Our Italians," regretted that these southerners were adding their numbers to those of the northern Italians already living in New York, who were "industrious and honest people from Genoa and the towns of the Ligurian coast, with a few emigrants from Piedmont and an occasional Livornese." The new arrivals, however, were "extremely ignorant, and have been reared in the belief that brigandage is a manly occupation, and that assassination is the natural sequence of the most trivial quarrel. They are miserably poor, and it is not strange that they resort to theft and robbery. It is, perhaps, hopeless to think of civilizing them, or of keeping them in order, except by the arm of the law."[22]

In a 1904 essay called "The Immigration Problem," one Robert De C. Ward made a racist distinction between two kinds of immigrants:

> A few years ago practically all of our immigrants were from northern and western Europe, that is, they were more or less closely allied to us racially, historically, industrially and politically. They were largely the same elements which had recently made up the English race . . . Now, however, the majority of the newcomers are from southern and eastern Europe, and they are coming in rapidly increasing numbers from Asia. These people are alien to us, in race . . . in language, in social, political, and industrial ideas and inheritances.[23]

Newspapers, magazines, and opinion journals routinely described southern Italian immigrants as lacking any ethical or moral sense, unassimilable, ineducable, irreducibly foreign. "That the Mediterranean peoples are morally below the races of Northern Europe is as certain as any social fact," declared the sociologist Edward Alsworth Ross. In the racist discourse of the times, the fair coloring of Anglo-Saxons and Nordics was a visible marker of their ethical superiority to the southern Italians. "Even when they were dirty, ferocious barbarians, these blonds were truth-tellers," claimed Alsworth Ross. "Be it pride or awkwardness or lack of imagination or fair-play sense, something has held them back from the nimble lying of the Southern races.

"The Northerners seem to surpass the southern Europeans in innate ethical endowment," the sociologist concluded.[24]

Italian immigrants in the 1880s were even accused of a conspiracy to inundate the United States with Italian fleas. Respectable publications gave credence to this ludicrous slander promoted by anti-Italian nativists. In an editorial of November 8, 1883, *The New York Times* announced that "the Italian flea has reached this country in company with other Italian immigrants, and is now present in great force in a small Pennsylvania town where Italian laborers are employed. Unless the importation of this infamous insect is checked the whole country will swarm with Italian fleas. Our own native flea will disappear before its formidable competitor."[25] The "Italian flea" served as a metaphor for the southern Italians themselves, and the supposed threat they posed to native-born Americans. Decades before Nazi propaganda dehumanized Jews by associating them with disease-spreading rodents, the mainstream American press propagated images of Italians as carriers of a foreign pestilence that, if unchecked, would run rampant throughout the nation.

These flea-carrying, uncivilized, and threatening Mediterraneans demonstrated their foreignness and inferiority the moment they arrived in America. Edward Alsworth Ross again:

> Before the boards of inquiry at Ellis Island their emotional instability stands out in the sharpest contrast to the self-control of the Hebrew and the stolidity of the Slav. They gesticulate much, and usually tears stand in their eyes. When two witnesses are being examined, both talk at once, and their hands will be moving all the time. Their glances flit quickly from one questioner to another, and their eyes are the restless, uncomprehending eyes of the desert Bedouin between walls. Yet for all this eager attention, they are slow to catch the meaning of a simple question, and often it must be repeated.[26]

The frankly racist nature of so much that was said about southern Italian immigrants seems startling today. After all, aren't Italians Caucasians? They are designated as such, by the U.S. Census and in general usage. But to the xenophobic nativists of early-twentieth-century America, the new arrivals from southern Italy hardly qualified as white folks. The arrival of Italians in large numbers coincided with the rise in popularity of Social Darwinism, which applied evolutionary doctrine beyond the realm of biology and into analyses of human behavior. The Social Darwinist outlook sanctioned racism, with its exponents teaching that the "Teutonic" and "Nordic" races were superior to all others. These purportedly superior races brought their institutions from Great Britain and Germany to the English colonies and to North America.

Social Darwinists, fearful of racial degeneration, regarded the newcomers of the post–Civil War years as weaker, more dangerous, less civilized, and, as noted earlier, inherently criminal.

"From this perspective," observes historian Salvatore J. La Gumina, "Italians, along with other representatives of new immigration, Jews, Poles, Greeks, etc., clearly remained undesirable. As the largest group of these newcomers, Italians seemed least likely to satisfy the requirements of assimilation."[27]

In parts of the American South, where slavery was still a fresh memory and descendants of slaves, "free" blacks, were subjected to the official racism of de jure segregation and Jim Crow laws, southern Italians occupied "a racial middle ground within the otherwise unforgiving binary caste system of white-over-black," according to the scholar Matthew Frye Jacobson.[28] To Southern racists, many of the Italian immigrants, with their dark hair and eyes and olive skin, did not look white. Moreover, they did not "act white." In New Orleans, for example, "Italian immigrants were stigmatized in the post–Civil War period because they accepted economic niches (farm labor and small tenancy, for instance) marked as 'black' by local custom, and because they lived and worked comfortably among blacks."[29]

The 1922 trial in Alabama of a black man accused of miscegenation provides a vivid example of the racial in-betweenness of southern Italian immigrants in the eyes of white America. Jim Rollins, the black man in question, had been convicted of the crime of miscegenation, but his conviction was overturned by an appeals court on the grounds that the prosecution could not conclusively prove that Edith LaBue, the woman in question, was indeed white. LaBue was a Sicilian immigrant, and her ethnicity, the court held, meant that she might be "a Negro or a descendant of a Negro." Although the court did not definitively state that Sicilians were nonwhite, the ruling "also made clear that she [LaBue] was not the sort of white woman whose purity was to be 'protected' by that bulwark of white supremacism, the miscegenation statute."[30]

By the early 1920s, there were already nearly four million Italians in the country, to the displeasure of many native-born Americans. "In opinion polls reflecting native-born Americans' preferences in new neighbors, Italians ranked near the bottom. They were seen as clannish, uncouth, instinctively criminal."[31] The Volstead Act, better known as Prohibition, was imposed on America in 1920 primarily by WASP "zealots of sobriety," and "lent credibility to the image of typically wine-drinking Italians, who were by nature lawless; and the American press, by making antiheroes of such bootlegging gangsters as Alphonse ('Scarface') Capone, heightened the notoriety attached to many people with Italian names."[32]

Nearly one-quarter of all Italians in the United States lived in New York City, but they did not constitute a significant voting bloc, either because they were not registered to vote, or, as noncitizens, were not eligible. In the early 1920s, there were no Republican or Democratic district leaders of Italian origin. Public high schools banned the teaching of the Italian language; the public school system offered no courses in Italian history or culture. Leonard Covello, an Italian-born educator and author, observed that for the children of immigrants, assimilation began with "learning to be ashamed of our parents."[33] Anti-Italian prejudice was so common that the Italian government sometimes protested it, as well as America's imposition, in 1924, of limits to immigration from southern Europe.

Faced with the intense hostility of nativist Americans, denigrated as racially inferior, dangerously radical, and prone to violent criminality, the southern Italian immigrants clung to the cultural construct and social institution that had sustained them in the harsh world they had left behind. "The only system to which the *contadino* [peasant] paid attention was *l'ordine della famiglia*; the unwritten but all-demanding and complex system of rules governing one's relations within, and responsibilities to, his own family, and his posture toward those outside the family. All other social institutions were seen within a spectrum of attitudes ranging from indifference to scorn and contempt."[34]

The concept of family embraced by southern Italians is expansive, including mothers, fathers, and siblings, but also aunts, uncles, cousins, and *comari* and *compari*. Every Italian family has *comari* and *compari*; often referred to as godmothers and godfathers, they are intimate but nonblood members of the extended family.[35] (Fans of *The Sopranos* are familiar with *comari*, pronounced "gumads," as the mistresses of the show's married mafiosi.)

"Sociability in Italy was family-based," as historian Robert A. Orsi observes in *The Madonna of 115th Street*, his study of the Italian American community of East Harlem, New York. And in America, the immigrants replicated, to the best of their ability in a strange land, the family system they had known. At the center of this system is the "domus," a concept referring both to the family itself and to the actual physical home. For southern Italians, the domus is "the foundation of their understanding of the good and the basis of their moral judgment."[36]

The domus, and its preservation in the New World, was the most important thing to the southern Italians. They didn't identify with Italy as a nation, but with their particular *paesi* and the domus-centered lives they had known in those towns and villages of the Mezzogiorno. "These people could not understand the proud *italianità* of Italian Harlem's middle-class immigrant professionals, who had managed to find some identification with the Italian nation . . . So their memories and images of Italy were memories of strict family order and discipline, of family loyalty and mutual support," says Orsi.

First- and second-generation Italian Americans "felt that their love and respect for the domus marked them out as a distinct and different people in American culture, and they frequently compared Italian and American values—to the great detriment of the latter. When the immigrants wanted to criticize their children's new ideas about themselves and the ways they wanted to organize their lives, they accused them of being American.[37]

"Individuals were warned that to violate the blood bonding of the domus meant disaster," Orsi observes. "There were a number of levels to this blood unity. It referred, first of all, to the blood-bond existing between mother and child, the essential blood tie; it also meant the special bonds that exist among siblings: the brother-sister relationship or the brother-brother relationship was thought to be closer than the father-son or father-daughter relationship because brothers and sisters were of the same blood, had suckled their mother's blood."

In the domus-centered worldview, a blood relationship existed among southern Italians from different regions, despite whatever antagonisms might have existed in the old country. Neapolitans might disdain Sicilians as superstitious peasants, and Sicilians might look down on Neapolitans as thieves and cutthroats, but better that their sons and daughters should marry each other than a non-Italian. If one married a non-Italian, one "might not be able to incorporate his or her children into the domus . . ."[38]

The domus mitigated the social isolation and feelings of alienation that the immigrants and their children might experience in a foreign environment, a new world. The individual human being "located in the world by blood ties was not, and could not be, an isolated self: the self in Italian Harlem was a self-in-connection." Individual ambition and needs for personal satisfaction were to be submerged in all-consuming loyalty to the domus. Children were the responsibility of all the members of the domus, not just the parents, because the successful education of the young into the domus-centered culture was "far too important a cultural task to be left to two people who might or might not be able to handle it."[39]

Orsi notes that the community could be quite cruel to those who by circumstances or choice lived outside the domus. Two groups came in for particular scorn, unmarried women and priests. Disdain for the clergy may surprise those used to seeing Italians as intensely devout Catholics loyal to their Church. But although they were passionately devoted to their faith, manifested in community rituals such as religious *feste*, in which they honored particular saints, they were far less wedded to the institutional Church than were Irish Catholics. Many Italians, in fact, were strongly anticlerical. My grandfather, not long before his death, warned my mother that if she had a church funeral service for him, he would come back to haunt her.

First-generation Italian Americans remembered the Church as an ally of the hated ruling classes in the old country. But their antagonism toward clerics also stemmed from the fact that they chose to live outside a domus. "Southern Italians were not always pleased when their sons decided to become priests; the church in this way became too intimate a rival to the domus."

In the domus, its members revealed the selves that had been formed and nurtured in the family crucible. The domus was "a theater of self-revelation: on this stage, a person showed the world his or her worth and integrity, responsibility, and devotion, the respect they gave and the respect they were due."[40]

Those Italian Americans who lived the domus-centered life de-

scribed by Orsi often recall it with nostalgic fondness. Katherine Narducci, an actress known to *Sopranos* fans as Charmaine Bucco, the
mobster-hating wife and business partner of restaurateur Artie Bucco,
grew up in East Harlem during the 1960s and '70s, by which time Italian Harlem had shrunk to a few blocks. But her recollections demonstrate that the culture Orsi portrays still existed for the remaining
descendants of the immigrants.

> I lived on First Avenue and I would say there were probably
> about seven apartment buildings on one street—from 114th to
> 115th Street, let's say. Everybody was so close; it felt like it was
> a huge one-family house. Because we were over the roofs and in
> and out of each other's houses. And the freedom—you felt so
> safe. It wasn't like today. We were allowed to wander off and my
> mother didn't think twice about it, letting me go out from morn-
> ing to night. The neighborhood, we would have feasts [religious
> *feste*] every year. All of the owners of the rides would let the
> poor kids of the neighborhood on the rides free. It was just very
> exciting. It was religious. We went to church, we had great
> morals. It was a fantastic way of life . . . I loved it.
>
> We would have barbecues right in the middle of the street.
> Everybody would cook together, eat together. They would open
> up a big table on Sunday and everybody would eat at the table.
> The jukebox would be in the street . . . and the music . . . It was
> so romantic. When you're young, I think a lot of times you don't
> realize the area you're growing up in, how great it is. I remember
> I used to say, "God, I love this neighborhood. I never want to go
> anywhere else!" It was just terrific. I lived on the second floor—
> and my bedroom was right in front on First Avenue—and I
> would hear all the Italian ladies talking and all the guys talking
> in the street. And the sound would put me to sleep 'cause I felt
> so safe.[41]

Narducci's golden memories notwithstanding, life in the domus-
centered community had its downside. Economic success was es-
teemed only if it helped to maintain and support the domus. It was
expected that individuals would refuse promotions at work if moving

up threatened the stability of the domus. If an upwardly mobile Italian-American decided to move out of the community, "the decision to do so could cause real pain in the domus."[42]

The family culture that Narducci remembers so fondly could also be oppressive to women, who were expected to be the protectors of the domus, willing to sacrifice and suffer on behalf of their families, and to submit to male authority. Like the revered figure of the Madonna, the Italian wife and mother wielded power, but it was circumscribed and defined by men, and limited to the realm of the family.

The priority on protecting the domus also could lead Italian American communities to indulge, even excuse, the gangsters in their midst, as long as they were seen as guardians of this realm. "For many Italians who grew up in East Harlem, gangsters are romantic figures, characters like those in southern Italian legends and folktales," notes Robert Orsi. "They are said to have kept the community safe, looked after poor people, and watched over the women of the community. They made sure that people coming home from work late at night were safe in the streets, according to the legend."[43]

Katherine Narducci's memories of the mob's presence in East Harlem bear out Orsi's observations. Charmaine Bucco may despise gangsters, but the actress who plays the honest and put-upon working woman recalls them as a positive force in the community.

> I didn't really . . . at that time realize that they were mob guys . . . but I knew it was a strong group of men who took care of the neighborhood and they had a lot to do with the safety of the neighborhood. I didn't realize "mob." In my older years, my teen years, I started to realize . . .
>
> My truth and my perception was that they were the best guys ever. They did everything for the kids in the neighborhood. Every single holiday, we were taken care of. If you didn't have a Halloween costume because you were too poor, they'd buy you one. So, they were just terrific. They were Santa Claus on Christmas . . . You know it's like what they say about John Gotti. The people in the neighborhood didn't know the details of what went on. They just knew that this guy took care of the neighborhood. He had parties on the Fourth of July, he helped so many

people in the neighborhood. I know one story: this homeless woman went to his house. He set her up in an apartment, bought her furniture. And he barely knew her. This is what the people know, that's how they know him—the smiles, the generous guy, the glamorous guy, the good-looking guy. How could you not like this guy?[44]

Narducci's familiarity with gangsters was, in fact, familial; her father, Nicky Narducci, was a local mob figure who was "whacked"—shot to death in front of the Upper East Side bar he owned—when she was ten years old. *On the Pad*, a 1973 book about a rogue New York City cop who testified before the Knapp Commission, which was investigating police corruption, describes Nicky Narducci as "a flip, tough hood . . . Narducci had a lot of arrests in his record, more than twenty, but had served fewer than three years in prison." Narducci "had to have had a hook, influence, that extended into the office of New York District Attorney Frank S. Hogan . . . How else explain . . . the felony charges reduced to misdemeanors, the acquiescence of the DA's office to Narducci 'walking away' from arrests . . . ?" According to the book, Narducci "hobnobbed . . . with top Mob figures."[45] But at thirty years old, he ended up dead, a photo of his corpse appearing on page 5 of the New York *Daily News*.

"My father died at an early age," continues Katherine Narducci, "and I had, like, twenty other fathers. I just felt very safe. These guys treated me like a daughter. Not knowing who they were or what they did, I just knew they kept everything safe. They were very giving."

Narducci as a child might not have understood how gangsters made their money. (And she surely cannot be taken seriously when she says that John Gotti's neighbors were unaware of his criminal exploits.) But according to Robert Orsi, "Everyone in the community knew that local mobsters spent most of their time in Italian Harlem extorting Italian merchants and running numbers games that took money away from the community." But community members were able to reconcile this knowledge with the apparently incompatible perception of gangsters as men who defended the domus. "Why," Orsi asks, "did the community make heroes out of these mobsters, if only in the tales they told, when they knew full well the reality of their crimes?"[46]

The gangsters, he believes, served the symbolic function of representing both "the violence that individuals knew they had to do to their own aspirations and plans in deference to the domus, and the violent fantasies they sometimes entertained against the domus itself." In the stories Italian East Harlemites told about the gangsters in their midst,

> The guns of these cruel men are aimed against violators of the domus: in this way, the mafiosi also articulate the rage that people inevitably turned inward in their struggles against the demands of the domus and the guilt they suffered for struggling. In the tales, the domus is always successfully defended: these myths allowed the people to express their rage against it while both assuring them that the domus was safe against that rage and reminding them of what was necessary for their submission . . . Symbols of aggression and repression, the mythical mafiosi embodied the complexity of feeling and anxiety which the people of Italian Harlem bore toward the domus.[47]

Dedication to the values of the domus, when narrowly conceived, could also foster an us-against-the-world mentality that could be used to legitimate hostility toward other ethnic groups, for instance, the intense rivalry and occasionally violent clashes between Italians and blacks and Puerto Ricans in East Harlem during the 1950s and '60s. Fierce loyalty to the domus, in fact, has been partly responsible for more recent racial attacks by young Italian American males—some of them aspiring mafiosi or errand boys for gangsters—against black males who venture onto Italian turf. "Protecting the neighborhood" is a familiar rationale offered by these misguided youths and the adults who condone their behavior, because blacks and other nonwhite strangers who venture into Italian areas must be up to no good.

But it would be a mistake to say that the values of the domus-centered community necessarily foster tribalism. Mutual support and concern, especially during crises, shared sacrifice and the sense of communal responsibility for children and the needy, loyalty, and the primacy of face-to-face relationships over the pursuit of material wealth—all these are qualities that can inform progressive politics as well as ethnocentrism. As Robert Orsi observes, the world of the domus produced the gangster Frank Costello, but it also produced such champions of reform as Mayor Fiorello La Guardia.[48] Vito Marcantonio, the East Harlem–born radical who represented his community in the U.S. Congress for two decades, was also formed by the values of the domus.

If the experience of the first generation of Italian Americans, and to a lesser degree of the second generation, was prejudice and discrimination, by the time World War II broke out, "a climate of acceptance of Italians had developed in America."[49] Italian Americans by then had achieved some political power; Fiorello La Guardia and Angelo Rossi were the nationally prominent mayors of New York City and San Francisco. Hundreds of thousands of Italian Americans were members of the U.S. armed forces, and those Italian Americans not in uniform responded loyally and enthusiastically to the war effort. Many Italian Americans had admired Italy's fascist dictator Benito Mussolini, believing that he had gained international respect for Italy. But when the United States entered the war, Italian Americans had no hesitation in choosing sides: their new country got their loyalty, despite whatever attachments they may have had to the old country.

Popular culture reflected the changed perception of Italians. In the films of the 1930s, Italians generally were depicted as Prohibition-era mobsters, usually portrayed by non-Italian actors such as Edward G. Robinson (*Little Caesar*) and Paul Muni (*Scarface*). World War II brought a respite from the gangster image, as Italian American boys— who usually hailed from Brooklyn—proved themselves loyal and heroic fighters.[50] The Italian American soldier usually was part of an ethnically representative (of white ethnics, that is) platoon—a Goldberg, an O'Hara, a Smith, and a Martino. *From Here to Eternity*, a World War II film made a few years after the war's end, featured a character who was to become the best-known Italian American movie GI, Angelo Maggio, a tragic figure hounded and eventually killed by a sadistic, Italian-hating sergeant played by Ernest Borgnine (né Borgnino).

But a decade later, even a sympathetic character like Maggio came to be linked to the mafia in the popular consciousness. Mario Puzo's

The Godfather, with its thinly veiled Sinatra character, the singer-actor Johnny Fontane, made millions of readers (and later, moviegoers) believe that Sinatra had won the role of Maggio because of a horse's head in a producer's bed.[51]

During the postwar years, Italians came to be accepted as Americans, as they achieved greatness in sports, politics, and the arts and sciences. But in one respect they remained haunted by the immigrant past and its tribulations. The passage of two or three generations since the era of mass migration from Italy had not swept away the association of southern Italians with organized crime. The widespread notoriety attached to organized crime in the 1950s and 1960s, with highly publicized Congressional investigations and public hearings, further entrenched this connection in the popular imagination.

> To put it another way [wrote Salvatore La Gumina in the early 1970s], a "mystique" has evolved around the "Mafia" and "Cosa Nostra" theme with influence on both popular and official notions of the validity of criminal phenomena. The public has been so saturated with the Mafia theme that, in effect, a conditioning process has taken place around the term. The mental picture of the Mafia in the public mind, made up as it is of myth and fact, has tended to blur our vision of the real world. The Italian term "mafia" has come to be synonymous with organized crime.[52]

Italian Americans who enter politics often find themselves the object of "insinuations or brazen lies about Mafia connections" that can derail or hinder their aspirations.[53] Rumors of wiseguy skeletons rattling in family closets plagued the vice presidential campaign of Geraldine Ferraro in 1984 and Mario Cuomo's gubernatorial reelection bid in 1986. Such leading newspapers as *The Philadelphia Inquirer*, the *New York Post*, and *The Wall Street Journal* insinuated that Ferraro and her family were "connected," but no evidence was ever brought forth to support the accusations.[54]

Mario Cuomo found vindication when Nicholas Pileggi, a well-known journalist whose book *Wiseguy* is a milestone in mob-lit, reported that the rumors had been "passed around by cops, media people and others in a kind of shadow network of gossip and loose talk." Pileggi found that most of the rumors had been spread by two people, a Long Island public relations man who worked for the Right to Life candidate in the 1986 gubernatorial campaign, and a conservative aide in the state legislature.[55]

Gay Talese maintains that although Cuomo ultimately was vindicated, the rumor-mongering was effective; it "basically kept him from challenging Bill Clinton for the Presidential nomination.

"Clinton, a cracker from Hope, Arkansas, and Cuomo both came from poor circumstances, both were provincials, but Clinton was more likely to be accepted nationally as an American," Talese says. "Cuomo looked like someone who could be a character in *The Godfather*,"[56] which was what Clinton said about him. Americans like Italians as gangsters, but don't want one as president.

"Look at the anchormen for the three major networks—Brokaw, Rather, and Jennings. All are white, non-ethnic men who look like they could be occupants of the White House, or are potential matinee idols. You wouldn't see someone dark, like Pacino. You could not have an Italian, or a Jew, as a network anchorman. It's all about appearances and Cuomo didn't have it, nor does anyone of Italian origin." (Talese was right about the network TV news anchors, but there is now far more diversity among the ranks of cable news anchors and reporters.)[57]

And the ethnic profiling of Italian elected officials continues. The Order of the Sons of Italy in America (OSIA), the oldest Italian American watchdog group, found examples of the stereotyping of Italian American politicians in *The Wall Street Journal*, *USA Today*, and *Newsweek*. Two victims of media hits were New York gubernatorial candidate Andrew Cuomo and U.S. Senator Robert Torricelli of New Jersey, whose withdrawals from their respective races in 2002 were chalked up to their being made "offers they couldn't refuse."

In October 2002, *Newsweek* presented a two-page spread, "Tony and 'The Torch,' " by Jonathan Alter, that, the OSIA observed, "reads more like a *Sopranos* script than a news article thanks to its liberal use of mob-speak: Torricelli 'seemed likely to get whacked in November . . . because when you "rat out" New Jersey, the voters treat you like Big

Pussy' [a *Sopranos* character murdered for having become a government informant"]. The article drew other analogies between Torricelli's dire political situation and the characters and storylines of *The Sopranos*.

"The line between fiction and fact has become dangerously blurred to the detriment of Italian Americans in public life," the OSIA noted in a press release. Referring to a general tendency by media pundits to belittle Italian American complaints about stereotyping, the release concluded, "Instead of telling Italian Americans to 'lighten up,' the press's reporting should clean up."[58]

In Maine, 2002 Green Party gubernatorial candidate Jonathan Carter ran a TV advertisement opposing legalized gambling that linked his opponent, former state legislator John Baldacci, a Democrat, to the mafia. "Casino gambling in Maine? You got a problem with that?" an unseen announcer says in a stereotypically mafioso accent. The gangster-announcer notes that although Baldacci says he's opposed to casinos, he voted in favor of them when he was in the Maine legislature. "If he can flip, he can flop, bada bing, bada boom, know what I mean?" Declaring that Carter is unalterably opposed to legalized gambling, the announcer insists, "we ain't gonna be Vegas or New Jersey [Tony Soprano's home state], not now, not ever, never. In other words, fuhgedaboudit."

"Bada boom, bada bing" is a phrase that has become a cliché of movies and TV shows about the mafia, and the Bada Bing is the name of the strip club on *The Sopranos* where Tony and his crew have their headquarters. "Fuhgedaboudit" is also a staple of mob lore. In the 1997 film *Donnie Brasco*, the title character, an undercover FBI agent investigating organized crime, delivers an amusing soliloquy on the various meanings of the expression.

But Jonathan Carter and his campaign denied that the commercial was in any way defamatory. Advocacy groups, and not all of them Italian-American, disagreed, as did some in the Maine media who deplored the ad as ethnic stereotyping that had no place in a political campaign. Baldacci, an astute campaigner, garnered sympathy from those offended by the Carter commercial. And he won the election, with Carter coming in a distant third.

2

The Mafia: Mediterranean Menace,
American Myth

t the end of 1950 and early in 1951, some 20 to 30 million
Americans interrupted their normal routines to watch a real-life
police lineup on television. The Special Committee to Investigate Organized Crime in Interstate Commerce, known to posterity as
the Kefauver crime committee, was in business, and during its tele-
vised public hearings at Foley Square in Manhattan, organized crime
figures, hit men, and corrupt politicians appeared before the committee to testify about a nationwide criminal conspiracy called the mafia.

In May 1950 the Senate established the five-member special committee, appointing a freshman senator from Tennessee, Estes Kefauver,
as its chairman. The committee visited fourteen major cities in fifteen
months, just as increasing numbers of Americans were purchasing
their first television sets. During the hearings, Americans got to see and
hear actual gangsters like Frank Costello and Joe Adonis, although in
Costello's case, only his big, callused hands were shown—a theatrical
touch that made America's reputed top crime boss all the more compelling a TV character.

The Kefauver committee produced a report with numerous alarming claims about Italian American organized crime and the failures of
the government to combat it. The committee charged that the Bureau
of Internal Revenue had not made "a real effort" to crack down on
fraudulent income tax returns of "known gangsters and racketeers." But
the report's most dramatic claim was that organized crime indeed was
organized, and it was governed by a national commission. The committee was convinced that there existed a "phantom government" of the

underworld which "enforces its own law, carries out its own executions and not only ignores but abhors the democratic process of justice which are [sic] held to be the safeguards of the American citizen."[1]

Kefauver's hearings acquainted Americans with such purported mafia lingo as *capo regime* and *capo di tutti capi*, these exotic terms reinforcing the notion of a foreign conspiracy engaged in subverting the American Way. The committee also produced the first charts of names that allegedly constituted the mafia. But how credible were the Kefauver findings? The committee had different evidentiary standards than that of a trial or court proceeding and was allowed to accept hearsay evidence that would not have been permitted in a court of law. It also ignored testimony from twenty-odd Italian American witnesses who denied the existence of a centralized organization called the mafia. The committee's report disregarded these demurrals, attributing them to the fearsome power of *omertà*, the mafia code of silence. The committee failed to produce irrefutable evidence that there indeed existed an organization called the mafia, leading an attorney to fault its report in the *Stanford Law Review*: "The cumulative denials and professed ignorance . . . suggest that it is either a *very* elusive, shadowy sinister organization—or else, equally credible, a romantic myth."[2]

Daniel Bell, in his famous study of American politics, *The End of Ideology*, also disputes the Kefauver committee's findings. "Unfortunately for a good story—and the existence of the Mafia would be a whale of a story—neither the Senate Crime Committee in its testimony, nor Kefauver . . . presented any real evidence that the Mafia exists as a functioning organization."

"One finds," Bell continues, "police officials asserting before the Kefauver committee their *belief* in the Mafia; the Narcotics Bureau *thinks* that a world-wide dope ring allegedly run by [Lucky] Luciano is part of the Mafia; but the only other 'evidence' presented . . . is that certain crimes bear 'the earmarks of the Mafia.' " Bell also notes that the Senate crime committee did not conduct any original research and its staff "was incredibly small." He concludes:

The salient reason, perhaps, why the Kefauver Committee was taken in by its own myth of an omnipotent Mafia and a despotic

[Frank] Costello was its failure to assimilate and understand three of the more relevant sociological facts about institutionalized crime in relation to the political life of large urban communities in America, namely: (1) the rise of the American Italian community, as part of the inevitable process of ethnic succession, to positions of importance in politics . . . (2) the fact that there are individual Italians who play prominent, often leading roles today in gambling and in the mobs; and (3) the fact that Italian gamblers and mobsters often possessed "status" within the Italian community itself and a "pull" in city politics. These three items are indeed related—but not so as to form a "plot."[3]

But despite the warranted skepticism about the Kefauver committee's findings, the investigation and the drama of its televised hearings, with testimony from reputed mafiosi, succeeded in establishing in the public mind the existence of a sinister, well-organized, and dangerous conspiracy of men with vowel-heavy names whose activities threatened American institutions. And, in fact, long before Kefauver, the American public had been introduced to the persona of the Italian hoodlum through the medium of film.

As early as the 1930s, American gangsters with Italian names were already the image and symbol of organized crime. The success of the gangster movies *Little Caesar* and *Scarface* contributed to "the public's vision of crime syndicates that were dominated by men with marked, no matter how stilted, Italian accents. In such films, the Italian was well on his way to replacing the Irishman as the symbol of the hood."[4]

If, by the early 1950s, the connection between Italians and organized crime had been well established in the mind of America, due both to the actual criminality Americans learned about through the media and through the fictional representations of the movies, the latter part of the decade produced the most sensational, and to many, most compelling evidence to date of the existence of an organization called the mafia.

In November 1957, the New York State Police raided a meeting at the rural home of one Joseph Barbara, in the south-central New York town of Apalachin. The police arrested fifty-eight men, all Italian, and many of them immigrants. Perhaps as many as fifty other of the re-puted mobsters at the meeting fled into the nearby woods. The names of those arrested or later identified as having been at the Apalachin meeting made up a roll call of the most notorious underworld figures known at the time; they included Tommy Lucchese, reputedly the head of one of New York's "five families" of organized crime, Chicago boss Sam Giancana, Stefano Magaddino of Buffalo, and Joe Zerilli of Detroit.

The next summer, the Senate Select Committee on Improper Ac-tivities in the Labor or Management Field, chaired by Senator John L. McClellan of Arkansas, with Robert Kennedy as its chief counsel, held hearings just on Apalachin and the mafia. The hearings, which contin-ued until the summer of 1959, heard from such high-profile witnesses as Lucchese and Vito Genovese, head of the Luciano "family."

But it was Joe Valachi, a lowly soldier in the Luciano organization, who became the McClellan committee's prize catch. In 1962, while in-carcerated at the federal penitentiary in Atlanta, Valachi walked across the exercise yard, grabbed a piece of pipe, and bludgeoned a fellow in-mate to death. When asked to explain the assault, Valachi said he had mistaken his victim for a man he thought his cellmate, Vito Genovese, had ordered to kill him.

Valachi subsequently bought protection from his fellow criminals by becoming "the first Mafioso ever to sing at length, on the record, and finally in public."[5] The petty hood found himself the star of tele-vised hearings held in 1963 before the McClellan investigations sub-committee. As he told his tales of old, unsolved murders, and of the structure, history, and culture of organized crime, he blew away "omertà, the traditional code of silence that had generally protected the Mafia's inner workings."[6]

Valachi also introduced a new, unfamiliar term into the national dis-course about Italian American organized crime. Members of the crimi-nal fraternity, Valachi revealed, didn't say they belonged to the mafia. They called their enterprise La Cosa Nostra—Italian for "Our Thing." This organization, he claimed, was governed by a national body known as the Commission.

But, as with the Kefauver report, the veracity of Valachi's testimony has been undermined—some would say demolished—by a close examination of what he actually told McClellan's committee. Valachi contradicted himself on a number of key points, including the subject of mafia initiations and the structure and operations of Cosa Nostra. He also spoke about purported mafia misdeeds of which he could not have had firsthand knowledge. Valachi's evidence of a centralized, nationwide criminal conspiracy overseen by a Commission simply was not credible. The star witness who supposedly blew the lid off a criminal conspiracy's well-guarded secrecy told the McClellan committee exactly what it wanted to hear—and what would win a career criminal a place in the federal witness protection program.

Author and investigative journalist Nick Tosches explores the connection between show business and organized crime in *Dino: Living High in the Dirty Business of Dreams*, his 1992 biography of Dean Martin. Skeptical about Valachi's revelations, he writes:

> Spectacularly orchestrated for the media by Bobby Kennedy, Valachi's testimony was used to corroborate the picture of organized crime that the government had devised in its own image, the only image that it could truly comprehend: that of an ordered, homogeneous entity, an imagined ideal bureaucracy. Valachi's testimony popularized the Italian phrase *Cosa Nostra*. It carried an air of inside knowledge that the well-worn *Mafia* now lacked. It was new and improved.[7]

Despite the unreliability of Joe Valachi's testimony, there is no denying the fact that the McClellan committee and its star witness brought unprecedented public attention to the subject of the mafia, or the Cosa Nostra, as Valachi called it. Since the 1930s Americans had gone through periods of intense fascination with organized crime. But in the 1960s a national mythology about Italian American crime solidified, with a focus on the shadowy, powerful men who led crime "families."

Valachi's testimony even had a major impact on national politics. The Republicans, with Barry Goldwater as their presidential candidate, mounted a law-and-order campaign in 1964. The victorious Democrat, Lyndon Johnson, announced a war on crime that would include a Presidential Commission on Law Enforcement and Administration of Justice, which would appoint a special task force on organized crime.

Post-Valachi, references to the mafia in *The New York Times* escalated from two in 1962 to sixty-seven in 1963 and 359 in 1969.[8] Publishers issued quickie biographies of infamous celebrity mobsters such as Frank Costello, Vito Genovese, and Carlo Gambino. Peter Maas, a magazine writer, took Joe Valachi's handwritten manuscript of his memoirs and shaped it into *The Valachi Papers*, published in 1969. That year also saw the publication of the book that to this day has done more than any other popular culture creation to establish a mythology of the mafia: Mario Puzo's novel *The Godfather*.

In the decades since, the media and popular culture have portrayed Italian American organized crime in ways varied enough to recall the old Indian tale about the six blind men and the elephant—the nature of the thing varies depending upon one's perspective. Movies and television, fiction and reportage, have depicted the mafia as:

- A national criminal conspiracy governed like a corporation, with a board of directors called the Commission, which extends its tentacles into legitimate business, politics, and labor;
- A transnational criminal enterprise, with its home office in Italy and overseas divisions in the Americas;
- A more raffish version of capitalism, which meets demand for services, and vices, that our puritanical government foolishly proscribes;
- A temporary means by which impoverished ethnic groups achieve economic mobility, before moving on to become legit;
- A family business that sons enter out of loyalty to their powerful, domineering fathers;
- A way for blue-collar men without education and prospects to make fast money;
- The vehicle by which an immigrant group, or certain members of it, refuse the deal offered by America—assimilate, play by the rules, and relinquish the Old World—choosing instead to maintain their "ancient traditions";
- A means by which men who don't want to work for a living,

greedy men with an appetite for violence bordering on the psychotic, can get rich;

• Not a single, unified organization, but rather a bunch of gangs scattered across the country, united only in the fact that their members are of Italian background and engage in illegal enterprises.

Some of these depictions are mutually contradictory, others not. But the one thing they share is this: there are Italian American criminals who organize their criminal exploits, giving them a certain rationality and a degree of order. But beyond that, what are we talking about when we say "mafia"? How much of what we "know" about Italian American organized crime is real and how much mythology?

As any *Godfather* fan knows, the phenomenon we know as the mafia originated in Sicily, or more precisely, western Sicily, in the capital city, Palermo, and its environs. It is not an ancient association with deep roots in Sicilian culture, as is commonly believed, but instead emerged relatively recently in the late nineteenth century, as Italy, which had been a collection of states ruled by foreigners and the Vatican, became a united, modern nation.

In feudal Italy, *latifondisti* (major landowners) controlled the economy and enjoyed a monopoly on the use of violence.[9] But the Risorgimento changed the pattern of land ownership in Sicily, dispossessing the Church from its holdings and splitting up the vast feudal estates. The abolition of feudalism transformed land into a market commodity, with legally defined property rights. Members of the rising middle class were able to buy land, thereby unsettling the old order and unleashing "a degree of energy, mobility, negotiation and accompanying social tension unthinkable under the ancient regime."[10] Mafia scholarship often identifies the new proprietors from the rural middle class, along with the estate managers they hired, as constituting the original mafia.

Anton Blok, a Dutch anthropologist and author of one of the best-known studies of Sicilian organized crime, *The Mafia of a Sicilian Village* (1972), maintained that the men known in Sicily as mafiosi originally were *gabelloti*, "violent peasant entrepreneurs" hired by absentee landlords to maintain order on their large estates. During the late nineteenth and early twentieth centuries, these estate managers hired other local men, forming associations called *cosche* that were similar to the vigilante groups that rose up during the settling of the American West. Each village or town had its own *cosca*, and these organizations, better known outside Sicily as "families," collectively constituted "the mafia," according to Blok.

But, as Blok notes, "the various local *cosche* maintained loose relationships with each other without, however, yielding their relative autonomy to any overarching or sovereign power."[11] In other words, these groups did not constitute one centrally organized, united organization known as the mafia.

The *gabelloti* performed several important functions: they were a point of contact between the peasants, the landlords, and the government; they provided land and employment to peasants, which made them indispensable to economic survival; they managed the large estates, or *latifondi*, thereby making money for the landowners; and they became in effect the only means of social control in a society lacking effective public administration and law enforcement.[12] In its origins, then, it was less a criminal organization than an economic and police organization that provided jobs and social control and settled disputes.

The private use of unlicensed violence (that is, violence not sanctioned by legal authority) as a means to control the public arena is the central characteristic of the mafia, according to Blok.

Much of his thesis, however, has been convincingly rebutted by the Italian sociologist Diego Gambetta, who argues that "the mafia is a specific economic enterprise, an industry which produces, promotes, and sells private protection. The mafia represents this industry as it has developed in Sicily over the last one hundred and fifty years."[13] Whereas Blok's analysis is based on his observations of rural mafiosi in the village where he lived and studied during the 1960s, Gambetta's study draws on the invaluable evidence yielded by the aggressive anti-mafia campaign waged in the 1980s by the Sicilian magistrates Giovanni Falcone and Paolo Borsellino.

Gambetta rejects Blok's contention that the chief characteristic of the mafia is its private use of unlicensed violence: "Violence is a means, not an end; a resource, not the final product. The commodity that is really at stake is *protection.*" He notes that protection is an "ambiguous commodity" that can connote both security and threat. This commodity proves useful in economic transactions in which at least one party does not trust the other to play fair. Gambetta observes that "every time the state decrees a particular transaction or commodity illegal, a potential market for private protection is created. Trading becomes by definition vulnerable, and illegal dealers have an incentive to seek the protection of other agencies."[14]

In both legal and illegal markets,

> Those who enlist mafiosi to sort out their disputes, to retrieve their stolen property, or to protect their cartels from free riders and competitors do not perceive that protection as bogus. They may feel dissatisfied because they are forced to pay often for a service they seldom use, as with insurance, or because they pay extortionate prices for it as they do for other monopoly goods. Still, this practice differs from extortion proper, where the payment aims only to avoid costs directly threatened by the "protectors."[15]

Gambetta argues that the mafia is most accurately compared to a business. It is, however, not a centralized industry but instead comprises many "individual firms united by a brand name and, intermittently, a cartel."[16] Though he maintains that mafia protection differs from extortion per se, the distinction between the two seems minor, in that mafiosi often offered "protection" from themselves. In Paul Ginsborg's words, the mafia "created a 'racket' in which it consciously injected elements of uncertainty into market conditions, and then extorted payments for protection from these same conditions."[17]

Ginsborg, an eminent historian and analyst of contemporary Italy, has written that this unique and uniquely perverse business can be seen as a service organization that managed to expand its operations from localities to the national and international levels. Locally, it specialized in providing protection and privilege in the markets it controlled, as well as extortion rackets. Nationally, it offered a political service by delivering votes in exchange for being able to function without government interference. On the international plane, it controlled networks for illegal trafficking in goods, including drugs, and for money laundering.[18]

Rejecting the argument of some commentators that the mafia constitutes its own self-regulating legal order, with norms similar to those of the state, Gambetta declares that "the norms adopted by the cartel are often breached and manipulated, and in no way are they part of a fixed and universally agreed-on code; nor is there any moral justification for them."[19]

Ginsborg notes that the mafia "did not even resemble a pre-modern state, for it had no absolute monarch and no dependence on a landowning class. Rather, it had grown side by side with the development of capitalism in Sicily and had acquired its identity, both urban and rural, in contradistinction to the modern state, and not in imitation of it."[20]

Gambetta disputes Blok's conflation of mafiosi with *gabelloti*, the estate managers, noting that it is impossible to reconcile "the fact that the mafia supposedly provides private protection to all classes on the one hand with the *gabelloti* as a rural class on the other hand—a class, moreover, whose aim was ostensibly to achieve a higher social status as farmers and landowners." He acknowledges that some *gabelloti* resorted to violence, either directly or through thugs they hired, and that some mafiosi became *gabelloti*. But Blok's violent peasant entrepreneurs are not synonymous with mafiosi:

> The world is full of violent entrepreneurs. Mafiosi are different. If we confuse them with entrepreneurs, no matter how vicious, engaged in manipulating the market to their own advantage, then the mafia evaporates and we are left with nothing to define it except cultural, ethnographic, racial or other nebulous distinctions. Thus, when certain unscrupulous acts are performed by Sicilians . . . these are automatically perceived as cases of mafia activity, whereas if a Piedmontese or an Englishman acts in the same way, it is simply an example of unfair dealing.[21]

What distinguishes mafiosi, Gambetta says, is their *autonomy*—the fact that a successful mafioso is an independent agent with so many customers that "no individual buyer is essential for business to succeed." A mafioso is even more autonomous if he supplies protection to a variety of customers rather than having to rely on one type of buyer. That way, his protection "becomes abstract currency, a credible commodity in more than one area."[22]

Gambetta observes that in parts of Sicily where landowners were present and united, rather than absent from their properties and living in urban areas, they were able to supply their own protection. But elsewhere on the island, a new industry supplying protection emerged in the nineteenth century, developing further as commerce linked the countryside with the coastal areas and urban markets. Against the claims of Blok and others that mafiosi migrated to cities at a relatively late stage in their history, Gambetta notes that they had always traveled back and forth between town and country. The mafia of Sicily didn't emerge fully formed from the *latifondi*, nor did it simply spring up where commerce was most vibrant. Instead, "it evolved where the two worlds met."

Gambetta concludes, "In this encounter of rural and urban, force and cunning, lower and middle classes lies the secret of the mafia's origin, the energy that turned it into an industry."[23]

In *Honor Thy Father*, his book about the Sicilian-born gangster Joe Bonanno and his criminal organization, Gay Talese observes, "For centuries their [Sicilians'] region's poverty and pestilence was ignored by the Sicilian government, by the parliament in Rome, by dozens of previous rulers overseas; so finally [mafiosi] took the law into their own hands and bent it to suit themselves, as they had seen the aristocrats do."[24] Talese notes that although the mafiosi recognized that the established order was exploitative, they had no interest in reforming it; instead, they "had learned to work within the system, to exploit it while it exploited the country."[25] Blok similarly notes that the mafiosi were allies of the landowning aristocracy, to whom they posed no threat, and therefore were an inherently reactionary force in society.[26]

That pattern continued to the late twentieth century, with mafiosi allied with conservative political parties, particularly the now-defunct Christian Democrats, and opposed to liberal reform or leftist political currents. (The body count of Sicilians murdered by the mafia in the decades after World War II included numerous Communist Party members and other leftists.) During a visit to Sicily in the mid-1990s, I saw a graffito on a building wall that read CHRISTIAN DEMOCRATS = COSA NOSTRA. The scrawling bespoke the widespread and, as demonstrated by the investigations of the magistrates Giovanni Falcone and Paolo Borsellino, accurate perception among Sicilians that the political party favored by the Vatican was in bed with organized crime.[27]

Falcone and Borsellino, two heroic public servants, knew all too well that their success in prosecuting and jailing hundreds of mafiosi had sealed their own death warrants. Both were assassinated in 1992. These atrocious crimes were breathtaking in their sheer audacity— Falcone, his wife Francesca, also a magistrate, and several bodyguards were killed on the highway from the Palermo airport by explosives hidden in a culvert, Borsellino by a car bomb in front of his mother's apartment building. The murders ignited the simmering rage of long-suffering Sicilians, who, in mass demonstrations in the streets of Palermo and elsewhere on the island, demanded justice. The Italian state subsequently came down hard on the mafia, even sending several thousand troops to Sicily to suppress criminal violence and to protect members of the judiciary.

The troops were still there in 1995 when I visited the island for several weeks. I was stunned by the sight of so many soldiers from all over Italy, many of them just youths, patrolling the Palermo area in military vehicles or standing guard outside official residences, clutching big guns. To appreciate the enormity of the Falcone and Borsellino assassinations and the severity of the Italian government's response, imagine if New York gangsters had murdered the mob-busting prosecutors Rudolph Giuliani and Edward McDonald (of *Goodfellas* fame), and the federal government had sent thousands of National Guard troops to patrol entire boroughs of the city.

In September 2002, accompanied by a Sicilian friend who is a university professor, I visited the Giovanni and Francesca Falcone Foundation, established in Palermo by the martyred magistrate's sister. The foundation, housed in offices that had been occupied by a mafia-connected business shut down by the local government, is a United Nations–recognized nongovernmental organization that works to foster a *"cultura antimafiosa."* It supports research, conducts conferences, and engages in various educational and cultural activities, with a particular focus on reaching and supporting youth, both those who have been affected by mafia violence and those who are at risk for becoming involved with organized crime.

The office manager of the foundation, a soft-spoken but voluble young *palermitana*, gave me and my friend Giovanni a tour of the premises. Holding my arm, she told me, with considerable warmth and sincerity, that it was wonderful that I, a Sicilian American, felt such an affinity for Sicily and for the struggle of its people to liberate themselves from the scourge of the mafia. Her words moved me, but the real emotional wallop came when we entered a room in which Falcone's quarters in the Prosecutor's Office of Palermo had been reconstructed. His desk was there, covered with neatly arranged stacks of paper, folders, and books, as if he had just stepped away for a break from work. The walls were covered with photos, plaques, and framed letters from various governmental and law enforcement agencies, Italian and international, including one from the FBI.

But what really got to me were the ducks. The window ledge was packed with hand-carved and painted duck figurines, which, as the manager explained, Falcone liked to collect. These whimsical carvings, seemingly at odds with the fierce image of the illustrious mafia fighter, brought him more potently to life than did all the accoutrements of his profession. My emotions welled up—affection for this man I never knew, sadness over his loss, and anger at the mafia and those misguided consumers of gangster entertainment back in America who think there's something cool and rebellious about mafiosi.

And I admit, I also thought of another Italian male with a sentimental fondness for aquatic fowl: the fictional mobster Tony Soprano, a brutish killer humanized by the inexplicable sorrow he felt when he discovered that the family of ducks whose presence he took pleasure in had disappeared, abandoning his suburban swimming pool, and him.

If scholars now agree that the criminal associations collectively known as the mafia emerged late in the nineteenth century, there remains some dispute regarding the etymology of the word. Some historians

THE MAFIA / 53

have claimed that it originated as an acronym during the Sicilian rebellion against French rule in the thirteenth century. *Morte alla Francia, Italia anela!* (Italy longs for death to France) purportedly was the rebels' motto. This is unlikely, since the term was not used before the 1860s. It has also been said that the word was an acronym for the battle cry of a Sicilian secret society, dedicated to the revolutionary Giuseppe Mazzini, that waged sabotage against Bourbon officials in the 1860s: *Mazzini Autorizza Furti, Incendi, Avvelenamenti* (Mazzini authorizes theft, arson, and poisoning). Yet another version of the term's origins claims it is an Arab word meaning "cave" or "place of refuge," because Sicilians who rebelled against Arab rule took refuge in caves.[28]

Whatever its genesis, Sicilians have long used *mafia* as an adjective, with a small *m*, to connote an ideal of "courage, strength, agility, quickness, endurance, and intelligence." In this context, *mafia* has nothing to do with crime or criminal societies.[29]

Diego Gambetta declares that "all etymologies which posit a direct origin of *mafia* are wrong, for it is almost certainly a late derivation from *mafiusu*," a Sicilian dialect word that can designate someone who is arrogant or a bully but also "brave, bold, courageous, no-nonsense, handsome."[30]

But Sicilians also used *mafia* to refer to local criminal groups in their homeland, and it is of course this usage that took hold in the United States. As noted earlier, Americans in the late 1800s could read newspaper accounts of the exploits of criminal societies in southern peninsular Italy and Sicily. There were the Neapolitan *camorre*, terroristic gangs that specialized in extortion, blackmail, smuggling, and kidnapping, and the Calabrian 'Ndrangheta (the Brotherhood), whose members engaged mainly in banditry and smuggling.

"Mafia" became the designation applied to all Italian American organized crime because of two notorious murders. In 1890, Police Superintendent David Hennessey was shot to death in New Orleans. Hennessey had made a name for himself investigating the Black Hand extortion rings that preyed on the Sicilian immigrant community. (These gangs bore no similarity either to the Sicilian mafia or to the so-called American Cosa Nostra. The Black Hand extortionists thrived in the poverty, discrimination, and despair of the Sicilian immigrant ghettos.) Although these crimes involved Italians victimizing other Italians, they fed the xenophobia of the native-born population, alarmed at the arrival of so many poor, and to them, strange and threatening Mediterranean immigrants.[31] At the time he was killed, Hennessey was investigating murders that had occurred as part of a bloody fight between rival gangs for control of the Black Hand extortion rackets in New Orleans.

Local bigots and the gutter press not surprisingly blamed Hennessey's murder on the Italians, although they were never able to prove their accusations. (Hennessey's murder remains unsolved to this day.) Fourteen Italians were indicted and imprisoned, and in March 1891 a lynch mob of more than six thousand men broke into the prison. They beat, hanged, and shot to death eleven Italians, several of whom had not even been on trial for the Hennessey murder. Though many members of the mob were identified—the leaders included some of the most prominent citizens of New Orleans—no one was ever held accountable for the lynching, the largest in American history.[32]

Richard Gambino, whose book *Vendetta* and its Showtime cable TV film adaptation of the same name chronicled the Hennessey case, noted that although some public officials and newspapers denounced the lynching, others, including Theodore Roosevelt and *The New York Times*, approved. "Lynch law was the only course open to the people of New Orleans to stay the issue of a new license to the Mafia to continue its bloody practices," the *Times* editorialized.[33]

In the wake of the Hennessey incident, newspapers increasingly published sensational but unsubstantiated stories about the purported exploits of Italian crime outfits. More sophisticated journals wondered whether Italians were predisposed to criminality by dint of genetics, culture, or both. Articles with such titles as "What Shall We Do with the Dago?" and "Are the Italians a Dangerous Class?" articulated and fueled the debate about the supposed predilection of Italians, particularly Sicilians, for criminal activity.[34]

Twenty years later, another murder dispelled any doubts among Anglo-Saxons that the southern Italian immigrants were a lawless bunch bent on establishing their old-world crime syndicates on American soil. In March 1909, Joseph Petrosino, an Italian-born detective in the New York Police Department, was shot to death in Palermo. The press reported that Petrosino was on a mission to investigate purported links between American hoodlums of Italian origin and the Sicilian mafia. But Petrosino's police work in America had convinced him that criminals among the Italian immigrant populations acted alone or with small groups of accomplices, not as members of a well-organized, foreign-based association. Petrosino had actually gone to Sicily to check on the activities of criminals who had returned to Italy from America, and to examine the police records of Italian-born criminals then living in the United States.[35]

But when a prominent Sicilian mafioso claimed credit for killing the detective, the existence of a Palermo connection seemed indisputable. (The actual circumstances of Petrosino's death, however, remain uncertain, and no evidence was ever found to tie the boastful mafioso to criminal activity by Italians in America.)[36] Petrosino's murder became a calamity for Italian Americans. Protestant America, feeling threatened by what it perceived to be a criminal conspiracy that somehow involved virtually every southern Italian, lashed out. There were massive police raids on Italian neighborhoods; Chicago police in 1909 raided the city's Little Italy, jailing 194 Italian Americans. The men were later released when the authorities could not produce any evidence linking them to crimes.[37]

A little more than a decade later, as the Roaring Twenties reached full pitch, the syncopated rhythms of jazz and the rat-tat-tat of machine-gun fire supplied the era's soundtrack. During the 1920s thirsty Americans chafed under the forced abstemiousness of Prohibition, which, as Gay Talese has observed, was imposed on America primarily by Anglo-Saxon zealots. Gangsters, always ready to exploit any need made illicit by government, stepped in to meet the demand for bootleg booze.

"The dagoes . . . they ruined this town!" an Irish cop (played by Sean Connery) rages in Brian De Palma's 1987 film *The Untouchables*. The cop's ire is directed at the notorious Chicago gangster Al Capone, who built a criminal empire on bootlegging. But until Capone came along, the Prohibition-era gangs were generally controlled by Irish and Jewish gangsters; Italians joined as low-level members.[38] The violence and political corruption of the Prohibition era did not originate with Italians.

But eventually Italian American hoodlums did seize control of boot-legging and other rackets financed with profits from bootlegging. The historical roots of an American Cosa Nostra, rather than a criminal syndicate imported and overseen by Sicilian immigrants, purportedly trace back to Prohibition, and specifically to a war between two groups of mobsters, one an Italian-Jewish alliance led by Joseph Masseria and whose members included Vito Genovese, Frank Costello, Meyer Lansky, and "Bugsy" Siegel, the other made up of Sicilians, including Joe Bonanno, Joseph Profaci, and Salvatore Maranzano. The press called the clash between these two groups "the Castellammarese War," because a number of the Sicilians had come from the coastal town of Castellamare del Golfo, near Palermo. (Many years later, Joe Valachi claimed that in early 1930, Masseria and his associates decreed death for any gangster who came from the western Sicilian coastal town.)[39]

The prime casualty of the "war" was Salvatore Maranzano, the leader of the Sicilians, who was killed in September 1931. Maranzano, according to legend, was one of forty-odd "Mustache Petes," old-time Sicilians who were whacked by the younger, Americanized Italians. Once the old-timers' bullet-riddled bodies had cooled, the new Italian American group took control of organized crime in America.

This creation myth of the American Cosa Nostra is, however, not credible. Humbert Nelli, a historian who has specialized in the Prohibition era, disputes the idea that there was a bloody purge, noting that the idea that more than forty leading mobsters could have been killed in two days defies logic.[40] Word of these assassinations would have spread rapidly throughout the underworld, most likely resulting in a counterattack. Moreover, the notion that Maranzano's murder was related to an "Italian civil war over the creation of a new corporate hierarchy in organized crime" makes little sense given that the group responsible for arranging the hit included Meyer Lansky and "Bugsy" Siegel.[41] Why would they involve themselves in an Italian vendetta unless non-Italian hoodlums were likely to reap substantial benefits? And if Jews were part of the group that struck down Maranzano, the idea that organized crime was entirely Italian obviously is untenable.

Nativists did smear Jews and Irish with the notion that their respective groups had inherent criminal tendencies. But, as Richard Gambino points out, "there were no legends of secret criminal societies in the European roots of these groups, and no Gaelic or Yiddish word equivalent to 'Mafia' . . ."[42] The media had used the term "mafia" since the Hennessey and Petrosino cases, and the usage became more widespread during the 1930s, the existence of non-Italian criminals and crime groups notwithstanding. The notion that there was one national organized crime network controlled by men of one ethnic group took hold. Hollywood took notice, and was quick to exploit the sensationalism of what Salvatore La Gumina has called a mafia mystique.

During the 1970s, the concept of "the Mafia" as a centralized, ethnically homogeneous, national crime organization presided over by a board of directors–like Commission faced increasing challenges. Federal law enforcement agencies, students of organized crime,[43] and the media continued to propagate what had been conventional wisdom since the Kefauver hearings, and had been reinforced by the McClellan committee, Joe Valachi, and Lyndon Johnson's Task Force on Organized Crime. But some critics claimed that organized crime, rather than an alien conspiracy that threatened the American socioeconomic system, was integral to the economy because it made available goods and services the law had deemed illicit.

Francis Ianni, an anthropologist and author of several books on organized crime, expressed the emerging counterview:

A small but growing number of law enforcement officials, journalists, and social scientists who have been studying organized crime interpret these same facts quite differently. They see organized crime as an integral part of the American social and economic system, involving: (1) segments of the American public who demand goods and services which are defined as illegal, (2) organized groups of criminals who are willing to take the risks involved in supplying them and (3) the corrupt public officials who protect such individuals for their own profit or gain.[44]

"In this crucial relationship," Ianni said, "the criminal is permitted to produce and provide those illicit goods and services which our morals publicly condemn but which our mores privately demand— gambling, stolen but cheap goods, illegal alcohol, sex, and drugs." In return for being allowed to operate, the criminal was obliged to pay tribute to the political establishment; the history of organized crime testifies "to how gangsters and racketeers paid heavily into the coffers of political machines in exchange for immunity from prosecution." Ianni, echoing Daniel Bell's point about organized crime and upward mobility, noted that "ghetto dwellers and their children have found organized crime an open route to escaping poverty and powerlessness. The successful gangster, like the successful politician, has become a neighborhood model, in addition, proving it is possible to achieve rapid and dramatic success in spite of the police and a variety of oppressors . . ."[45]

Until the 1970s, the Hobbs Act of 1946 was the legislation most often used to indict organized crime figures. The act made the interference with or obstruction of interstate commerce subject to criminal prosecution. Anyone who engaged in such criminal activities as gambling or drug trafficking by using interstate facilities (such as the mail or telephone) was subject to federal prosecution.[46] Later, the 1968 Omnibus Crime Control and Safe Streets Act established a standard and procedure for legal electronic surveillance, which in subsequent decades the FBI used to "spin a thick web of wiretaps and electronic bugs around the organized crime families."[47]

In 1970 Congress enacted what would become the most important anti–organized crime statute, the Racketeer Influenced and Corrupt Organizations Act (RICO), as part of the Organized Crime Control Act. RICO revolutionized the prosecution of organized crime by making it possible to bring to a single trial entire criminal groups for their participation in a criminal enterprise that is "engaged in a pattern of racketeering activity." The law defines a "pattern of racketeering activity" as any two federal or state crimes committed within ten years of one another; an "enterprise" is any individual, organization, or group of individuals legally constituted or associated in fact.

Before RICO, guilt was individual: gangs of criminals could not be prosecuted as gangs unless conspiracy could be proven. If conspiracy could not be proven, prosecutors were forced to prosecute criminals individually. RICO removed these roadblocks, permitting law enforcement authorities, notably U.S. attorney Rudolph Giuliani, to indict hundreds of gangsters. RICO provides draconian penalties—in addition to a twenty-year maximum sentence for violation of both the substantive and conspiracy provisions, the statute levies heavy fines and requires the forfeiture of the defendant's property that is traceable to racketeering activity.[48]

The FBI and federal prosecutors didn't really take advantage of the law until the early 1980s, when "practically every significant organized-crime prosecution was brought under the statute."[49] The government's use of RICO during that time constituted a successful attack on organized crime without precedent, resulting in the convictions of more than a thousand mobsters between 1981 and 1987.[50] Giuliani, then the U.S. attorney for the Southern District of New York, and two U.S. attorneys in New York City, successfully prosecuted the bosses of all of New York's organized crime "families" under RICO provisions.

In his book *Gotham Unbound*, criminologist James B. Jacobs chronicles the government's successful efforts to drive gangsters from their key industrial and labor rackets and to purge urban politics of their influence. He focuses on New York City and in particular on mob penetration of the garment and waste-hauling industries, the construction trade, the Fulton Fish Market, JFK Airport, and the Javits Convention Center. But Jacobs maintains that the city's experience is not unique; the "main themes" of New York's story "could also be told for Boston, Buffalo, Chicago, Cleveland, Jersey City, Kansas City, Las Vegas, Los Angeles, Miami, New Orleans, Newark, Philadelphia, and many other large and small U.S. cities" in which "Italian organized-crime groups have a long history of extensive industrial and labor racketeering and of having functioned as important players in urban politics and in the urban power structure."[51]

Though Jacobs interchangeably uses the terms "Cosa Nostra" and "mafia," his usage is a linguistic convenience. He argues that the empirical evidence to support the existence of a nationwide syndicate called by those names, and governed by a ruling council, does not exist.

"It is best to think of Cosa Nostra as a mélange of locally-based crime families, each of which has exclusive jurisdiction in its territory," he writes. However, this does not mean that there is no communication or cooperation among crime groups. And as Jacobs notes, electronic surveillance in the 1980s revealed that at least several of the New York City families sometimes used a council or a commission, but its jurisdiction and authority remain unclear. It apparently has functioned "like a court called upon to solve occasional disputes."[52]

Jacobs, during an interview at New York University, where he is a law professor and director of the Center for Research in Crime and Justice, endorsed Francis Ianni's assertion that like a shadowy doppelgänger of the capitalism that fuels America, Cosa Nostra has endured because it provided goods and services people wanted.

"The mafia is not all bad," he says. "It's not monolithic evil or anything like that. It's an institution in American society. It provided things that people wanted but were not able to obtain—like alcohol during Prohibition, and gambling, and so forth. They stepped into the breach . . . and loans in the loan-sharking area. So, the mafia was functional. That's why it lasted so long, why it was so powerful, because it served needs."

Jacobs also supports the claim made by actress Katherine Narducci and others that "mobbed-up" neighborhoods were safe places. "[Mafiosi] were a force for stability in neighborhoods," he says.

> They were not involved in random street violence or street crime. They wanted to live in safe neighborhoods, and because they had a reputation for violence and a willingness to use violence, the neighborhoods in which they had a presence were safe. There was no question that what made these organized crime families so powerful was their aura of being willing to use violence—extreme violence. So that was always in the background. They traded on that reputation. But because the reputation was so credible, they didn't often have to use it with common citizens.
>
> So, from my standpoint, I guess [Cosa Nostra] is a more complex phenomenon that I don't think has been adequately

analyzed. What's bad about organized crime? What's the evil? I think that's something that really needs to be thought about. I have some sympathy with this point that sometimes we just paint it with an evil brush. If the mafia engages in cartels and price fixing, we see it as much worse than if there are businessmen doing cartels and price fixing. We ought to stop it, but it's not uncommon. It doesn't become the biggest problem in the nation just because some people associated with Cosa Nostra do it.

People do need credit, and credit, in my mind, is no different than gambling. If we have a law that says that credit can't be provided above a certain rate and there are certain people who don't qualify at that rate because they're too risky, then there's a demand for credit at higher rates, and the mob provided that credit. And I'm sure a lot of people benefited from that credit. Some people didn't benefit. That's true of alcohol, it's true of gambling.

The drugs were a major mistake. I think if you took out the drugs, then the Italian American organized crime families look a lot different. They look a lot more functional. They look a lot more like they're providing useful services. And the things that they did didn't generate huge punishments and penalties, for the most part. Talk about gambling, when [prosecutors] brought in these gambling cases, nobody took them seriously. For many years, there were laws against gambling, but there was no real fear of gambling in the sense of doing something serious about it. But the drugs were different. I think that really hurt the mafia families a lot. Some of the leaders apparently realized that, and wanted to keep their members out of it. But the money was so great . . . So the mafia was always involved in drugs . . .

I think it's interesting that we've never had a grassroots movement that's really seen organized crime as a horror that has to be eradicated. Look at how we look at the drug dealers, and the way we look at pedophiles . . . I think that tells you something. Or even drunk driving. The main momentum for dealing with

organized crime came from professional law enforcement themselves, which saw organized crime as an affront, but didn't really
come from the public or from business or from labor. It tells you
something![53]

The veteran newspaper columnist, reporter, and author Pete Hamill
makes a point akin to Jacobs's about the similarities between some organized crime activities and those of "legitimate" businessmen, but
more pungently. Presenting a roll call of corporate malefactors whom
he says constitute an "axis of sleaze"—among them Enron, the Hal-
liburton Corporation, Adelphia Communications, Kmart, Global Crossing, Qwest, Lucent, Xerox, Tyco, and Martha Stewart's dealings with
ImClone—Hamill says, "If you added up all the illegal profits gathered
by the mob over the past century, you wouldn't come close to what
these corporate sleazebags have won for themselves in the past two
years."[54]

Vittorio Zucconi, an editor and columnist for the Italian newspaper *La
Repubblica,* has called the current era of the American mafia's history
"il declino del padrino," the decline of the Godfather. He maintains that
in America, one can observe "the funeral of the dying Mafia,"[55] and
considering the imprisonment and death of so many top mobsters from
the mid-1980s to the present, it's difficult to argue with him. The most
notorious Italian American mobster, John Gotti, died in a prison hospital of cancer in June 2002. A figure for whom the term "media whore"
could have been invented, Gotti loved the press of TV reporters and as-
sorted paparazzi that would inevitably surround him when he appeared
in public, whether at a nightclub or a courtroom.

Less than a year after Gotti's death, and just weeks after the FBI
won its first defections from the seemingly impenetrable Bonanno
crime family, federal prosecutors indicted the elusive man they claimed
was the family's boss. Joseph C. Massino, known to his confreres as
Big Joey (a nickname he acquired when he weighed four hundred
pounds) and to the media as "the Last Don," was the only one of the
bosses of New York's so-called five families of La Cosa Nostra to evade

prosecution over the previous decade. Now that racketeering and seven murder charges had been filed against him, prosecutors said that virtually all the heads of the "five families" of New York organized crime either were awaiting trial or had been convicted of racketeering crimes.

Brooklyn U.S. attorney Roslynn Mauskopf and other officials, as *The New York Times* reported,

> crowed over the indictments, calling them a capstone of a decade of prosecutions against organized crime bosses that have helped loosen the mob's stranglehold over industries in the New York area. "In the early years, the middle years of the 20th century, the structure of traditional organized crime was formulated, in large measure right here in Brooklyn," she said. "At the beginning of the 21st century, as a result of federal law enforcement's efforts—their determined, their sustained and their outstanding efforts—the heads of the five families and a significant portion of their members have been brought before the bar of justice."[56]

Seven months later, a jury convicted Massino on all charges, including the murder of Dominick Napolitano, a mob chief better known—to his colleagues, to the FBI, and to movie audiences—as Sonny Black. Big Joey had Sonny whacked in 1981 for allowing their organization to be infiltrated by the FBI agent Joseph D. Pistone. Posing as a jewel thief named Donnie Brasco, special agent Pistone had won Sonny's trust and favor so completely that the family nearly offered him full-fledged membership as a "made" man.

Two months after Massino's arrest and indictment in early 2003, the government convicted Peter Gotti, John's elder brother, of racketeering, conspiracy, and money laundering, in "a case that prosecutors described as a historic blow to the mafia and its control of the New York waterfront."[57] Law enforcement officials said that "Uncle Peter" had clung to power in the Gambino organized crime family as a way to ensure Gotti family control of millions of ill-gotten dollars.

During the trial, jurors heard wiretap evidence that demonstrated just how much real mafia life had blended with its cinematic and other pop culture representations. After the *Godfather* films came out in the 1970s, prosecutors noticed that gangsters caught on electronic surveillance had adopted the film's argot, using terms and phrases from the memorable dialogue crafted by Mario Puzo and Francis Ford Coppola. In the Peter Gotti case, surveillance tapes revealed mobsters "expressing a degree of self-awareness about their chosen path that outsiders might find surprising." In an exchange that sounds like dialogue straight from Puzo-Coppola, one mafioso tells a friend that a Gambino associate had just been arrested, and then ruefully observes, "What are you gonna do? That's life. That's the life we chose."[58]

James B. Jacobs in *Gotham Unbound* writes that because of vigorous law enforcement, "Cosa Nostra's survival into the next millennium . . . can be seriously doubted."[59] But successful crime control strategies can't fully explain *"il declino del padrino."* The American mafia's decline has a lot to do with the fact that "the life we chose" today is not the life chosen by young Italian Americans, with the possible exception of those few *disgraziati* whose greed and sociopathy impel them toward crime and those unfortunate enough to have grown up in gangster families.

During the heyday of organized crime, young Italian American males growing up in the ethnic enclaves of Brooklyn or the Bronx, Chicago or Philadelphia, could rub shoulders with actual gangsters. Chazz Palmintieri, recalling the mob's presence in the Bronx of his youth, said, in an interview, "Oh, it was all over the place, it was all around. It was on the corners, it was in every social club." Two decades later, Joseph Pistone, undercover as "Donnie Brasco," discovered that the street culture that had sustained the mafia was dying out.[60] For most Italian Americans, the socioeconomic conditions that had fostered organized crime—poverty, discrimination and social isolation, lack of economic opportunity—are history.

Since the 1960s, many Italian Americans have left the mean streets of their urban neighborhoods for the suburbs. Decades have passed since storefront windows bore signs saying NO ITALIANS NEED APPLY. Italian Americans are no longer condemned to a life of exhausting manual labor; they are now more likely to be lawyers, doctors, teachers, corporate executives, and elected officials. The mafia has not disappeared, but it certainly is disintegrating with the economic ascent of Italian Americans.

Tom Fontana, a Sicilian American from Buffalo, New York, is a successful television producer and writer, whose credits include the HBO prison series *Oz* and the long-running NBC cop drama *Homicide: Life on the Streets*. Growing up in Buffalo, a "mobbed-up" city that was the hometown of Stefano Magaddino, one of the most notorious of the old-time gangsters, Fontana learned early on that his ethnicity conjured up certain images in the minds of non-Italians.

"When I was in grade school," he recalls,

I was standing in the lunch line and one of the other kids said, " 'Fontana,' what kind of name is that?" I said, "Oh, I'm Sicilian." And he goes, "Oh, so your father's in the mafia." Now, this is God's honest truth. I had never heard the word "mafia" before—or if I'd heard it, it had never registered and never meant anything. So I go home and I say to my mother and father, "Are we in the mafia?" and my mother said, "No, honey. They didn't want us." Which was the family joke, because my mother's father was actually from Castellamare del Golfo. And even though he knew a lot of those guys and every once in a while he was asked to do something, it was never anything illegal, at least that my mother can remember. He was an honest businessman and so he never did anything past the minimal amount he needed to do to survive in the neighborhood.

We were raised with a real sense of "That's not a life." I went to high school with a lot of those guys. I went to grade school with the sons of a lot of those guys. But I don't know if it also was that my family was so intent on being American and so intent on moving up, because my parents were Depression-era babies, and they really felt that their children were going to have choices way beyond those that they had been allowed in this several-block radius that was their entire world.

Buffalo is a *very* serious mob town. But somehow, it seemed, at least for our family, that life was an old option, as opposed to the new options that were opening up. The truth is, when I said to my father—this is a long time later—"I'm going to go to New York and be a playwright," he didn't know what the fuck being a playwright meant. But—God love them both—they supported me. I mean, literally—financially as well as emotionally—to come to New York and take this chance—so in that regard, I owe them whatever I've become. Whatever success I've had is a result of them saying, "You not only can move out of the neighborhood, you can move to another city."

I think that without being simplistic about it, the mafia existed in this country for a specific need. There was a very specific need in the immigrant population for this kind of an organization to exist, and the reality is, we Italians are Americans now. We are homogenized. Not that we've lost our culture, but we're judges and lawyers and doctors and senators. It's like in *The Godfather*, when Vito Corleone says, "I wanted something better for you, Michael," and Michael says, "We'll get there, Pop." Well, we got there! We got there! The strength of the mafia came out of a need for it during a period of time. In the same way that the Russian gangsters right now are the meanest motherfuckers on the planet Earth. That's because their need is . . . that's their immigrant population's need. We don't have that need anymore.[61]

Martin Scorsese, in his celebrated Italian American trilogy of *Mean Streets*, *Raging Bull*, and *Goodfellas*, depicts gangsters as members of working-class, ethnic communities rather than as isolated outlaws. The filmmaker's recollections of his youth in Manhattan's Little Italy attest to their function in the economy of a blue-collar, immigrant neighborhood whose members overwhelmingly are law-abiding.

I have to tell you, when I was growing up in the 1940s and 1950s, I was part of a world that had that [organized crime] as an element. Sometimes my mother would ask, "Hey, what fell off the truck today?" Not that she's a thief, but you buy it. "Yellow sweaters! Hey, look what the guys got off the truck," you know, and you bring it around. You gotta beat the system somehow. [Scorsese drew on this experience for a scene in *Goodfellas* in which mobsters all are wearing the same "off the truck" yellow sweaters.]

They were not educated. A lot of the Sicilians, the Italian Americans, were very, very suspicious about the government. That's one of the reasons they ran away from Sicily. They certainly weren't going to put themselves in the hands of an American police force. You have to understand the cultural issues there. They wouldn't trust it. They just basically stayed with the family and everything else.

And so for the first, and into the second generation, I think, it was difficult to get them to understand about taking advantage of America, the opportunity for education, which gives you power, makes you move and that sort of thing. I never thought the things that I put on film could've been put on film when I was growing up. Despite the fact that you had the majority of the people down there [in Manhattan's Little Italy] being hardworking, working-class families, going to the garment district every day to work and coming back, you know. They were not underworld characters, the majority were really good, decent people. But it's that odd combination of knowing people and liking them, and then finding out later what they did. Or knowing some people and not liking them, and finding out what it was they did.[62]

By the mid-1980s, the mafia that Martin Scorsese had known and observed when he was growing up in Little Italy was devolving into something else, an entity more violent, venal, and unpredictable. The late veteran reporter Jack Newfield pinpointed John Gotti's assassination of mob boss Paul Castellano, on December 16, 1985, as the beginning of "the modern mob's New York meltdown." "This transfer of power through gunfire became emblematic of the mob's brain drain, and the loss of its old-world codes of respect, secrecy, and discipline,"[63] wrote Newfield in *New York* magazine. The "unauthorized cowboy assassination" of Castellano hastened the disintegration of the mob, its loss of power and cohesion.

Newfield disapprovingly notes that "Gotti and his crew were into topless bars, steroids, drugs, swagger, and immediate gratification"—in other words, the Teflon Don's gang was more like Tony Soprano's crew than Don Corleone's heroin-eschewing "family." Newfield's article begins as a reasonably straightforward account of the decline of Italian American organized crime in its capital city. But it quickly becomes an exercise in mafia mythology, as Newfield unfavorably compares the new Gotti-era mob to the older, more dignified and disciplined Cosa Nostra. He claims that Salvatore "Sammy the Bull" Gravano, Gotti's top killer, was the first underboss "to abandon the Sicilian blood oath of silence" when he testified against his former boss. Gravano is of Sicilian descent, but his boss was the grandson of Neapolitans. Publicity hound and voluble star of numerous FBI surveillance recordings, John Gotti wasn't too rigorous about maintaining musty old-world traditions of discretion and silence. But the real reason *omertà* collapsed is the prospect of extraordinary long prison sentences. The old-time gangsters, with their industrial and labor rackets and involvement in illicit gambling and prostitution, rarely faced sentences of forty or fifty years.

To Newfield, no single figure epitomizes the contemporary mob's decline more than John Gotti, Jr., who actually kept a typed list of his supposedly secret organization's members in his basement, where federal investigators found it in 1997. "DUMBFELLA," proclaimed the New York *Daily News* front page headline. Newfield says, "DUMB-FELLA will stand forever as the final epitaph for the modern mob in New York."[64]

If Newfield is too taken in by mafia mythology to clearly see the larger structural reasons for the mob's decline, Gay Talese believes that the mafia today is little more than the mythology, which is sustained by institutional interests. "*The New York Times* will run an organized crime piece about someone in Queens being shot in a disco by a member of the Bonanno family, and there hasn't been a Bonanno family since 1971," he scornfully says. "It's remarkable how familiar these names are, since most of these guys have either been dead for some time or are senile. But this mafia mythology will never die because the crime families have been established" for five decades in the mind of the American public by "the Justice Department, the FBI, and journalists.

"There are vested interests in keeping [Cosa Nostra] alive and identifiable," Talese argues. "The Justice Department since 1957 has defined five families and has invested a hell of a lot of time and money in defining" organized crime in these familial, and familiar, terms. "Organized crime must exist to justify the budget to fight it," Talese says. "So it's kept alive for much the same reasons Disney keeps Dumbo alive—to keep the franchise going."[65]

Talese overstates his case; Italian American organized crime groups, though battered by law enforcement and in decline, still exist. But in a larger sense he is correct: these days "the Mafia" thrives only in its representations, in the mythologies of law enforcement and popular culture.

3

A Genre Is Born: The Appeal of Pure Power

The gangster film is a genre like pornography and the horror film, held in contempt socially and intellectually not because it may corrupt and not because it is artistically inferior to other kinds of films but because it realizes our dreams, exposes our deepest psychic urges.
                                        —Jonathan Munby, *Public Enemies, Public Heroes*

Mobsters have everything you don't: power, money, women, cars, security, and most of all, a certain leverage.
                                        —Chris Messenger, *"The Godfather" and American Culture*

Mob stories are always hot.   —Christopher Moltisanti in *The Sopranos*

W ho's Attila? The leader of some wop gang?"
        Bull Weed, a bank robber, poses this question in the 1927
        film *Underworld* when another crook makes a comment about "Attila at the gates of Rome." Directed by Josef von Sternberg and written by Ben Hecht, *Underworld* is regarded by cinema historians as the first modern gangster film. But despite the allusion to ethnic crime groups, Hecht's Oscar-winning script does not feature Italian American criminals; his hoodlums are native-born Americans.

For Hecht, "gangsters were not just good copy, but legitimate heirs to the robber barons of the nineties, to be cultivated and enjoyed and not too reluctantly admired."[1] Hecht's appreciation of Prohibition-era hoods sounds no different from that of mob movie fans in successive decades, who have cultivated, enjoyed, and not too reluctantly admired godfathers and goodfellas in the movies and on TV.

The "floridly sinister figure"[2] of the Italian American gangster that began to appear on movie screens in the late 1920s and early 1930s was embodied by characters with such names as Nick Scarsi, Tony Camonte, Louis Beretti, and Rico Bandello.

But since Prohibition-era organized crime was multiethnic, movie mobsters also included Bennie Horovitz, Tommy Doyle, and Nicky Solomon. Despite the near-total identification of Italians with gangsterism that persists to this day, most of the early gangland leaders were Jewish or Irish; Italians joined their gangs as low-ranking members. It was Alphonse Capone who established Italian dominance in the Chicago underworld, deposing the Irish and their leader Bugs Moran.

Hollywood's association of gangsterism with Italian American ethnicity did not begin, as is often assumed, with *Little Caesar* (1931), which was based on the rise and fall of the Sam Cardinelli gang in Chicago. The first real Italian mob movie, *Doorway to Hell*, was released the previous year. The genre's inauspicious debut was a romanticized portrayal of Johnny Torrio, a Chicago gangster who in 1925 turned over the keys to his crime kingdom to his protégé Al Capone. Besides being clunky and unexciting, *Doorway to Hell* lacked a charismatic star; instead it had the bland, WASPy Lew Ayres as Louis Ricarno, the Torrio character. Ayres was simply unbelievable as a murderous criminal: "In place of a gangland executive with a Napoleonic complex, there was a cute collegian who, when he talked about a killing, sounded and looked like a frat brother describing an initiation."[3]

No one could say the same about Edward G. Robinson's portrayal the following year of Cesare Rico Bandello, the eponymous mobster of *Little Caesar*. Robinson, short and bulldoggish, with a perpetual glower on his heavy-featured face, made a brooding and convincingly dangerous gangster. Compared to later movie mobsters, Robinson's Rico displays little overt *italianità* beyond a fondness for spaghetti and membership in the Palermo Club. But the Romanian-born Jewish actor brought a brutish physicality and impatient energy to his portrayal of a small-time thug who rises to the heights of the underworld, only to lose it all, including his life. At his violent death, he offers the cri de coeur that, until Vito Corleone's unrefusable offer, was the most celebrated gangster utterance: "Mother of Mercy! Is this the end of Rico?"

The other definitive portrait of the Italian American gangster in the 1930s is *Scarface* (1932), produced by Howard Hughes, directed by Howard Hawks, and written by Ben Hecht. Tony Camonte, the eponymous villain played by veteran Yiddish stage actor Paul Muni, was based on Al Capone, who, when the film was released, was residing in a federal prison in Atlanta, serving time for income tax evasion. Hecht's script drew on a novel of the same name, and a New York *Daily News* reporter who was an authority on Capone was retained as technical adviser.[4] Hawks, however, wasn't aiming for strict realism. He suggested to Hecht that the Capone crime organization be depicted as a contemporary Chicago version of the *la famiglia Borgia*. This meant primarily a suggestion of incest between Camonte and his sister, according to film historian Carlos Clarens, who says that ultimately the Borgia angle "was barely visible in the film as released."[5]

But for other critics, the Borgia motif with its hint of sibling incest is integral to the film's "atmosphere of conspiracy and violence."[6] Critic Robert Casillo argues that Hecht's approach "repeats the longstanding identification in the Anglo-Saxon mind of Italians with Renaissance duplicity. Similarly, the identification of Italians with incest confirms the horror of the native core culture towards seemingly atavistic Old World familialism." Casillo observes that "Tony Camonte first appears as a lowbrow simian with oily hair who speaks pidgin English riddled with malapropisms; as he rises in the world of crime he becomes more professional, more 'American,' and more human."[7]

We get our first look at Camonte when he emerges from under a barber's towel. He's hardly a pretty sight, with his apelike visage and oiled hair, a nasty-looking scar on his cheek, and speaking in an Italian accent that was more (Chico) Marx than Mezzogiorno. He gradually becomes Americanized, losing the accent and acquiring a more expensive wardrobe, "so that at the picture's end Camonte is almost accent-free and tuxedo-sharp—even his hairline seems to have receded from the Neanderthal brow."[8]

But the depictions of Italians in *Scarface* are not all unflattering; Casillo singles out the "superior morality" of Tony's mother, while Camonte's police nemesis is named Guarino, a detail that "anticipates those later films in which, to avoid the suggestion of an ethnic slur, the gangster is balanced by a policeman or priest of the same ethnic origin."[9] Summarizing the images that appeared in these two seminal films, Casillo notes, "Paradoxically, the Italian American gangster either is too familial or else non- or anti-familial—a misconception that Coppola, in *The Godfather*, worked hard to dispel."[10]

Scarface is much more violent than *Little Caesar*, with some fifteen killings. The opening sequence reenacts Capone's 1920 murder of "Big Jim" Colosimo, whom Capone shot to death in a phone booth under orders from his mentor Johnny Torrio. The film also re-creates the notorious St. Valentine's Day Massacre, in which seven men associated with gangster Bugs Moran were lined up against a garage wall and executed. Though graphic for the times, the film could not fully convey the sheer gruesomeness of the actual killings—Capone's hit men fired more than one thousand machine-gun bullets at the luckless hoods, resulting in near-decapitations and severed limbs. The slaughter spurred public outrage, leading to the federal tax investigation that resulted in Capone's conviction in the fall of 1931.[11]

Scarface does not, however, include one of Capone's best-known acts of violence, his beating of one of his associates with a baseball bat during a testimonial dinner. The omission is odd, given that Hawks said that this anecdote is what interested him in Capone in the first place. But the baseball battering later turned up in Nicholas Ray's 1958 film *Party Girl* (with Lee J. Cobb as the Capone character) and in Brian De Palma's 1987 *The Untouchables*, with Robert De Niro wielding the bat. De Niro's portrayal ranks as perhaps the best—certainly the most frightening—of the Chicago crimelord, with the possible exception of Ben Gazzara's work in *Capone* (1975). Rod Steiger did a creditable job in the 1959 film *Al Capone*, but only Gazzara and De Niro created Capones that were convincingly Italian. Others who have played the gangster, or characters based on him—Jason Robards, Jr., Neville Brand, and Paul Muni—haven't come close.

Every era seems to get the gangsters it needs and desires. The Corleone family appeared on the pop-culture landscape during the late 1960s–early '70s, when war was raging in Southeast Asia and generational conflict and radical cultural change roiled the home front. At a time when traditional authority—government, family, church—was under siege, *The Godfather* upheld patriarchal power, filial loyalty, and cultural tradition. *Part II*, however, was far more iconoclastic, mercilessly exposing the corrupt, repressive underside of these values.

Brian De Palma's *The Untouchables* (1987) was in tune with the zeitgeist of the 1980s, but in a surprising way. De Palma, a Hitchcock devotee and imitator whose sensibility—luridly sexual, ultraviolent, and anti-establishment—yielded films like *Sisters, Carrie*, and *Dressed to Kill*, made a gangster movie that extolled Reaganite "family values." His Eliot Ness, played as a straight-arrow WASP by Kevin Costner (Ness actually was Jewish), is a happily married man and father, and the script, by man's man playwright David Mamet, makes repeated reference to the joys of domestic life. De Niro's Al Capone, unlike the Corleones, is defiantly antifamilial. His lack of family ties, in fact, is a marker for his general viciousness and inhumanity. (The real Capone, however, married an Irish woman married Mae Coughlin when they were both in their early twenties, and they had a son, Albert Francis.) Encountering Eliot Ness, he sneeringly delivers the ultimate taunt, "I fuck you and your family!" Ness is heroic not only because he represents the law but because he's an upright family man, with a wife and winsome children who adore him.

Though De Palma's *Untouchables* tendentiously contrasted conservative "pro-family" values to gangster amorality, the film did offer a more realistic depiction of gangsters than Coppola's Corleones. "I don't like to make my criminals family men who are only in it because their father's dying," he said. "I love *The Godfather*, but it's not my image of mobsters."[12]

The Sopranos, which debuted in 1999, presents mafiosi as suburbanites, struggling with the same postmodern problems as other members of the noncriminal middle class: changes in gender relations in the wake of feminism, economic uncertainty, a sense that the American dream isn't what it once was and perhaps was a chimera all along.

Scarface was a huge hit with audiences in 1932, and its popularity wasn't due solely to Ben Hecht's vivid script and Howard Hawks's powerfully expressionistic visual style. In the 1930s, film scholar Jonathan Munby observes, "The gangster hero was a big box-office draw, and it is clear that far from disturbing audience empathy, the gangster's misfit status was key to his attraction." Like the Depression-era audiences in the thirties, the gangster wanted to escape poverty; Italians and Jews could also relate to the struggle of a Rico Bandello or a Tony Camonte to break out of the immigrant ghetto. Munby continues: "What made the early 1930s Hollywood gangster appealing, then, was not the degree to which he reflected the bad side of real gangsters. Rather, the recourse to realism was part of a concerted attempt to address the real social experiences and desires of a Depression- and Prohibition-era audience. Gangster movies stylized gangsterdom (albeit in the name of documentary realism) in order to bring Hollywood closer to its audience."[13]

The gangster's rebellion against society's rules, his relentless drive to move ahead, to get somewhere, resonated with Americans burdened by hard times. For those among the Depression's countless victims who would have liked to lash out at economic and social oppression in the same fearless, uncompromising way as movie mobsters, but were not inclined to break the law, the gangster functioned as a "projection of a collective resentment."[14] And one of the things Americans most resented was Prohibition.

The Volstead Act, under which the sale and consumption of alcohol was illegal for thirteen years, was foisted on the country mainly by Anglo temperance crusaders, as Gay Talese has observed.[15] The huge wave of immigration from southern and eastern Europe unsettled Anglo-Saxons, challenging their social, cultural, and political hegemony. On the one hand, the growth of American industrial capitalism required the labor of these uprooted peasants, artisans, and unskilled workers. But their cultural and perceived racial differences threatened Anglo-Saxon dominance and thus had to be managed, regulated, *controlled*.

Prohibition was rooted in the emerging philosophies of Taylorism, with its emphasis on worker efficiency, scientific management, and social engineering, all of which were intended "to rationalize not only work but the laborers themselves."[16] Booze threatened the productiveness and efficiency of workers, which was bad enough, but the places where it was consumed, such as bars, dance halls, workers' clubs, represented leisure—free time that would be used irresponsibly and dangerously by the new, non–Anglo-Saxon ethnic working class.

If, as Jonathan Munby claims, Prohibition "was an attempt to control the new consumer culture [generated by modern industrial capitalism] in terms of the puritan ethic,"[17] Italian immigrants were most in need of such regulation. Prohibition was introduced in 1920, and in the Roaring Twenties there were already four million Italians in America, much to the displeasure of nativist Americans. WASP elite opinion viewed Italians as wine drinkers who were lawless by nature, as well as clannish and uncouth. The press helped reinforce this image with their copious coverage of the notorious bootlegger Al Capone, who was portrayed as an antihero, simultaneously deplorable and irresistibly fascinating.

But what the WASP establishment disapproved, moviegoers ate up. The American entertainment industry, through gangster pictures, not only articulated the desires of the working-class and ethnic "other"; it also lent its sanction to those desires.[18]

In *Scarface*, the lure of success, American capitalist–style, is beamed to the city's inhabitants in the form of a travel agency sign that proclaims THE WORLD IS YOURS. Tony Camonte takes the sign seriously; he is impatient to grab what its message promises. As he ascends the criminal hierarchy, he lives large, buying silk shirts, tailored suits, and lots of jewelry. When his girlfriend scorns his taste in jewelry as gaudy, even effeminate, Tony is wounded. He desperately wants to be legit and leave behind the Old World, symbolized by his traditional southern Italian mamma. Recognizing that being able to read and write English and to speak it well are necessary to acquire status and power, Camonte yearns to be literate and takes elocution lessons to lose his accent. He even sets up his office in imitation of a legitimate business, with a telephone and a secretary. Tony Camonte's struggle to break free from the constraints of the Old World, and to win acceptance in the New, is not only that of Italians but of all ethnic Americans.

Besides functioning as figures expressing a collective resentment of injustice and the struggle of working-class ethnics to make it, 1930s gangsters provided a useful object lesson to the moviegoing public. As film critic Robert Warshow explains it, "In the end it is the gangster's weakness as much as his power and freedom that appeals to us; the world is not ours, but it is not his either, and in his death he 'pays' for our fantasies, releasing us momentarily both from the concept of success, which he denies by caricaturing it, and from the need to succeed, which he shows to be dangerous."[19]

Audiences in the 1930s identified so strongly with movie mobsters that the producers of *Scarface* were not permitted to release the film until they added a scene "featuring a moral diatribe by a press representative and moral custodians against the gangster."[20] After resisting pressure from censors, Howard Hughes eventually gave in. (The film's director, however, did not go along; Howard Hawks refused to shoot any additional scenes.)

There are two scenes in which the established Anglo order asserts its moral and policing authority over gangland. In the first, a detective denounces the notion that a gangster is a "colorful character." "Colorful? What color is a crawling louse? Say listen, that's the attitude of too many morons in this country. They think these big hoodlums are some sort of demi-gods."[21]

The second intrusion of established society comes in a scene set in the office of the publishers of the *Evening Record*, a Mr. Garston. As the scene begins, representatives of local civic groups are complaining to Garston about what they perceive as his paper's excessive coverage of gangsters, which they believe serves only to glorify them. The publisher urges the good citizens to protest not his paper's reportage but the laxness of government: "Instead of trying to hide the facts, get busy and see that laws are passed that'll do some good . . . Pass a federal law that puts the gun in the same class as drugs and white slavery. Put teeth in the deportation act."[22]

The civic leaders include an Italian, who, in a fresh-off-the-boat accent, agrees with the publisher's condemnations of gangsters: "Thatsa true. They bring nothin' but-a disgrace to my people."

The *Scarface* released in 1932 offered these corrective scenes, in which, as Jonathan Munby observes, the dominant Anglo culture "manifests itself as a policing agency" that chastens the audience's enjoyment by imposing bourgeois moralism on the raffish, blue-collar gangland tale.[23] In the same censorious spirit, two violent sequences, including the reenactment of the St. Valentine's Day Massacre, were cut from the version seen by Depression-era audiences, though later restored.

Whatever the gangster may have signified to American moviegoers in the 1930s, including Italian Americans, to the first generation of Italian American antidefamation activists, characters like Tony Camonte, Rico Bandello, and other fictional Mediterranean mobsters represented the dominant WASP culture's attempts to subordinate their ethnic group by controlling its cinematic portrayals. Fred Gardaphé, a leading figure in contemporary Italian American studies, identifies the portrayal of gangsters in the early mob movies like *Little Caesar* and *Scarface* with blackface minstrelsy. In a similar vein to the wearing of blackface by black and white performers, "the early use of the gangster figure was a means of exploiting and controlling a variant culture through performance . . . In this way, the majority culture could co-opt and control the subculture while defusing any threat posed by the difference the Italian immigrant brought to American culture."[24]

The threat, Gardaphé argues, lay in the ethnic gangster's swaggering sexuality and his demonstrated mastery as "the man with the plan, the man of action"[25] who says *vaffanculo* to society's rules and gets things done his way. To Gardaphé, the gangster minstrelsy is evident in several key distortions of *italianità* common to mob movies, including "the repression of the role of women in Italian culture and the replacement of the mother/son paradigm with the father/son paradigm."[26]

The first protests against the association of Italians with organized crime emerged in the 1930s. And although organizations such as the Order of the Sons of Italy in America failed to have *Scarface* banned, "they exerted enormous influence against the invidious portrayal of their brethren."[27] Section 10 ("National Feelings") of the Hollywood production code of 1933 specified that "no picture shall be produced that tends to incite bigotry or hatred among people of different races, religions, or national origins." Even when a movie character was based on an actual Italian gangster, such as the mobster modeled on Lucky Luciano in *Marked Woman* (1937), his name was anglicized. The production code also fostered a shift in focus from gangsters like Tony Camonte and Rico Bandello to the lawmen who pursued them: "Films that featured the gangster were relegated to B-movie status as the former stars of gangster films began taking on the roles of the G-men and police."[28]

The boom years in gangster movies lasted from 1930 to 1942; but in the decade that followed the gangster virtually disappeared from screens. World War II "had brought about years of patriotic machine gunning . . . and the absence of the gangster from the screen went practically unnoticed."[29] After the war, the genre known as film noir emerged. The term has been used somewhat indiscriminately to characterize just about any movie depicting crime and which has a "dark" tone and unhappy ending. Originally it was applied by French critics to the "tawdry-glamorous, big-city, low-life thrillers" made in Hollywood after the war. As film historian Carlos Clarens notes, the underworld as seen in the film noir—"not exactly a class, a group, or a milieu"—bore little or no resemblance to actual organized crime in America. In fact, "No real-life criminals were portrayed in American films from Dillinger in 1945 until Baby Face Nelson in 1957, roughly the heyday of the film noir."[30]

When Italian American gangsters did appear in movies made after World War II, the lingering influence of the Hollywood production code often "led to the balancing of negative and favorable images in the same film," as in *Cry of the City* (1948), where the Italian criminal finds his antithesis in an Italian policeman. The film, directed by Robert Siodmak and written by Richard Thorpe, was a "doppelgänger narrative" about two Italian Americans who grew up together, one turning to crime, the other to law enforcement.[31]

Kiss of Death, also from 1948, was "one of the few films of its period," notes Robert Casillo, "to convey a plausible rather than a grotesque view of Italian family attitudes." The protagonist, Nick Bianco, is a small-time criminal who steals to support his impoverished immigrant family. Victor Mature, who often came across as dull and wooden on-screen, gave one of his better performances as Bianco.[32]

Bianco becomes an informer at the urging of an ambitious district attorney named Di Angelo (played by Brian Donlevy). But Di Angelo cannot protect Bianco from the mob, and he is nearly killed. *Kiss of Death* managed not only to "undercut the usual antithesis between the good Italian American and the Italian American criminal," it also made audiences sympathize with an informer.[33]

But the same period also produced films in which Italian American characters were unmitigatedly bad. Sociologist Richard Gambino, commenting on *Detective Story* (1951), says "virtually every criminal shown in the movie's presentation of police life in New York from ordinary thug to wealthy gangster was depicted in the crudest, most insulting stereotypes of Italian-Americans."[34] *Key Largo*, from 1948, features Edward G. Robinson as the vicious gangster Johnny Rocco, who, in his limitless greed, is another Italian American criminal, like Scarface or Little Caesar, "identified with endless, aimless desire, a threat to the disciplined business mentality of the American core culture."[35]

The Black Hand, from 1950, is notable less for its cinematic quality than for its attempt to portray the origins of Italian American organized crime. Directed by the reliably undistinguished Richard Thorpe and starring Gene Kelly and J. Carrol Naish, *The Black Hand* was inspired by New York detective Joseph Petrosino's attempt to investigate purported connections between the extortionists operating in Little Italy and criminal syndicates in Sicily. (Petrosino believed that most of the New York hoods were expatriate mafiosi who had fled Sicily.) Although Petrosino was shot to death in Palermo shortly after his arrival, the connection between Old and New World criminals was never proven. The film, however, strongly suggests such a link; a disclaimer at the beginning states, "This story deals with the hard, angry days when these new citizens began to place their stake in the American dream—when they purged the Old World Terror of the Black Hand."[36]

Carlos Clarens notes that the word "purged" signifies a view of organized crime as a foreign import, not a social problem that arose spontaneously in America due to specifically American conditions. Italians had to eradicate the vestiges of the bad Old World from their ranks before they could achieve respectability as assimilated Americans.[37] In *The Black Hand*, the purging is performed by Johnny Columbo (Kelly), whose father, an honest attorney, has been murdered by gangsters. Columbo—a name that evokes the Genoese explorer who "discovered" America and thus symbolizes the "good Italian"—is meant to be a hero. But his methods are pretty much indistinguishable from those of the mobsters he battles. He extracts information at knifepoint from *omertà*-silenced and terrified immigrants, blows up the Black Hand headquarters, and murders the local mob boss.

The Black Hand suggests that Italians have a special propensity for crime, a sanguinary heritage that they must reject to become American. The film's condescension, however, is slightly tempered by a heartfelt speech delivered by J. Carrol Naish as Lorelli, the Petrosino character: "No dagos, no wops, no guineas allowed. They don't think we're good. All they read in the papers is about murder. Are we an inferior race as they say?"[38] Lorelli's speech, though it may have been intended to soothe sensibilities abraded by the film's association of Italians with criminality, does powerfully convey one Italian's resentment over the prejudice and defamation his people encountered in WASP America.

The Black Hand went into movie theaters the same year that the glowing box in American living rooms would bring the public the Kefauver committee's revelations of the vast and well-organized criminal conspiracy known as the mafia. In that context, the movie appeared as a report on the origins of a contemporary threat.

A year later, Warner Brothers, known for its gritty urban social dramas, released *The Enforcer*, with Humphrey Bogart as Ferguson, a tenacious Manhattan assistant DA out to bust the head of a gang of professional killers. The movie mob was based on a Jewish-Italian gang from Brooklyn that the press dubbed "Murder Incorporated." Though the actual Murder Inc. was led by Louis "Lepke" Buchalter, a Jew, the film's fearsome gang boss is inaptly named Mendoza. (Perhaps the studio, not wanting to offend either Italians or Jews, settled on a Spanish surname for the villain because there were no Hispanic counterparts of the Anti-Defamation League and the Sons of Italy to contend with in 1951.) Mendoza's gang is an ethnically mixed bunch; two characters, Joe Rico and Tom Zaca, have Italian names, but there's also a Duke Malloy, an O'Hara, and one Big Babe Lazich, played by Zero Mostel.

The characters most clearly defined as Italian, interestingly enough, are victims of Mendoza's gang. The voluble, heavy-accented immigrant, Tony Vetto—a "Mustache Pete," as American-born Italians often called the "old-timers"—is murdered because he witnessed a killing by Mendoza's gang. His daughter Angela, who also saw the murder, comes out of hiding and agrees to be Ferguson's star witness: her testimony will send Mendoza to the electric chair.

The Enforcer is a workmanlike film that hardly qualifies as a milestone in gangland movie history. But one aspect makes it more than just a footnote. Ferguson and the cops, as they investigate Mendoza's outfit, are puzzled by the gang's argot of "contracts" and "hits." In successive years, reporting on organized crime syndicates and movies about mobsters would render these terms commonplace. But in 1951, it was a revelation—to both law enforcement and the public—that they referred to murder for hire.

During the postwar years, Hollywood not only depicted Italians as gangsters but also as hapless proles whose ethnic traits condemned them to social inferiority. *Marty* (1955), directed by Delbert Mann and written by Paddy Chayefsky, portrays the dull, lonely life of the title character, an Italian American butcher from the Bronx, played by the Italian American actor Ernest Borgnine, who won an Oscar for his performance. Marty, homely and shy, is afraid that no woman will ever love him. He eventually does meet and fall in love with a woman with a comparable lack of self-esteem, but unfortunately she is not Italian. The two lovers' ethnic mismatch causes problems with Marty's family, but the obstacles are overcome and the butcher and his girl marry.

Though regarded in its day as a compassionate portrayal of working-class ethnics, *Marty*, as Robert Casillo has noted, "reeks of sentimental condescension and liberal pity toward the 'little people.' " The film's Italian characters, Casillo aptly observes, are "amusingly crude but indolent, aimless, and ineffectual."[39] The verbal exchanges between Marty and his pal Angie convey what Chayefsky saw as the emptiness of their sad little lives: "Whaddya wanna do, Angie?" "I dunno, whaddya wanna do, Marty?"

Another film from the same period, *Somebody Up There Likes Me* (1958), pretended to be the biography of the Italian American boxer Rocky Graziano—with blue-eyed, Jewish-WASP Paul Newman improbably cast in the lead role. Newman's risible attempt to portray a tough, streetwise Italian American provides some unintended amusement in a film packed with invidious portrayals of Italian Americans. The hero is likable, but he "still resembles the thugs and brutes he leaves behind"[40] as he rises from his impoverished and crime-ridden Italian American social milieu. His attainment of fame and riches comes from his success in a sport that not only relies on violence and brutality but that is controlled to a considerable extent by gangsters.

In 1961 a B picture titled *The Most Dangerous Man Alive* mentioned the 1957 gathering of reputed organized crime figures in Apalachin, New York. This reference was unusual in that movies about the mafia as an organization, rather than individual criminals like Scarface or Rico Bandello, were fairly rare. Hollywood heretofore had produced only three films about Sicilian and Italian American crime organizations—*The Black Hand* and *Pay or Die* (1960), both based on the Joseph Petrosino story, and *The Brotherhood*, a 1968 crime family saga starring Kirk Douglas as a Sicilian mafia patriarch.[41] Critical reaction to the Douglas film was generally favorable, but it was a resounding flop at the box office. That commercial failure, and a budding Italian American campaign against an anticipated film version of Mario Puzo's bestselling novel, almost prevented another movie about a Sicilian mafia patriarch from being made.[42]

Films about gangsters appealed to moviegoers during the Prohibition and Depression eras because they articulated the resentments and desires of working-class and ethnic audiences, and sanctioned those resentments and desires, even as they dramatized the ultimate consequences of gangsterism—imprisonment and violent death. The early gangster films, as cultural critic Robert Warshow explained, depicted the gangster's weakness as much as his appealing power and freedom, telling us that "the world is not ours, but it is not his either."

Warshow wrote his two most famous essays about movie gangsters, "The Gangster as Tragic Hero" and "Movie Chronicle: *The Westerner*," in 1948 and 1954 respectively, before the emergence of the mafia genre, with its godfathers and their families (consanguine and sanguinary), and its obligatory Italian American ambience, or, as *Sopranos* creator David Chase calls it, "the tomato sauce."[43] Warshow's subtle and persuasive readings of the gangster film center on the professional criminal as a figure who "speaks for us, expressing that part of the American psyche which rejects the qualities and demands of modern life, which rejects 'Americanism' itself."[44] He writes about the gangster as a solitary urban creature, not as a member of a particular ethnic group engaged in organized criminal activity with others of the same ethnicity. And these particular ethnic criminals, in both real life and reel life, don't so much reject Americanism as seek success in America, but strictly on their own terms.

As Jonathan Munby has observed, the appeal of gangster films is connected to the appeal of genres themselves, and their ability to "realize our dreams" and "expose our deepest psychic urges." Genre films— horror, science fiction, detective stories, musicals, westerns, even pornography—rely on particular conventions of plot, style, and character. Each genre has its common characteristics, with which fans are intimately familiar. Horror exploits and exorcises our fear of death; vampire films in particular tell us that though we must die, there are worse things than mortality. Westerns evoke a lost world in which lone, rugged men, unencumbered by women and the refinement and civilization they represent, live by their own moral codes, dispensing rough justice. Science fiction envisions worlds yet to be, or depicts confrontations between our world and alien realms; in both instances, the vision tends to the dystopic.

For fans of genre films, it is the familiar—or rather how a particular horror or gangster or sci-fi film juggles, combines, or manipulates the familiar elements—that determines whether the movie or TV series satisfies. "The joy in genre is to see what can be dared in the creation of a new form or the creative destruction and complication of an old one."[45] But the pleasure of genre isn't only aesthetic. Superior genre works orchestrate their conventions so that they not only entertain us but also penetrate and expose our psyches, our complicated and contradictory dream lives.

The mafia genre's conventions are relatively new: *The Godfather*, published in 1969, is the template. Francis Ford Coppola's adaptation of Puzo's novel, and its first sequel, *The Godfather, Part II*, created a new cinematic form, the Italian American mafia genre, and creatively destroyed and complicated the older gangster genre. Though hardly the first artful gangster movie, *The Godfather* surpassed all its predecessors. Much has been written about its operatic qualities (Vito Corleone's famous speeches are compared to spoken arias), Gordon Willis's superb cinematography, the haunting score by Nino Rota, and the indelible performances of Brando, Pacino, De Niro, et al. The Corleone family saga, centering on a sovereign of sorts and the favored son to whom he bequeaths his kingdom, has the resonance of myth, and the decline of the shining prince into a conscienceless killer gives the family saga a tragic dimension.

But, as agitated Italian American antidefamationists pointed out, there was more to Coppola's films than splendid artistry. More than any previous film depicting Italian mobsters, *The Godfather* establishes a symbiotic relationship between *italianità* and organized criminality. Not only are these gangsters the most Italian-defined of any movie hoodlums, speaking in Sicilian dialect and singing "La luna mezzu' mari," eating capicola sandwiches and engaging in the bloody vendettas that decimated the male populations of entire villages back in Sicily. The *Godfather* films identify the organization and values of a mafia clan with those of the southern Italian/Sicilian family. The profits of the Corleone crime "family" nourish the Italian immigrant family, and the Italian family culture sustains the crime family.

The Godfather, by brilliantly reinventing the gangster genre, influenced every mafia movie that came after it. It became the touchstone by which all its successors were measured. It's not an exaggeration to say that *The Godfather* is the Torah, and everything else is commentary. Mafia movies made post-*Godfather* cribbed from it, paid homage to it, imitated it, parodied it, and even challenged its version of the mafia. (Martin Scorsese's brutal, darkly funny, and entirely unsentimental films about mob life collectively constitute an anti-*Godfather*.) But now, three decades later, the hallmarks of the genre established by Coppola's films—the swarthy "family" men in the dark suits, the remorseless violence, the conniving and duplicity, the soundtracks, with their minestrone of vintage Italian American pop, Neapolitan standards, and operatic arias—have become pop culture clichés, ripe for parody and satire.

But long before *Analyze This* and *The Sopranos*, the first sign that the Godfather had become such a familiar American pop-culture icon that he could be played for laughs was John Belushi's Vito Corleone spoof on *Saturday Night Live* in the late 1970s. Belushi's Vito is a reluctant group therapy patient who can't get in touch with his feelings about the Tattaglia family, the rival mob clan that murdered his son

Santino. When the other group members accuse Vito of "blocking" his "true feelings," the therapist gently chides them, "Vito will tell us what he's feeling when he's ready." Besides the dead-on accuracy of Belushi's impersonation, the laughs come from the incongruity of Vito Corleone, an old-fashioned, tight-lipped mafioso committed to *omertà*, blabbing about the family business to a shrink. This was an exceedingly outré comedy concept at the time.

Prizzi's Honor, director John Huston's 1985 adaptation of Richard Condon's novel, depicts the eponymous Sicilian-descended mafia clan as a bunch of bumblers. Led by a cadaverous old don who possesses none of Vito Corleone's austere authority, the Prizzis have no outlaw allure and elicit no terror or pity. One by one the Prizzi brothers are "whacked," and by a Polish-American hit woman, no less, who falls in love with, and is later killed by, a Prizzi assassin played by Jack Nicholson, whose mushmouthed speech seems a parodic homage to Don Corleone.

If the test of a genre's vitality is its continuing relevance, the ability of its conventions to "still express themes and conflicts that preoccupy its audience,"[46] then the stunning success of *The Sopranos* proves that the mafia genre, notwithstanding its familiarity, still has life in it. The voluminous commentary that seeks to explain our long-running attraction to mafia stories locates the appeal of the cable TV series in several basic themes: power and powerlessness, an ambivalent identification with outlaws, nostalgia, and the visceral thrill of screen violence.

"The key to the Mafia mania," notes Richard Gambino, "is that Americans yearn for the aura of *l'ordine della famiglia* [Italian family culture] that emerges from Mafia stories. Values of belonging, loyalty, control of one's life, canny ability to assess people and events, and palpable rather than abstract human relations radiate through the criminal sensationalism of the tales."[47] Gambino, though he deplores the stereotyping of Italian Americans as criminals, evidently does not regard these depictions as ipso facto manifestations of an anti-Italian bigotry; in his interpretation "Mafia mania" bespeaks an admiration for Italian American values.

He also observes that "the myth of an extrasocietal, almost omnipotent power has great appeal in a complicated American society in which people are exasperated by feelings of confusion, impotence, and defeat."[48] The late playwright and actress Julie Bovasso, best known to moviegoers for her roles in *Saturday Night Fever* and *Moonstruck*, maintained that mafia dramas, with their powerful protagonists, tap into the yearnings of members of highly technological and bureaucratized societies for autonomy and control over life's unpredictability.[49]

Mafiosi also appeal to that urge among us good citizens to beat the system, whether it's by winning the lottery or pulling off some get-rich-quick scheme. Gangsters, at least in their pop-culture representations, enjoy the fruits of success *all'americana*, but they do it their way, to paraphrase that ode to self-aggrandizement made famous by a certain blue-eyed Italian American crooner.

"The mob image represents a dark version of the American Dream, in which there is a little bit of defiance of America," says Flavia Alaya, a professor of literature and cultural history, political activist, and author of *Under the Rose* (Feminist Press, 2001), an acclaimed memoir of her clandestine affair during the 1960s with a Roman Catholic priest. "It's like, 'We do our thing while you do your thing, and we get away with it.' If you want to be against the government, you can still look like a model citizen. I think all Americans in their hearts want to do that. It was what the Western was about, it was what the Wild West was about. It was about being an outlaw and getting away with it."

"Everyone traveling the middle of the road loves the fantasy of living on the edge," observes *New York Times* columnist Matthew Purdy, in an article comparing the "gangsta" imagery of rap to the old-school gangsterism of the mafia. "Gangsta or gangster, the attraction is the entrepreneurial lifestyle. Let someone else punch the clock; I'll sit around, punching up associates on my cell phone and punching out anyone in my way." Purdy quotes Tommy Jones, a young man "wearing extra-baggy pants and a wool hat pulled low," who admires gangstas/gangsters because "They're independent. They don't pay taxes. They live well. Sex. It's not 9 to 5. It's freedom."[50]

"I've liked gangster movies since I was a kid," acknowledges Fred Roos, coproducer of *Godfather II* and *III*. "I don't think it's the violence that makes them so compelling—I think it's the way these guys take things into their own hands. They're not victims. They stand up to people. We live in an era where it's easy to feel powerless. So you can identify with someone who can solve your problems. It's the ultimate fantasy. If you've been done wronged, wouldn't you want to have a Godfather who could fix everything?"[51]

Nostalgia—for a bygone period in American history in which the social order seemed more cohesive and crime less threatening because it seemed less terrifyingly random and more *organized*—underlies our fascination with "the Mafia."

Ray De Felitta is a Bronx-born filmmaker whose *Two-Family House*, an evocative and understated look at working-class Italian American life in Staten Island during the 1950s, won the Audience Award at the 2000 Sundance Film Festival. The film starred three actors known to audiences for their roles in *The Sopranos*—Michael Rispoli, Vincent Pastore, and Katherine Narducci—but there are no gangsters in *Two-Family House*, just blue-collar paisans with credible flaws and virtues. De Felitta muses:

> I think one of the reasons that people like going automatically to the mob place is that there's nostalgia to it. People probably don't consciously know it or want to cop to it, but there is a sort of relief in the way something used to work, and it once worked okay. What you're basically telling people with that portrayal of Italians is, They had a social order that worked this way. You had the satisfaction of killing somebody if they fucked it up, or you had the satisfaction of telling your wife, "I'm going to go sleep with my mistress." There's something sort of quaint about it— the more you keep replaying it and caricaturing it, the more it becomes comfort food. You put the right Dean Martin song behind it, you put the right suits on and get the right Cadillac, and I think everybody finds it, like, a nice world to revisit somehow. Even if it's being done today, it feels period no matter when you do it. The mob feels eternally and fatally stuck in the fifties somehow.[52]

Novelist Ann Patchett sounds a similar note. "There is a reason we love *The Sopranos* and all the mafioso gore that came before it. Somehow crime is acceptable as long as it's organized. Someone may get whacked for an incredibly stupid reason, but they knew what they were doing. They broke the code. By watching the program, we learn that code and can feel that we would be smart enough not to insult the boss or cheat him or sleep with his daughter. There we are, safe from crime."[53]

Lorenzo Carcaterra, the Bronx-born author of the novels *Sleepers* and *Street Boys*, was raised in a mobbed-up neighborhood, and he knows from experience what De Felitta, Patchett, and others, like criminologist James B. Jacobs, have described.

> When there was a problem that needed to be solved beyond the walls of our apartment, I was taught from the earliest age to seek the help of men like John Gotti. This may be why I am not as disturbed as other Italian Americans are by the public fascination with the Mafia. I understand their concerns, that the actions of a small fraction (at the height of its power, there were less than 5,000 members in the Italian branch of organized crime) taint the accomplishments of 20 million. I look upon them neither as heroes nor as people we should emulate, and I know that their stay among us is always shaded in darkness.
>
> But I have seen the other side, the one Gotti so willingly exposed to the press, and have always been comfortable in that company, under those conditions. It was their presence in my neighborhood that allowed my mother to walk free of any worry about muggings, allowed me to play outside with my friends long after summer nights had turned to early mornings, and enabled us to rest in our beds at night, warm and secure. If money was required, it was to their pockets we turned. If a dispute needed to be settled, we looked to them to serve as judges. If a job was what we wanted, it was their social club we walked into. It is easy for people to scoff at such notions, to write them off as the simple romanticism of street thugs. But I lived on those streets as a child, and I knew who those men were and heard what it was they did for a living, and none of it mattered. I felt at ease with them and safe under their gaze.[54]

Carcaterra quotes Sonny Grosso, a former New York Police Department detective turned television producer, who, although he "put a lot of those guys in jail," evinces nostalgia for the days when crime was organized by Italians, because now "what's replaced organized crime is disorganized crime. And that's something even worse." Grosso grew up in East Harlem, New York, when mafiosi had a major presence in the neighborhood, and, like actress Katherine Narducci, recalls the safety: "I knew that my sister could go out and buy a quart of milk and not come back with an ax in her back." But today, Grosso complains, poor neighborhoods in New York are plagued by "kids and grandmothers dealing dope. Drive-by shootings."[55]

There is an unmistakable racial subtext to Grosso's remarks. When Italians were in charge, crime wasn't such a terrible thing. It wasn't random, and it didn't destroy the quality of life in neighborhoods where mob guys lived and worked. But in today's poor—meaning black and Latino—neighborhoods, crime is out of control, anarchic: *dis*organized. Where there were mafiosi, mothers and sisters were safe from the dangers of the streets; in the ghetto 'hoods, the residents whom mob guys refer to as "citizens"—mothers, grandmothers, sisters, kids—are the agents of misrule.

But at least Carcaterra and Grosso acknowledge that mafiosi are criminals "whose stay among us is always shaded in darkness" and who should be locked up. Other outsiders succumb to a romantic view of mafiosi as colorful members of an exotic urban subculture. *Donnie Brasco* (1997) is one of the best of the recent films about contemporary Italian American organized crime. Based on the memoirs of Joseph Pistone, an actual FBI agent who infiltrated a New York mafia family, *Donnie Brasco* powerfully depicts the fearsome brutality of mob life. But Mike Newell, the film's British director, was charmed by the mobsters he met while preparing the film. He recounted his experiences in an interview with the *Los Angeles Times*.

Q: Is it true before production began you hung out with mob members in Brooklyn for research?
A: I had a wonderful time. The thing at which they are best is dealing with you one-to-one. They leave school at age 10, 11 or 12. But what they lose in formal education, they more than make up for it. It isn't just street-wiseness. They are something midway between a doctor and a neighborhood therapist. They

were wonderfully charismatic and charming and fun to be with. To get drunk with the mob . . .

Q: Did it take you a long time to gain their trust?

A: It probably took me six to eight weeks before I was talking to the real thing. All of this time, there was one particular man, Rocco, who would take me around. He is the son of an old mob family. We spent a long time drinking in the right bars and eating in the right restaurants. Then one day he just said, "I have some people for you to meet." We knocked on the door of a place that looked like a hairdresser salon and inside there were the lads. I ran with them for a couple of months. It was very interesting. It really is like a tribe up the Amazon. There are basic ground rules that have nothing to do with the way we live. The people trust one another or they don't trust one another.[56]

Now that *The Sopranos* and the hit movie *Analyze This* (and its sequel, *Analyze That*) have shown us mafia dons in psychotherapy, it may be time to put the genre's fans on the couch. Psychiatrists and other mental health professionals regularly weigh in on the verisimilitude of the therapy sessions on *The Sopranos*, the general consensus being that the show presents the most accurate depiction of the talking cure of any film or TV show. Psychoanalyst Ethel Spector Person, in the *Journal of the American Psychoanalytic Association*, offers an intrapsychic explanation for the appeal of the mafia don to audiences.

Focusing on the popularity of the *Godfather* films, she sees two "interlocking fantasies embedded in the plot line."

For a few, the godfather fantasy is about becoming the Godfather, procuring for oneself a secular version of the godhead. For many more the fantasy is about seeking vicarious power through a connection to one or another mortal—a godfather or godmother, a titan of industry, a mentor, a totalitarian leader—whom they imbue with the mystique of power and to whom they pledge obeisance. For them the fantasy is primarily about securing riches, knowledge, and vicarious authority in the here and now through attachment to a powerful godfather figure.[57]

Person says the Godfather's power consists of "miracle, mystery, and authority." "Put another way," she writes, "his power lies in our need for him to be powerful." She provocatively compares the Catholic Church during the Inquisition to the mafia in the United States: "Through their respective versions of miracles, mystery, and authority, they both wielded . . . economic, psychological, and political power." She concludes that the Godfather fantasy is so compelling "not just because we have a wish to dominate and command but because we have a wish to attach ourselves to power through submissiveness and obedience. The godfather fantasy allows us to imagine a world in which both tendencies can be lived out to the hilt, directly and vicariously."[58]

This analysis seems apt when the Godfather in question is a commanding figure like Vito Corleone, who, in both his literary and cinematic incarnations, seems less a gangland chief than a feudal lord, or even God himself, as he dispenses his particular brand of justice and solves his supplicants' problems. Puzo's novel, in fact, encourages us to see the Godfather as perhaps even greater than God, or at least more responsive to his followers than the disinterested divinity in Heaven who leaves countless fervent prayers unanswered. Vito Corleone, he tells us in the book's first chapter, "was a man to whom everybody came for help, and never were they disappointed."[59]

But it's a stretch to associate "miracle, mystery, and authority" with less lofty figures such as Tony Soprano and the various mob bosses in the films of Scorsese, and of lesser filmmakers and TV series. These fictional mafiosi—and their real-life counterparts like John Gotti—derive their power from their organizational abilities, but also, probably more so, from their ability to instill fear, their cunning and ruthlessness, and their willingness, even eagerness to commit murder.

The leftist social critic Michael Parenti agrees with other commentators that the appeal of mafia tales to the general public lies in their outlaw mystique, in the genre's depictions of "a breed of people who live outside the law with a powerful law of their own, who kowtow to no one, who are powerful and effective . . ."[60] For Italian American fans of the genre, "Mafia movies also offer the appeal of empowerment; they portray Italians in positions of strength and dominance, able to get things done as they want, in direct and forceful ways, not unlike the frontier cowboy hero. For powerless people, the Mafia don, with his army of hit men and network of lawyers, obliging politicians, and big business friends, becomes an appealing figure." Although many Italian Americans "find the association with crime offensive, some are finding a kind of group recognition" in mafia dramas. Parenti says that Italian Americans, like other ethnics, "have been starved for acknowledgment from the dominant culture," so many are responsive "to any kind of media representation, even a derogatory one."

But audiences of whatever background can experience this identification with gangsters only because the mafia genre distorts the ugly realities of organized crime; it "tells us nothing about the mob's role in union-busting, extortion, and shakedowns, and nothing about its victimization of workers, consumers, women (as wives or prostitutes), and small-business owners—including many Italians . . . Instead," Parenti charges, "hoodlums are transformed into folk heroes, loveable patriarchs who want nothing more than a decent life for their families and a steady income from their often unspecified 'business' ventures."[61]

Parenti is obviously referring to *The Godfather*, and his indictment carries some weight—but only in terms of the first film of Coppola's trilogy. *Godfather II* largely eschews these distortions, presenting Michael Corleone as the monstrous head of a corrupt multinational corporation, a CEO from hell. It's surprising that Parenti, a Marxist, entirely overlooks the anticapitalist critique in *Godfather II*, which depicts the Corleone empire not as an aberration but as rooted in the American political economy. Or, as Michael Corleone coolly replies when Senator Pat Geary, an old-line WASP, decries the Corleones as a sinister and foreign cancer feeding on the American way of life, "We're both part of the same corruption."

Moreover, it appears Parenti has never seen a Martin Scorsese film. There are no "loveable folk heroes" to be found in *Mean Streets*, *Raging Bull*, *Goodfellas*, or *Casino*. Scorsese's hoods are working-class strivers at best, the rest being cunning malefactors and outright psychotics.

But Parenti's essential point, that the mythic status of gangsters in American popular culture is based, at least in part, on downplaying their venality and the corrosive effects of their activities on society, rings true. "The hard truth is that these guys were pieces of (garbage)," says novelist James Ellroy, who has placed mobsters Mickey Cohen and Johnny Stompanato as characters in his books *The Big Nowhere* and *L.A. Confidential*.

"You always see Bugsy Siegel portrayed in movies as this capitalist visionary—the guy who invented Las Vegas," says Ellroy. "In reality, he was a psychopath. If you did the real story of gangsters, it would be a stupid, fatuous tale of greed and corruption. But Hollywood only shows the sensuality of seeking pure power. It doesn't show the scum that comes with it."[62]

A well-established convention of the genre first cited by Carlos Clarens also helps explain our fascination with mafiosi and other gangsters. Early in the history of crime films, Hollywood realized that outlaw narratives capture the public's imagination when they are told not from the point of view of the established order but from the criminals' perspective. That realization had consequences that are evident in contemporary mafia dramas: "Stay close to a character, whether in print or on the screen, and that character ran the risk of turning into a protagonist," as Carlos Clarens puts it.[63] We are drawn to a Michael Corleone or a Tony Soprano despite their awful crimes because a bond has been created between them and us, the spectators. We see them as the protagonists of their own stories, and we come to see something of ourselves in them. Michael will do anything to live up to the trust his father has placed in him; Tony seeks relief in psychiatry and Prozac from the debilitating pressures of his work and his domestic life. The particulars of their lives may be alien to us, but because their creators have brought us so close to them, they, unlike the faceless proletarians in the Rolling Stones' classic "Salt of the Earth," do look real to us, and not so strange.

4

Don Corleone Was My Grandfather

The *Godfather* is the broadest representation of this [Mafia] myth in our days; it made it into a popular culture staple with worldwide appeal.
—Alessandro Camon, *"The Godfather* and the Mythology of Mafia"

The *Godfather* is the I Ching. The *Godfather* is the sum of all wisdom. *The Godfather* is the answer to any question.
—Tom Hanks in *You've Got Mail*

I never met a real honest-to-god gangster.   —Mario Puzo

Keep your friends close and your enemies closer.
Oh, Michael, you are blind, it was an abortion, Michael, an abortion.
This Sicilian thing that's been going on for two thousand years . . .
Leave the gun, take the cannoli.
Michael, we're bigger than U.S. Steel.
I never wanted this for you—Senator Corleone, Governor Corleone, or something.
I'm with you now.
It was you, Fredo! You broke my heart.
I'm gonna make him an offer he can't refuse.

These lines of dialogue from the *Godfather* films are imprinted on the collective consciousness of American moviegoers, mine included.

I've watched the first two films many times over the years, and my knowledge of *Godfather* arcana is as extensive as any hardcore fan's. But when I saw the first film in Francis Ford Coppola's trilogy in 1972, I was a college student, with shoulder-length black hair and a full beard. My hirsuteness, along with my prominent dark eyes and olive skin, earned me nicknames like Swami and the Sheik.

The baby boomer son of an auto mechanic and a housewife, themselves children of poor Neapolitan and Sicilian immigrants and survivors of the Great Depression and World War II, I identified with the counterculture and the New Left. There was a war to protest, lots of dope to be smoked, and back-to-nature acid trips in the woods. The Stones' *Sticky Fingers* was on my stereo and a Black Panther poster adorned my dorm room wall. My identity was radical hippie freak, resisting and refusing the establishment in my politics and my partying. My ethnic background was just that, background.

I was born in Bridgeport, Connecticut, a fading industrial city, to a working-class family, and I lived my early years mostly among Italian Americans. My family went to a church that, in the 1960s, still offered a Sunday Mass in Italian. Family and social events, like wedding receptions and First Communion and Confirmation parties, were held at an Italian catering hall just a few doors from the Italian bakery. Going out to eat inevitably meant eating Italian, at places with names like Venetian Gardens and Conte's. Holidays, particularly Easter and Christmas, required "making the rounds"—after Mass we'd visit the relatives, an extended family that still included a few of the "old-timers," Italian-born grandparents and other elderly kin who'd crossed the Atlantic in steerage decades earlier. Sunday dinners at my Aunt Lina's house in Queens were hours-long affairs featuring course after ample course of southern Italian *cucina casalinga*, unpretentious and satisfying home cooking.

I grew up in a familial world where ethnicity was both taken for granted and central to our identity. We always called ourselves Italian, not Italian American, even though my parents were born in America (my father was stationed in southern Italy during World War II; my mother has never seen the *madrepatria*) and we were indisputably Americans.

But although *italianità* was all around me, I was almost entirely ignorant of many aspects of "the Italian American experience." I knew that my maternal and paternal grandparents had been among the wave of millions of impoverished peasants and workers who fled southern Italy to find *pane e lavoro* (bread and work) in America. I knew they had come from places called Napoli and Sicilia. But I knew nothing of these lands they'd left, or the privations they'd endured. What were their lives like in the "old country"? What had made up their minds to uproot themselves from the humble places where they and their ancestors had dwelled for centuries to begin new lives in a new, non-Italian world? And what had they found when they arrived?

My family and relatives never spoke about these things. When I recall their reticence, it seems to me that the *miseria* my grandparents had known in Italy and their escape from it must have been such wrenching experiences that, once over, they were not to be spoken of; they were the traumas of a history that ended at Ellis Island. Nor did the American public schools I attended teach me about the Italian immigrant experience. The only reference to the arrival of so many of my forebears that I can recall from my textbooks is a line about "long-headed Sicilians" being among the newcomers to America in the early twentieth century. (Was my head of unusual length? I wondered. I did take a large-size hat. Could non-Sicilians pick me out by comparing their craniums to mine?) When I was a kid, America didn't celebrate multiculturalism or champion ethnic identity; the story we told ourselves was that immigrants came here to build better lives, proved their good faith by shedding the remnants of the Old World, and assimilated into the American melting pot.

But even though we Italians had accepted America, it seemed like America hadn't wholly accepted us. We were no longer the desperately poor immigrants whose arrival en masse had so discomfited WASP society. But, as my memories of growing up in the late fifties and sixties remind me, we were still considered foreign, different from other Euro-Americans, and quite possibly not fully "white." From non-Italians I leaned that we were not supposed to be intelligent or well read: those were Jewish traits. We were supposed to be loud, low-class, and prone to excessive emotionalism and violence.

From television shows like *The Untouchables*, I learned that the government, personified by Eliot Ness and his posse of FBI agents, had its hands full trying to bring to justice bad guys with Italian last names, the only Italians I recall seeing on TV except for the occasional comic type, like the voluble barber speaking broken English. It wasn't until the seventies that Italians were seen on the other side of the law, in cop dramas like *Baretta* and *Columbo*.

In my adolescence I came to see Italian American life as limited and limiting, too centered on family, work, and religion. My intellectual curiosity and rebellious temperament were leading me far from Italo-America, into new territory—black music, the counterculture, and radical politics. The cultural and political upheaval of those times made Italian American culture seem old-fashioned and corny. Faced with a choice between Sinatra and the Stones, I sided with the skinny English boys my father called "queers."

I willfully bucked my family's expectations of what a *ben educato* (well-brought-up) Italian boy should be. Rather than respectfully defer to adult, and especially adult male authority, I questioned everything, much to my parents' dismay. And fueling my profound and deepening alienation from family and convention was a burgeoning awareness of my homosexuality. I knew well that Italian boys weren't supposed to be queer. We were supposed to be *maschio*, not *finocchio*.

So when I, radical hippie freak and closeted young gay man, walked into that Pennsylvania movie theater in 1972 with my college roommate and a few other friends to see this new, highly anticipated, and controversial movie about Italian gangsters, the last thing I expected was to see myself. But, as would be true of so many Italian Americans, I felt an immediate shock of recognition as I watched Coppola's Corleones. These were the most Italian Italians I'd ever seen in an American movie.

The opening scenes are set in 1945, years before I was born. But it didn't matter. I knew these people, and their world. At Connie Corleone's wedding, the guests lustily sing "La luna mezzu' mari," the bawdy Sicilian ditty familiar to me from wedding receptions I'd been to as a child. (The old Sicilian man who leads the song even makes the requisite suggestive hand gestures to accompany the verses about the fisherman who comes to his *innamorata* with his "fish" in his hand, the butcher with his "sausage," etc.) Among the guests are paisans who could have been my relatives: old women with corsages pinned to their heavy bosoms and somber, reserved old men; all alongside loud gavones and others who maintain a proud reserve and dignity. And the noisy kids running around everywhere, indulged by the adults.

The guests are eating capicola sandwiches, and I laughed out loud to hear an exuberant young paisan call the spiced meat "gobbagoal," the typical southern Italian dialect pronunciation favored by my family and every other Italian American of my acquaintance. Of course no Italian father would offer the guests at his daughter's wedding only capicola sandwiches. Don Corleone provides a lavish feast of typical southern Italian *abbondanza*, with yardwide trays of lasagna, huge fruit baskets, barrels of beer and gallons of wine, countless biscotti, and the elaborate four-tiered wedding cake.

The Godfather is, in other words, drenched in *italianità*. This, of course, was fully intended, not only by Francis Ford Coppola and Mario Puzo, coauthors of the screenplay, but also by the redoubtable Robert Evans, who at the time was vice president in charge of production at Paramount. In the documentary *The Kid Stays in the Picture*, Evans recalls that before *The Godfather*, mob films "all starred Jews, not Sicilians." (He must have been thinking not only of Paul Muni and Edward G. Robinson but also of Kirk Douglas, who played a Sicilian mafia patriarch in the unsuccessful 1968 mob drama *The Brotherhood*.) Evans was determined to make a mafia film "so Sicilian you could smell the spaghetti sauce."

Francis Ford Coppola, a native of Detroit who had earned a master's degree in film studies from UCLA, boasted a less than impressive résumé when he was hired to direct *The Godfather*. He'd made the commercial and critical failures *Dementia 13* and *Finian's Rainbow*, and *The Rain People* and *You're a Big Boy Now*, which received mixed reviews. But Coppola had had greater success as a writer or script doctor for various projects. His breakthrough as screenwriter was his script for *Patton* (1970), which won him an Academy Award. That success helped persuade a skeptical Paramount to ask him, in the spring of 1970, to direct *The Godfather*.[1]

But Coppola rejected the offer; it smelled to him like "a typical Hollywood project under tight studio control," which the independent-minded filmmaker wanted to escape.[2] Not only that: he had read the first fifty or so pages of the novel and hated it, calling it "cheap and sensational."[3] Robert Evans has said that Coppola believed that taking the job would "blacken his Italian heritage."[4] Coppola had grown up in a home steeped in Italian culture and had a strong sense of *italianità*. But, given his monetary woes—his production company American Zoetrope was floundering financially, its first film, George Lucas's *THX-1138*, having flopped—he accepted Paramount's offer when asked a second time, and reread the entire book.

"I got into what the book is really about," he said, "the story of the family, this father and his sons and questions of power and succession—and I thought it was a terrific story, if you could cut out all the other stuff,"[5] particularly the bizarre subplot about Lucy Mancini and her oversized vagina. (Mancini, Sonny Corleone's mistress, winds up in Las Vegas after his death, where she meets a nice, if mobbed-up, Jewish doctor who surgically tightens what he calls her "big box." She and Sonny had been perfectly matched sexually, as he possessed a huge penis, which Puzo describes in such explicit and loving detail—"an enormous, blood-gorged pole of muscle"—that I began to wonder if he didn't have a touch of the *finocchio* in him.)

If the *Patton* script helped Coppola get the director's job, other factors were more decisive: ethnicity and money.

"I was Italian American, which is to say I might be able to bring some authenticity to the Italian families," Coppola observes in the documentary film *A Decade Under the Influence*.[6] Coppola here greatly understates the importance of his background to Paramount. Coppola had a number of advantages, in Paramount's view: he came cheap ($125,000 plus 6 percent of gross rentals), he was available, and, after initially rejecting Paramount's offer, he was willing. It also didn't hurt that he had developed successful screenplays, but his ethnic background was the clincher.

Robert Evans "was glad to have a director with the strong knowledge of Italian heritage that only a lifetime of cultural immersion can create."[7] Mario Puzo remembered, "It was [Paramount executive Peter] Bart who came up with the idea of using Coppola. Mainly because he was Italian and young."[8] But Coppola's *italianità* was valuable to Paramount not only because of whatever authenticity he could bring to the material. His name, the studio felt, could also serve as insurance against protests by Italian American organizations.

This turned out to be too optimistic, as the protests did come, the largest organized by the Italian American Civil Rights League, headed by Joe Colombo, himself a reputed mobster. In 1970 the league held a rally in Madison Square Garden that raised nearly $600,000 to stop production of the film.[9] League members sent a form letter protesting the book and the proposed film to every elected official in the federal government, with copies to Paramount. The league, claiming to represent tens of thousands of Italian Americans, dominated the protests, but it wasn't the only aggrieved organization. The Sons of Italy weighed in against the film, as did other groups representing business people and professionals, the kind of Italians (legitimately employed, noncriminal) the Corleones would disdain as *pezzonovanti* (big shots).

Even before he had written the novel, Mario Puzo envisioned *The Godfather* as a film. By the late 1960s Puzo had written two literary novels: *The Dark Arena* (1955), set in post–World War II occupied Germany, and, a decade later, *The Fortunate Pilgrim*, inspired by his striving immigrant mother and the Puzo family's hardscrabble life in the Hell's Kitchen section of Manhattan. Critics gave both books favorable reviews, *The New York Times* calling the latter "a small classic" while *New York* magazine likened the author to an Italian American Bernard Malamud.

The critical acclaim didn't translate into robust sales; both books were commercial failures, with *Pilgrim* selling less than 5,000 copies.[10] At forty-five years old, his career seemingly stalled, Puzo was broke, in debt, and desperate.

But in *The Fortunate Pilgrim* lies the genesis of *The Godfather*. Lucia Santa, the earlier novel's protagonist, immigrates to New York from a mountain village in southern Italy. Her hopes for a better life take a beating in the tough urban neighborhood, where she endures two failed marriages that leave her with six children to support by herself. Her eldest son, Lorenzo, falls in with some neighborhood gangsters, who enlist him to collect payoffs to the mob from local businessmen.

An editor told Puzo that *The Fortunate Pilgrim* might have sold bet-

ter if it had only had "a little more of that Mafia stuff in it."[11] That settled it for the author. His next novel would be a gangster story, and he
intended it to be a commercial blockbuster.

Puzo's publisher, G.P. Putnam's Sons, paid him a modest advance
of $5,000 for his proposed gangster novel. But some two years before
the book's publication, Puzo pitched the evolving project to Paramount.
This was a shrewd move on the author's part, as Paramount "was one of
the few studios that nurtured an idea through formative stages by col-
laborating with authors, even if they weren't working on a screenplay.
Peter Bart would guide a project through development over a period of
years, supporting writers through the lean times with an advance or a
payment for rewrite."[12]

What Bart bought, with approval of his boss, Robert Evans, was a
114-page treatment and outline of a book to be called *Mafia*. In
1967–1968, "Paramount helped Puzo along, bringing him to the West
Coast from time to time, buying development rights to the project, and
keeping the author afloat with occasional checks to support his efforts."[13] In 1968, Puzo finished the novel, which was now retitled *The
Godfather*. Paramount got a great deal; in January 1969, three months
before the publication of the book, the studio acquired the movie rights
for $80,000. "For only a few thousand dollars, plus some care and feed-
ing of a struggling author, Bart and Paramount found itself controlling
the rights to a book that was not only a blockbuster, but potentially the
blockbuster of the decade."[14]

The book remained on bestseller lists for more than a year, eventually selling tens of millions of copies worldwide. But despite the novel's
enormous success, Paramount's interest in the film began to wane,
largely because of the failure of *The Brotherhood*. The financial losses
Paramount incurred from the Kirk Douglas vehicle left the studio skittish about taking on another picture about the mafia. Paramount, its
qualms about the project notwithstanding, decided to move ahead in
late 1969, largely on the strength of the book's mass popularity and the
fact that some independent producers attempted to buy the property
from the studio. But having seen that other bestselling books did not
translate into hit films—*Portnoy's Complaint* and *Catch-22* were among
the titles that flopped as films—Robert Evans and Paramount had

modest plans for the movie. They wanted to make it on the cheap, for $2 million, at a running time of only an hour and forty-five minutes, and to shoot on a back lot in Hollywood, not in New York City and certainly not in Sicily.

The movie was budgeted at $2.25 million but ended up costing some $6.5 million. The cost overruns put Coppola in a bad light with Paramount. "I was in deep trouble," Coppola noted, "very serious trouble till the film turned out to be successful."[15] Robert Evans, despite his stated intention to make an authentically Sicilian mafia movie, was particularly concerned about Coppola's and Puzo's intention to film in Sicily. Evans asked whether the Sicilian sequences were really necessary. Puzo and Coppola insisted that they were, and Evans, along with Peter Bart and Paramount president Stanley Jaffee, went along in the end. "They did listen to the creative point of view when they didn't have to," Puzo noted.[16]

Once Coppola took on the project, he quickly determined how he would interpret the source material. "I have a belief that in so-called work for hire that you fall in love with the movies you have to make," he said.

You find what about that film that you love. So with *The Godfather*, I said, this is a classic story, this is like Shakespeare. I'm going to do it like the story of a king. He has three sons and each son has gotten some part of his talent. One is cunning and cold and one is violent and emotional and the third is sweet but sort of dumb. And the Godfather, the father, had all of those qualities. That's why he was a great king. And I'm going to tell it sort of like a story of succession, and it'll be very classical. So out of whatever you've chosen to fall in love with comes the style.[17]

Coppola also decided, according to Evans, to make the Corleone story a metaphor for capitalism.

As a politicized college student, I got the critique of capitalism, which was hardly understated. But what captivated me—besides the compelling narrative and exceptional acting—was the ethnic verisimilitude, in which I recognized my family and myself. There was something qualitatively different about these Italians and Italian Americans from previous film representations.

In movies like *Scarface* and *Little Caesar*, the *italianità* is depicted negatively, as old-world baggage that needs to be discarded. The condescension and derision of those portrayals reflected the status of Italians in America during the 1920s and 1930s, which, as discussed in Chapter 1, was that of a despised and often feared minority. The early gangster movies "bespeak a cultural bias created by the 'white' film makers, and dominant society as well," as critic Vera Dika observes.[18] In other words, the Italianness of a character like Tony Camonte is a "marker" for his "primitive depravity."[19]

The Godfather represents a radical break from these invidious depictions. It's not only the physical and behavioral aspects of ethnicity that Coppola gets right. Dika writes that Coppola's and Puzo's Italians "embody a return to 'la via vecchia,' or to the old Sicilian ways. The Italian Americans who are constructed here are ones who embody the mores of an ancient society, and so take on a nostalgic quality."[20]

Dika, like so many other commentators on Italo-America, is indebted to Richard Gambino's landmark study *Blood of My Blood* (1974). The book, a leading text in Italian American studies courses, has been criticized on a number of counts. Some have said that Gambino sometimes confuses social class and the vicissitudes of history with ethnicity, as when he attributes the paucity of Italian immigrant women in domestic service compared to Irish women to a purported Italian cultural bias against working in the homes of strangers.[21] Others have criticized Gambino for stereotyping both African Americans and Italian Americans.[22] But, its shortcomings notwithstanding, *Blood of My Blood*—published the same year as the release of *Godfather II* and just two years after the first film—helped explain Italian Americans to themselves and to a broader audience.

Gambino describes *la via vecchia* in gendered terms, limning the qualities of the masculine ideal, the *uomo di pazienza* (a man of patience and self-control, with a pragmatic approach to life and a canny assessment of situations and other people), and the feminine, the *donna di seriatà* (a virtuous woman who embodies the seriousness required to handle both the privileges and responsibilities that come with being the center of *la famiglia*). In the first *Godfather* film, Vito Corleone, and even the apparently "Americanized" Michael, embody the ascribed traits of *pazienza*. Sonny Corleone, hot-tempered and unable to rein in his violent impulses, transgresses the ideal of *pazienza*, and pays for it with his life.

In Mamma Corleone, one sees—or rather, glimpses—the *donna di seriatà*. As Fred Gardaphé notes, *The Godfather* distorts the typical Italian family dynamic by replacing the mother/son dyad with the father/son relationship. In the film, Mamma Corleone, whose first name, Carmela, is never spoken, is practically a cipher, a mostly silent and reactive character, which, as any Italian American can attest, runs counter to reality, even for an immigrant Sicilian woman in the 1940s.

The Corleones, as well as the other Italians in the first film, such as the undertaker Bonasera and the baker Nazorine, cling to the old ways, despite having left Sicily. As first-generation Italian Americans, they are more Italian than American. Vera Dika acutely observes that *la via vecchia* not only dominates the film, it also performs an exculpatory function as it "diminishes the characters' association with crime and its squalid realities, and instead foregrounds acts made punishable precisely because they are reactions against the breach of an ancient masculine code."[23] The characters who commit *infamie*—the pedophile Hollywood producer Jack Woltz, or Carlo Rizzi, who beats his wife, Connie Corleone, get just what they deserve because they have transgressed the protocols of the Old World.

This code was familiar to me, growing up in Italo-America, even if my immediate family and our relatives never used the terms *la via vecchia* or *l'ordine della famiglia*. Though a third-generation Italian American, I was still Italian enough to see that there was more to *The Godfather* than "the greatest gangster movie ever made," as Pauline Kael proclaimed, or a metaphoric rendering of capitalist corruption, as Coppola stated. I recognized these people, their appearance, mannerisms, behavior, and attitudes. And I identified with them, as representative figures of the great migration from Italy and of the Italian diaspora. Vito and Carmela Corleone were my grandparents, the immigrant generation; their children, Michael, Sonny, Fredo, and Connie, my parents' generation; and the grandchildren, Anthony and Mary, my cousins, the second generation born in America.

Although I recognized the figures in the Corleone family portrait, there was just one thing wrong with that picture: All the main characters were criminals. Conniving, remorseless killers who could chat amiably with an associate one minute and blow his brains out the next. It was as if my Sicilian grandfather, a thoughtful, politically progressive man who loved jazz and classical music and played the guitar, had a hidden violent life that had suddenly been exposed to the world's scrutiny.

The Godfather presented us with a paradox: the most vividly realistic and lovingly detailed depiction of Italian American life in the history of the movies was framed through the singular experience of an atypical group, a secret society of outlaws. The irksome image that Italian Americans had decried since the 1930s, when the Sons of Italy assailed *Scarface*, was now, thanks to Mario Puzo and Francis Ford Coppola, more compelling, and, for many Americans, more persuasive than ever. *Italianità* and *criminalità* were now inextricably fused together in the popular imagination. And that is why the woman in the Southern state whose office I had called could say to me upon hearing my surname, "Why, you must know the Godfather!"

And yet countless Italian Americans love *The Godfather*, and I'm one of them. Despite its stereotypical baggage, the novel and the films (the first two, anyway) had an enormous impact on our cultural consciousness and sense of identity as "ethnic" Americans. Puzo's novel, according to Fred Gardaphé, "has done more to create a national consciousness of the Italian American experience than any work of fiction or nonfiction published before or since. It certainly was the first novel that Italian Americans as a group reacted to, either positively or negatively, perhaps because it appeared at a time when Italian Americans were just beginning to emerge as an identifiable cultural and political entity."[24]

The book, Gardaphé claims, "created an identity crisis for Italian Americans throughout the nation,"[25] eliciting such disparate reactions as outraged denunciations from antidefamation groups to unabashed identification with both the novel and the movies. Organizations like the Sons of Italy and UNICO National fumed. But countless Italian Americans ardently embraced *The Godfather*. On an innocuous level, young Italian Americans formed *"Godfather* clubs," bought tons of movie memorabilia (souvenir shops in New York's Little Italy still do a brisk trade in *Godfather* merch), and danced to the movie's "Love Theme" (by the veteran Italian film score composer Nino Rota) at their weddings.

But Italian Americans took to *The Godfather* for other, more profound reasons. The Puzo-Coppola pop-culture juggernaut may have revived and reinforced distasteful stereotypes of Italians, but "the book and film had, at least, made their community visible."[26] By the late sixties and early seventies, Italian Americans had become the largest and most vocal contingent in that era's "white ethnic" revival, a movement of cultural self-assertion that arose in emulation of—and sometimes in competition with—the black civil rights crusade and other movements built on racial, ethnic, gender, and sexual identities.

The Godfather, marshaling the strengths of classic Hollywood filmmaking—tightly constructed narrative, epic sweep and grandeur, superb cinematography, and evocative musical score—gave unprecedented exposure to Italian American history and experience (albeit in the context of a crime melodrama), spanning the decades from immigration to assimilation and upward mobility.

Allen Barra, a cultural critic and author who is Italian American, calls Mario Puzo a "lousy writer" who made all of America believe the lie that organized crime equals "the Mafia," an ancient, all-powerful conspiracy exported from Sicily to the United States, where immigrants and their descendants turned the old-world family business into a corporate monolith. Puzo, according to Barra, invented a "grim fairy tale world" that had little to do with actual organized crime in America. "The annals of organized crime are dominated by names like Arnold Rothstein . . . but the only Jews in Puzo's book are silent partners in gambling casinos," Barra fumes. But if Puzo misrepresented gangsters, he did understand "Italian families, who, like Woody Allen's old Jews, are 'like everybody else, just more so.'

"The godfathers' murders, betrayals, and bloody tragedies," Barra notes, "were immediately understood to be a metaphor for Italian family life, especially by Italian-Americans. They, finally, were able to bask in the attention of mainstream America, while secretly enjoying a little thrill from the hint of fear accorded to anyone with an Italian name by the very thought of the Mafia."[27]

Richard Gambino, writing in *The Village Voice* shortly after the release of *Godfather II*, claims that the Puzo-Coppola enterprise "carried a benefit with the [mafia] stereotyping" by providing "millions of Americans with an introduction to the Southern Italian's view of tragedy." The deprivations southern Italians had endured in the Mezzogiorno— poverty, political disenfranchisement, weak civil society, and nonexistent social justice—gave rise to a *weltanschauung* that emphasized the tragic absurdity of life. Maturity, and a degree of existential freedom, came from accepting this absurdity while also "having the will and emotion to live life and enjoy it."[28]

Gambino presents this worldview as more realistic than "the sense of progress and optimism" characteristic of Protestant northern Europe. Southern Italians, he maintains, understand that "good is inextricably woven with evil, and that few motives or events are of unmixed moral quality."[29] This view of life enables them to make sense of seeming paradoxes, such as the head of a brutal crime syndicate being a loving father, and how his college-educated, ostensibly assimilated son can become a more ruthless don than his old-world father.

What Gambino overlooks, however, is that this realistic orientation toward life can breed cynicism and political apathy. If all human action is compromised by base or evil intent, then why bother to try to change things for the better? The most one can do is to accept reality as it is and make the best of it. This is perfectly consistent with the mafia's own attitude toward Italy's economic and political systems, as described in Chapter 2. Mafiosi recognized that the establishment was corrupt and oppressive, but since they were not reformers they set out to manipulate and exploit it to their own advantage rather than pursue change. Some of that northern European optimism and belief in progress would have immensely benefited southern Italy and Sicily.

If Gambino believes *The Godfather* carries benefits along with its stereotypes, Bill Tonelli goes even further: rather than defame Italians, the Corleone chronicles actually flatter them. Tonelli, an author and former editor at *Esquire* and *Rolling Stone*, loves to ruffle the feathers of Italian American antidefamationists, and his comments about their greatest bête noir (until *The Sopranos* came along) are a case in point. Noting that the first film opens with the undertaker Bonasera's entreaty to Vito Corleone to grant the justice that has been denied him by an American court, Tonelli states, "This radical notion—that even in America, one's own tribe might provide a power structure superior to that of civil authority—is what's really at the heart of *The Godfather*'s appeal. It's why Italian-Americans in particular love the saga, for how it glamorizes and glorifies our values and customs above all others. The Corleones are our Kennedys, except with better morals."[30]

Tonelli says the rest of America was so taken by *The Godfather* for the same reasons Italians were. Its depiction of ethnic solidarity and family cohesion offered a "vision of an alternative to late-20th-century middle-class mistrust and malaise."[31] "Remember," says Tonelli, "the book and the movie were released during the era of Vietnam and Watergate; Don Corleone's lack of reverence for legitimate power, which in the '50s might have seemed atavistic, suddenly appeared wise. *The Godfather* also arrived just as the American nuclear family began its meltdown due to rising divorce rates."[32]

The Godfather depicts one ethnic group's particular experience, and a narrow slice of it at that. How is it, then, that this tale of an ethnically defined criminal subculture came to enjoy such broad-based appeal, to inspire identification and a devotion that for some shades into fanaticism, among so many people with no personal connection to Italy or Italian culture?

Robert Viscusi, like so many Italian Americans, felt that shock of recognition when he first saw *The Godfather*—"Shit, that's us!"—while simultaneously feeling the distance between him and the on-screen paisans. "We're *not* gangsters," he says. "So, to me, it was always a puzzle why *The Godfather* worked so well. And after thinking about it for many years, the conclusion that I've come to is that it's really a kind of political fable, and that's why it rings such bells."[33]

Bill Tonelli and others have explained why the first film connected with audiences in the early 1970s, a period of political and cultural upheaval in which legitimate authority behaved so illegitimately, at home and abroad, that Puzo's and Coppola's mafia seemed not as bad, and even more honest, than the government. But *The Godfather* remains immensely popular today. The novel continues to be read and the first two films continue to be seen by millions. The original film received a twenty-fifth anniversary re-release to theaters in 1997, all three films have been released on video and DVD as *The Godfather Trilogy*, and *Godfather I* and *II* are ubiquitous on cable and satellite TV networks.

The Corleones are also thriving on the Internet. Besides the numerous *Godfather* and other mob-related Web sites created by fans (Unofficial Homepage of the New York Mafia, Cosa Nostra, The Mafia Page, The New Mafia Order, Gangsters!, to cite just a few), an online marketplace offers a diverse menu of *Godfather* merchandise: books, DVDs, art prints and posters, T-shirts, and computer screen savers bearing the likenesses of the films' stars.

A *Godfather* for gamers will come on the market in 2006, created by Electronic Arts, a California-based studio. The *Godfather* video game doesn't reiterate the first film of the trilogy. It instead uses the familiar characters and scenes to produce a "wide-ranging virtual universe in which players can create their own narratives." Gamers experience key moments from the film from the perspective of a mafia soldier, an up-and-coming Corleone family member who builds "respect" by taking over rackets and "serving his masters" in the criminal organization.

The game's developers recruited James Caan and Robert Duvall to voice their characters, Sonny Corleone and Tom Hagen. Al Pacino, however, declined to participate. Marlon Brando did agree to voice Don Vito, but the recordings Electronic Arts made with the actor shortly before his death turned out to be unusable. A vocal mimic used them to guide his own performance as the Godfather.

Nick Earl of Electronic Arts acknowledged that *Godfather* fans might not appreciate his company's tampering with "probably the most beloved, most iconic film of all time." But it was the film's director who passed judgment on the game even before it was released. "The game has taken the work we all did on the film, and transformed it into a 'kill and be killed' slaughter session," Francis Ford Coppola said. "I did not cooperate with its making in any way, nor do I like or approve of what I saw of the result."[34]

As Robert Viscusi notes, it's the fablelike or mythic aspects of the Corleone saga that have given this highly specific story its universal appeal. Certainly many immigrants and Americans of immigrant backgrounds could identify with the Corleones as ethnic outsiders in a white-bread world. Still, that doesn't explain why "a Mafia family's intergenerational struggle is probably, pace Huck Finn, the most familiar story in American culture," or why "Don Vito Corleone surely keeps company with Huck and Jay Gatsby as one of the most indelible icons of American fiction."[35]

The extraordinary and undying popularity of *The Godfather* lies in the seeming paradox that the story of an Italian American organized crime family has superseded the western, now a near-extinct genre, as "the most enduring and revealing American myth, the one that most explains us to ourselves. It's the great story of assimilation and upward mobility . . . and also a fantasy of fairness and justice in which everyone receives exactly what he deserves, even (or especially) if that means getting whacked."[36]

Mario Puzo was modest, even self-deprecating, about the merits of his novel. "The book got much better reviews than I expected," he wrote. "I wished like hell I'd written it better."[37] But he recognized that in Vito Corleone he had created "a central character that was popularly accepted as genuinely mythic."[38]

An organized crime chief modeled mostly on the real-life gangster Carlo Gambino, Don Corleone hardly seems a criminal at all. Puzo likens him to a great ruler, a lawgiver, a farsighted statesman who devises the idea of the Commission, described in the novel as a "loosely bound confederated council" that adjudicates Cosa Nostra disputes. He rules over his world far more effectively and with greater wisdom than the *pezzonovanti*, the corporate, political, and law enforcement leaders who rule mainstream society. He's akin to a Roman emperor, and appears as godlike to his subjects as they did to theirs."[39]

The film incarnation of Vito Corleone attests to the influence of Italian director Luchino Visconti on Francis Ford Coppola. The Godfather, like the Sicilian prince Don Fabrizio in Visconti's classic film *The Leopard*, represents "an order about to pass."[40] Visconti's nobleman stands on the cusp of great historical change, the unification of Italy and the end of Sicily's feudal order. Vito Corleone represents the last of the old mafiosi, a ruthless but courtly crime chief who, with organized crime's move into the narcotics trade, has become an anachronism.

In the person of Don Corleone, several related myths converge: that of the Mafia itself, its own self-created mythos; the mythic saga of immigration and assimilation to a new way of life; and that of the organized crime family as a repository of ethnic solidarity and resistance to any authority except its own.

In Italy, the criminal organizations collectively known as the mafia have defined their identity in mythic terms. The Mafia myth relies on "mystery" (concerning its origins and even the origin of its name) and "ambiguity" regarding what and who is "mafia." Alessandro Camon, an Italian-born film producer and author, observes that "there is no activity, no area of society that is inherently the Mafia's concern, but they all can be."[41] Another source of ambiguity, says Camon, is the fact that "there is no easy way to set the Mafia apart from the general culture it operates within."[42] This is why I and other Italian Americans can imagine the Corleones as our relatives: they look, talk, and in most ways behave like "us."

The intertwining of mafia and not-mafia in Sicily leads some scholars to warn about the dangers of anti-mafia campaigns that don't take into account that poor and working-class Sicilians depend on mafia-infiltrated industries, particularly construction, for their livelihoods.[43] Just as the economic survival of coca-cultivating South American farmers would be jeopardized by an antidrug campaign that did not compensate them for the loss of their cash crop, many lower-class Sicilians fear their way of life could be endangered by "too much legality."[44]

The Mafia myth has at its core what Camon calls a "radical schism" in the character of the mafioso: "absolute ruthlessness against his enemies, but absolute devotion to his family and friends."[45] This double morality, which enables its practitioner "to function from one level to the other—from murder to family, from extinguishing life to protecting it—and even more specifically, to do one *because* of the other, could be the quintessential credo of the Mafia myth."[46] The mythical mafioso, then, is "a mysterious man and a man of contradiction."[47]

Vito Corleone and his American-born son Michael fully embody these qualities. Vito commissions a hideously brutal act of intimidation—decapitating a prize stallion and placing its severed head in the bed of its owner—to keep a promise to his beloved godson. In *Godfather III*, when denounced for his crimes by his ex-wife Kay, Michael insists, "I spent my life protecting my family . . . I did what I could, Kay, to protect all of you, from the horrors of this world."

And the Corleones of course are family men. "The mutual loyalty of fathers and sons is the emotional core of the story: fathers 'do what they have to do' to grant their sons a better life; sons inherit the mantle to defend the achievements and honor of their fathers. The affirmation of this bond is the ultimate value; profit and power are just means to an end."[48] This, of course, is myth in the sense of a useful fiction. As Camon acknowledges, the mafia's real credo is making money. But, he cautions, it would be a mistake to regard the mafioso's embrace of this familial myth as disingenuous: "The myth would have no power if its messengers didn't buy into it."[49]

Mario Puzo, whose novel and scripts (cowritten with Francis Ford Coppola) have made the Mafia myth fascinating to millions of readers and moviegoers, did no firsthand research on organized crime, either in the United States or in Sicily. He acknowledged never having met a real gangster. His knowledge of the mafia came mainly from records of United States Senate hearings. "You can write and get transcripts of all their investigative committees . . . For ten bucks, I got 100 volumes."[50] Puzo presumably was referring to transcripts of the Kefauver hearings in the early 1950s, and the later hearings led by Senator John McClellan in the late fifties and early sixties. As discussed in Chapter 2, the findings of these Senate investigations have been challenged, even debunked. Puzo therefore based his novel on information of dubious provenance.

But regardless of *The Godfather*'s veracity—and Puzo admitted that "my Mafia is a very romanticized myth"[51]—after the novel became a hit, the author "was introduced to a few gentlemen related to the material" who "loved the book."[52] And they weren't alone. "In different parts of the country I heard a nice story; that the Mafia had paid me a million dollars to write *The Godfather* as a public relations con."[53]

Whatever the reading habits of gangsters, it seems likely that far more of them saw the films than read the novel. Sammy "the Bull" Gravano, the former Gotti associate and later prosecution witness, recalled how he reacted to seeing the first film: "I left that movie stunned . . . I mean, I floated out of the theater. Maybe it was fiction, but for me, then, that was our life. It was incredible. I remember talking to a multitude of guys, made guys [initiated mobsters], who felt exactly the same way."[54]

"Wiseguys love movies about wiseguys," says former FBI undercover agent Joseph D. Pistone, aka Donnie Brasco. "They love being depicted on the big screen . . . *The Godfather*? That movie makes wiseguys look like philosophers and noble warriors. Wiseguys know that movie better than most film students."[55]

It's not surprising that the film appealed to the vanity of mobsters. *The Godfather* made the life of a mafioso, as Alessandro Camon describes it, "big, powerful, glamorous, and complex enough to provide the audience not just a vicarious thrill, but an inspiration: he couldn't help wanting that life. And so the real Mafiosi began taking after their on-screen counterparts at the same time they were inspiring them. Even if most movies depicted them as cruel and unrefined, the classy aura of *The Godfather* seemed to stick to the tale enough to make this semiotic exchange possible."[56]

But in the past quarter-century, the *declino del padrino* has set in. Camon attributes the decline to the mafia's having become "addicted to consumerism" and turning "shallow and nihilistic," no longer believing "in the once cogent fiction of its 'code': honor, respect, silence."[57] Although at times in Camon's analysis it isn't clear whether he is referring to the Sicilian mafia or to Italian American organized crime, in both cases there has been a breakdown of the value system and discipline that had made the gangster's world cohesive. In America and in Italy, gangsters betray each other readily to avoid lengthy prison sentences. During the 1980s and early '90s, Sicilian mobsters who turned government witness and revealed family secrets became so numerous that they were collectively known as *pentiti*, penitents.

Alessandro Camon's analysis of the mythical mafioso as a "sort of hero" who, "in the landscape of popular culture [is] a relative of any battle-scared soldier, any benign but unyielding ruler, any fearless gunfighter," offers insights that are valuable to an understanding of this contradictory creature. He's less credible when he argues that the familial core of mafia culture is inconsistent with the familiar claim—made not only by critics but by the films' director—that *The Godfather* is a metaphor for capitalism. Capitalism's ethos is individualistic, Camon avers; in a capitalist society, each person is considered to be capable of and responsible for his or her own success. But the mafioso is associated with a group known as a family, "whose collective interest is inseparable from that of the individuals."[58] Mafia ideology, therefore, is more properly associated with the working class and the aristocracy than with the middle class.

But what are the Corleones if not bourgeois? Their New York home, for example, is neither ostentatious nor shabby; it exudes subdued, decorous middle-class taste. And what are the Corleones if not businessmen? Theirs is a parasitic, nonproductive capitalism, but it certainly operates on the profit motive. To state that family values and capitalist ideology are fundamentally at odds is a strange claim for an Italian to make, given that in Italy industrial capitalism has been largely a family affair—the Agnellis (Fiat), the Olivettis (typewriters to telecommunications), and the Tanzis (the food megacorporation Parmalat, which Tanzi family greed and corruption drove into insolvency) are just some of the better-known corporate clans. And similarly in the United States, families with names like Rockefeller, Morgan, and Ford have played not insubstantial roles in the development of industrial capitalism. The business practices of these Italian and American capitalist dynasties have at times made the Corleones—and real Sicilian mafiosi—look like followers of Gandhi.

Mafia culture may valorize family and the interdependence of family members, but as Camon himself observes, the real raison d'être is making money. Family ideology can bind members together and provide justification for any misdeeds they may commit. But although mafia crime groups may be called families, their structures are militaristic (with bosses, captains, "soldiers," etc.) rather than familial. And like big capitalists elsewhere, Sicilian mafia families amorally pursue their own interests in complete disregard for the effect of their activities on society as a whole. The effects of mafia control of the construction industry are depressingly evident in the ugly housing projects hastily thrown up on Palermo's *periferia* during the 1960s by mob-controlled firms. The chaotic jumble of hazardous slum housing in the western Sicilian city of Agrigento, within sight of the area's magnificent Greek ruins, is another testament to the ruinous social consequences of the mafia's familial business practices.

The first two *Godfather* films brilliantly explicate the continuity between small-scale, family-controlled mafia enterprise and corporate capitalism. The films depict the clan or small association, known by the sociological term "gemeinschaft," as superior to a large institutional collectivity, the "gesellschaft." The Corleone business is indeed a family venture, wholly owned and operated. It is ethnically homogeneous, and closed to outsiders, like a secret society. It is its own world, a counterculture, an alternative social order in which ethnic solidarity is a means to resist corporate control and, indeed, assimilation to American society. Don Corleone forcefully articulates the mafia philosophy in the famous peace meeting of the heads of the "five families":

> "As for our own deeds, we are not responsible to the .90 calibers, the pezzonovanti who take it upon themselves to decide what we shall do with our lives, who declare wars they wish us to fight in to protect what they own. Who is to say we should obey the laws they make for their own interest and to our hurt? And who are they then to meddle when we look after our own interests? *Sonna cosa nostra*," Don Corleone said. "These are our own affairs. We will manage our world for ourselves because it is our world, *cosa nostra*. And so we have to stick together to guard against outside meddlers. Otherwise they will put the ring in our nose as they have put the ring in the nose of all the millions of Neapolitans and other Italians in this country."[59]

Puzo describes the leaders of this world: "They were those rarities, men who had refused to accept the rule of organized society, men who refused the dominion of other men. There was no force, no mortal man who could bend them to their will unless they wished it. They were men who guarded their free will with wiles and murder.

Their wills could be subverted only by death. Or the utmost reasonableness."[60]

The mafia, or at least Don Corleone's piece of it, is a well-run concern that takes better care of its members than does legitimate society. In the novel, as World War II rages, "the Don could take pride in his rule. His world was safe for those who had sworn loyalty to him; other men who believed in law and order were dying by the millions."[61] Don Corleone is shocked and uncomprehending when members of his organization—and his own son, Michael—volunteer to serve their country, an abstraction the Godfather can't understand. When told that one of the enlistees had said, "America has been good to me," the Don curtly replies, "*I* have been good to him."[62]

But ultimately the Corleone enterprise, which had seemed "a hermetically enclosed world of a secret society and its ethnically encoded local traditions,"[63] is revealed as another manifestation of the capitalist business ethic, as part of "the current economic and political praxis."[64] Over the course of the first two films, "the archaic, relatively honorbound order of Don Corleone" gives way to "the more pragmatic and less scrupulous regime" of his younger son Michael, who builds the family business into a national corporation.[65] (In Puzo's novel, Don Corleone anticipates this transformation, telling his assembled mob confreres, "We have to be cunning like the business people, there's more money in it and it's better for our children and grandchildren.")[66]

In *The Godfather*, the New York–based Corleone crime family is an insular Sicilian realm, defending its interests within a larger, hostile society. In *Godfather II*, with the family's move to Las Vegas and its economic expansion into hotel ownership and casinos, the loss of the old Sicilian world becomes evident.

At the lavish resort party given in honor of the confirmation of Michael's son Anthony, Frank Pentangeli, an old Corleone associate from New York, realizes how much things have changed—there is no Italian food at the party, most of the guests aren't Italian, and the orchestra can't even play a tarantella. Even worse, Michael refuses to allow Pentangeli to whack the Rosato brothers, errant hoodlums who flout the old rules, selling drugs, employing "niggers and spics," and committing violence "in their grandmothers' neighborhood." Michael denies his old family friend this "justice" because the Rosatos are aligned with Hyman Roth, the Meyer Lansky–like underworld financier with whom he is setting up a major business deal. Money clearly has become more important than the old Sicilian blood ties.

Critics and fans were quick to realize how much *The Godfather* broke with the conventions of earlier gangster movies. It wasn't only its greater ethnic authenticity or its topflight production values. Until *The Godfather*, crime movies were constrained by the repressive morality of the old Hays Code. When the Code began to break down in the 1960s, films that were more morally complex, even ambiguous, could be made, a development crucial to *The Godfather*.

Before Coppola's film, crime movies viewed the criminal from the perspective of law-abiding society, from "an external, legalistic viewpoint and an attitude tinged with outrage."[67] *The Godfather* reversed this point of view, "looking from inside the underworld out into a hopelessly corrupt society from which tradition, loyalty, honor, and respect for one's elders had almost totally vanished."[68]

Vincent Canby, reviewing *The Godfather* in *The New York Times*, welcomed this change, saying Coppola's film represented "the gangster melodrama come of age, truly sorrowful and truly exciting, without the false piety of the films that flourished forty years ago, scaring the delighted hell out of us while cautioning that crime doesn't (or, at least, shouldn't) pay . . ."[69] *The Godfather*, Alessandro Camon observes, was the first major film "that unabashedly chose to embrace the Mafia myth and portray the protagonist as a fascinating, multilayered hero."[70]

Some argue that this strategy never would have worked—we in the audience never would have found Vito or Michael Corleone fascinating and multilayered—had not Puzo and Coppola engaged in considerable dissembling about the nature of organized crime and its social costs. Bill Tonelli may be right to argue that pervasive disillusion with established authority and the breakdown of the nuclear family rendered Americans, Italian and otherwise, receptive to Corleone family values. He doesn't explore the political implications of this argument, but other commentators have. Carlos Clarens, one of the most astute critics of *The Godfather*, charges in his influential 1980 book *Crime Movies* that the film glorifies the mafia, endorsing "a sexist, patriarchal, repressive subculture . . ."[71]

Others argued that Puzo and Coppola had perversely transformed vicious criminals into ambitious immigrants guilty of little worse than pursuing "the American dream by alternative means." British critic Mike Bygrave, writing in the liberal paper *The Guardian*, charged that the novelist and director had perpetrated a massive public relations fraud on behalf of organized crime, having "cloaked the Mob in the leading myths of American life." In the mythopoetics of Puzo-Coppola, "Law-abiding America became an illusion. The Mafia became the real America, the authentic guardians of honour, decency and justice for all."[72]

Where, Clarens asks, does the Corleone family income come from? In the first film there is much talk of Vito Corleone's power and influence. But, says Clarens, there is "not one word about such bread-and-butter activities as prostitution, hijacking, loan sharking, or the numbers racket. At times Coppola went soft on his characters in a way Puzo never did."[73] Clarens sees in *The Godfather* a lamentable nostalgia for the heyday of organized crime and for powerful patriarchs like Don Corleone.

Stephen Fox, in a feature written for the American Movie Channel's Web site, makes a similar point:

> In the first film, gangsters often behave quite badly, betraying each other and killing with casual insouciance. But they only harm each other; the focus is relentlessly internal to the point of claustrophobia. The movie offers no sense of just what gangsters do to make their money: nothing about labor rackets, extortion, loan-sharking or gambling. The Sollozzo character does refer to the politicians that Don Vito has in his pocket, but the point is left dangling.[74]

Jerry Capeci, a reporter who covered the organized crime beat for the New York *Daily News*, notes that the film depicts a mob family that "resorted to violence only to defend itself . . . It didn't show their musclemen pounding a poor degenerate gambler who was behind on his loan shark payment or mobsters torching a restaurant or garbage truck of an extortion victim. There is no blue-collar worker shot to death after killing a son of a gangster in a tragic car accident."[75] (Capeci's last reference is to a neighbor of John Gotti, who disappeared after accidentally running over one of Gotti's children with his car.)

Capeci acknowledges enjoying *The Godfather*, but he maintains that all three films "failed to capture the reality of day-to-day Mafia life." He pronounces sentence on the mob: "The daily routine involves grit, grime, self-interest, lying, cheating, backstabbing, pettiness, spontaneous violence, stupidity, betrayal, and many other acts that conjure up the idea of killers without honor who will do almost anything to make a buck . . . *The Godfather's* fabulous profits and the film's artistic merits have nothing to do with reality,"[76] Capeci concludes.

Coppola's first *Godfather* film is evasive about the Corleone business, but Puzo's novel makes clear the sources of the family's wealth: "The Corleone group depended on gambling for most of its income."[77] The Corleones are also involved in labor racketeering. They invest profits from their illicit activities in legitimate enterprises such as real estate and construction. There's the Genco Olive Oil importing company, the original Corleone business and the legitimate front for the empire. Even in the novel, the Corleones, or at least Vito, appear as less venal and violent than other mafiosi, those who make their bread through prostitution and narcotics. The Corleones, as depicted by both Puzo and Puzo-Coppola, are the aristocracy of the underworld.

Fox overstates (but not by much) when he writes that the *Godfather* gangsters only harm each other. In the first film, the movie producer Jack Woltz is terrorized into giving a coveted role to Johnny Fontane, the Sinatra-like singer who is godson to Vito Corleone. In *Godfather II*, the Corleones arrange to have a senator caught in a compromising situation—with a dead prostitute in his bed—the better to blackmail him.

But both films load the dice in favor of the Corleones, since Woltz and Senator Pat Geary are both depicted "as racist [toward Italians], uncouth, venal, and more significant, as sexual perverts."[78] Woltz is a pedophile who violates young girls; Senator Geary enjoys rough sex with hookers. The proclivities of these scoundrels "clearly offend the

Corleones, abstemious family men . . . The producer and the senator appear guilty of crimes against nature, next to which the Corleones are merely granting justice without resorting to the law, or at worst transacting business in an unorthodox way."[79]

Michael Corleone's transformation from a straight-arrow collegian and soldier to his father's cold-blooded successor strikes some as implausible and as another instance of the film's gloss on gangster brutality. "The first film turns on Michael's decision to join the family business," writes Stephen Fox. "The Don had hoped his war-hero college-educated son would go straight and redeem the family's reputation. Instead, after the Don is shot, Michael whispers, 'I'm with you now.' He becomes a criminal because he loves his daddy—nobody could object to that."[80]

"Most hoodlums," Fox continues, "embark on a life of crime because they wish to make a living without working, except in occasional intense spurts, and they see nothing wrong with killing, stealing, and scaring people. The theme is consistent: Nothing is ever a Corleone's fault. Instead, the culprit is the ancient blood feuds of Sicily, or the white-suited neighborhood boss in Little Italy, or plotting rival gangsters, or politicians, or capitalism itself."

The book makes Michael's transformation much more plausible. Despite his aloofness from the family business, he is his father's son, more so than his two brothers, the volatile Sonny and the hapless Fredo. Puzo describes Michael as having "all the quiet force and intelligence of his great father, the born instinct to act in such a way that men had no recourse but to respect him."[81] When Michael proposes to kill the drug dealer Sollozzo and the corrupt police captain McCluskey, Sonny says to him: "I always said you were the toughest one in the Family, tougher than the Don himself. You were the only one who could stand off the old man."[82] When angry, Michael exudes an icy calm that unnerves even hardened gangsters. Michael's relinquishing of his conventional life to become his father's successor is credible in the novel because Puzo has prepared us for it.

There are dissenters from the view that the film glorifies the mafia. Harlan Lebo, in his *The Godfather Legacy*, insists that it does exactly the opposite. In the Puzo-Coppola script for *The Godfather*, the "plot points were honed to razor edges to characterize the fear, treachery, and endless suspicion that is the hallmark of life in the criminal underworld."[83]

"To be sure," Lebo writes, "the script also brought out favorable points about family, loyalty, honor, and respect. But the scenes that coldly and calmly characterized the dark side of the Mafia offered the most important commentary on society and the human condition."[84]

Lebo argues that the movie is even more hard-hitting than the novel in its critique of the savagery of organized crime: "Page after page of the heartless scheming of the Mafia family that Puzo worked so hard to develop in his book were actually amplified considerably by distilling them into a few well-chosen scenes,"[85] such as Sonny Corleone ordering the murder of driver Paulie Gatto right after inquiring about his health, or Tessio plotting the murder of Michael Corleone, whom he had known since Don Vito's favorite son was a baby.

In response to those who say the film glorifies the mafia, Lebo responds, "None of these critics would recognize that in the film's exploration of the Corleone family, behind the laughter, the bonding, and the dynamic personalities, every human encounter in *The Godfather* was a portrait of treachery."[86]

Yes, but Lebo's two examples actually support Stephen Fox's point that the *Godfather* gangsters "only harm each other." Moreover, since the films place us within the Corleone universe, where we are "looking from inside the underworld out into a hopelessly corrupt society," we can't help but think Paulie (who set up Vito Corleone to be killed) and Tessio (who planned the same fate for Michael) get their just desserts.

Puzo's novel is much harder on the Corleones and on organized crime than is the film. He does romanticize the mafia, as he has acknowledged. (Coppola claimed to be surprised when he was accused of glorifying the mafia. He was especially shocked by comments that he had romanticized Michael Corleone, whom he felt he had unambiguously depicted "as a monster.")[87] But in the book's Sicilian scenes, Puzo succinctly recounts the terrible conditions that gave rise to the mafia and describes organized crime as a blight on Sicilian society.

"Sicily was a land that had been more cruelly raped than any other in history," he declares. "The Inquisition had tortured rich and poor alike. The landowning barons and the princes of the Catholic Church exercised absolute power over the shepherds and farmers. The police were the instruments of their power and so identified with them that to be called a policeman is the foulest insult one Sicilian can hurl at another."[88]

Faced with such overwhelming oppression, Sicilians learned not to make themselves vulnerable by betraying their anger or making threats; any such efforts would result in quick reprisal. Sicilians learned that the establishment was their enemy, so to obtain redress they went to "the rebel underground, the Mafia."

This is a somewhat idealized account of the mafia's origins. As described in Chapter 2, the mafia bands (*cosche*) that arose in rural western Sicily did provide jobs and other services, but they always had a predatory and violent character. In the Sicily of the 1940s, the period Puzo describes, mafia families to some extent still fulfilled the role of Robin Hood–like dispensers of justice to those whom the justice system oppressed. While hiding out in Sicily, Michael Corleone learns of this aspect of the "honored society" from one of his hosts, Dr. Taza, a spectacularly incompetent physician who obtained his medical degree through the mafia's intercession.

But Michael also learns about the reality that Taza conceals from him: the mafia was "the illegal arm of the rich and even the auxiliary police of the legal and political structure. It had become a degenerate capitalist structure, anti-communist, anti-liberal, placing its own taxes on every form of business endeavor no matter how small."[89]

Puzo is absolutely clear about the corrosive effects of the mafia on Sicilian society: "Merit meant nothing. Talent meant nothing. Work meant nothing. The Mafia Godfather gave you your profession as a gift." The corrupt, undemocratic sociopolitical structure that nurtured and protected the mafia resulted in Sicily becoming "a land of ghosts, its men emigrating to every other country on earth to be able to earn their bread, or simply to escape being murdered for exercising their political and economic freedoms."[90]

The historical tragedy of Sicily is what forced my grandparents to emigrate; "Nothing changes there," I can recall my *nonno* saying. Puzo's novel and the *Godfather* films are more accurate than not about the mafia's exploits in Sicily. The distortion comes with the implication in both that the mafia was exported to America from Europe, that Italian American organized crime is an overseas branch of La Cosa Nostra, and that organized crime in America is exclusively an Italian affair. Organized crime existed in America before Sicilians and other southern Italians arrived, and it has always been multiethnic. Al Capone and Lucky Luciano, to cite two of America's most notorious mobsters, were not the heads of mafia "families" but ran criminal organizations that also comprised Jews and Irish. It's hard to argue with Allen Barra's claim that the *Godfather* novel and films "did more than anything else to create a myth of the all-powerful Sicilian-American crime syndicate."[91]

Mob expert Jerry Capeci acknowledges enjoying the *Godfather* movies, but as entertainment, not as a credible portrait of organized crime. He regards Martin Scorsese's *Goodfellas* (1990) as "the best depiction of real Mafia life yet filmed . . . *The Godfather* makes the hoods too noble," Capeci says. "In *Godfather, Part II*, the mob guys were darker, more evil. The violence was messier, the cameras lingered on it longer, and it was more realistic. *Goodfellas* got it right the first time."[92]

Goodfellas, based on Nicholas Pileggi's book *Wiseguy*, depicts the bloody exploits of a New York mob crew that made its biggest score with the $6 million Lufthansa heist at Kennedy Airport in 1978. Scorsese's brutal, darkly comic film doesn't lend a mythic aura to these hoods, instead depicting them as violent to the point of psychosis, greedy, and not too bright. There are no somber scenes of dark-suited men discussing business in tasteful, wood-paneled offices, no soulful father-son conversations, no joyous family celebrations. There's just unvarnished avarice, backstabbing, and killing.

Goodfellas is a superb film and one that has many enthusiasts among fans and critics. It is extraordinarily effective in its demolition of Mafia mythology and the false glamour that mobsters have accrued over some thirty years, thanks to Puzo and Coppola. But as a portrait of a milieu rather than an individual, it lacks at its center a charismatic protagonist. Henry Hill (played competently but without inspiration by Ray Liotta) narrates *Goodfellas*, and though we see the film's incidents from his perspective, he never becomes a fascinating, enigmatic character like Vito or Michael Corleone. He's just a hood.

This is why *Goodfellas* hasn't generated the same broad popularity and devotion as *The Godfather*—it deconstructs the Mafia myth instead of perpetuating it. The *Godfather* films offer historical sweep, grandeur, nostalgia, and the aura of tragedy; *Goodfellas* presents grubby, unglamorous reality. And when it comes to our movie mobsters, we prefer the Godfather to the mafia soldier, the mythic to the mundane.

The first two *Godfather* films are universally admired, but *The Godfather, Part III*, released sixteen years after *Godfather II*, has become a punch line. In an episode of the NBC television drama *Third Watch*, an Italian American cop declared his ethnic bona fides by saying he loves pizza, pasta, and "the first two *Godfathers*." The members of Tony Soprano's mob crew revere *I* and *II*—Silvio Dante (Steven Van Zandt) frequently quotes lines of dialogue from the films—and disdain *III*.

Likewise, *Godfather III* isn't a critics' favorite.

"Francis Ford Coppola's 'The Godfather Part III' isn't just a disappointment, it's a failure of heartbreaking proportions," according to Hal Hinson of *The Washington Post*. Roger Ebert, writing in the *Chicago Sun-Times*, declared that "it lacks the confident forward sweep of a film that knows where it's going." Of major critics, *The New York Times*'s Janet Maslin was virtually alone in her opinion that *The Godfather, Part III*, was "a valid and deeply moving continuation of the Corleone family saga."

The third and from all appearances final installment in the *Godfather* series indeed is a flawed film. The narrative at times is convoluted and confusing. Pacino, so mesmerizing in the first two films, is a somewhat recessive presence as the sixtyish Michael. And a very young and inexperienced Sofia Coppola, as Michael Corleone's daughter Mary, is utterly miscast in the role—a first for the trilogy.

I saw *Godfather III* on its opening night in Manhattan. The theater had sold tickets in advance, and every showing was sold out. The excited anticipation of the fans was palpable, and the moment the first, familiar notes of the mournful trumpet theme sounded, the theater erupted in applause and cheers. Three hours later, the deflated mood of the audience was as tangible as their earlier excitement. "That sucked" and "What a disappointment" seemed to be the general verdict, one with which I concurred.

But *III* has its strengths. Though not an achievement on par with the first two *Godfathers*, it is a better film than generally recognized—a conclusion I reached after recently watching it again for the first time since its premiere. At the very least, one immediately experiences the pleasure of being back in the company of old friends: Michael, Kay, Connie; *consigliere* Tom Hagen is gone, but stone-face hit man Al Neri is still around, hovering on the sidelines. Anthony and Mary, Michael and Kay's children, are attractive young adults now; *figlio* and *figlia* respectively are an aspiring opera singer and the director of the Corleone family charitable foundation. Vincent Mancini (played by Andy Garcia), the son of Sonny Corleone and his mistress Lucy Mancini, is a welcome addition to the Corleone clan, his sexed-up volatility making him a true chip off the old block. Eli Wallach is also a delight as the sly, duplicitous Don Altobello, a longtime family friend who has changed sides. The film is graced by Gordon Willis's elegant cinematography, with its dark earth tones, and by the Carmine Coppola–Nino Rota score.

The third film's most striking aspect, though, is its political stance. If the earlier films portrayed the Corleone family business as a metaphor for capitalism, *III* brings the analogy to an international stage, focusing on collusion among the Sicilian mafia, the Vatican, and the Italian state, with the narrative based on actual events of the 1980s.

The film opens with the camera panning through the Lake Tahoe compound, now in disrepair and abandoned. Then, flash forward to New York City, 1979, where the Catholic Church is bestowing the prestigious Order of St. Sebastian on Michael. The honor, the highest that can be given to a layman, is the culmination of Michael's twenty-year effort to achieve respectability and legitimacy for his family.

Anthony and Mary attend the award ceremony, which gives the former don the opportunity to wax sentimental about children as "the only wealth in this world . . . More than all the money and power on Earth, [they] are my treasure." Kay, now remarried (and not to an Italian), comes too, but only to support her son in his dispute with his father over his education and career. Michael wants Anthony to study law; Anthony wants to dedicate himself to music.

Michael and Kay argue this point, but when she blurts, "He knows that you killed Fredo," Michael visibly wilts. He relents and agrees to give Anthony his freedom. (This scene echoes one from Puzo's novel that did not make it into the first film. When Don Vito chastises a young Sonny for his violent impetuousness, he exclaims to his father, "I saw you kill Fanucci," the Black Hand gangster whom Vito murdered years earlier in Little Italy. The don subsequently gives up trying to rein in his oldest son.)

The initial encounter between Michael and Kay, who have not seen each other for some time, is one of the film's best scenes, as Kay, fighting for her son, unleashes years of anger and resentment on her ex-husband. "You know Michael, now that you're so respectable I think you're more dangerous than you ever were," she says, disgusted by the Vatican award. "In fact, I preferred you when you were just a common mafia hood."

When Michael protests that his main concern had always been to protect her and the children from "the horrors of this world," she coldly replies, "But you became my horror."

"I don't hate you, Michael," she adds. "I dread you."

Michael donates $100 million to the Church for the poor of Sicily; receiving the thanks of the corrupt Archbishop Gilday, he piously says, "Let's just hope the money gets to the people who need it." A nice irony there, a mafioso and a churchman, figures historically aligned in Sicily to the detriment of the downtrodden, posing as the benefactors of the Sicilian poor. Of course the money won't go where it's needed, but it will buy greater respectability and influence for Michael, who is now legit, having divested the Corleone family of all its illicit businesses.

Whatever his charitable concerns, his real intent is to gain majority control of the European real estate holding company International Immobiliare ("the largest landlord on earth"), a $6 billion corporation of which the Church owns 25 percent. The Church has a huge deficit, and Michael agrees to bail the Vatican out and take majority control of Immobiliare for $500 million.

The devious Archbishop Gilday ups the ante to $600 million, telling Michael that the price is a bargain because with this money "your whole past history and the history of your family will be washed away." Michael plans to transform Immobiliare, a venerable European corporation, into a diversified conglomerate. This joint American-European venture, he says, "will defeat any competition." The Vatican's representative, pleased with the deal, declares, "International Immobiliare will be safe in Michael Corleone's hands."

But Michael's old underworld associates are angry at being cut out of the Immobiliare deal. Michael brings the discontented dons together for a meeting, at which he tries to assuage them with cash payouts, the millions he received from selling the Corleones' casinos. Left out of the largesse, and furious at the snub, is Joey Zasa, a preening, publicity-loving John Gotti–like hood whom the newspapers call "the best-dressed gangster."

Zasa storms out of the meeting, followed by Don Altobello. Moments later, a helicopter appears outside the high-rise where the meeting is being held, and unseen gunmen launch a massacre from the air. Vincent, who rescues Michael from the carnage, is certain that Joey Zasa poses the main threat to Corleones. But Michael has enemies far more formidable than Zasa or any of the other mob bosses. And they come from the world of Italian politics and finance.

The biggest of the *pezzonovanti* is an ascetic, taciturn figure called Lucchesi, who is modeled on an actual Italian politician, the Senator for Life and former Christian Democratic Party leader Giulio Andreotti. Lucchesi is said to be the only man who could have orchestrated a hit as spectacular as the helicopter assault. Lucchesi is called "don," a blurring of the term's original meaning as a title of respect and its mafia meaning. Lucchesi, a "man of finance and politics," combines respectability and corruption, and on a far grander scale than Michael Corleone.

As Michael wearily remarks to his sister, Connie, "All my life I kept trying to go up in society, where everything higher up was legal, straight. But the higher I go, the crookeder it becomes." Michael comes to the somewhat self-serving conclusion that "Italian politics—they're the true mafia."

The film's two central themes, the sins of fathers and the inescapability of destiny, converge in Sicily, where Michael is to be killed by a father-and-son assassin team hired by Don Altobello. But with

Michael's blessing, Vincent whacks the Corleone enemies, including Lucchesi. (Connie takes care of Altobello with some poisoned cannoli.) Michael once again has triumphed over his foes. But as the family leaves the Palermo opera house, having enjoyed Anthony's successful debut in *Cavalleria Rusticana*, the father assassin takes his shot at Michael. He is wounded, but Mary catches the fatal bullet.

The promise Michael had made to Mary—"I would burn in hell to keep you safe"—is mocked by the implacable *destino* he set for himself the moment he decided to kill Sollozzo and Captain McCluskey. His sins have been visited on his beloved child, striking her down. Michael howls inconsolably, like Lear, at the center of a tableau of wild grief, surrounded by Kay, Connie, Anthony, and Vincent. The film's denouement on the steps of the Palermo opera house is riveting, and not even Sofia Coppola's amateurish performance can vitiate its power.

Coppola and Puzo based their script for *Godfather III* on a major scandal of the early 1980s involving the Vatican, Sicilian mafiosi, and Italy's largest bank, Banco Ambrosiano, of which the Church was the major stockholder. The Rome-based bank was close to collapse, burdened with millions of dollars in unsecured debts. Those losses were linked to the Vatican's financial arm, the Institute of Religious Works (IOR), forcing the Catholic Church to later acknowledge a "moral responsibility" in the bank's collapse.

As the circumstances surrounding the scandal emerged, it became clear that Roberto Calvi, the Milanese banker who was president of Ambrosiano, was at the center of a spider's web of corruption linking the bank not only to the mafia but also to the Institute of Religious Works. Offshore tax havens, cold war politics, and a politically influential right-wing Masonic lodge, known as P2, also figured in the debacle.[93]

An investigation by Rome prosecutors determined that these connections had a direct bearing on the 1982 death of Calvi, who was found hanging from the Blackfriars Bridge in London. (*Godfather III* depicts Calvi's death with a brief shot of a body dangling from a bridge. But this image is inscrutable unless the viewer is familiar with the actual event, which the film never explains.) The prosecutors concluded that Sicilian mafiosi (with some Neapolitan *camorristi*) killed Calvi, acting not only in their own interests—Calvi apparently pocketed money they had asked him to launder—but also to ensure that the banker could not blackmail "politico-institutional figures and [representatives] of freemasonry, the P2 lodge, and the IOR with whom he had invested substantial sums of money, some of it from Cosa Nostra and Italian public corporations."[94]

Calvi's son, Carlo, said all along that the mafia was responsible for his father's death. "From the beginning we had identified criminal elements of the Mafia living in London, as having organised my father's murder," he told the BBC. "Of course we think that this is at the level of the executioner and that the murder was organized by politicians. The Mafia had simply the role of carrying out the murder."[95] The higher one goes, the crookeder it becomes.

Godfather III, as a few critics have had the perspicacity to see, deglorifies and deglamorizes the Italian American gangster, showing him to be motivated not by honor or venerable Sicilian codes of behavior but purely by greed and a lust for power. (That is how movies had typically portrayed gangsters, until the first two *Godfather* films.) As Vera Dika observes, "In Part III the characters are presented in such a way that they no longer embody the ways of 'La Via Vecchia.'"[96] Michael, in fact, becomes "the symbolic exploiter of his own people" by aligning himself with northern Italian businessmen and the Church.[97]

At the conclusion of *Godfather II* Michael is sitting outside the Lake Tahoe house in autumn, desolate and utterly alone. Both of his parents are dead, his wife has left him, and, having just murdered his brother Fredo, he is the only surviving Corleone son. The question he asked his mother earlier in the film—"Can a man lose his family?"—has been answered in the affirmative.

But though Michael has lost his soul he has gained the world. He has defeated all his enemies and, at the film's end, he is Mafioso Numero Uno, the unrivaled king of the underworld who has enough wealth and influence to gain entrée to the highest circles of the "legitimate" business world. The *pezzonovanti* of the established order have attempted to crush him, as have his underworld rivals, but he has beaten all of them. The *Godfather* fantasy of absolute personal power has been realized (albeit at a tremendous cost).

Godfather III shatters that fantasy. At the end of the film, a defeated Michael dies alone in Sicily, a death nothing like his father's demise among the tomato plants in *The Godfather*. There are no grandchildren or other family members around him, only a dog that sniffs his corpse as it lies on the ground. This conclusion to the saga delivers a message that devotees of the first two films were loath to accept: this is how it all ends, in defeat, isolation, and lonely, unmourned death.

Nicholas Pileggi, author of *Wiseguy* and a journalist who has covered organized crime for *New York* magazine, has said, "If you're Italian American and looking for a clue to your background and to the world your parents came from, the whole history of organized crime is an interesting source."[98] Some of my paisans doubtless will declare me anathema for saying so, but *The Godfather* inspired my first serious attempts to understand what Robert Viscusi has called our "complicated and difficult" heritage. Lacking that awareness, I had felt ambivalence and even some shame about my background.

Fascinated by the film and intrigued by the outrage it stirred among Italian Americans who said it defamed us, I began reading books like Gambino's *Blood of My Blood* and others that told me the stories that popular culture rarely told, in particular, those of immigrants like my maternal grandfather, who held progressive values and fought for social justice, belying the media cliché of southern Italians as tradition-bound conservatives who care only about *la famiglia*.

The Godfather was also a catalyst to my writing about Italian Americans and about Italy, beginning with an occasional newspaper or magazine article in the late seventies and leading to this book.

In *"The Godfather" and American Culture*, a savvy study of how the novel and films have captured the American imagination, author Chris Messenger states, contra Pileggi, "Italian Americans don't need to read or view *Godfather* texts to know their heritage or condition."[99] This is true today because an Italian American ethnic revival in the thirty-plus years since *The Godfather* has produced a voluminous literature, comprising historical studies, personal memoirs, fiction and poetry, and cultural criticism. Young Italian Americans now have far more opportunities to learn about themselves than I did. They don't have to discover their cultural heritage through the perspective of gangster dramas, as if the only Italians worth knowing are the "bad uncles of the barren cliffs of Sicily . . . that they transported in barrels like pure olive oil across the Atlantic."[100]

Critic Vera Dika maintains that *The Godfather* offers an "antiseptic dream of racial and ethnic purity" which was "enthusiastically consumed by a predominantly white society."[101] But then how does one explain the enormous popularity of the films with non-Italians, especially blacks and Latinos? Both rap music and salsa, for example, have paid homage to *The Godfather* by incorporating its imagery and themes. Movies about ambitious blacks and Latinos who turn to gangsterism owe a substantial debt to *The Godfather*, from 1970s "blaxploitation" flicks like *Black Caesar* and *Black Godfather* to Brian De Palma's Cubanized remake of *Scarface* to *New Jack City*. Chris Messenger is closer to the mark when he notes that "Mob narrative is not coextensive with Italian American narrative but is rather an offshoot from it, hybridized by the experience of many ethnic and/or oppressed groups that are suspicious of the law."[102] *The Godfather* doesn't belong only to Italian Americans or to Caucasians.

If further proof were needed that *The Godfather* is truly an American story, consider Mark Winegardner, a novelist and creative writing professor who, in 2003, was chosen by Random House and the estate of Mario Puzo to write a sequel to Puzo's classic pop epic. Winegardner announced that his book, whose title, *The Godfather Returns*, evokes a B-grade horror movie, would pick up where Puzo's bestseller left off, with Michael Corleone's ascent to Godfatherhood.[103] That *Godfather II* and *III* already have told that story apparently didn't concern Random House or the Puzo estate.

As is obvious from his surname, Winegardner is not Sicilian, not even Italian American. "I'm just a novelist with a vision of how to write this book," he told the British newspaper *The Guardian*. "I am, however, German-Irish, just like Tom Hagen [the Corleone family *consigliere*]. And he did just fine in this world."

Ah, "my Mick Kraut friend" (as sleazy Hollywood producer Jack Woltz calls Hagen the night before he wakes up next to his prize stallion's severed head), but Michael busted your paisan down to family attorney. Not being Sicilian, he wasn't up to the demands of being a "wartime *consigliere*." And neither were you up to this assignment.

In the sequel, published in November 2004, Winegardner attempted to fill in what he saw as gaps in Puzo's narrative, including the reason Fredo Corleone betrays Michael, and Michael's failure to keep his promise to his father and his wife Kay to go legit. But *Godfather II* already explained Fredo's betrayal, as a massive case of sibling rivalry and resentment. Fredo foolishly feeds information to Michael's enemies because "there was something in it for me," and the middle Corleone brother, in the late John Cazale's superb and heartbreaking portrayal, pours out his bitterness over his subordinate position in the family:

> I didn't know it was gonna be a hit, Mike—I swear to God I didn't know it was going to be a hit. Johnny Ola bumped into me in Beverly Hills—and he said that he wanted to talk—he said that you and—and—Roth were in on a—a—big deal together. And that there was something in it for me if I'd help 'em out. He said that—he said that—you were bein' tough on the negotiations. But if they could get a little help—and close the deal fast—it'd be good for the family.
> MICHAEL: You believed that story. You believed that.
> FREDO: He said there was something in it for me—on my own.
> MICHAEL: I've always taken care of you, Fredo.
> FREDO: Taken care of me? You're my kid brother and you take care of me? Did you ever think about that—did you ever once think about that? Send Fredo off to do this—send Fredo off to do that! Let Fredo take care of some Mickey Mouse nightclub somewhere! Send Fredo to pick somebody up at the airport! I'm your older brother, Mike, and I was stepped over!

Winegardner adds some backstory, in which Fredo is vulnerable to pressure because he is a self-hating bisexual with a weakness for drunken encounters with married men in grubby motel rooms. But none of his embellishments add anything of substance to what Puzo and Coppola came up with.

The Godfather Returns presents some new characters: Fausto

"Nick" Geraci, a mafia soldier who becomes Michael's rival; Francesca and Kathy Corleone, the twin daughters of Sonny and Sandra Corleone; and a few other mafia dons, including one whose phallic nose earns him the nickname "Fuckface." Tom Hagen has a larger presence than Puzo gave him, no doubt because Winegardner so identifies with him. But none of the new characters is the least bit compelling, and the old familiar figures, Michael included, are only pallid simulacra of Puzo's creations.

It's become conventional wisdom to say that Francis Ford Coppola transformed a junk novel into a work of cinematic art. *New York Times* critic Michiko Kakutani expressed this consensus in her pan of Winegardner's book: "Mario Puzo's 1969 novel . . . was really a trashy potboiler: fast, punchy, sometimes lurid reading, quite devoid of the gravitas and emotional undertow that Mr. Coppola . . . imparted to those classic films."[104]

The Godfather, though no literary masterpiece, had color, verve, and narrative drive. It was a good old-fashioned page-turner that carried the reader along from its memorable opening scene with the vengeance-seeking undertaker Bonasera to its conclusion, Michael's elevation to Godfather. By comparison, Winegardner's sequel has no consistent narrative line; it proceeds by fits and starts and never achieves anything like Puzo's compulsive readability.

Puzo's novel may have been pulp, but it was great pulp, and sometimes more than that, as in the Sicilian sequences. In Coppola's film, Michael courts and marries Apollonia while hiding out on the island after having killed McCluskey and Tattaglia. In Puzo's telling, however, there's much more to Michael's Sicilian sojourn. He also learns about the origins and the true nature of the mafia, how it is intertwined with Sicilian political economy, and how it corrupts Sicilian society. In these passages, his writing has the "gravitas" that Kakutani and others found lacking.

The Godfather wasn't an elegant exercise in literary style, but Winegardner—who directs the creative writing program at Florida State University in Tallahassee—serves up some truly awful prose. Here is Nick Geraci's father, Fausto Sr., clearing up his son's confusion over his having survived a suspicious plane crash: " 'Why do you think you're alive, you big dummy?' Fausto said. 'You think they'd've kept you alive if they thought you fucked up? How many guys you know pulled a stunt like you did in the lake there and didn't wind up taking two in the head, a meat hook up the ass, butta-beepa-da-boppa-da-boop?' "[105]

The Godfather Returns was a sequel no one needed. Random House, banking on the enduring popularity of the original novel and the films, apparently believed Winegardner's middling effort had the potential to be a major hit. But the book never caught fire with readers. It debuted at number seven on *The New York Times* bestseller list, and then quickly fell off. Whereas Puzo's novel remained on the list for sixty-seven weeks, Winegardner's sequel was sleeping with the fishes by mid-January 2005, only two months after its publication. *The Godfather Returns* was, evidently, a literary offering that was all too easy to refuse.

5

From Mean Streets to Suburban Meadow:
The Sopranos Rewrites the Genre

Like Westerns, gangster pictures have moved in and out of vogue in Hollywood with the regularity of tides, often disappearing for years before suddenly returning in the form of a smash hit.

—Harlan Lebo, *The Godfather Legacy*

The richest and most compelling piece of television—no, of popular culture—that I've encountered in the past twenty years is a meditation on the nature of morality, the possibility of redemption and the legacy of Freud.

—Ellen Willis, in *The Nation*

At this point in time it's a little bit hard to take mobsters all that seriously.

—David Chase, creator of *The Sopranos*

The next chapter in the long-running mythological saga of the Italian American mafia begins in a psychiatrist's waiting room in suburban New Jersey.

There, uneasily contemplating a sculpture of a naked woman, sits Tony Soprano, an overweight, fortyish Italian American husband and father who has been suffering from debilitating panic attacks. Confused and scared, he has reluctantly decided to do something unthinkable for someone in his line of work. A mafioso committed to *omertà*, the code forbidding any discussion of mob business with outsiders, Tony Soprano has turned to the talking cure for relief from his suffering. And this tough leader of men seeks help from a woman, no less, a primly sexy paisana named Dr. Jennifer Melfi whose forebears came from the same "part of the boot" as Tony's family.

What would bring a mob boss to such a state?

Both of his families, the one at home and the one at the job, are busting his *coglioni* big-time. He's trying to do the right thing by his widowed mother, Livia, house-proud wife, Carmela, and two spoiled kids, A.J. (Anthony Jr.) and Meadow, while taking care of business as a capo in the New Jersey mob. His marriage is shaky, mainly because of his repeated infidelities with a series of "gumads," or mistresses. (What ironists these wiseguys are, calling the hookers and strippers they keep on the side by the southern Italian variant of *comare*, or godmother.)

Tony's cantankerous mother is furious that he wants to move her into a nursing home. His bitter and volatile uncle, old-time mafioso Corrado "Junior" Soprano, wants to murder a rival in the restaurant run by Tony's childhood friend. Meanwhile, Czech gangsters are trying to break Tony's monopoly on garbage hauling in northern New Jersey. ("Waste management consultant" is how he describes his occupation to Dr. Melfi.) His loose cannon of a nephew Christopher deals with the upstart competitors by killing their representative—who also is a mob boss's nephew, and like Christopher, a member of the reckless, coke-snorting "new generation" of gangsters—and dumping the body on Staten Island, all without Uncle Tony's permission.

And if this wasn't enough *agità*, the feeling that the best days of "this thing of ours" have come and gone, and that he's not in the same league as the fabled mafia bosses of yore, haunts Tony. "Lately I'm getting the feeling that I came in at the end. The best is over," he tells Dr. Melfi. The psychiatrist's response is both clueless yet totally apt: "Many Americans, I think, feel that way."

All the above unfolded in barely a half-hour's screen time in the debut episode of *The Sopranos*, which aired Sunday, January 10, 1999, on the premium cable network Home Box Office. But the new series offered much more than efficient exposition. The writing—by the show's creator, the veteran television writer and producer David Chase, and others—was witty, multilayered, and as profane as is possible only on a premium cable channel. The acting, by a predominantly Italian American cast led by James Gandolfini, up to then a reliable supporting actor in movies and TV, was vivid yet nuanced. The camera work, by director of photography Alik Sakharov, was cinematic—the show is shot on 35-millimeter film stock instead of videotape—with naturalistic lighting giving compositions a painterly quality rarely seen on network television.

The show's opening credit sequence was a masterpiece of montage. To the pounding rock beat of the sinister theme song, "Woke Up This Morning," Tony Soprano drives his big black SUV from New York City through the Lincoln Tunnel and into northern New Jersey, past the hideous wasteland of oil refineries and truck stops, through an old ethnic working-class neighborhood, and on to his destination: his suburban home, with its manicured lawns, lush greenery, and swimming pool. Besides being technically accomplished, the superbly shot, edited, and scored sequence worked as metaphor for Italian American upward mobility over three generations, from poor immigrants to blue-collar residents of urban Little Italys to middle-class suburbanites.

The Sopranos from the first proclaimed itself both the heir to the tradition epitomized by the Godfather films (with a secondary debt to Scorsese's Goodfellas and the James Cagney classic Public Enemy) and a radical break from the Coppola-Puzo trilogy. The series, as critic Stephen Holden observed in The New York Times, "carries 'The Godfather's' epic themes into the present, turning tragedy into comedy and vice-versa."[1] David Chase also extends The Godfather's depiction of organized crime as a more raffish form of capitalism into the twenty-first century, with mob business once again part of a much larger corruption.

That The Sopranos never could have existed without The Godfather was obvious from the first episode, when Tony's nephew Christopher Moltisanti misquotes one of the film's most famous lines as he and another gangster dispose of a corpse. When Christopher mutters, "Lewis Brasi sleeps with the fishes," the other, older hoodlum disgustedly corrects him, "Luca Brasi. It's Luca Brasi."

The Sopranos is nothing if not acutely self-conscious about its debt to the Coppola-Puzo films and to other exemplars of the genre. Critic Chris Messenger, in "The Godfather" and American Culture: How the Corleones Became "Our Gang," observes, "No single vehicle has so well captured America's decades-long affair with mob narrative as does The

Sopranos." David Chase is "unrelenting in his portrayal of a culture and media industry so deeply imbued with what could be called Godfatherness—that there is no way out to an original or summary statement of influence and effect, origin and separation."[2] That awareness extends to the show's characters, who "live in an America that has been completely colonized by *The Godfather*."[3]

"Once I got started on writing the pilot, it became sort of central to the idea that these guys would have been shaped by especially 'The Godfather,'" David Chase has said. "They refer to 'The Godfather' all the time, that they would live 'The Godfather' in their heads. They would talk about 'The Godfather,' and they would compare things to 'The Godfather.' And to a certain extent, 'Goodfellas.' But mostly, I think, for a lot of wiseguys, 'The Godfather' is like the Koran."[4]

Chase and his writers deploy their life-imitates-art strategy so effectively that the show's characters seem to live within the narrative frame of the Mafia myth as much as they inhabit an actual geographic entity called New Jersey. When Christopher shoots a bakery clerk in the foot, the act evokes the incident in *Goodfellas* when Tommy De Vito, the psychotic hoodlum played by Joe Pesci, shoots Spider, a young waiter in a tavern, played by Michael Imperioli. In another episode, Carmela and her women friends attend a lecture about the accomplishments of Italian American women. The gung-ho speaker, in the midst of her paean to paisanas, deplores pop-culture portrayals of Italian American women as mob wives; the remark wounds the respectability-craving Carmela and outrages her friends. Jennifer Melfi's ex-husband Richard is a militant antidefamationist who complains incessantly about movies that depict Italians as gangsters. He's frustrated when Jennifer tells him he should be more concerned about ethnic cleansing, and his son says that mafia stories, rather than slurring Italian Americans, constitute an American pop-culture mythology, as the western once did.

The male psychiatrist whom Tony consults when Dr. Melfi won't see him justifies his refusal to accept Tony as a patient by saying, "I watch the news like everyone else. I know who you are. And I saw *Analyze This*. I don't need the ramifications that could arise from treating someone like yourself."

Tony's indignant rejoinder is priceless: "*Analyze This*? Come on, it's a fucking comedy!"

At the most mundane level, *The Sopranos*' debt to *The Godfather* is evident in the frequent allusions to the Corleone trilogy. Silvio Dante, Tony Soprano's *consigliere* and owner of the Bada Bing strip club, loves to quote Michael Corleone's "Just when I thought I was out, they pull me back in!" from *III*. The Luca Brasi allusions continue after the series's first episode and Christopher's mangling of the "sleeps with the fishes" line. In the second season, the older gangster who corrects him, Sal "Big Pussy" Bonpensiero, himself ends up sleeping with the fishes when Tony discovers he has been informing to the FBI and consequently "whacks" him. The killing takes place on Tony's boat, and he and his henchmen dump Pussy's body in the ocean. Not long afterward, as Tony uneasily celebrates his birthday with friends and family, his daughter Meadow gives him Billy Bass, a mechanical fish that "sings" the Al Green soul classic "Take Me to the River."

Chase has paid homage to the *ur*-mob movie in several of his casting choices. Dominic "Uncle Junior" Chianese played Johnny Ola, a partner of the Meyer Lansky–like Hyman Roth, in *Godfather II*. An episode titled "The Weight" features Richard Bright, who was the stone-faced Corleone hit man Al Neri—the guy who whacked poor Fredo in the boat on Lake Tahoe—in all three *Godfather* films.

Just as actual gangsters like Salvatore "Sammy the Bull" Gravano are rabid *Godfather* fans, so is Tony Soprano. His wife Carmela tells the freeloading priest whom she keeps around as a spiritual adviser that Tony watches DVDs of *Godfather II* "all the time." Tony predictably is not a fan of *III*. (The priest, however, wants to know, "Where does he rank *Goodfellas*?")

But the show's relationship to *The Godfather* goes much deeper than clever allusions and casting choices. David Chase has spoken of his long-standing desire to create a gangster story; he and his father would avidly watch TV shows like *The Untouchables* and movies like *Public Enemy* while he was growing up in New Jersey. But what story would he tell? Where could he possibly take the genre, after not only *The Godfather* and *Goodfellas* but also *Donnie Brasco* (released in 1997, only two years before *The Sopranos* debuted), with its dispassionate view of the avarice, brutality, and sleaze of quotidian mob life? Hadn't it all been done?

Chase's struggle to carve out his own piece of fictive mob turf has him grappling with what literary critic Harold Bloom famously dubbed the anxiety of influence. Bloom's theory of the psychology of influence posits a conflict of Oedipal dimensions between an artist and his or her creative forebears. (Bloom cites the workings of influence on poets, but his theory applies to any artist.) Artists must struggle to find their own voice through an ambivalent and anxiety-ridden relationship with the precursors whom they most admire. The artist must "swerve" away from the admired forebears by taking a corrective action that implies that although the formidable precursor was correct up to a point, the "new" artist has surpassed the influence.[5]

David Chase swerved away from Puzo, Coppola, Scorsese, et al. by embracing the *declino del padrino* and relocating the gangster story from its traditional urban, working-class setting to the affluent suburbs. According to Fred Gardaphé, Chase has conceived *The Sopranos* in "the tradition and spirit of the U.S. gangster film," making it "a commentary on not only the genre but on contemporary life in the United States." By moving the gangster to the suburbs, where today most Americans live, Chase "has breathed new life into this cultural icon that has captured the attention of American audiences since his first appearance in the early silent films."[6]

Chase himself has observed:

The Godfather and *Goodfellas* . . . were neighborhood movies about the old neighborhood. This is a suburban story. This is about mobsters in suburbia. And for me that's not farfetched because I grew up in the suburbs in New Jersey and that's where the mobsters were. They had begun, where I lived, to move out of the city of Newark, New Jersey, into the surrounding, sort of leafy suburbs. And that's what I grew up with.

. . . I mean, it doesn't take place in Little Italy. You don't have sit-downs in New York . . . He's [Tony Soprano] in the suburbs, he goes to the garden store and has a house with a lawn and all that. His kids go to a suburban school. He drives a Suburban, as a matter of fact.[7]

"When you think of the mob, you immediately think the Lower East Side, Little Italy or the Bronx," says actor Michael Rispoli, who played the terminally ill mob boss Jackie Aprile in the first season of *The Sopranos*. "But instead they put it in suburbia, which made it accessible to all suburbanites, so they can't say, 'Well, that's not a world I know about.' It is a world they do know about, and [organized crime] is happening in their midst."[8]

Relocating the mob narrative from urban mean streets and social clubs also links *The Sopranos* to other pop-culture works about suburban malaise, including films such as *American Beauty* and director Todd Solondz's *Welcome to the Dollhouse* and *Happiness*. Chase's gambit resonates for yet another, real-world reason: it makes sense for criminals to leave the city because the 'burbs offer more opportunities for enterprising crooks.

The New York Times reported during the summer of 2004 that a popular school superintendent in Roslyn, Long Island, had been indicted for stealing millions of dollars in school district funding. "Our enduring image of government corruption has to do with big-city pols and the golden era of Tammany Hall, but there aren't any Boss Tweeds navigating Lexus sport utility vehicles along Main Street here," the *Times* reporter observed.[9] The influence of Boss Tweed and Tammany was on the decline back in the 1920s, and New York City government has been "relatively clean" for decades. "Not so suburbia. In fact, to read the news these days is to survey a sprawling realm of suburban malfeasance that would leave the Tammany pols humbled."[10]

The *Times* cited a range of crimes, from school funding rip-offs to costly insurance scams to travel voucher fraud to sexual abuse, perpetrated by public officials and their accomplices. But these Long Island misdeeds pale in comparison to what's been happening in Tony Soprano's home state. In a subsequent article, the *Times* jocularly tallied instances of fraud and other corruption in New Jersey politics, most involving associates of Governor James McGreevey—a major fund-raiser indicted for soliciting campaign contributions in exchange for government favors, appointments of ethically challenged and/or incompetent persons to high posts, and, most egregious, the indictment of the governor's top campaign contributor, whom McGreevey unsuccessfully supported to be head of the Port Authority of New York and New Jersey, on charges of hiring a prostitute to try to thwart a federal investigation.

Twice in the article the correspondent, Peter Appelbome, reached for *Sopranos* analogies to give the paper's readers a sense of the degree of the sleaze and alleged criminality of Jersey politics. The pertinent pop-culture referents for suburbia have changed, as now *The Stepford Wives* has been supplanted by *The Sopranos*. The scandal involving the top campaign contributor offered, according to Applebome, "enough familial amity and Machiavellian moxie for a month's worth of intrigue at the Bada Bing."[11]

But New Jersey isn't the only state whose quiet, tree-lined streets have attracted wiseguys. In September 2004 federal prosecutors indicted Anthony Megale, a resident of Stamford, Connecticut, on racketeering, illegal gambling, and extortion charges, claiming that he was the underboss of the Gambino organized crime organization. The U.S. attorney for Connecticut said that the presence of the Gambino crime family underboss in Stamford "troubles us," but another federal prosecutor observed, "Organized crime is in the suburbs because suburbs are nice places to live . . . There's no reason why the chief executive officer of an organized crime family does not want to live nicely in Wilton, Conn. There are just as many opportunities in the suburbs as there are in cities, and probably less competition."[12]

(The usually au courant David Chase thus far hasn't exploited the possibilities for Tony and company to conspire with corrupt officials to get a piece of the suburban spoils. The closest he's come is a plotline about New Jersey mobsters, including the Sopranos, colluding with a Newark city councilman on a waterfront development project.)

But David Chase's relocation of the gangster story wasn't only geographic. Well aware that the genre needed reinvention—"Who cares about a mob crew in Brooklyn or New Jersey; we've seen that and seen that and seen that"[13]—Chase ventured into new territory: the domestic and intrapsychic lives of his gangsters, and their conflicts in both realms.

The Sopranos hardly ignores the daily business of organized crime. We see Tony and his crew conning and hustling. We watch them hijack trucks, perpetrate insurance and stock market scams, run high-stakes poker games, deal drugs, connive with corrupt politicians. We witness the mayhem and murder they commit in the name of "business." But organized crime per se takes a back seat to the show's depiction of men engaged in coping with their families, lovers, the noncriminal world, and each other.

Sons and grandsons of poor immigrants from Campania, they and their friends and families struggle with some very American problems—an uncertain economy, rebellious children, fiercely competitive college entrance exams, the burden of caring for aging parents, substance abuse. The men and women in Sopranoland have been affected by the profound changes in gender roles and sexual behavior that have transformed America in the wake of feminism and the sexual revolution. They're well aware that the rules of engagement in what used to be quaintly called "the battle of the sexes" have been rewritten since Tony's cherished 1950s.

They also cope with the changes in America's racial order since the civil rights revolution of the 1960s. Tony and Christopher in particular cling to a racist view of blacks and other non-Euro-Americans as threatening outsiders. Tony is openly hostile to Meadow's half-black, half-Jewish boyfriend, and he takes sadistic pleasure from humiliating an African American cop who stops him for a traffic violation. But Tony will do business with blacks when it's expedient (he forms an alliance with a corrupt activist minister) and his intolerance also stops at the bedroom, when he takes a Latina gumad named Valentina.

The show's central themes—the decline of organized crime and its impact on the men and families who depend on this waning tribal subculture and its peculiar economy—converge in the fleshy figure of Tony Soprano. Despite all the trappings of "the good life" (cue the Tony Bennett tune) that he has accumulated, Tony is beset by feelings of loss and a belief that the good old days—for both America and the American mafia—have passed.

When, in his first therapy session with Dr. Melfi, she asks him, "Are you depressed?," Tony demurs, and then fumes.

"Whatever happened to Gary Cooper, the strong silent type?" he says. "That was an American. He wasn't in touch with his feelings. He just did what he had to do. See, what they didn't know is that once they got Gary Cooper in touch with his feelings they couldn't get him to shut up. It's dysfunction this, dysfunction that, dysfunction *vaffancul'*."

Though Tony is a baby-boomer Italian American who as a young man casually participated in his generation's cultural rebellion—long hair, drug experimentation, rock music—as a suburban paterfamilias he longs for the 1950s, with its cultural conservatism, political quietude, and moral certainties. When his daughter, Meadow, speaks frankly about sex at the dinner table, pointing out that the twenty-first century is about to arrive, Tony snaps, "In this house it's 1953."

Like many middle-class American white males of his generation, he's confused by what America has become and is uneasy about his status in a changed nation.

"All through the last part of the nineties—all the period that *The Sopranos* was gestating, you might say—was a period in which Americans didn't know where to turn, culturally and politically," observes Flavia Alaya, a New Jersey–based academic, political activist, and author. (Alaya's memoir of love and sex in the 1960s, *Under the Rose*, has become a feminist classic. In it she chronicles her relationship as a young Italian American academic with the Irish American Catholic priest and housing activist Harry Browne, with whom she had three children before Browne went public with their affair so they could marry.) Alaya is an unabashed fan of *The Sopranos* and has little patience with denunciations of the show by Italian Americans. "I really think this program is a wonderful cultural event—not one that we should loathe, but one that we should welcome," she says.

Really, we've been in a quandary—kind of a fog. As someone who considers herself on the American left, sort of sophisticated politically, I felt that even more. I don't know where Chase fits, but I don't think he's a conservative Republican! So I think he understands, or at least feels, that Americans are going through some kind of, "Where do we go from here? What do we do with ourselves?" The fact that it was the turn of the century, too, is also a condition of our malaise. So, everything should have been better, right? The millennium came, and it went, "Thud!" So, when Tony is having this nervous breakdown, it's like the entire country. To me, everybody's saying, "Yeah, that's me. That could be me. That's us!" That's all of us trying to deal with this.[14]

David Chase pinpoints a delicious irony in Tony's malaise: "The kernel of the joke, the essential joke, was that life in America had gotten so savage, so selfish even a mob guy couldn't take it anymore. That was the essential joke. And he's in therapy because what he sees everyday upsets him so much. He and his guys invented selfishness, they invented me first, they invented it's all about me. And now he can't take it because the rest of the country has surpassed them."[15]

Imagine Tony's response to the theft of millions in funding by that Long Island schools superintendent. "Stealin' from kids! *Madonn'*, can you believe that shit!" he might exclaim. (His indignation would no doubt be mixed with some admiration for the scale of the scam, not to mention envy.)

Tony Soprano is both exotic and familiar, an upper-middle-class family man "who, except for his occupation, is pretty much like the rest of us."[16] The show's focus on Tony's domestic and inner lives brings him closer to us. We can relate to his problems with his wife and children, his aging mother, and his other difficult relatives, and to his loss of certainty about his place in the world. His concerns, and those of the other men and women in his world, become ours, so much so that we see in "our mobsters, ourselves," as cultural critic Ellen Willis puts it.[17]

Critic Carlos Clarens's important insight—"Stay close to a character, whether in print or on the screen, and that character [runs] the risk of turning into a protagonist"[18]—explains how audiences can come to identify with malefactors like Tony and company. *The Sopranos* takes this tactic further than any previous mafia movie, novel, or television show. The show's format—a continuing television drama, with each episode approximately an hour long and uninterrupted by commercials—allows viewers to spend more time in the company of its characters than a two-hour film. (As of this writing, five seasons comprising sixty-five episodes have been shown, and one more season is planned.) We get to know much more about Tony and the men, women, and children in his world than we ever did about the Corleones. We know them far more intimately, too, being privy to their dreams and fantasies, their fears and desires, their strengths and frailties. Knowing them so well, we can be deeply affected by them.

That the show's protagonist is in psychotherapy, and that we the viewers are like flies on the wall in Tony's therapist's office, creates an even more intimate bond between us and a man whom most of us would go out of our way to avoid. And though not every episode of the show includes a session, the therapeutic relationship between Tony and Dr. Melfi is central to The Sopranos. As David Chase has said, the gangster in therapy conceit was the initial inspiration for the series.[19]

Chase, who has undergone psychotherapy, and with a female therapist, would have put cinema's two most famous mafiosi on the couch: "When I go back and look at The Godfather . . . I have a theory, which is that they were depressed. I think Don Corleone was depressed, and I think Michael was depressed. If you watch it those are two depressed guys! They really needed therapy and they never got it."[20]

But Tony Soprano is not the first fictional gangster to seek the talking cure. Before Tony met Dr. Melfi there were some half-dozen films in which a mobster consults a therapist to get in touch with his feelings.[21] These include Grosse Point Blank with a psychiatrist played by Alan Arkin treating John Cusack's mob hit man; National Lampoon's The Don's Analyst, with Robert Loggia as a neurotic mafia boss and Kevin Pollak as his analyst; and, of course, Analyze This. Released in 1999, the same year The Sopranos made its debut, the popular comedy starred Robert De Niro as a mafioso who, like Tony Soprano, is prone to panic attacks, with Billy Crystal as his reluctant therapist.

Analyze This and The Don's Analyst both offer a shticky, vaudevillian spin on two venerable pop-culture archetypes, the Italian mafia don and the Jewish shrink. The Sopranos instead gives its gangster an ethnically simpatico therapist in Dr. Melfi. But the common ethnic roots of analyst and analysand, though important to the series, are hardly its most innovative move. The Sopranos broke new ground by offering the richest, most complex, and most accurate depiction of psychotherapy of any film or television program. Glen O. Gabbard, a psychiatrist and author of The Psychology of the Sopranos, claims that the show's depiction of psychological conflict is the main reason we watch: "The human condition involves psychological conflict, the inevitability of strife in intimate relationships, existential loneliness and crises of meaning. These psychological struggles are writ larger than life each week on *The Sopranos*, and we are drawn to the show because of them."[22]

Gabbard writes that his colleagues "have shown a particular interest in *The Sopranos*."[23] "Obsession" might be more accurate. As he reports, many became Home Box Office subscribers solely to see the show. Shrinks love to argue over Dr. Melfi's therapeutic technique, debating everything from her diagnoses to her medication choices. Some insist Tony is a treatable sociopath, others say he's a violent psychopath better handled by law enforcement. Melfi's critics argue that she is simply enabling Tony to become a better gangster rather than forcing him to confront the evil he does. And why does she behave so seductively, wearing short skirts and crossing and uncrossing her shapely legs during sessions?

Melfi's defenders respond that her sessions with Tony have performed an invaluable public service by educating viewers about clinical diagnoses such as panic disorder and borderline personality disorder, and by revealing what actually occurs in a psychotherapeutic encounter. Jennifer Melfi, the argument goes, has done more to destigmatize mental illness and boost the image of psychiatry than any of the profession's public relations initiatives.

Rebecca Chianese Scarpati, a psychotherapist who is the daughter of Dominic Chianese, the veteran stage and film actor who portrays Corrado "Uncle Junior" Soprano, is one of Melfi's biggest boosters. She rejects the argument that her fictional colleague shouldn't treat Tony:

> In our profession we treat. We heal. We don't distinguish among people. You look at someone in pain, and you ask, do I hold out hope for that person? If I believe he can heal, I'll do everything I can to help him to do that. I think that not to treat somebody because of who he or she is doesn't make any sense. There are always legal issues in any type of treatment you do. If you work with batterers, if you work with youth offenders, you're always going to have the issue of criminality unless you're only treating neurotic people in the suburbs [who presumably aren't gangsters]. But if they beat their wives, or get arrested for some white-collar crime, you wouldn't refuse to treat them, so why would you treat Tony Soprano any different?

But can Tony be redeemed from the life he has lived? "That's a great question," says Scarpati.

Melfi doesn't know the answer to that. None of us knows the answer to that with our patients. If you have a client who is suicidal, if someone is really hell-bent on committing suicide, he'll do it. It takes place on suicide watch in hospital lockdown. They figure it out. Does that mean you don't treat them, you don't give it your best shot? You certainly don't give them a gun and say, "Here, go ahead." You work with him, you do what you can.

Scarpati, who admires *The Sopranos* for what she considers the unprecedented realism of its depiction of psychotherapy, defends Melfi's therapeutic approach. "I think she has not crossed her professional line and I'd be very disappointed with the writers if they had her do that. I just can't believe it'd go in that direction" of having Melfi act on her acknowledged sexual attraction to Tony, her "erotic countertransference," in psychoanalytic lingo.

When I, as a woman, look at the character of Tony Soprano, it's very hard for me to see the appeal there. I'm not one of those women who are dying to jump into bed with him! But if I were treating him, maybe I would have that countertransference. Melfi sees the vulnerability in him, she sees the little boy who needs a hug in him, but also that he's a very powerful man. But she never crosses that line, she takes it [the countertransference] where she's supposed to take it and she does what she's supposed to do with it.[24]

An encounter between Melfi and her patient in an episode of the series' fifth season supports Scarpati's point. Tony, after having left therapy, decides he wants to resume seeing Dr. Melfi. But not for more sessions. He informs Dr. Melfi that he wants to take their relationship "in that other direction." But Melfi flatly refuses. She won't violate her professional ethics. And despite having admitted to her own therapist that she found Tony "a little sexy," she is repelled by the things he does. "In a personal relationship," she tells Tony, "I don't think I could sit silent." Tony, who had been smugly confident that Melfi would accept his offer, is outraged and hurt, and he storms out of her office.

During the show's third season, the online magazine *Slate* gave a forum to Gabbard and three other psychoanalysts to discuss each episode. The discussion, according to Gabbard, "became popular beyond the wildest expectations of its editors, with hundreds of thousands of readers regularly following our dialogue."[25]

The American Psychoanalytic Association, in December 2001, honored the show for "the artistic depiction of psychoanalysis and psychoanalytic psychotherapy." Lorraine Bracco received an award at the same event for creating "the most credible psychoanalyst ever to appear in the cinema or on television." Dr. Melfi apparently is so believable that when Bracco appeared at the event, she felt the need to remind the assembled mental health professionals that she was not really one of them; she just played a therapist on TV.

Gabbard might be overstating things when he claims that we watch *The Sopranos* mainly for its depiction of psychological conflict. But there's no denying that Freud's analysis of the family as a site of deadly battles is central to the show. Tony Soprano's difficulties with his mother and his distorted understanding of his parents' marriage remind us how difficult it can be to free ourselves from our own "family romance" to see other people—especially our parents—as they are, rather than as characters in an Oedipal costume drama. Like anyone in psychotherapy, Tony must locate the source of his suffering if he is to gain insight and change his life. Since the source almost always is the family drama, he, guided and supported by his therapist, has to figure out who are the critical players among the dramatis personae—father, mother, siblings, or some combination of them.

Tony idealizes his late father, John, as a strong, hardworking man who cared for and protected his family. He sees his mother, Livia, as a miserable, destructive harridan who wore down her husband until he was nothing but "a squeaking gerbil." Tony remembers his mother threatening to poke his eye out with a fork, and he clings to the memory of her vowing to her husband that she'd kill her children if John insisted on moving to the West Coast.

We share his unremittingly negative view of his mother as an Italian

American Medea—until an episode in the series' fifth season compli-cates the picture. Visiting his father's grave, Tony discovers a dolled-up, sixty-something woman also paying her respects. She turns out to be one Fran Felstein, a former department store salesclerk who had been his father's mistress. The free-spirited Fran fascinates Tony at first, but he quickly realizes that she's manipulative and selfish. He finds her flir-tatiousness creepy and is further disenchanted when he finds out that she smoked around his father when he was dying from emphysema.

During therapy, Tony reveals that when he was a teenager he had lied to his mother to cover up for his father's infidelity. When Livia had been hospitalized after suffering a miscarriage, John Soprano, instead of being at his wife's bedside, had been with a girlfriend, whom Tony realizes was Fran. He understands that his father had betrayed his mother, and had forced him to be an accomplice to his betrayal. But even so, he refuses to recast Livia from villain to victim in his family drama. When Dr. Melfi suggests that Livia might deserve some sympa-thy, Tony thinks about it for a minute before bitterly replying, "You know what? Fuck her. She made my father give away my dog."

As seen in the probing of Tony's mother-dominated psyche, *The Sopranos* demonstrates a deep understanding of the nature of psychic conflict. But although Tony is the only character actually in therapy, he's not alone in his intrapsychic distress. In Glen Gabbard's analysis of Christopher Moltisanti, Tony's fuck-up of a nephew suffers "a sense of existential meaninglessness, a feeling of being doomed to an unob-served life where he is a pawn in a chess game beyond his comprehen-sion. He regards his very being as an inconsequential nothingness."[26] He is crushed when a television news item about the Soprano crime organization doesn't even mention his name. If he's that insignificant, what's the point of his life?

Christopher starts cracking up, having nightmares about the Czech gangster whose brains he blew out. He infuriates his Uncle Tony with that impulsive and unnecessary shooting of the bakery clerk. Christo-pher, who nurses an ambition to be a screenwriter, decides to write a script about his life in the underworld. ("Mob stories are always hot," he tells his fiancée, Adriana.) But when he fails, he sinks deeper into despair. Then providentially a reprieve arrives: a newspaper article calls him a "reputed gangster." Christopher runs out and buys as many copies of the paper as he can find and gives them to friends and family. The world's recognition—or at least a New Jersey newspaper's—means he's not a nobody. His life suddenly has purpose again, and all's well with his world.

Tony's son, A.J., the overindulged suburban prince, discovers the futility of existence around the same time he hits puberty. "Life is essentially meaningless," he announces to his parents, who are furious that he has taken his mother's car and crashed it. He has been reading "Nitch" (Nietzsche) in school and has concluded that God is dead and living is pointless. To Tony and Carmela's dismay, he also declares that his upcoming confirmation in the Catholic Church is an exercise in absurdity. (Tony's underling Big Pussy has his own view of A.J.'s adolescent angst: "At thirteen they start getting broody.") But it's not all that surprising that A.J. would be receptive to bleak philosophy: his grandmother Livia Soprano was the voice of cosmic despair. "What makes you think you're so special?" she once said to him. Life, she explained, is "all a big nothing."

Even hardened old gangster Corrado "Uncle Junior" Soprano is haunted by "existential loneliness and crises of meaning." Uncle Junior has lived his entire life in the mob; he knows no other existence. "Junior's family is the mafia," says Dominic Chianese, whose portrayal of Tony's uncle is a consistent highlight of the series. "That's where his loyalty lies. He doesn't have his own family. He's a gangster, he has the gang mentality."

Junior, he says, "is a narrow-minded old prick. There's nothing noble about him at all." What makes the character not only bearable but also entertaining is his humor. "He's funny. He's hilarious," Chianese says. "The writers love to write for Uncle Junior because he's a curmudgeon; he's a grumpy guy who says very clever things."[27] Junior bears out Glen Gabbard's observation that David Chase's creations are kin to Samuel Beckett's tramps in *Waiting for Godot*: they "entertain us by wringing humor and meaning out of the fabric of a bleak backdrop of nothingness."[28]

During the fifth season of *The Sopranos* tough old Corrado begins to come apart. He's managed to survive cancer, but house arrest and early Alzheimer's are making him miserable. He goes wandering in his old Newark neighborhood, looking for his long-dead brother Johnny. For a legitimate excuse to leave the house, he starts attending funerals. This works fine when the deceased is indeed a relative. But Junior, relishing the few hours' freedom, begins to scour the obituary pages for dead people with Italian names. Soon he's demanding that his attorney obtain his release to attend any Italian funeral within driving distance.

The first few times this happens we're amused: the wily old bastard has found a way to get around his government-ordered confinement. But during the eulogy for one of these deceased paisans, Junior breaks down. Sobbing uncontrollably, he pours out his soul-sickness, his deep despair over the life he has lived and its emptiness. He is now old, sick, and alone, with no wife or children to comfort him, to tell him that his life was worth something. When his doctor suggests adjusting his anti-depressant medication, Junior replies, "I'm trapped, what's the goddamn point?"

No matter how up close and personal *The Sopranos* gets to its mobsters and their kin, the show never lets us forget that Tony and his crew are criminals, and brutal, remorseless ones at that. Former FBI undercover agent Joseph D. Pistone states the obvious: "Wiseguys are not nice guys. Wiseguys aren't even close to being nice guys . . . Wiseguys are barbaric."[29] Tony Soprano can be funny, charming, and even compassionate. But he also kills people for a living, sometimes with his bare hands, which makes him monstrous.

Tony lets us know that if you spend enough time with him you'll meet "the beast in me," to quote the song by British rocker Nick Lowe used to powerful effect on the show's soundtrack. Chase and his writers have used other animal imagery to define Tony. In the show's fifth season he is likened to a bear prowling the grounds of his suburban manse. Earlier in the show's run, Tony explains to an old friend who has become what mobsters call a "degenerate gambler" why he allowed the friend to ruin himself and his business: as in the old story about the scorpion who stings the frog who allowed him to ride on his back, Tony "stung" the gambler because it was his nature to do so.

Early in its first season, *The Sopranos* forced viewers to face Tony Soprano's dual nature in a memorable episode titled "College." His whip-smart daughter, Meadow, is checking out campuses, and Tony takes her to Maine for some interviews. He stops at a gas station to refuel the SUV and there recognizes another customer as Fabian Petrulio, a former gangster who became an informer and entered the federal witness protection program.

After dropping off Meadow for her interview, he tracks down the mafia turncoat and strangles him to death with a wire, the garroting yet another *Godfather* allusion, to the fate suffered by Luca Brasi, before his underwater interment. Having exacted his vengeance, Tony once again becomes the dutiful dad, picking up Meadow and inquiring about her interview. Meadow, no fool, notices the bloody wound on her father's hand and receives his unconvincing explanation with candid skepticism.

David Chase has said that this bold, Brechtian gambit—forcing viewers to see the monstrous side of a character that they, over four episodes, had come to like and identify with—was not popular with executives at HBO. The conflicted antihero who seems "like us" but who does awful things that appall us is hardly a television staple. Vic Mackey, the rogue cop portrayed by Michael Chiklis on the Fox drama *The Shield*, is the only comparably contradictory lead character on a TV series. Mackey, however, can never be *too* nefarious; after all, he's supposed to be on the opposite side of the law from Tony Soprano. More to the point, *The Shield* is not a premium cable show; Fox FX sells advertising and therefore restricts the content of its programs.

Film critic Armond White, one of the few to dissent from the critical consensus in favor of *The Sopranos*, maintains that "Tony Soprano stands in the same position as 'All in the Family's Archie Bunker— a spurious Everyman who actually sentimentalizes national flaws, whether racism or exploitation."[30] Contrary to White's absurd claim, *The Sopranos* has consistently portrayed both Tony's racism and his business practices as morally repellent. Chase, however, was aware that *viewers* might sentimentalize the character, and he set out to ensure that viewers got the point about the kind of man Tony Soprano is:

I think it's important . . . everybody loves the Soprano family, we love Tony Soprano, what a great guy, he's so funny, and they're all so funny. I think it's important . . . to never forget what the reality is. And the reality is . . . there are two things. I don't think real wiseguys commit as many murders as any mob movie shows, but they will go that extra distance, and they do intimidate, brutalize, and murder people. So I think it's important to have that be part of the texture so we don't go merrily off this pier, oh these lovable funny mafia guys.[31]

"College," which Chase has called the "ultimate *Sopranos* episode,"[32] does more than remind us that Tony Soprano, suburban dad, is also a brutal killer. If we see ourselves in Tony, is it only his more mundane and sympathetic aspect? Or do we also share the dark side of his divided nature? Most of us don't settle scores by murdering people who piss us off. But the rage that in Tony festers and explodes in sudden bursts of fearsome violence is not so alien, especially to men.

If Tony and the other mobsters on *The Sopranos* are ourselves, as Ellen Willis, Stephen Holden, and numerous other commentators contend, then we also have the beast in us. We "civilians" (or "citizens," or "flag-salutin' motherfuckers," as Paulie Walnuts likes to call us) manage to keep the feral side of our natures under some degree of control. Or we channel it into more socially acceptable aggressions, like sports, or the predatory practices of corporate capitalism. But we like to watch Tony's violence—especially when it seems justified—not only because the show makes it dramatically compelling but also because all the killings and beatings satisfy our genre expectations. Tony and his crew embody "the traits that the dominant culture represses in reality, yet adores as entertainment."[33]

Tony of course has ready-made justifications for his violence. Committed to *omertà*, he must punish those who transgress this venerable mafia tradition, as Fabian Petrulio finds out, with Tony's judgment, "You took an oath!" being the last words he hears. Tony has absorbed mafia values and traditions not only from his father, the late Johnny Boy Soprano, but also from that master narrative of gangsterism, *The Godfather*. Like Michael Corleone, Tony has inherited codes of being and behaving, but he struggles to make sense of them in a situation in which they have less and less application. If one of the Corleones had gotten busted, he'd probably have faced no more than five years' jail time (if that), since gambling was the family's primary enterprise. Under those circumstances, keeping faith with *omertà* was relatively undemanding. But ever since the RICO statute made it easier for the feds to bust up entire mob families and put their members in prison for decades, wiseguys are increasingly forsaking silence in exchange for shorter sentences.

Born into "this thing of ours," Tony Soprano respects and upholds mafia tradition, as did Michael Corleone. But there's one big and insuperable difference. "He's not like Michael in the sense that his father isn't 'God,'" notes Robert Viscusi. Tony Soprano's father, Johnny Boy, was a Newark gangster, and although he led a crew, he certainly was no Godfather, as his nickname attests. "Don Vito Corleone" evokes a Sicilian grandee; "Johnny Boy"—coincidentally or not, the name of the crazy ne'er-do-well played by Robert De Niro in *Mean Streets*—sounds like a neighborhood punk.

"Don Corleone is not a gangster," Viscusi says. "It's like, that's what he does for a living. His real job is he's God." Viscusi, who has taught Puzo's novel to several generations of students at Brooklyn College, quotes one of its most famous passages: "'Don Corleone was a man to whom everyone came with their problems and never were they disappointed.' So Tony Soprano inherits two things: he inherits his father, and like all gangsters real and imaginary, in the current generation, he also inherits Don Corleone."[34] And he realizes not only that he isn't "worthy" of this inheritance but also that what's left of the legacy itself is pretty meager.

If *The Sopranos* is *The Godfather Redux*, the Mafia myth for our postmodern times, its relationship to its fabled forebear recalls Karl Marx's dictum about all facts and personages of importance in history occurring twice, "the first time as tragedy, the second as farce."[35] Whereas the first *Godfather* film presented the Corleone family business as a powerful empire headed by a wise king, the mob in *The Sopranos* is "strictly small potatoes, and it's fading."[36] In *Godfather II*, the criminal enterprise built by Vito Corleone and expanded by his son has become "bigger than U.S. Steel," as Hyman Roth exults to Michael. Tony Soprano and his men can barely maintain control of their carting business. In one episode in the series' fifth season, gangsters were reduced to lamenting the loss of a shipment of stolen provolone.

Vito and Michael had the grave, thoughtful Tom Hagen to advise them in business matters; Tony's *consigliere* Silvio Dante is a scowling, cartoonish hood in an obvious wig who runs the Bada Bing strip club and does bad Al Pacino impressions.

If the Corleones are the aristocracy of the underworld, Tony Soprano and his crew are the groundlings, the gavones, as Italian Americans call boorish and vulgar people.

A slave to his appetites for food, sex, and violence, Tony lacks the gravity and self-possession of Vito and Michael Corleone. Instead of the tragedy of an idealistic son full of promise devolving into a homicidal monster, there is the dark comedy of a fat and horny suburban dad struggling in vain to keep peace at home and on the job. His mother, Livia, is no Mamma Corleone, loving, nurturing, and reticent—she's a bitter, scheming termagant who puts a contract on her son as payback for his installing her in a nursing home. Carmela is no Kay Adams Corleone, the whiny WASP outsider shut out of her husband's affairs. Signora Soprano is a neighborhood Italian girl who knew exactly what she was getting into when she married Tony and is not above acting like a mafiosa herself when it suits her. Tony's bratty kids do seem to love him, but they rarely show him the respect and deference that Vito Corleone's children automatically accorded their patriarch. Meadow and A.J. challenge him, curse at the dinner table, and even call him "Mister Mob Boss" to his face.

The world of *The Sopranos* is unequivocally not the same one the Corleones inhabited, the one that taught Tony and us, the viewers, what being a gangster was all about. The show's gangsters, though hardly the most reflective of men, recognize this.

"I'm talkin' about the year 2000, the millennium," says Christopher Moltisanti. "Where do we go from here?" In the same first-season episode Tony and his men watch a TV interview with "a former soldier in the Gambino family turned government informer and bestselling author." Talking about the new breed of gangsters, the younger men with their "disregard of the rules that served the old dons so well," the former hood declares, "The golden age of the mob is gone and it's never coming back, and it's their fault."

Tony is acutely aware that he is living in the twilight of the mafia. During his first therapy session with Dr. Melfi he complains, "Things are trending downward." It's not like it was in his father's day. (For one thing, Johnny Boy Soprano would have used much more pungent language than his son's middle manager lingo.) His father had "his people, standards, pride." More to the point, in those halcyon days, wiseguys who got busted kept their mouths shut and served their time. Today's mobsters, says Tony, have "no room for the penal experience."

But despite his nostalgia for mafia tradition and his dismay over its decline, Tony Soprano is very much a man of the moment, a conspicuous consumer heedless about the future. "Tony talks about the future of the family, and about his place in history, but what Tony wants is stuff," says David Chase. "He wants to be successful and get as much as he can out of the family. But I don't think he has much sense of follow-through about it. He would never say that; he would never admit that. But what happens to that family after he's gone doesn't interest him. It's all lip service."[37]

More than an uncommonly entertaining and well-wrought television series, *The Sopranos* qualifies as a cultural phenomenon. The echoing encomia of critics like Ellen Willis and Stephen Holden of *The New York Times*—"The richest and most compelling piece of television—no, of popular culture—that I've encountered in the past twenty years"; "so perfectly attuned to geographic details and cultural and social nuances that it just may be the greatest work of American popular culture of the last quarter century"—have been seconded by many other representatives of the chattering classes.[38]

The show quickly became a must-see for all who prided themselves on being tuned in to the cultural zeitgeist. HBO has gained thousands of new subscribers thanks to the series, which has also spawned a publishing mini-industry of books with such titles as *"The Sopranos" Cookbook, The Tao of "The Sopranos," The Psychology of "The Sopranos," "The*

Sopranos" on the Couch, A Sitdown with "The Sopranos," Bright Lights, Baked Ziti: The Unofficial, Unauthorized Guide to "The Sopranos," and "The Sopranos" and Philosophy: I Kill Therefore I Am. Other Sopranos merch includes a line of men's clothing, bus tours of the New Jersey locales that appear in the show, and CDs of the show's soundtrack. The Sopranos is a mass media phenomenon, but the show's fans—many of them Italian Americans—are as fanatically devoted as those of such cult hits as Buffy the Vampire Slayer, and perhaps even more so, as their loyalty has withstood the long waits between seasons and the weaker episodes, which became more frequent as the series wore on.

The Sopranos has not only revised and resuscitated a venerable genre but has also changed the medium of television itself. Broadcast network executives despair over the loss of viewers not only to the mob series but also to HBO's other cutting-edge programs: Six Feet Under (this comedy-drama about a family of funeral directors has at times even surpassed The Sopranos in quality), the bawdy, goodhearted comedy Sex in the City, the ultraviolent and homoerotic prison melodrama Oz, the gritty and complex cop drama The Wire, and the revisionist western Deadwood. The cable network doesn't always strike gold—the less said about duds like Project Greenlight and The Mind of the Married Man the better—but at its best HBO's programming has set a standard that broadcast networks, with their commercials and "standards and practices" (censorship rules), can't approach.

HBO programs have not only cleaned up in the ratings—the fourth-season finale of The Sopranos beat out all competition, and only a National Basketball Association game drew higher ratings than the fifth-season finale—but also in Emmy Award nominations and wins. The show's twenty nominations for the 2003–2004 Emmy Awards included four in Outstanding Writing for a Drama Series, "a category the broadcast networks once ruled." In fact, every nominee in the category was for an HBO program.[39] The worst fears of broadcast executives were fulfilled when The Sopranos won Emmys not only for its writing but, after four years, its first for Best Dramatic Series. Best Supporting Actor and Actress Emmys went to Michael Imperioli and Drea De Matteo, for their performances as the warring lovers Christopher Moltisanti and Adriana La Cerva.

For David Chase, the Emmys provided a mythic moment. "This is really great," he said. "Seeing Michael Corleone and Tony Soprano shake hands really blows my mind." Chase was referring to the fact that Al Pacino, who won an Emmy for his portrayal of Roy Cohn in HBO's adaptation of *Angels in America*, met James Gandolfini for the first time at the awards ceremony.[40]

Network television's few attempts to capitalize on the success of *The Sopranos* were short-lived failures: CBS's *Falcone*, based on Joseph Pistone's years as an undercover agent, lasted less than one season, in 2000; and *Kingpin*, about a Latino mobster and his crime *familia* that ran for six episodes on NBC in 2003. Neither show was terrible, but compared to *The Sopranos*, both seemed pallid and uninspired.

Chase's accomplishment is sui generis, as these failed cash-in attempts attest. The uniqueness of *The Sopranos* doesn't reside only in its relocation of the Mafia myth from city to suburb or in its focus on the inner and domestic lives of its characters. Neither innovation would seem so striking were it not for the verisimilitude for which the show strives, and more often than not, brilliantly achieves. The psychoanalytic sessions, the suburban New Jersey settings, the way the characters talk and the things they say to each other, the Soprano family dynamics, the show's keen and satiric awareness of such phenomena of contemporary American life as Prozac, 9/11, stock market fraud, and children with attention deficit disorder—all these are rendered with striking realism.

Stephen Holden, one of the show's most ardent boosters in the media, observes, "*The Sopranos*, more than any American television show, looks, feels, and sounds like real life as it's lived in the United States in the cluttered environment of the Internet, mall shopping, rap music and a runaway stock market."[41]

Had the show not had this panoramic scope, and instead focused on the criminal doings of the Soprano crew, it's doubtful it would have won the critical hosannas and devoted audience it has enjoyed since its debut. The online newspaper *U.S. Italia Viewpoints* (an English-language counterpart to the Italian print publication *America Oggi*) sent a correspondent to a preview screening of the first episode of *The Sopranos'* fifth season. The reporter, an Italian, observed, "The lovers of the series cross all the significant social categories—age, social status, sex, and ethnicity." This diverse audience, she noted, isn't even particularly interested in "mob-related issues." At the screening she attended, "The topics that were discussed were mostly related to the happenings in the Soprano household; Tony's problems with his wife, his daughter, his fears, his guilt, and his therapy sessions."[42]

But ultimately the show *is* a gangster story, one that honors the genre's conventions even as it departs from and comments on them. Its popularity is due in no small part to its vivid and accurate depiction of organized crime in the new millennium. David Chase admits that his knowledge of gangsters is secondhand, as was Mario Puzo's. "I don't know anybody in the mob," he says. The closest he came to firsthand acquaintance was a high school friend whose father was a New Jersey wiseguy. During the show's first season, he relied on veteran television writer Frank Renzulli, who "contributed a lot of that marinara sauce . . . He knew the financial pyramid that makes up mob life, the actual business of it."[43]

Chase, however, has drawn on actual events in mob history for the story lines. The starting point for the show's fifth season was an article he read in the *Newark Star-Ledger* about the RICO trials of the 1980s. The Racketeer Influenced and Corrupt Organizations Act (RICO), passed by Congress in 1970, helped the government to put many mobsters behind bars. "[A] lot of those guys are now getting out of jail," Chase says. "They've served their time and they are hitting the streets again, and so the show begins with what we call the Mafia Class of 2003 hitting the streets."[44]

These "grads" include one Feech La Manna, a terrifying old thug played with coiled ferocity by Robert Loggia, and Tony Blundetto, a cousin of Tony Soprano, played by indie film veteran Steve Buscemi. Both men cause Boss Soprano no end of grief when they return to pick up where they'd left off. Tony realizes that these vexing personnel problems demand different solutions. He handles Feech, who has been annoying other mobsters, by having him sent back to prison. Cousin Tony, a belligerent and disruptive hood who nearly provokes a war between New York and New Jersey gangsters, merits a harsher punishment: a single shotgun blast to the head, delivered by the boss himself. The latter action illustrates an essential point about wiseguys made by Joseph D. Pistone: "The guy that kills you will most likely be the guy who's closest to you."[45]

The high body count on *The Sopranos* is actually one of the less realistic aspects of the show. Contract killings, or "hits," occur far less frequently in organized crime than on the show. When real mobsters get into a "beef" with each other or with some hapless "citizen," they're far more likely to settle disputes with their fists than with pistols.[46] In the real world, gangsters usually carry a piece only when they have a "job" to do; to be constantly armed is to be vulnerable to arrest.[47]

But in just about every other way, *The Sopranos* offers a strikingly accurate depiction of organized crime and of government efforts to combat it. And excessive body count notwithstanding, the show is dead-on in portraying why mobsters and those in their orbit get whacked.

His years posing as Donnie Brasco taught undercover FBI agent Joseph Pistone what not to do if he wanted to stay alive:

> There are certain mob rules that must never, ever be broken. They are not hard to understand, and there is no mystery to them at all—they are laid out for you going in so that you will not break them by accident. These are the things that will get you whacked by a wiseguy: Not sharing money from illegal activities will get you killed . . . Testifying before a grand jury will get you killed . . . Talking to cops will get you killed . . . Laying your hands on another wiseguy will get you killed . . . Speaking of girlfriends, the quickest way to catch two in the head is to mess around with a wiseguy's girlfriend, wife, or daughter. That is maybe the dumbest thing you could ever do . . .[48]

As any *Sopranos* fan knows, characters who transgress these rules end up whacked. But more often the characters' behavior is shaped by their knowledge of what would happen if they broke these rules. Furio Giunta, a mob soldier imported from Naples to work for Tony's crew, returns to Italy to prevent the only two possible outcomes of his budding romance with Carmela Soprano: Tony will kill him or he will have to kill Tony. Four characters thus far have been whacked for informing: mobsters Fabian Petrulio, Jimmy Altieri, and Sal "Big Pussy" Bonpensiero, and Adriana La Cerva, Christopher Moltisanti's pathetically trusting fiancée.

Pistone cites one more transgression that will lower the life expectancy of a wiseguy: "Apparently being gay will get you killed, too."[49] He offers as evidence the fate of one Johnny Boy D'Amato, acting *consigliere* of the New Jersey–based De Cavalcante crime family. After his girlfriend let it be known that she believed Johnny Boy was more *finocchio* than *maschio*, the family had him whacked, as a queer *consigliere* could only be a cause for shame and dishonor.

The Sopranos hasn't yet incorporated this incident but it has come close: during the show's fifth season, Meadow Soprano's boyfriend happens to catch mob captain Vito Spatafore giving a blow job to a security guard. At the conclusion of the season the rotund fellator was still alive and well. But as of this writing, there will be a sixth season of the series, with thirteen more episodes. And since the De Cavalcante family is generally considered, even by its own members, to be the model for the Soprano organization, Vito may yet pay the ultimate price for not keeping his mouth shut.

The verisimilitude of *The Sopranos* extends to its depictions of mafia business practices. Tony and his crew have their hands in all the traditional mob enterprises—trash hauling, truck hijackings, stolen merchandise or "swag," strip clubs, loan sharking—plus a few newer ones, like stock market scams and health insurance fraud. Gambling is also a major profit center for the Soprano organization, because, as former special agent Pistone observes, "Of all the various scams and operations orchestrated by wiseguys, none is as profitable and as dependable as illegal gambling."

This is because of a perfect balance between supply and demand: gambling is "a 365-day-a-year proposition" (there is always some sporting event to bet on) and "the world is full of lousy, degenerate gamblers." Besides being a reliable income source for the mob, gambling is often the weapon they use to seize control of legitimate businesses.[50]

"Hostile takeover has a whole different meaning when it comes to wiseguys," Pistone cracks. "Perhaps they learn that the owner of a particular business has some kind of weakness. Say he's a degenerate gambler." Predatory mobsters move in to handle his bets, allowing him to run up huge debts. When the wiseguys tell him to settle up, and he can't, the wiseguys demand part of his business as settlement. "Once you have your hooks in the business, you suck all the money you can out of it until you milk it dry. You leave the ravaged carcass of a once-thriving enterprise in your wake."[51]

Tony Soprano's high school friend Davey Scatino, a legit businessman who owns a successful sporting goods mall store, is a classic "degenerate gambler," that is, one who, as Pistone puts it, would "bet their grandmother's last set of dentures on the outcome of the Florida–Florida State game." Scatino's weakness, however, isn't college sports but "executive" card games run by Tony Soprano and his associates. (The high rollers who play in these games aren't all gangsters or "connected" types; there are celebrity gamblers, too, including Frank Sinatra, Jr., and over-the-hill rock star David Lee Roth.) Scatino quickly gets in over his head, incurring huge losses.

Tony Soprano, in need of some quick cash himself, initiates a "bust out"—planned bankruptcy—of Davey Scatino's business. To collect the gambling debt Davey owes, Tony takes over the purchase of merchandise for Davey's store and then takes the goods for himself. This means that Scatino's debt eventually will be paid off—at the cost of his livelihood and, most likely, the loss of his wife and kids. When the shattered Scatino pitifully asks Tony how he could ruin an old friend, the mob chief calmly relates the story of the scorpion and the frog. You could hardly ask for a more chilling cautionary tale about the folly of getting involved with gangsters.

The Sopranos rings true in other ways. The mob's economic structure, what Chase calls "the financial pyramid," in which soldiers and captains kick up a portion of their "earnings" to the boss, is credibly rendered. Christopher Moltisanti's drug habit (and Tony's occasional cocaine use) reflects a trend that Joseph Pistone has described. In the past mobsters sold drugs but didn't consume the merchandise. Nowadays, "Lots of wiseguys become addicts and get careless and sloppy."[52]

Dysfunction among once-cohesive mob families is one of the main tropes of *il declino del padrino*, and here again *The Sopranos* is on the money. Tony has his hands full trying to keep order among his fractious troops, whether it's cleaning up anarchic Christopher's various messes, whacking an errant cousin, or dealing with trusted associates who have become informers. One of his captains, Paulie "Walnuts" Gualtieri, seems perpetually discontent, over Tony's favoritism toward Christopher, over his "earnings," and, most galling, over the fact that no one visited his dear mama while he did a short stint in jail.

A real-life mafia trial drove home the potential consequences of a mob boss failing to look after the kin of imprisoned wiseguys. Testimony from a disgruntled brother-in-law was key to the conviction of New York mobster Joseph Massino, who, in July 2004, was found guilty on seven counts of murder. Massino's former underboss, Salvatore "Good Lookin' Sal" Vitale, was motivated to testify against his sister's husband in no small part by his outrage at Massino for neglecting his family responsibilities. When Vitale was arrested, "No one called my wife and children and asked if they needed anything," he told the jury.[53]

The Massino trial itself was a media event, "with news organizations from Los Angeles to London using it to evoke the mob of television and movie lore."[54] The media mob and the mob in the media converged around the trial of the sixty-one-year-old mobster known as "Big Joey." An episode of *The Sopranos* had mentioned him as a model of the old-school gangsters who are becoming extinct. During the trial, the judge often asked potential jurors whether they thought *The Sopranos* was realistic.

The line between real mob and media mob became even fuzzier as the prosecutor, Assistant U.S. attorney Robert Henoch, detailed the various murder charges against Massino. Big Joey had two celebrity victims whose names are well known to mob movie fans: Alphonse "Sonny Red" Indelicato, and the much bigger star, Dominick "Sonny Black" Napolitano, both of *Donnie Brasco* fame.

Massino had Sonny Black killed for permitting the Bonanno crime organization to be infiltrated by Pistone. Sonny Black had the misfortune not only of being shot to death and having his corpse dumped in a Staten Island swamp, his killers also chopped off his hands, purportedly as a warning to other mobsters not to shake hands with informers. To add insult to injury, he was played by the taller, paler Irish American actor Michael Madsen in a lackluster performance in *Donnie Brasco,* the 1997 film based on Pistone's bestselling book.

The characters on *The Sopranos* embody other fundamental mob traits and values identified by Pistone. "Wiseguys love their mothers to death,"[55] and Paulie "Walnuts" Gualtieri, one of Tony's captains, is fanatically devoted to his mama. He'll murder one of her friends to get the money he needs to stay in Tony Soprano's good graces, but anyone who even looks cross-eyed at the sainted Mrs. Gualtieri might not live to tell about it. "Stupidity and greediness" also rank high on Pistone's checklist. *The Sopranos* offers numerous examples, with Christopher Moltisanti reliably providing many of them.

Wiseguys are politically conservative and proudly patriotic, Pistone says, because "Where else but in this great, freedom-loving country could they get away with as much shit as they do?"[56] When Christopher asks his fiancée, Adriana, what stress could possibly be causing her irritable bowel symptoms, she lies, "War, Christopher? Ya know, the Middle East?" (The actual source of her somatic suffering is that she's been informing to the FBI.) Christopher, with Dubya-esque bravado, declares, "You don't listen to the president? We're gonna mop the floor with the whole fuckin' world. The whole world's gonna be under our control. So what are you worked up about?"

(If there were any doubts about David Chase's political stance, his putting this right-wing rant in the mouth of a homicidal gangster should have dispelled them.)

The Sopranos achieves its greatest verisimilitude in its portrait of its protagonist. Tony Soprano's character has a fissure, or, as Glen O. Gabbard put it, a "vertical split,"[57] which permits him to be both a loving father and a vicious criminal. This split, this "radical schism," is the very core of the Mafia myth, as Italian critic Alessandro Camon has observed. The mafioso demonstrates "absolute ruthlessness against his enemies, but absolute devotion to his family and friends." This double morality enables its practitioner "to function from one level to the other—from murder to family, from extinguishing life to protecting it."[58]

The "mystery and contradiction" that Camon pinpoints as the essence of the mafia gangster intrigues and ensnares us, and keeps us watching Tony as he navigates his two distinct yet overlapping worlds. How is it, we wonder, that he can lovingly chauffeur his daughter to college interviews and then go off and choke the life out of a former associate? How can he calmly arrange the murder of Adriana La Cerva, for whom he had tender feelings, cold-bloodedly duping her into taking a ride with Silvio Dante, her executioner? How can he pride himself on being a solid family man when he casually destroys Davey Scatino and his family's livelihood?

We can turn to history, sociology, and psychology to try to understand men like Tony Soprano, and they do yield insights. We also have their own self-concept of themselves as soldiers. Like uniformed combatants, they are trained to take and protect life, to kill in the service of preserving life. The structure of organized crime groups itself is quasi-military, with lowest-ranking made men designated as soldiers and their leaders as captains. Tony has justified his behavior by saying, "It's a war out there." But of course gangsters are not really soldiers, and they're not engaged in a genuine war. There is ultimately something inexplicable about the character of the mafia gangster. Though a successful wiseguy manages to balance the demands of family and "family," the mystery and contradiction in his psyche, or soul, if you prefer, are ultimately irresolvable—except with death, an omnipresent reality in their lives.

The radical schism in the mafioso's character, his mystery and contradiction, finds its mirror image in our often ambivalent reaction to gangsters, fictional and real. We are fascinated and repelled, amused and horrified. And this ambivalence isn't only that of the average pop-culture consumer. Joseph Pistone, with all of his detailed insider's knowledge of organized crime, all his firsthand experience of its brutality and corruption, equivocates when he writes about gangsters.

"I did not see them as especially evil or loathsome; to me, they were just guys who grew up in a particular culture and under particular economic conditions and chose to become wiseguys, like other guys choose to become bakers or businessmen," he comments in *The Way of the Wiseguy*. "I had no great score to settle with them when I joined the

FBI. Neither did I have any inclination to cut them slack. I knew who they were, understood how they thought, and when it became my job to help put them behind bars, I did it like anybody does a job they take seriously."[59]

But this does not jibe with much of what he's written, in both *Donnie Brasco* and *The Way of the Wiseguy*. In the latter he declares, "Wiseguys are the meanest, cruelest, least caring people you'll ever meet."[60] And in both books, he graphically recounts mafia misdeeds that can only be called evil and loathsome—victims impaled on meathooks, or force-fed their own genitals before being killed, or slashed and hung up over bathtubs until all the blood has drained from their bodies.

Mob dramas—the *Godfather* films, *Goodfellas*, *Donnie Brasco*, *The Sopranos*, and many others—have served up generous portions of this atrocious violence in different tonal registers: Coppola's somberly shocking tableaux, Scorsese's unpredictably eruptive mayhem, Chase's visceral brutality tinged with dark comedy. Grisly violence is so fundamental to gangland stories that an analogy to another genre besides the western seems apt.

Critic Catherine Don Diego claims that the gangster genre offers a type of realist horror, with hoodlums as monsters in human form. "Considering the violence inherent in fictional and nonfictional narratives of organized crime activities, the horrific nature of shakedowns, hits, and scare tactics that contribute to the morbid fascination audiences have with these films places many (though not all) of them at least within the periphery of the horror genre."[61]

It's not much of a leap to see mobsters as kin to that venerable popcult archetype, the vampire. The mafioso, like Nosferatu, has his origins in a "foreign" culture, which makes him an alien threat, but his Old Worldliness also makes him an exotic outsider. Like the undead, mobsters are us—or used to be, before they departed from normal human society to become something else. They are parasitic, draining their victims of cash; as Joseph Pistone notes, "They suck up money like vampires suck blood."[62]

They're also notorious for their literal bloodlust. Though not actually nocturnal, wiseguys are most active at night. Most men, notes Pistone, "aren't going out every night when they are in their forties and fifties." Wiseguys, though, "go bouncing pretty much six out of seven nights a week."[63]

And to some, they are fascinating predators, alluring and repellent at the same time. In 1992 director Jon Landis made the analogy literal and married the two genres in his comedy-drama *Innocent Blood*. French actress Anne (*La Femme Nikita*) Parillaud plays Marie, a vampire with a conscience: she only bites bad guys. One of her victims is Sal Macelli, a mafia chief played by Robert Loggia, the veteran character actor whose numerous gangster portrayals include Feech La Manna, from season five of *The Sopranos*. After Marie feeds on him, Macelli wakes up in a morgue, confused and very thirsty. He soon figures out what's happened to him, and he's delighted by the transformation. In one of the film's funniest moments, the newly undead Sal, elated to be unharmed after being struck by a bus, gleefully cries "*Vaffancul'!*" at the driver as he gives the Italian hand-on-arm fuck-you gesture.

Sal realizes that a family of undead gangsters would be unstoppable, and he proceeds to give his crew members what *Vampire Chronicles* novelist Anne Rice calls "the Dark Gift." Besides Loggia, the cast of *Innocent Blood* includes mob movie veterans Chazz Palmintieri and Anthony LaPaglia, and three character actors who would become *Sopranos* mainstays: Tony Sirico ("Paulie Walnuts"), David Proval ("Richie Aprile"), and Tony Lip ("Big Carmine Lupertazzi").

The blood-lusting ferocity that invites comparisons to vampires may be the most appallingly sensationalistic element of mob life, on- and off-screen. But the everyday business of thievery and scamming "pretty much violates any standard of decency and goodness that our society relies on to function smoothly."[64] Tony Soprano once defended his line of work by claiming that La Cosa Nostra's crimes pale in comparison to the "theft of a nation" by the Anglo-Saxon robber barons of the late nineteenth and early twentieth centuries. Fair enough. But Italian American organized crime indisputably has had a corrosive effect on society, whether mobsters flood African American communities with heroin, exploit women through prostitution, corrupt labor unions, or impose a "mob tax" on legitimate businesses, inflating the costs of goods and services to the general public. Organized crime plainly is not just another career choice, *pace* Joe Pistone.

The former FBI agent's inability to recognize that mystery and contradiction are fundamental to the character of the mafioso leads him to make a categorical statement that his own writing refutes. "Wiseguys have no friends," he claims in *The Way of the Wiseguy*. "Being someone's friend means trusting them and sharing your deepest thoughts and fears with them. In the Mafia, you cannot afford to be that vulnerable."[65]

But in *Donnie Brasco*, Pistone frequently describes close and intimate relationships among the gangsters whose world he penetrated. Benny "Lefty" Ruggiero gets furious at "Donnie" when he believes the younger man is not adhering to mafia rules of comportment. But his affection—even love—for his young "protégé" is unmistakable. The same goes for Dominick "Sonny Black" Napolitano, the capo who ultimately paid with his life for bringing Pistone into the Bonanno family.

Pistone observes that every married wiseguy keeps at least one gumad, or mistress. But by his own account, these outlaws "preferred spending the night bullshitting with each other to spending it with their girlfriends." Visiting their gumads "almost became an obligation, just like going home to the wife." Mobsters, Pistone writes, are happiest when "they are hanging out with each other, talking sports, planning scores, shooting the shit."[66] As Pistone observes, wiseguys do turn on each other, and when someone does get whacked, the killer is often someone the victim knows and trusts. But if no real friendship exists among wiseguys, then why do they enjoy each other's company so much?

Tony Soprano's relationships with his mob cronies and associates exemplify the wiseguy way of friendship. He frequently refers sincerely to other mobsters as his friends, even as he bellyaches about the loneliness of being a leader. He obviously loves his errant nephew Christopher, his longtime crony Big Pussy, and even his Uncle Junior. But if one of them breaks any of the mob's unbreakable rules, like informing to the FBI, Tony will not hesitate to have him whacked. This "thing of ours" is bigger than any individual.

The concept of a suburban paterfamilias who is also a violent criminal would be an abstraction had the character not been incarnated in the burly frame of James Gandolfini, who makes the radical schism credible and compelling. Until *The Sopranos*, Gandolfini had been a supporting player whose work I enjoyed in films such as *Fallen* and *Get Shorty*. None of his film roles, however, prepared me for his extraordinary performance as Tony Soprano.

David Chase, when asked how *Sopranos* fans can root for a malefactor like Tony Soprano, acknowledged, "It wouldn't work if it wasn't Jim Gandolfini . . . he just has this . . . well, we all know what it is—he has this quality that you empathize with him, despite everything. I mean, the writing has something to do with it. I'm not being foolish about it. But it would not work if it wasn't him—specifically him!"[67]

Ray De Felitta, a New York–based director and screenwriter (*Two-Family House, Café Society*), says of Gandolfini, "I think as an actor he can do no wrong. He's just a wonderfully funny, original, simple presence. A great deal of that show's success I attribute to his presence. You can't separate these things out. They all work with each other. But, there's something about him—his hangdog simplicity and his torturedness . . . It's a strangely perfect melding of the actor and the character."[68]

The heavyset and balding Gandolfini registers Tony Soprano's complex emotions with subtlety and delicacy while still imbuing him with the flamboyance and swagger we expect from our Italian American gangsters (and the actors who play them). He's the little boy lost and a murderous brute, the fearsome commander of a criminal enterprise, and the jocular good-time guy. When enraged he's terrifying, but he faints at the sight of a slice of capicola because the sandwich meat brings back a traumatic memory from his childhood.

As a mob boss, he knows what's expected of him, and most of the time he can deliver. But he's haunted by his realization that he's not as tough as he appears; for all his macho bluster, he's still a *soprano*. Tony is the reluctant heir to a family tradition born in the poverty and oppression of southern Italy; his forebears were *camorristi* in the Campania region. He has been forced by history and circumstances into a life he wouldn't have chosen for himself, and that's his tragedy, if such a man can be seen as tragic. He is a warrior in an ignoble cause, and he could have been something better.

In season five of *The Sopranos*, we discover that his charisma and leadership abilities might have been channeled into a career in athletics. Tony dreams of his high school basketball coach, who rebukes him for the life choices he's made. "I told you many times, Anthony, you were special," the coach admonishes him. "You had smarts, personality, leadership potential. All the prerequisites to lead young men onto the field of sport." Tony points a pistol at Mr. Molinaro—it's no coincidence that the voice of conscience belongs to a fellow Italian American—but when he pulls the trigger, the gun goes limp. He tries again, and the clip falls out. The coach tells him, "You'll never shut me up." And it turns out that this isn't the first time the coach's reproachful voice has come to him in his sleep. "I had another of my Coach Molinaro dreams," he tells Carmela upon awakening.

In late 2004, newspaper headlines reinforced the uncanny correspondence between mob life as depicted on *The Sopranos* and real-life organized crime. The New York *Daily News* reported that John A. Gotti, Jr., son of the notorious "Teflon Don," had denounced the mafia and his father in conversations with close friends that were taped by the FBI: "In dozens of prison tapes, John A. (Junior) Gotti told visitors how he never wanted a Mafia life and how he hoped for better for his son."

Like his fictional counterpart Tony Soprano, "Junior" Gotti was forced into the mob life. He likewise adored his father and craved his love and respect. But in prison, away from the streets, the doubts that long had troubled him crystallized into bitter regret and rage. "I know my father loved me, but I got to question how much, to put me with all these wolves," Gotti admitted to his friends. "This is the world you put your kid in? So much treachery . . . My father couldn't have loved me, to push me into this life."[69]

Will any *Sopranos* fan be surprised if Tony utters something like Junior Gotti's cri de coeur (whether in a prison visiting room or Dr. Melfi's office) before the series reaches its conclusion?

When I first saw *The Godfather* I was stunned by the unprecedented realism of its depiction of first- and second-generation Italian Americans. I was hardly alone in my reaction; the film captivated countless paisans because they recognized themselves and their kin in the characters.

And for some, the shock of recognition was tinged with dismay: yes, that's us, but we're *not* criminals!

Sandra Mortola Gilbert, a poet and critic, was also struck by the "persuasive Italian Americanness . . . so vividly dramatized in *The Godfather*." She, however, was not charmed by what she saw: "Was it the *plausibility* of these people—their unnervingly familiar ways of dancing, laughing, dressing, eating, and drinking—that so distressed me?"[70]

The Sopranos achieves an even greater realism in its depiction of third- and fourth-generation Italian Americans. The show's more rabid Italian American critics insist that the drama serves up a grotesque distortion of their community and culture, but Robert Viscusi is dead-on when he says, of the show's characters, "They *are* Italian Americans!" *The Sopranos* actually outdoes the *Godfather* films, as well as those of Martin Scorsese, in the depth and variety of its *italianità*.

Sometimes it's seemingly small details that hit home with us paisans. In one episode, Carmela, upset with Tony about the lack of sex in their marriage, says, "Sometimes I think you skeeve me." Tony's reply: "How can I skeeve you, you're the mother of my children!" Non-Italians can easily figure out that Carmela is hurt because she thinks Tony finds her physically unappealing. But to Italian American ears, Carmela's accusation cuts deeper. To skeeve something means you find it repulsive; the term derives from the Italian *schifoso*, disgusting. (Italians also say, *mi fa schifo*, "it makes me sick.") I grew up hearing my parents, relatives, and other Italian Americans go on about how they "skeeved" a person, place, or thing—"I skeeve that restaurant, it's filthy," or, "I skeeve Mary's lasagna, she uses cottage cheese instead of *ricott'*"—but until *The Sopranos*, I'd never heard this southern Italian dialect expression in any pop-culture medium.

"Skeeve" is only one example. Tony's boat is named the *Stugots* (a common southern Italian vulgarism, derived from *questo cazzo*, this dick). Livia Soprano calls someone she despises a *facciabrut'* (from *facciabrutta*, ugly face). *Vaffanculo* (go fuck yourself), *strunz* (from *stronzo*, turd), *mannaggia* (damn), and others have added spice to the show's dialogue while amusing Italian American viewers like me. *Madonn'*—from *Madonna mia*, an all-purpose exclamation—is now probably as familiar to pop-culture consumers as "oy vey," thanks to *The Sopranos*.

"The way that the characters talk and the research that's done by those writers—most of whom are not Italian or Italian American, by the way—it's just amazing," laughs Annabella Sciorra, whose performance as Tony Soprano's tempestuous mistress Gloria Trillo riveted viewers during the series' third season. "And *pucchiacca*, it's a terrible word"—its closest English equivalent would be "cunt"—"I haven't heard anybody say that since I was a kid!"[71]

"We make donations of these words," says Dominic Chianese. "The show's Italian American actors share these with the writers. And some of them come from David [Chase] and [Frank] Renzulli." Chianese has his own favorites: "*Incazzat'*, so passionate you can't think straight, you blow up. And *gabbadotz*, hardheaded. We use them and others on the show, and I think it gives it flavor, it's as if you were using Yiddish on a Jewish program."[72]

But the show's treatment of Italian American ethnicity is much more incisive than just its knowing use of southern Italian dialect.

Like Martin Scorsese in *Mean Streets* and *Goodfellas*, David Chase has made brilliant use of music—rock, hip-hop, rhythm and blues, Italian American pop and opera—to create atmosphere and to comment on the action. He has also used specifically Italian music—to signify passion, a familiar trope, but also to signify Italian American connection to old-world ethnic roots.

In the episode titled "The Weight," Carmela, without Tony, goes to a party of her husband's relatives and mob associates. Carmela is powerfully attracted to one of them, Furio Giunta, a member of Tony's crew imported from Naples. Furio, with his sleek black hair pulled into a ponytail, and his aura of Mediterranean sensuality, seems to have leaped from the cover of an Italian romance novel. When he asks Carmela to dance, the music is neither American pop nor sentimental Italian Americana but a raucous, intensely rhythmic number by Spaccanapoli, a contemporary neo-roots band from Naples. "Vesuvio" is the name of the piece, and its pounding percussion and raw, wailing vocals stir up the roiling magma of dangerous passion threatening to erupt between the mob boss's wife and his henchman. Surly Soprano son A.J. mutters that he's "bored as shit," but the music from the *madrepatria* moves the more intelligent and sensitive Meadow.

"I know that people have issues with *The Sopranos*," Annabella

Sciorra adds. "But I feel that the show has opened up a whole new level of what being Italian American is. I think that David Chase claimed this Italian American territory and said, 'Wait. There's a lot more to explore here. There's a lot more to offer.' He set it in a mafia family, but I think he could have done it in another situation. I think the fact that he set it in this mafia family makes it kind of funny, that they deal with issues that all middle-class Italian Americans, all middle-class families deal with."[73]

Michael Rispoli, who portrayed cancer-stricken mob boss Jackie Aprile, agrees with Sciorra that the show's focus on a mob family that happens to be upwardly mobile both reinvigorates the organized crime genre and depicts a heretofore unexplored slice of Italo-Americana. Rispoli realized early on that this new spin would have broad appeal. He recalls:

> Early in the show's first season I was in Utah, having breakfast with my wife. The waitress said to me, "I saw you on TV the other night. You're an actor, right?" I said yeah. People usually recognize me from *While You Were Sleeping* [a 1995 comedy-drama with Sandra Bullock]. But she said no, "It was a mafia thing." I said, Oh, *The Juror*, where I played a gangster. She said no, it was a television show . . . *The Sopranos*, I said, and she said, "Yeah, that's it! My mother loves that show!" This is about four weeks into the run, the first year. I went home and called up James Gandolfini, and I said, "Jimmy, your show's a hit—even the Mormons are watching it!"
>
> It's a crossover thing. You got Tony Soprano and Carmela Soprano. But their kids . . . the kids are a hybrid, a new generation. You got A.J. as they call him, and Meadow. Meadow Soprano! What Italian would ever call a kid "Meadow"? But it's perfect because it shows these are suburban Italians.[74]

America finds Italian Americans fascinating, in large measure because a century of assimilation into American life hasn't eradicated our ethnic distinctiveness. Social scientists may argue that Italian Americans are living in the "twilight" of their ethnicity, or that Italian

American ethnicity is now purely "symbolic" rather than "functional." But as discussed earlier, in the Introduction, Americans of Italian descent have remained "ethnic" to a degree unequaled by other groups of European origin.

The Sopranos live in an affluent suburb that would have been off-limits to their immigrant grandparents; the WASPs would have let them in only to mow lawns or build stone walls. But though they've climbed up the socioeconomic ladder, they're only two generations from the immigrant era, and something of steerage, and of their struggling blue-collar days, still clings to them.

They live among and interact with other Italian Americans who came from humble immigrant roots: their neighbors the Cusamanos, surgeon Bruce and his classy wife, Jean, Jennifer Melfi and her family and friends, a Columbia University dean, a nursing home director who quotes old-world proverbs in flawless Italian. Most of the FBI agents who are pursuing Tony and his crew have Italian names. These Italian Americans are law-abiding, college-educated professionals, and they regard paisans like Tony with a mixture of contempt and fascination.

In an episode from the first season titled "A Hit Is a Hit," Dr. Melfi urges Tony to widen his circle of social contacts. Carmela, an avid social climber, readily agrees. Tony has his misgivings, but he and Carmela start socializing with their respectable Italian American neighbors, including the Cusamanos. They are welcomed at backyard barbecues and Dr. Cusamano even invites Tony to play golf at his country club. But Tony quickly realizes that these high-class Italians don't consider him their equal. They're only interested in hearing stories about the mob, and whether "*The Godfather* was really accurate." The "Wonder Bread wops," as Tony calls them, want to make him their dancing bear, a semidomesticated brute performing for their titillation and amusement.

An episode from the fifth season dug deeper into class-based culture conflict among Italian Americans. Carmela throws a seventy-fifth birthday party for her father, Hugh De Angelis, and among the guests are Dr. Russ Fegoli, a professor and retired "assistant to the Ambassador to the Vatican," and his wife, Lena. The Fegolis, friends of Carmela's mother, are the kind of *haut bourgeois* Italian Americans who look to Tuscany, and what they consider to be the glamour and sophistication of northern Italy, for their sense of *italianità*.

Carmela's mother joins the Fegolis in praising Tuscany, and effuses about such glorious dishes as bollito misto and osso buco. Mamma De Angelis and her friends clearly regard these creations of *cucina toscana* as superior to Neapolitan baked ziti. But the joke is that both are humble dishes—the former is just boiled meat, the latter is a veal shinbone, and neither is Tuscan in origin.

Tony, having been expelled from the Soprano manse by Carmela because of his infidelities, was banned from the birthday party. But partly as a rebuke to Carmela and partly because he's fond of her father, he shows up, wearing a string of sausages around his neck like a Hawaiian lei. The birthday boy, Carmela's father, is delighted to see Tony. But Carmela's mother is plainly mortified that her mobster son-in-law has appeared, and, even worse, that he intends to grill "sazeech" near her cultured friends the Fegolis.

After the party, a furious Carmela confronts her mother, accusing her of being ashamed of her southern Italian roots. Carmela reminds her that the pretentious, Tuscany-loving Fegolis actually grew up on Arthur Avenue, in a working-class (southern) Italian American neighborhood in the Bronx. Mamma De Angelis protests that she's never denied her heritage, but Carmela has her number: she's embarrassed by her gavone relatives, Carmela, her husband and two children, and the rest of the Soprano clan.

Thoroughly *incazzat'*, Carmela then opens an old wound that obviously has aggravated her for years: when Meadow was born, Mrs. De Angelis said of her black-haired and olive-skinned granddaughter, "Why does she have to be so dark?"

I gasped, taken back to one of my sharpest childhood memories—my mother's anger at my paternal grandmother for her suggestion that my brother and I be kept out of strong sunlight so we wouldn't look like "eggplants." I was also certain that the episode hit home for other Italian Americans with memories of color consciousness in their families, of a racial anxiety bubbling just below the surface of the prized white identity attained over decades of assimilation.

Carmela's accusation reminded us that although many of us have

repressed the memory of having been regarded as "less" than white—
and of darkness being associated with lower socioeconomic status—we
haven't entirely erased the "mark of the Turk" from our collective consciousness.

Both episodes bear out Robert Viscusi's claim that *The Sopranos*
disturbs because "it's so naked and raw in its depictions of the class humiliations that go along with being an Italian American on the rise."[75]

But what does it mean that the defense of southern Italian honor
comes from a character as morally compromised as Carmela Soprano?
Her tirade, for all its righteous indignation, betrays not a little defen-
siveness about her own life and the choices she has made.

The series also presents Tony Soprano as some kind of southern
Italian Everyman. His physical presence—his way of speaking in
Neapolitan cadences, his facial expressions and body language—all
mark him unmistakably as a third-generation Italian American of proletarian origins, as do the things he holds dear: family, loyalty, and his
wife's baked ziti. Tony demonstrates a proud *italianità* that he strives to
impart to his daughter. He brings Meadow to a Catholic church built
by his grandfather and other Italian immigrant laborers to show off
their accomplished handiwork; he informs her that Antonio Meucci,
not Alexander Graham Bell, actually invented the telephone. When he
makes the decision to see a therapist, it is important to him that the
doctor is an Italian American. And Tony consistently seems more vital,
more down-to-earth, more *real* than his "Wonder Bread wop" neighbors.

Is David Chase implying not only that the choice for Italian Americans is to be either a gangster/gavone or a bleached-out bourgeois, but
also that the former is actually preferable? Chase has expressed disdain
for bourgeois values and for the capitalist mass media that extol them.
Having worked in network television before *The Sopranos*, he regards
its offerings as "propaganda for the corporate state—the programming,
not only the commercials . . . What I mean is, it was ramming home
every week the message that 'life is nothing but great,' 'Americans are
great' and 'heartfelt emotion and sharing conquers everything.' "[76]

Given Chase's iconoclasm and his keen sense of irony, it's not surprising that his murderous crime boss would embody qualities preferable to the pretentiousness and snobbery of the Italian American

borghesia. But Dr. Jennifer Melfi seems closer to his idea of a representative or admirable Italian American. Melfi is an intelligent and capable professional. Though prone to self-doubt and overintellectualizing, she is confident and comfortable in her own skin.

She is a serious person who makes sound ethical judgments. She will not violate her personal and professional ethics by acting on her sexual attraction to Tony Soprano. After she is raped by a young thug, she furiously fantasizes about having her assailant killed. But when she has the opportunity to enlist Tony as her avenger, she refuses his brand of rough justice.

Though thoroughly upper-middle-class by dint of her education and profession, she's no snob. When Jean Cusamano criticizes the Murano glass knickknacks in Carmela's home as proof of Signora Soprano's tacky, nouveau riche taste, Melfi speaks up: "I like Murano glass." Melfi, no "Wonder Bread wop," acknowledges and is proud of her southern Italian roots. But she has no time for the tunnel vision and self-pity of her ex-husband, Richard, the perpetually outraged ethnic warrior.

The Sopranos, the richest, most complex and artistically satisfying mob drama in the history of the genre, affirms the capaciousness of the Mafia myth and shows how talented artists can use it to explore not only organized crime but also class, culture, psychology, and national identity—and what it means to be Italian American in the twenty-first century, long after the Sopranos and De Angelises, the Cusamanos and Melfis arrived in the strange new world of *Lamerica*.

6

Act Like a Man: Sex and Gender in the Mafia Myth

The distance from Michael [Corleone] to Henry Hill to Tony [Soprano] can be plotted in terms of their relation to women.
—Cindy Donatelli and Sharon Alward, " 'I Dread You': Married to the Mob in *The Godfather*, *Goodfellas*, and *The Sopranos*"

What's with you, you think everybody's gay. Maybe *you're* gay!
—Carmela Soprano, to Tony

You can act like a man!   —Don Vito Corleone, in *The Godfather*

Johnny Fontane, the Sinatra-like pop crooner in *The Godfather*, needs help from Vito Corleone, who is his actual godfather. He joins the other supplicants seeking the Don's assistance at his daughter Connie's wedding reception, because, as son Michael observes, "no Sicilian will refuse a request on his daughter's wedding day."

Fontane, his once red-hot career having cooled, desperately wants a film role that he knows will put him back on top. But the film's producer, he sorrowfully informs Don Vito, won't even consider him for the part. "Oh, Godfather, I don't know what to do, I don't know what to do," Fontane sobs.

"You can act like a man!" Don Vito bellows, as he slaps his weepy godson in the face. "What's the matter with you? Is this how you turned out? A Hollywood *finocchio* [homosexual] that cries like a woman?"

The encounter between the distraught pop star and his gangster godfather is one of the film's most famous moments. It is beautifully acted by Al Martino as Fontane, and Brando, of course, is magisterial; in a matter of seconds he captures Don Corleone's volatile emotional chemistry, going from loving solicitude to dismay and rage to gentle mockery. But the scene does much more than dramatize the relationship between the two men, one dangerously close to has-been status, the other at the peak of his considerable power. Don Corleone, in admonishing his godson, was laying down the immutable law of gender, Sicilian-style: acting "like a man" means you don't lose control of your emotions and blubber. That's for women, and for homosexuals, who are like women, and are therefore not real men.

The Mafia myth, as we have seen, encompasses much more than the sordid business of organized crime. The big three creative talents of the mob genre, Francis Ford Coppola, Martin Scorsese, and David Chase, have used the genre's conventions to comment on economics and class, family dynamics, culture and ethnicity. But their works also ask: What does it mean to be a man? What does it mean to be a woman? What constitutes masculinity and femininity, and what burdens do these socially constructed categories impose on men and women? These artists explore relations between the genders, the power imbalances between men and women, and how women cope with male dominance.

And although Coppola, Scorsese, and Chase have anatomized mafia sexual mores and gender relations most thoroughly and with unparalleled insight, other artists, Italian American and not, have explored the territory. Jonathan Demme's *Married to the Mob* and John Huston's *Prizzi's Honor*, for example, feature strong-willed women who rebel against their assigned roles as wives and daughters. In Abel Ferrara's *The Funeral*, it is the lead female character who delivers the film's condemnation of organized crime and its oppressive culture of "honor" and vengeance.

Sociologist Richard Gambino, in his landmark 1974 book *Blood of My Blood*, describes a gender taxonomy and ideology born in the context of Mezzogiorno poverty and underdevelopment that southern Italian immigrants, largely agricultural workers and unskilled laborers, brought with them to America. The *uomo di pazienza* literally is a man of patience, and of emotional self-control, who demonstrates a pragmatic approach to life and cannily assesses situations and other people. The feminine ideal, the *donna di seriatà*, is that of a virtuous woman who embodies the seriousness required to handle both the privileges and responsibilities that come with being the center of *la famiglia*.

Gambino downplays the degree to which this gender system was based on male dominance. He claims that rather than being a simple patriarchy, it was a role-based system in which labor was more or less equitably divided between the genders. But this just isn't credible. Men simply were valued more: Luca Brasi's Sicilian wedding wish for Connie Corleone and Carlo Rizzi, "May your first child be a masculine child," says it all. Males were regarded as stronger, more responsible, and, because they possessed rationality, capable of transcending biology and its constraints. God and nature—which were the same thing—had assigned to them the roles of leader and protector.

Women were defined in terms of their capacities for reproduction and motherhood; biological functions become social characteristics. The southern Italian woman may have been the center of the family, upon whom the other members depended for physical, emotional, and spiritual sustenance. But her power was limited to the domestic sphere. And even there, the man ultimately ruled the roost. A typical southern Italian expression conveys the sense of male proprietorship: *Tengo una famiglia*, I hold or keep a family.

The southern Italian immigrants regarded sex as an explosive force whose potential for subverting the gendered social order was so great that it had to be channeled into marriage. Female virginity was a matter of family honor and economics: a "fallen" woman would not be able to make a good marriage that brought benefits to both families. (Children born out of wedlock had a particularly hard time, as they belonged to no family.) There was a word for women who flouted the sex/gender codes: *puttana*, whore. Dressing in a fashion regarded as immodest, wearing makeup, behaving in public in too free or flirtatious a manner could result in a young woman being called a *puttana*. Such labeling proved an effective means of social control.

Men learned that there were bad women, *puttane*, and good, virtuous women, who presumably included their mothers. The maternal ideal of unstinting love, nurturance, and self-sacrifice was embodied by Jesus' mother, the Madonna. Though such perfection was unattainable by ordinary human beings, southern Italian women were supposed to emulate her example. Thus was born the Madonna/whore dichotomy that has so vexed Italian men (because they wanted, but couldn't get, both aspects in the same woman) and oppressed Italian women.

(When Madonna Louise Veronica Ciccone became an international superstar in the 1980s, her ascendancy carried a particular frisson of transgression for Italians: here was a Madonna who looked and acted like a *puttana*!)

Although homosexuality was rarely spoken about, same-sex attractions were not rare in the Mezzogiorno, at least among men. Male prostitution was common in southern cities, particularly Naples. In the nineteenth century, northern European homosexuals sought refuge from the harsh Protestant morality of their home countries in what they saw as the more tolerant culture of the Italian South, which retained to some extent the pansexual attitudes of classical Greece and Rome.

The Sicilian town of Taormina was especially popular with foreign same-sexers, the most famous being the German nobleman Wilhelm Von Gloeden, who somehow managed to persuade dozens of Sicilian youths and men to strip naked for his camera during the late 1800s and early 1900s. Baron Von Gloeden managed to avoid scandal, maybe because of his hundreds of photos, only a very few were overtly sexual. He tended to shoot his models, sons of fishermen and peasants, in kitschy tableaux meant to evoke classical Greece and Rome and North Africa. (The naked young Sicilians displayed their uncircumcised and generally large penises for the baron's camera, but the laurel wreaths and Arabic headdresses they wore connoted Art, not porn.) He paid them, too, and even set up some of them in their own businesses. Von Gloeden adopted the classical Mediterranean model of homosexuality, of erotic and financial mentorship between an older man and a younger, generally heterosexual male. Today one can purchase his photographs, as postcards and in expensive coffee table books, in shops all over Sicily.[1]

As the Von Gloeden story suggests, a certain social tolerance toward homosexual behavior prevailed, provided that the *omosessuale* did not make a *brutta figura*, that is, cause a scandal by being too public about his sexuality. Homosexuals who contravened the status quo of silence and invisibility quickly discovered the limits of "live and let live." Like a "bad" woman labeled a *puttana*, the "obvious" homosexual was censured as a *finocchio, culattone, frocio*, and *disgraziato* (literally, disgraced or wretched one), and regarded as a potential threat to *l'ordine della famiglia* (family system).

(Such attitudes are by no means a thing of the past, however. In 2004, Rocco Buttiglione, from the southern Italian province of Puglia, was nominated by the right-wing government of Silvio Berlusconi to a commissioner's post in the European Union. Buttiglione previously had decried homosexuality as a "sin" and said that women would be better off staying home as full-time wives and mothers. Buttiglione's benighted comments caused a furor throughout Europe and in Italy, and he was forced to withdraw his candidacy.)

Italian immigrants to America structured their domestic and public lives according to these ideals and practices. They also inculcated them in their American-born children, with mixed results. Members of my parents' generation tried to be dutiful and loyal *figli* and *figlie* and proper men and women, as defined by their parents' old-world culture. But the sex/gender system of the Mezzogiorno was inevitably undermined by immigration and Americanization. Italian American family histories are full of stories of second-generation daughters resisting family control, chafing at having to be chaperoned on dates, refusing to marry men from the old country whom their parents picked for them, or seeking freedom and autonomy by working outside the home.

Southern Italian culture strictly defined gender roles and sexual morality, but southern Italians themselves were not necessarily prudish about sex. In fact, the "old-timers"—the immigrant generation—could be downright bawdy, in ways that embarrassed their American-born descendants. When I was on the verge of adolescence, my great-grandfather would ask me about the size of my *pesce* (penis), to my mother's mortification. Southern Italian immigrants didn't understand why the Irish priests who ran the Catholic parishes sermonized so fervently against the sins of the flesh. Sex was not something to be ashamed of or to fear. It was a natural, albeit potentially disruptive force, that had to be managed and domesticated.[2]

The Sicilians and other southern Italians who established organized crime groups in America were products of the same culture as their law-abiding compatriots, who constituted the vast majority of the immigrants. They by and large shared the same attitudes and followed the same social practices about gender and sexuality. As noted earlier, they even justified their criminal activity by claiming it served to protect the southern Italian family structure.

Near the end of Mario Puzo's novel, Tom Hagen tracks Kay Corleone to her parents' New Hampshire home, where she has fled after realizing that Michael has lied to her about his role in Carlo Rizzi's death. Hagen explains to her why both Carlo, and Corleone family turncoat Tessio, were killed: both had proved themselves to be treacherous, Carlo having set up Sonny, Tessio planning Michael's death, and such betrayal could not go unpunished. Michael would "be shirking his duty to you and his children, to his whole family, to me and my family, if he let Tessio and Carlo go free. They would have been a danger to us, all our lives."[3]

Michael Corleone's fictive descendant Tony Soprano gives the go-ahead to one of his captains to whack Jackie Aprile, Jr., the feckless mob wannabe who is his daughter Meadow's boyfriend. He knows Jackie's death will devastate the boy's mother and Meadow. But the kid is bad news for both of Tony's families—his irresponsibility endangers the Soprano crew and makes him an unsuitable suitor for Meadow. Tony doesn't hesitate to have him killed to protect himself and his own.

This familism, warped as it is, differentiates the Italian and Italian American gangster from his non-Latin counterparts. In the gangster movies made during the Depression, family life was a prison to avoid or escape. The gangster, notes Carlos Clarens, was the "romantic male figure of the period,"[4] and women, representing domesticity and routine, had to be put in their place when they tried to impede his freedom and fun.

No movie demonstrates the gangster genre's misogynistic streak better than *Public Enemy*, in which James Cagney smashes a grapefruit into the face of his girlfriend, played by Mae Clark. Carlos Clarens observes that in the context of the Depression, this act took on a specific meaning: "The girl became a nagging, simpering mate trying to restrain the man from taking to the road or to crime or some such alternative, any of which were vastly more attractive and romantic than sex-denying domesticity and a nine-to-five job. This was an appeal that men could identify with."[5]

The Italian mobster, however, can have his freedom and his *cucina casalinga* (home-cooked meals), too. His wife will manage hearth and home, while his gumad (or gumads) gives him sex, companionship, and momentary escape from the demands of domestic life.

Pop-culture representations of "the Mafia"—movies, TV shows, books—have portrayed gangsters and their significant others living within the "regime" of sex and gender, as philosopher-historian Michel Foucault would put it, that emerged in the peculiar circumstances of the Mezzogiorno. These mob tales depict, sometimes with startling depth and accuracy, other times in gross caricature, men and women whose attitudes and behavior have been shaped by this historical legacy, which has been changed—modified, distorted, resisted—but not eradicated by Americanization.

The genre, like the sex/gender regime it portrays, is male-dominated. Yet women are hardly peripheral to it. The popular conception of women in mob dramas is of wives and mothers who stir the tomato sauce, raise the kids, and put up with their men's philandering, striving to maintain a normal home life in the profoundly abnormal circumstances of being married to the mob. Think of Mamma Corleone, a saintly but mostly silent figure in the first two *Godfather* films, or Theresa in *Mean Streets*, whose main ambition in life is to set up house with Charlie, her small-time hoodlum boyfriend.

Then there are the girlfriends and mistresses—*puttane*, in the harsh reckoning of the Mezzogiorno—who attend to the sexual needs of their gangster men. As Joe Pistone notes, virtually all mobsters have a gumad. Sonny Corleone has Lucy Mancini, with whom he has vertical intercourse against a closed door while his wife gossips with the other mob women at Connie Corleone's wedding party. Henry Hill, in Scorsese's *Goodfellas*, has two gumads, Robin, a partner in his drug business, and Linda, whom he installs in an apartment not far from the home he shares with his wife, Karen. Bobby "Baccala" Bacillieri on *The Sopranos* is the only member of Tony's crew who is so happily married that he doesn't have another woman, an anomaly the other wiseguys regard with amused incomprehension.

The typology of mothers, wives, and gumads, however, can be too simplistic. Whatever their relationship to the gangsters in their lives, their actual behavior can't be reduced to these roles. Women in the Mafia myth can be victims, but also victimizers, enablers of their men's bad behavior and accomplices in it. And sometimes, they are even rebels, refusing to obey the rules of the aberrant society of La Cosa Nostra.

It has become a critical cliché that the *Godfather* films, whatever their virtues as cinema, are retrograde in their portrayals of women. Two feminist critics, Cindy Donatelli and Sharon Alward, argue that "in Francis Ford Coppola's saga, women are inevitably road kill . . . the *Godfather* films represent a revolting wet dream of female degradation."[6] This is rhetorical overkill: the *Godfather* films present a number of female characters who, though victimized, aren't just victims. Though secondary characters, they nonetheless play significant roles in the Corleone trilogy: Carmela Corleone, matriarch of the family; Constanzia (Connie), the only daughter among her and Vito's four children; Kay Adams, the New England WASP who marries Michael; and Kay and Michael's daughter, Mary.

Apollonia, the demure beauty Michael marries while hiding out in Sicily, is killed not long after the wedding, by a car bomb meant for her husband. But Apollonia's significance exceeds her brief moment in the Corleone saga, as she represents the traditional Sicilian ideal of womanhood: obedient to her parents, modest in dress and demeanor, and, until her marriage, a virgin. Her death signals the loss of that world and, for Michael, further assimilation into American life, as his second wife is an *echt*-American, one of the WASPs whose forebears were so horrified by the arrival on American shores of millions of southern Italians.

Apollonia's death also portends the loss of the romantic and sexual passion that humanized Michael. When he first encounters her, he is stunned, *colpito dal fulmine*, struck by a thunderbolt, as Sicilians say. He has no doubt that she is *the* one, his destiny, and he pursues her with his usual single-minded intensity. Their brief marriage is a passionate one, full of frequent and fervent lovemaking; the two devour each other in bed. (Puzo's novel is more forthcoming about this than the movie.) Michael's marriage to Kay, the educated, upper-middle-class New England girl, seems more a business arrangement by comparison. He says he loves her, but her main value to him seems to be as a mother to his two children and as a social asset—she's the kind of "classy" American spouse an immigrant's ambitious son would need to ascend in American society. A trophy wife.

Diane Keaton's performances as Kay in the three *Godfather* films have left us with indelible images, of her college-girl ingenuousness before she marries into the family from hell, her stunned look as doors are shut in her face, her tremulous expression as she bravely challenges her dictator of a husband. Mistreated by Michael, Kay also has been misunderstood and maligned by critics. Donatelli and Alward claim that Kay "plays out the role of bored suburban housewife—she pretends that her husband's 'business' is beneath her, that she has no knowledge of any of it, that the business is going to go legit—but I don't see her walking away from the mansion on Lake Tahoe."[7]

This is a near-total misreading of the character. Rather than act oblivious to her husband's business, she demands answers. Near the end of *The Godfather*, after Michael has "settled the family's accounts" by murdering all his rivals, she no longer believes her husband's lies. Seeing him receive tribute from the men who used to serve his father, she realizes that he is indeed Don Corleone now, and that his sister Connie's denunciation of him as a cold-blooded killer is true. Moreover, in *Godfather II* she does walk away from the Lake Tahoe mansion and her cosseted but precarious life as the Don's spouse, even at the cost of the loss of her children.

Carlos Clarens has criticized Coppola for "almost total suppression of the godfather's criminal dimension," claiming that the Corleone family's crimes were "transmuted into retaliatory action, correction of power abuse, business transactions of a more ethical nature than seemed customary among mobsters."[8] He maintains that the role of

Kay offers another instance of the director's "sleight of hand." In the novel, she functions as "a representative of the non-Italian, non-criminal world she left behind to marry into the Corleone family."⁹ But "her role gave Coppola the worst trouble, since to admit the honest outside world would have imperiled his airtight universe." Kay, there-fore, "was made to act unduly stupid, asking questions that no sensible mafioso wife had the right to ask her man."¹⁰

But Kay Adams is not of the Sicilian mafia culture, so she doesn't accept the unwritten rule of wifely silence. Michael married her be-cause he wanted a real American wife, who would give birth to Ameri-can kids. But he still expects her to follow the Sicilian rules for female comportment. Kay struggles with this impossible bind, and ultimately breaks free.

The Kay of the films, that is. The Kay Adams of Puzo's novel, whom Carlos Clarens characterizes as the representative of the noncriminal, non-Sicilian world, actually accommodates herself to being a mafia wife with relatively little discomfort. After she learns that Michael has lied to her and is responsible for the deaths of Carlo Rizzi and others, she takes her children and flees to the bosom of her upright family in New Hampshire. But her rebellion is short-lived; Corleone family lawyer Tom Hagen easily persuades her to return. At the novel's end, she is reconciled to Michael and her life as his wife.

Near the end of *Godfather II*, Kay tells Michael that she is leaving him and is taking the kids. He icily replies, "Do you expect me to let you take my children from me? Don't you know me? Don't you know that that's an impossibility—that that could never happen? That I would use all my power to keep something like that from happening—don't you know that?"

Thinking that Kay is just upset over having had a miscarriage, he tries to assure her that they can have another child. Exasperated, Kay decides to go for broke. "Oh, Michael you are blind," she says. "It wasn't a miscarriage. It was an abortion, Michael, an abortion. Just like our marriage is an abortion. Something that's unholy and evil. I didn't want your son, Michael—I wouldn't bring another one of your sons into this world. It was a son, Michael, a son and I had it killed—because this must all end."

Carlos Clarens argues, "Once this tiresome tactic [of Kay's foolish inquiries] had made her presence expendable, there was the unexpected revelation that she has willingly aborted Michael's third child." Clarens says this is "truly the unkindest blow to the character," and when "Michael slammed the door in her face, his action had all the force of justifiable rejection, and audiences were bound to accept and even applaud it."[11]

I don't recall the audience applauding the scene Clarens cites. I know I wanted to applaud Kay when she delivered her devastating news. By driving home the point that it was a male heir—"a masculine child"—she had aborted, she wounds Michael to the quick, shattering his facade of implacability and self-control. "I know that it's over now," she tells him. "I knew it then—there would be no way, Michael, no way you could ever forgive me. Not with this Sicilian thing that's been going on for two thousand years"—at which point Michael strikes her, something he has never done before. Kay knows what she has done is unforgivable, and that's exactly why she chose to do it.

Clarens absurdly claims, "Kay had no place in the cinematic saga of the Corleones." She definitely does have a place, as an outsider and a rebel. The Kay of the novel who functions as the reader's surrogate, the representative of the noncriminal world, submits to her husband, as a good 1950s housewife was supposed to. But the Kay of the film trilogy evolves, from a naive girl who loves her fiancé and wants to believe his disavowals of involvement in the family business, to the trapped mafia wife surrounded by treachery and violence, to the strong-willed woman who escapes from her "unholy and evil" marriage, albeit at great cost.

We next encounter Kay in *Part III* of the trilogy, some twenty years later. Now remarried, she meets with Michael after the Catholic Church has given him its prestigious Order of St. Sebastian award. Her purpose is to intervene with him on behalf of their son, Anthony, so that Michael will relent and allow the young man to pursue a career as an opera singer rather than attend law school. During their meeting, Kay is merciless with her ex-husband, scornfully rejecting all his justifications for the life he has led. She's disgusted by his newfound respectability as a philanthropist, saying she preferred him when he was just "a common mafia hood." During their marriage, he was her "horror," but now she says she doesn't hate him, she dreads him.

The aged and frail Michael Corleone who slumps behind his desk as he absorbs her rage and disgust seems a shadow of the fearsome cobra of old. Her words do wound him, and he begs her not to dread him. For the sake of their son, and perhaps because she feels some lingering affection for the man she once loved, she goes to Sicily, where Anthony is to make his operatic debut in a production of *Cavalleria Rusticana*. But the joy over Anthony's triumph turns to grief, as daughter Mary is killed outside the Palermo opera house by a bullet intended for Michael. Implacable *destino* has struck him down, ensnaring Kay, too.

Constanzia "Connie" Corleone, Don Vito's youngest child and only daughter, is another female character who is portrayed in greater depth in the films than in the novel. She initially appears as the sheltered mafia princess, doted on by her indulgent father, whose lavish wedding opens the first film. She makes a bad marriage to her brother Sonny's friend Carlo Rizzi, who cheats on her and beats her. After Michael has Carlo killed for setting up Sonny to be murdered, she confronts Michael, in Kay's presence, wailing that he stood as godfather at the baptism of her and Carlo's child all the while he was plotting her husband's death. And that's not all—she tells Kay that the screaming newspaper headlines about a spate of brazen gangland murders have everything to do with Michael.

"There's your husband!" she cries, demanding that Kay face the truth about the new Don Corleone.

In *Godfather II*, Connie makes a declaration which, note critics Donatelli and Alward, flew in the face "of all the rhetoric and images of the women's movement" at the time the film was released, in 1974: "Michael, I'd like to stay close to home now, if it's alright . . . you need me, Michael. I want to take care of you."[12] Connie decides to make peace with Michael and the Corleone family only after she's gone through a binge of self-destructive behavior fueled by her grief over Carlo's death and her fury at her brother. She has remarried, got divorced, and thrown herself into demeaning affairs, acting, in short, like a *puttana*. "You fly around the world with men who don't even care about you, and use you like a whore!" Michael reprimands her.

In the novel, Connie's distress over Carlo's murder dissipates quickly; only a week after she has denounced Michael she apologizes to him, saying she didn't mean any of it. She also finds a replacement for Carlo whom she quickly marries, "a fine young fellow who had come to work for the Corleone family as a male secretary . . . a boy from a reliable Italian family but graduated from the top business college in America."[13] The film *Godfather II* at least permits Connie a little rebellion before she returns to her toxic clan.

In the third film, she has become the family matriarch, a dark, witchy figure clad all in black. Still protective of Michael, she dutifully reiterates the official family fiction that Fredo drowned in Lake Tahoe when her brother laments that his son Anthony (rightfully) blames him for his uncle's death. Michael has divested himself of the family's businesses, mainly the enormously profitable casinos, but Connie has her own godmotherly ambitions. She becomes the sponsor of her nephew Vincent Mancini, the son of Sonny Corleone and his gumad Lucy, who longs to become his uncle's right-hand man and protector.

Connie convinces Michael to put his fate in Vincent's capable, if trigger-happy, hands, and to bestow the Corleone name, and hence legitimacy, on him. Connie has become an enabler and an accomplice in the family business; the young widow once horrified by her brother's cold-bloodedness now dispatches a family rival with some poisoned cannoli. (*Godfather III* nods to the original film in linking the luscious Sicilian pastry with death; Corleone captain Clemenza delivered the immortal line, "Leave the gun, take the cannoli," after his hit man has whacked Paulie Gatto, the traitorous chauffeur.)

Against the notion of women-as-roadkill, critic Vera Dika offers another, more persuasive interpretation of their function in the *Godfather* trilogy. The women, she writes, represent the traditional Sicilian culture, *la via vecchia*, which the men fight to protect. Dika perspicaciously observes, "Much of the men's violence is intended to protect the family, of which the woman is the center."[14] She notes that Fanucci, the Black Hand thug from the Little Italy sequences in *Godfather II*, is killed because "his depriving young Vito Corleone of his job strikes at his ability to feed his family, and Fanucci also threatens to slash the face of a young woman." The murder of the young Vito (Andolini) Corleone's mother in Sicily, the disfiguring of the undertaker Bonasera's daughter, and the assassination attempt on Michael while he is with Kay in their bedroom ("where my wife sleeps, and where my children play with their toys") all provide justification for the men's violence.

The fate of Mary Corleone (who, incidentally, doesn't exist in the novel, where Michael and Kay have two sons who go unnamed) provides the exception to Dika's otherwise accurate assessment. Rather than serve as a justification for violence, Mary's death drives home the horror of the premeditated violence that has been her family's stock-in-trade. The sins of the fathers are visited on an innocent, the young daughter to whom Michael vowed, "I would burn in hell to keep you safe." Mary becomes the instrument through which a merciless *destino* finally strikes down Michael Corleone, the killer and corrupter who, in his hubris, believed he had escaped reckoning for his crimes.

In contrast, Maerose Prizzi, the formidable schemer of *Prizzi's Honor*, a 1985 black comedy directed by John Huston, makes her own destiny, and she's nobody's victim. Adapted by Richard Condon from his own novel, *Prizzi's Honor* boasts a terrific, Oscar-winning performance by Anjelica Huston as Maerose, the daughter of Brooklyn mob boss Dominic Prizzi. Huston hilariously plays up the incongruity between Maerose's exotic beauty (the novel describes her as "Arab Sicilian") and her honking and decidedly inelegant Brooklyn accent.

Some four years before the film's action, Maerose suffered a major *disgrazia*. She had expected to marry Charley Partanna, the Prizzis' top hit man (played unconvincingly by Jack Nicholson), whom she had known since childhood. But one night Charley paid too much attention to another woman, and Maerose, in a fit of jealousy, ran away to Mexico with a man she barely knew. Her enraged father sent some wiseguys to retrieve her, but when she returned to Brooklyn he exiled her from the family because she had behaved like a *puttana*: "You shamed yourself with this zero guy in a shitty Mexican hotel room."

After four years in Sicilian purgatory, Maerose finds a way to reunite with her family and win back Charley. One night he calls her— for only the second time in four years—and insists on seeing her. Confused and distraught, he needs advice from his childhood friend. He tells her that he has fallen in love with Irene Walker, a blond

Polish-American and self-described tax consultant who is actually a contract killer. Irene has not only deceived Charley about her true occupation; she has scammed the Prizzis out of nearly a million dollars. As distressed as he is, he still adores Irene, and he turns to Maerose for advice. "Do I ice her? Or do I marry her?" he asks.

"Marry her," Maerose replies. "Just because she's a thief and a hitter doesn't mean she isn't a good woman in all the other departments." Maerose reminds him that the fact that he and Irene are "in the same line of business" bodes well for their future as husband and wife: "If she was some fashion model it couldn't last thirty days."

But before they get down to their heart-to-heart, Maerose seduces Charley, just moments after he arrives at her apartment. "Let's do it," she says. "Right here. On the Oriental. With all the lights on." What strikes Charley as spontaneous lust on Maerose's part is in reality pure calculation, as she intends to use their tryst to further her scheme to get revenge on her father and reclaim Charley. She then writes a letter to her grandfather, the ancient but still commanding Don Corrado Prizzi, begging that she be allowed to return to the family, particularly so she can care for her ailing father. The Don, usually the cagiest of men, is a sucker for such expressions of filial devotion, and he convinces his son Dominic to reconcile with Maerose.

The errant daughter prepares for her reunion with her papa by making herself look like a ruined spinster, her glossy black hair pulled into a bun and her face powdered to simulate a deathly pallor. The illusion fools Dominic, who exclaims, "My beautiful daughter is turned into an old woman! Charley Partanna did this to you! He had a chance to marry into the Prizzi family, but he had no use for you."

"He had a use for me, Papa," she sadly tells him. "He came to my place in New York the night before he left to marry the woman in California and he forced himself on me and did it to me. He screwed me," Maerose says—or as it comes out in her braying Brooklynese, "He schrewed me. T'ree times. Maybe four. I can't remember."

Maerose's disclosure has its desired effect. Dominic slaps her for speaking so coarsely to him, but he's foaming-at-the-mouth furious at Charley. Maerose then goads him further: "Papa, you should see the size of him . . ."

A seething Dominic interrupts, yelling, "How can you say such things to your father? Where is your honor?"

Maerose, playing the disgraced *puttana*, replies, "Papa, I have no honor anymore."

Maerose expertly exploits her father's mafioso obsession with "honor" to get what she wants. She knows Dominic will take action to avenge the family's good name, and that this inevitably will "schrew" things up for Charley and his bride. She helps matters along by giving Don Corrado some photos that prove that Irene not only ripped off the Prizzis but in the process murdered one of their men.

This sets off a series of maneuvers and countermaneuvers by the Prizzis, Charley, and Irene, all of them scrambling to protect their positions and stay alive. Dominic puts out a contract on Charley, hiring Irene as the contractor, not knowing that this talented freelance assassin is married to the intended victim. His hypertension and ulcers exacerbated by Maerose's revelations, Dominic begins to lose control. He foolishly antagonizes a rival mafia gang and ends up murdered. Don Corrado, meanwhile, decides to bring Charley back into the fold. He will make him boss of the Prizzi family, but only if he whacks Irene. Charley balks, but eventually comes around: "The family is the only place I can be. I know that," he says, accepting the inevitable.

The denouement occurs in Irene's California home, where she and Charley meet for the last time. They undress for bed, but both are prepared not for sex but for murder. Irene, no fool, realizes that Charley's lifelong ties to the Prizzis trump his loyalty to her. She emerges from the bathroom pistol in hand, but Charley is quicker: he hurls his concealed knife at her, with such force that she is pinned to the wall.

A bachelor once again, Charley returns to New York, calls Maerose, and asks her to dinner. He tells her that Irene will not be joining them. "How about it?" he dully says to Maerose.

"How about it?" squeals the triumphant Maerose, all girlish enthusiasm. "Holy cow, Charley! Just tell me where you want to meet!"

Maerose Prizzi, the spurned fiancée and disgraced daughter, proves herself a master strategist capable of outscheming men who consider themselves the ultimate schemers. In the famous image from *The Godfather* movie poster, a hand manipulates puppets on a string. In *Prizzi's*

Honor, it is not some all-powerful don who has everyone dancing; this time the puppet master is a woman.

Compared to Maerose Prizzi, Angela De Marco is an innocent. The heroine of *Married to the Mob*, Jonathan Demme's 1988 gangland spoof, Angela lives in wedded unbliss with Frank "the Cucumber" De Marco, a mafia hit man. Angela is played by Michelle Pfeiffer, and surprisingly enough, what seems like absurd miscasting—Pfeiffer's blond, blue-eyed Nordic beauty would have made Hitler swoon—actually works. Pfeiffer convincingly pulls off the transformation into an Italian American suburban princess—or rather, a comically exaggerated version of one, complete with nasal Long Island accent, big hair, press-on nails, and appliqué sweaters.

Angela may look like a caricature, but beneath the flashy facade there's genuine anguish. She has come to hate her existence, with its corruption and violence and constant threat of prison. "I want a normal life!" she yells at Frank. "Everything we wear, everything we eat, everything we own, fell off a truck . . . Everything has blood on it," she shouts at her husband. Frank, played by Alec Baldwin with delicious comic flair—he's deeply impressed by his own studliness and skill with a pistol—is unmoved. When Angela pleads for a divorce, Frank laughs at her and tells her to take a Valium, the mother's little helper favored by the other gangster wives of their acquaintance.

Seeing no way out, Angela resigns herself and her son Joey to a life of crime. But fate, in the person of mob boss Tony "the Tiger" Russo, suddenly intervenes. When Tony discovers that Frank has been putting the moves on one of his gumads, he has Frank killed. And with Frank out of the way, he can pursue Angela, whom he's coveted for years. Not wasting any time, he approaches Angela at the reception following Frank's funeral. After she rebuffs him, she decides the time is right for her and her son to escape the life she has come to loathe. They flee Long Island and move to a funky little apartment on Manhattan's Lower East Side.

Angela naively thinks she's finally free. But in reality, she's being pursued not only by an amorous Tony, despite her rejections, but by

Mike Downey (Matthew Modine) as well, an undercover FBI agent. Mike at first believes that Angela is Tony's new girlfriend, and can lead him to the mob boss. But he falls for Angela, as she does for him, setting off some mildly engrossing plot complications that are resolved in a shoot-'em-up in Miami.

Married to the Mob is an innocuous but generally entertaining entry in the mob movie canon. Its pleasures are chiefly the performances of Pfeiffer, Dean Stockwell as Tony Russo, and Mercedes Ruehl, who nearly steals the film as Tony's ball-breaking wife, Connie. Demme also makes good use of music to comment on the action and to accompany Angela's metamorphosis, from reggae to pop to new wave, not to mention "Mambo Italiano," the campy Rosemary Clooney number that opens the film ("Go, go, go, you mixed-up Siciliano!").

Demme's film is a lightweight confection, but it nonetheless leaves an unpleasant aftertaste. When Angela moves to the Lower East Side, she finds a hip, multicultural community that accepts her as a kindred spirit. She falls in with Rita Harcourt, a West Indian beautician (played by reggae singer Sister Carol East) who transforms her mall hair into a new, sleeker cut, and gives the suburban refugee her first real job at her salon.

Angela manages to flee the poisonous mob clan on Long Island and create a groovy new family in downtown Manhattan—where apparently she is the only Italian American. She not only escapes the mob, she also escapes her ethnic background, which is equated with organized crime. The possibility of friendship and community with other Italian Americans doesn't exist for Angela because there are no decent Italian Americans. In Demme's scheme, the Italian men are all dangerous hoods, the Italian women are all tacky, greedy, and neurotic. Angela can thrive and find happiness only with hipsters—and an FBI agent—in an urban bohemia, seen here as a wop-free zone.

Abel Ferrara, the Bronx-born, Italian American director known for lurid, ultraviolent films such as *The Driller Killer* and *King of New York*, made his foray into the organized crime genre with *The Funeral* (1996). Ferrara and his longtime screenwriter Nicholas St. John, both from Roman Catholic backgrounds, typically use film genres—supernatural horror in *The Addiction*, the detective story in *Bad Lieutenant*—to explore knotty moral and spiritual questions. In *The Funeral*, they strip away all the self-serving justifications for the mob life to show how the mafioso's obsession with honor and revenge devastates an Italian American family.

The story, set in the late 1930s, centers on the three Tempio brothers, Ray (Christopher Walken), the eldest and the leader; Chez (Christopher Penn), mentally unstable and a walking time bomb; and Johnny (Vincent Gallo), the youngest, a sensitive type with a passion for movies and books. The Tempios were born into organized crime. (Their surname means "temple," a nice irony given that their crimes have defiled what are supposed to be the sacred bonds of family.) Their father, Ray Sr., initiated his eldest son into the family's culture of violence by forcing him to commit murder when he was only a youth. The Tempio brothers live by their father's credo that you should never show mercy to your enemies because if you do, they will come back to kill you.

The film opens with the funeral of Johnny, who has been shot to death by an unknown assailant outside of the movie theater where he has just seen *The Petrified Forest*. (The 1936 Warner Brothers drama would appeal to Johnny: it stars Humphrey Bogart as Duke Mantee, a gangster who despite the blood on his hands clings to some decency and integrity.) Ray suspects Gaspare Spoglia (Benicio Del Toro), a rival gangster, mostly because Johnny was having an affair with Spoglia's wife. Faithful to the code drummed into him by his father, Ray must track down Gaspare and take his revenge.

But Gaspare and Johnny also had bitter political differences. Johnny, who had hoped to break free from the family business, was a Communist sympathizer who opposed Spoglia's strikebreaking tactics against unionized workers. Ray doesn't share his younger brother's politics, but he seems to respect them. When Ray confronts Gaspare, the suspected killer denounces Johnny as an anarchist. Ray immediately corrects him: "No, my brother was a Communist."

A left-wing, pro-union gangster is an interesting conceit, but not a credible one. Mafiosi exploit the existing order; they are not out to reform it. Gangsters historically have violently opposed reformist and rev-olutionary movements, in America and in Italy, and when they have political allegiances, they tend to be conservative, as Joseph Pistone has noted. Carlo Tresca, the great radical labor leader of the 1930s, was assassinated in New York by a mafioso. The leaders of American la-bor purged Communists, but not the gangsters who infiltrated and corrupted unions, particularly the building trades. Sicilian mafiosi, un-alterably opposed to any change in the status quo, were killing Com-munists and leftist labor leaders as late as the 1980s. But if Ferrara's historical revisionism defies reality, it is nonetheless a novel element that flouts the usual mob movie clichés.

As the two surviving Tempio brothers seek to avenge their brother's murder—Ray with a degree of calm and rationality, explosive Chez tee-tering on the edge of insanity—the women in their lives suffer the con-sequences of living with these violent men. The two main female characters—Ray's wife, Jean (Annabella Sciorra), and Chez's wife, Clara (Isabella Rossellini)—are intelligent, well-spoken, and painfully aware of their own victimization. Jean keeps a statue of Saint Agnes next to her bed, to remind herself of "what happens when you say no." (Agnes, whose name means "lamb" or "victim" in Latin, was an early Christian martyr, who, legend has it, was beheaded at age twelve be-cause she refused to renounce her faith.) Clara similarly keeps a fig-urine of Saint Dymphna, the patron of the mentally ill.

Both women have had enough of vengeance and violence. After Johnny is killed, Jean tells Johnny's fiancée, "We ought to be throwing you a party because of this. You ought to be celebrating the fact that you're not going to become one of their wives." Annabella Sciorra, a powerful actress whose intelligence always illuminates her perfor-mances, creates a Jean who sees clearly and tells the truth about the Tempios. She is, in fact, the moral center of the film. She has had some college, and she realizes what she has given up to marry into a world that she now desperately wants to escape. She pleads, in vain, for Ray to forgo the vengeance that his "honor" demands.

It is Jean who delivers the film's devastating verdict on the Tempios, and by extension on organized crime in general and its twisted men-of-honor mystique. "Tempios pass themselves off as tough, rugged individuals, and we fall for it," she bitterly observes. "But they're criminals. They're criminals because they've never risen above their heartless, il- literate upbringing. And there's nothing, absolutely nothing romantic about it."

In *Goodfellas*, Karen Hill, like Kay Corleone, is an outsider, a Jew in a predominantly Italian American world. Karen is married to Henry Hill, the half-Sicilian, half-Irish protagonist of Martin Scorsese's 1990 film based on the exploits of the Brooklyn-based mob crew that pulled off the $6 million Lufthansa Airlines heist at Kennedy Airport in 1978. Unlike Kay, she isn't disgusted by mob life. Her perspective is more complicated.

When she and Henry begin to date, Karen is dazzled by Henry's world and the perks they enjoy because of his connections. Even so, she views this peculiar tribal subculture with a critical and at times be- mused eye. But with total immersion in mob life, she gradually loses her outsider's perspective and comes to love the high-rolling lifestyle her husband provides. Even when things go bad and the consequences of living outside the law come crashing down on her, she never jumps off the ride. She is a forceful personality who gives as good as she gets. In Lorraine Bracco's sexy-smart performance, Karen is a "bad" girl "who enjoys danger, sex, and drugs."[15]

Henry and Karen's courtship gets off to a rocky start. When Henry (Ray Liotta) fails to show up for a date, Karen forces Tommy De Vito, the psycho killer memorably played by Joe Pesci, to drive her to track him down. Spotting him at a taxi stand in Brooklyn where he is hanging out with his hoodlum pals, she leaps out of the car screaming, "You've got some nerve! Standing me up. Nobody does that to me. Who do you think you are, a big shot?"

Which is exactly what he thinks he is. Henry is embarrassed by be- ing called out by a woman in front of his friends, but he's also capti- vated: "She's screaming on the street and I mean loud, but she looked good."

Henry introduces Karen to his world of nightclubs, of wiseguys and their flashily dressed women. She's impressed by the deference people show him and the special treatment he gets, like ringside tables at the Copacabana. His life strikes her as glamorous and exciting, and she wants to be a part of it. (When she asks him what he does, he tells her that he's in construction.) One night, early in their relationship, Henry pistol-whips a young Jewish guy from her neighborhood after Karen tells him the neighbor had tried to sexually assault her. He gives her the pistol to hide, and, as the camera closes in on the gun in her hand, Karen speaks to the audience in voice-over: "I know there are women, like my best friends, who would have gotten out of there the minute their boyfriend gave them a gun to hide. 'Feh, you and your gun. Get out of here. Who needs you?' That's what they would have said. But I didn't. I've got to admit the truth. It turned me on."

Karen marries Henry, to her parents' dismay. Similarly, his relatives are far from overjoyed that he's married a Jew. But Karen soon learns that her husband's blood relations aren't his only kin. "It was like he had two families," she says. "The first time I was introduced to them all at once, it was crazy. Paulie [Paul Vario, the mob boss played by Paul Sorvino] and his brothers had lots of sons and nephews and almost all of them were named Peter or Paul. It was unbelievable. There must have been two dozen Peters and Pauls at the wedding. Plus, they were all married to girls named Marie, and they named all their daughters Marie. By the time I finished meeting everybody I thought I was drunk."

If Karen doesn't immediately get that her husband's second family is La Cosa Nostra, she soon realizes what kind of life she married into. For one thing, her husband stays out all night bouncing with his buddies, and doesn't call home. Her distraught mother wails, "Normal people don't live this way!"

Up to this point, Henry has narrated *Goodfellas*. But once he marries Karen and brings her into his world, the film's perspective shifts to hers. Karen goes to a get-together given by one of the mob wives, and in voice-over describes what she sees. "We weren't married to nine-to-five guys, but the first time I realized how different it was was when Mickey [another mob wife] had a hostess party."

One woman complains about being sexually harassed at her job, but she won't mention it to her husband because she knows he'd kill the harasser and would be sent away for life. "It's disgusting what you have to put up with," she says. Another wife endures even worse travails. Her older son has shot another kid in "a lousy ten-dollar card game." When the grandmother of the shooter hears that her grandson has been arrested, she dies of a heart attack. "Now Jeannie's got a husband and son in jail and a mother in the funeral parlor," remarks one of the woman's friends.

Karen gives us more of her unsparing observations of the mob wives: "They had bad skin and wore too much makeup. I mean, they didn't look very good. They looked beat-up." This ugliness, which extends to bad teeth and poor dress, permeates their domestic lives: "They talked about how rotten their kids were and about beating them with broom handles and leather belts, but that the kids still didn't pay any attention."

But when Karen voices her misgivings about their way of life to Henry, he dismisses them and tells her he's about to come into big money. "Do you think I'm going to walk away from that?" He tries to calm his wife's fears about the likely consequences of his line of work: "Nobody goes to jail unless they want to, unless they make themselves get caught."

"After a while," Karen tells us, "it all got to be normal. None of it seemed like crimes. It was more that Henry was enterprising. That he and the guys were making a few bucks hustling while other men were sitting on their asses waiting for handouts. Our husbands weren't brain surgeons. They were blue collar guys, and the only way they could get extra money, real extra money, was to go out and cut a few corners."

Karen finds herself drawn deeper into mob life, and enjoying it. Her narration makes this society of outlaws sound like a cult: "And we were also very close. I mean, there were never any outsiders. Absolutely never! And being together all the time made everything seem even more normal." She repeatedly uses "normal" to describe her and Henry's lives, as if she were trying to convince herself and also to silence the nagging voice of her mother screaming, "Normal people don't live like this!"

Sure enough, Henry is eventually arrested, after he and another hood threaten to throw a bookie who owes them money into the lions' cage at a Florida zoo. (*Goodfellas* is nothing if not colorful.) He is sentenced to ten years in prison, and Karen dutifully visits him, smuggling in Italian cold cuts and cheeses, and marijuana. During his imprisonment the affluence Karen had enjoyed turns to hardship. She complains to Henry that she receives no support from his associates, not even from boss Paulie Vario. Karen at this point could have decided to divorce Henry and go back to her parents, but she's too stubborn for that, and she still loves her husband. So she waits, like a good mob wife.

And when Henry is released after serving four years of his sentence, he immediately goes back to his old ways, dealing cocaine and heroin and eventually becoming addicted. The drug profits enable the Hills to become bourgeois once again; in one sad-funny scene, Karen proudly shows off her garishly overdecorated home to her friends. Karen now is no longer ambivalent, no longer the outsider whose enjoyment of her life is colored by the occasional misgiving. She becomes her husband's accomplice, hiding guns for him and helping herself to the drugs that support her comfortable lifestyle. When the feds raid her home, she tucks a pistol in her panties and flushes coke down the toilet.

Henry's second arrest, on federal drug charges, sends the Hills on a downward spiral. Money, or rather the lack of it, once again becomes a problem. But this time the couple has more to worry about than how to pay the bills. Henry is in serious trouble with his mob confreres. Paulie Vario is furious at Henry for disobeying his order not to get involved with drugs. Jimmy Conway, who engineered the crew's Lufthansa Airlines heist at Kennedy Airport, fears Henry will rat on him and the rest of the gang in exchange for leniency from the feds. Henry realizes that with his and Karen's lives in danger from his fellow gangsters, his only option is to inform and, with Karen and their kids, go into the federal witness protection program.

The government successfully prosecutes Henry's associates, sending Conway, Vario, and others away for lengthy prison sentences. The Hills suffer their own form of incarceration: they are relocated to some nowhere town in the Midwest, where, as Henry laments, it is impossible to find decent Italian food. The film's narrative voice once again becomes Henry's. *Goodfellas* began with him announcing, "As far back as I can remember, I always wanted to be a gangster." It ends with him bemoaning the fact that "I'm an average nobody. I get to live the rest of my life like a schnook."

The last time we see Karen is in the offices of the feds, where she and Henry are trying to negotiate the terms of their existence as protected witnesses. Karen only asks that their kids' education not be disrupted and that the Hills not be relocated to a cold place because Henry is "very bronchial." But what does she want for herself? We never find out, though it's hard to imagine this New York good-time girl enjoying her new life. We can be pretty sure that while she's glad to be alive and that her family is intact, she, like Henry, misses the thrills from the good old bad old days, when, as Henry says, "We had it all for the asking."

The history of the gangster genre includes a few women who refused to be silenced or shunted aside by the men in their lives, but it wasn't until *The Sopranos* that a full female chorus emerged to cut through the high-testosterone din of the wiseguys. If "the distance from Michael to Henry Hill to Tony can be plotted in terms of their relation to women," as Donatelli and Alward claim, then the genre traveled light-years to end up in suburban New Jersey.[16]

For the first time, women are not secondary characters in the Mafia myth; they are an integral part of the show's dense, novelistic texture. The women of *The Sopranos* are mothers and wives, but they're not confined by those roles, which, moreover, are no longer lived the way they were in the 1950s, when Michael and Kay were young marrieds. They are also conniving sisters and headstrong daughters, volatile gumads and tragic strippers, dedicated psychiatrists and other accomplished professionals, mob associates, and even bosses. Women are victims and victimizers; they suffer from male power and violence, and they are complicit with it and reap its material rewards. They take the dominance of men for a fact of life, but they also resist it. And as the show's alpha male knows all too well, they wield power, too, not through violence (with the exception of Tony's out-of-control sister Janice), but in subtler and often more effective ways.

"Carmela Soprano, Livia, Janice, or even Meadow dreading Tony—please! No one is ever again going to slam the door in the face of these powerful, angry women, or he will regret it," note Donatelli and Alward, invoking the women of the Soprano family.[17]

The show's complex and ever-surprising treatment of gender relations is, in fact, one of its most original elements. That and the show's candor about sexuality, and not only the hetero variety, are as essential to its reinvention of the gangster genre as the suburban setting and the focus on the intrapsychic and domestic realms.

Women are so central to the series that the online journal *Salon* asked, "Is *The Sopranos* a chick show?"[18]

Regina Barreca, a feminist academic and *Sopranos* fan who has edited a book of essays about the series, says that at various times she has identified with almost every female character, admiring their "intelligence, wit, and the absolute refusal to be played for a sucker . . ."[19] She also identifies with them because "they are familiar and because they are unpredictable."[20]

"These two elements," Barreca observes, "are rarely paired in the development of women on television or on film. If the female characters run to types we know—the elderly mother, the cuckolded wife, the recently educated daughter—we imagine we can predict precisely how they will react within any framework." But "when we meet these characters in *The Sopranos* . . . all bets are off." The mother, instead of "weep[ing] and cring[ing] in fear of abandonment," schemes to have her son killed because he moved her from her longtime abode into a nursing home. The wife, "upon discovering her husband waist-deep in infidelity . . . embarks on a shopping spree while at a four-star hotel in Rome." The daughter goes to Columbia University, where she loses her virginity to her half-black, half-Jewish boyfriend, and "learns to despise her father not only for his lack of ethics but for his lack of sophistication."[21]

By being "courageous enough to braid together the domestic and the sexual, the educated and the nurturing, the Machiavellian and the maternal," David Chase "clears new ground for the women," says Barreca. "Neither madonnas nor whores (even the whores are not your ordinary whores—they too have complicated inner lives), the female characters in *The Sopranos* make life difficult for their men—and for their viewers, even those of us who identify with them."[22]

Taking exception to those Italian Americans who have derided the show's characters as crude and insulting caricatures, Barreca says, "When I watch *The Sopranos*, it's as if I'm watching a documentary about my relatives—except of course, for the Mafioso business and money stuff. Which, as far as I am concerned, are the least interesting parts" of the show.[23]

Barreca's point about the believability of the characters is entirely missed by the show's Italian American critics, who decry them as mere stereotypes foisted on the public by the supposedly self-hating David Chase and HBO. Though their behavior is often extreme and hardly admirable, both the women and the men on the show are real enough to give Italian American viewers a powerful shock of recognition.

Let's start with Livia, the Soprano matriarch. Tony's mom is "the mother of nightmares," says Barreca, "the pitiful, dependent, unloving woman who demands but never offers pity, support, or love."[24] She indeed is "fiendishly malignant," as Barreca describes her. But is she unbelievable, a cartoon of malevolence, as critics of the show have charged? Not to Barreca. "I knew Livia," she asserts. She likens Tony's mother to one of her own critical, downbeat, nonnurturing aunts.

Regina Barreca, meet Kenneth Ciongoli. A surgeon by profession and an antidefamation activist by avocation, Ciongoli is the vice chairman and a former president of the National Italian American Foundation (NIAF), the Washington, D.C.–based organization that has been at the forefront of the opposition to David Chase's series.

"*The Sopranos* gives me an ulcer," he says. "I cannot watch that program without being infuriated by it. Particularly because of the outrageous casting and the stereotyping—particularly of the mother, who, as I have said publicly, would not exist in our culture. She is an interfering woman who uses incredible profanity when speaking to her son and put a contract on her son's life. The reason it's important to be specific about that is because the mother-son bond is the strongest sociological bond in our culture. It defines our culture in many ways. David Chase should be ashamed of himself, and his mother must not be Italian."[25]

Ciongoli is wrong about Chase's mother, who is an Italian American, and his assessment of Livia Soprano is equally wide of the mark. Neither stereotype nor anomaly, Livia represents a type of southern

Italian woman described by the great Sicilian author Leonardo Sciascia (1922–1989), whose novels and stories probe the insidious effects of mafia violence and corruption on his homeland's entire social order. "The Mezzogiorno woman has that *terrible* quality," he wrote. "How many crimes of honor has she provoked, instigated, or encouraged! Women who are mothers, mothers-in-law. They are capable of the worst kinds of wickedness just in order to make up for the vexations they themselves were subjected to when they were young, as part of a terrifying social conformism."[26]

This is Livia Soprano to a T. But as Sciascia wisely reminds us, such women are not born that way; their "terrible" quality is produced by oppression, by a sex/gender regime that subjects women to innumerable "vexations."

Livia certainly experienced hers, as the daughter of immigrants who no doubt maintained Mezzogiorno traditions of male dominance and female subordination, and as the wife of a gangster who enjoyed the prerogatives of his world. A typical wiseguy, John Soprano, as previously mentioned, had women on the side, and he was with one of his gumads the night Livia had a miscarriage and was hospitalized. Her children grew up feeling the full force of her self-pity and rage, her selfishness and lack of compassion. In a flashback sequence, a young Livia threatens to murder her children rather than move to Nevada, as her husband would like, and it's no idle threat. She is Medea in a housedress, ready to avenge the slights and humiliations of her life on her children.

Livia Soprano is the descendant of another Mediterranean matriarch, her Roman namesake, known to fans of *I, Claudius* (both the Robert Graves novel and the celebrated television series) as the grasping and dangerous grandmother of the title character. Compared to her forebear, the New Jersey mob mother is a pussycat. She just poisons the air of family life; Livia of antiquity literally poisoned her enemies and rivals.

Tony and his sister Janice, faced with such a vindictive and unloving mother, responded differently. (Barbara, the third Soprano sibling, was smart enough to flee the family, returning only for Livia's funeral.) Janice truly is a piece of work. An ex-hippie who lived on a commune and called herself Parvati, she's unmistakably her mother's daughter—

"neurotic, caustic, manipulative, and irresponsible, bent on attributing to others the failures and problems of her own life and blind to her own part in the creation of these problems."[27]

Livia is a classic passive-aggressive type, constantly moaning that she's just a helpless old lady while she wreaks psychological and emotional havoc. Janice is just aggressive, and she's unafraid to go to extremes. She purports to be a feminist, but she puts up with her fiancé Richie Aprile's sexual perversity—he likes to hold a gun to her head during sex. She has her limits, though. One evening over dinner, when Richie expresses his displeasure at something she says by belting her in the mouth, she grabs his gun and blows him away. Some time later, she complains to Tony that she "was supposed to be married at this point in my life . . . the man I loved died," as if she had had absolutely nothing to do with his demise.

Janice subsequently has an affair with Ralphie Cifaretto, a viciously misogynistic mafia captain and sexual masochist who, according to Janice, "can't even get a hard-on unless he's in some kind of pain." And when she's decided she's had enough of creepy Ralphie, she dismisses him by shoving him down a flight of stairs.

After Livia dies, Janice moves into her house, certain that she'll find a mother lode of hidden wealth. She is indignant when she learns that Livia has bequeathed her valuable record collection to her former housekeeper Svetlana, a Russian émigré. She demands it back; Svetlana refuses. Janice then ups the ante. Svetlana is an amputee, so Janice steals her artificial leg, relinquishing it only after some Russian thugs rough her up. When Tony picks his sister up from a hospital emergency room, she tells him she has experienced an epiphany. Stealing a prosthetic limb was the lowest thing she'd done, and the only way she can redeem herself is by dedicating her life to God. Not surprisingly, Janice's born-again phase lasts about as long as her engagement to Richie.

After Richie and Ralphie (why do these guys always have *boys'* names?), Janice finally finds a good man. Relatively speaking, that is, since Bobby "Baccala" Bacillieri is a member of Tony's crew. Bobby is so devoted to his wife, Karen, that he, alone among Tony's boys, does not have a gumad, and when Karen is killed in a car accident, he is inconsolable. Impressed, even touched by Bobby's unabashed grieving, Janice sets her sights on him, fending off all competitors, including other mob widows. She impatiently waits for Bobby to let go of "his dead, idealized wife." When he finally agrees to let Janice serve the last baked ziti Karen had left in the freezer, she knows she has won.

Bobby and Janice wed, but bliss is in short supply. Janice, like her mother, is no font of maternal love and nurturance, and she has a hard time adjusting to her new status as stepmother to Bobby and Karen's two kids. And marriage to the calm, easygoing Bobby does nothing to temper her Soprano rage. At a peewee soccer game, Janice becomes infuriated when a member of the opposing team trips her stepdaughter Sophia. She attacks the kid's mother and ends up under arrest for assault. "That bitch is lucky I didn't kill her," Janice mutters.

Bobby tells Janice that although he likes "a spitfire type," he has had it with her violent temper. He delivers an ultimatum: either Janice seeks help from an anger management specialist, or "this thing with us ain't gonna work out." Janice reluctantly consults a therapist, who during a session asks, "You're angry—what are your actual physical sensations right now?" Janice, in touch with her feelings, replies, "I'd like to punch you in the face."

The Sopranos reverses the typical patriarchal trope of the mob genre: this time it is the mother's sins that are visited upon the son. Tony, the big bad gangster who strangles mob traitors, has been permanently scarred by Livia's emotional violence. She menaced him when he was under her roof—in therapy Tony recalls her threatening to poke his eye out with a fork—but now that he's an adult she has become literally lethal to him. In classic mafia style, she gives tacit permission to Corrado Soprano, her brother-in-law and Tony's uncle, to whack her son—all because he moved her into a nursing home after she absentmindedly caused a fire in her kitchen and accidentally ran over one of her friends with her car. Raised by this scary mother and forced into his father's way of life, he is wracked with rage, which he turns on others in acts of brutality and turns inward on himself, resulting in depression and panic attacks so severe that he blacks out.

Tony, though, is fortunate to be married to Carmela De Angelis Soprano, who genuinely loves him and their children. Carmela—as played superbly by Edie Falco, a soulful performer who is a "genius at moods," as Pauline Kael once said of the Australian actress Judy Davis—is the most complex and compelling woman character in the history of the gangster genre.

Through Carmela, *The Sopranos* explores issues affecting women more incisively and fearlessly than any program on the women's cable TV networks Lifetime and Oprah Winfrey's Oxygen. Carmela struggles constantly with "the trade-offs between fidelity and cold cash, Catholic guilt over divorce, stifled professional and sexual desires, a biting jealousy that threatens to overtake her happiness for a daughter on the brink of a much happier life than she will ever know," as Rebecca Traister observes.[28]

Carmela is the soul of *The Sopranos*, and she moves us more than any other character. She has been victimized by her husband, and particularly by his sexual indiscretions with his various gumads. But she revels in the upper-middle-class lifestyle his illicit earnings provide her and their children. She suffers genuine anguish over the life she has chosen, even admitting that she has sold her soul to the devil. "I have let evil in my house," she says, truthfully but disingenuously, since she knew who Tony was when she married him.

In *Reversible Destiny*, their study of Sicilian mafia groups, the American academics Jane and Peter Schneider observe, "A mafia wife cannot be ignorant of her husband's status and may well play an active role in promoting that status by hosting his friends, running some of his affairs, and generally basking in the reflection of his prestige and the goods his money buys."[29]

Carmela's conflicts notwithstanding, this sad-eyed, sympathetic woman has more in common with her Sicilian counterparts than she'd care to admit. At times she has been Tony's willing accomplice; in one episode, she helps him hide some heavy artillery from the FBI. She's also unafraid to trade on Tony's fearsome reputation when it suits her.

In one of the show's most famous episodes, Carmela requests a letter of recommendation to Georgetown University for her daughter Meadow from her neighbor Jean Cusamano's sister, a high-powered attorney and a Georgetown alumna. The sister is reluctant, but when Carmela shows up bearing a freshly baked ricotta pie and a none-too-subtle reminder of who her husband is, she promises to write the letter. Carmela smiles sweetly, enjoying her triumph. But she's too much the tough cookie to trust a verbal promise. When Jean Cusamano later tells Carmela that the letter has been written, Carmela demands a copy.

No feminist, Carmela stays in a marriage that often demeans her. She regards herself as a good Catholic, so divorce is out of the question. But that doesn't mean that she doesn't long for some extramarital sexual and romantic fulfillment. She responds to the overtures of Furio Giunta, the passionate, pony-tailed Neapolitan who busts heads for her husband. "He looks at me like I'm beautiful," Carmela sighs to her friend Rosie Aprile, who sagely advises her, "If you haven't slept with him yet, don't." Furio, realizing that he can have Carmela only if he kills Tony, flees to Napoli.

Carmela gets another chance at romance during the series' fifth season. She and Tony are no longer living together; she threw him out after his Russian gumad Irina called her to say, "Tony loves me. If it wasn't for his kids, you would be out on street." Tony arrived home to find his golf clubs thrown in the driveway and Carmela ready to do the same to him. "You've made a fool of me for years with these whores," she screamed, "and now it's come into our home!"

During her separation from Tony, she accepts a dinner invitation from Bob Wegler, a counselor at her son A.J.'s school. After dinner, they end up in bed. For the first time in twenty years, Carmela has sex with a man other than Tony Soprano, and she's ecstatic. The tryst becomes a full-fledged romance, and she intends to pursue it, despite her own misgivings and the disapproval of Father Intintola, her confessor. But one night after sex, Bob unexpectedly announces that they should "take a time-out." He's angry at himself and at Carmela because he strong-armed one of A.J.'s teachers into inflating the underperforming brat's grade on a term paper. He claims Carmela had sex with him to get him to do it. "You used your pussy to get what you wanted," he bluntly tells her. Wounded but furious, she storms out, and the affair is *finito*.

Unlike the incident involving the ricotta pie and the implicit threat to Jean Cusamano's sister, this time being married to the mob hasn't worked to Carmela's advantage. She sinks into depression, and when her father comments on her mood, she tells him, "Whatever I say, whatever I do, because I was married to a man like Tony, my motives will always be called into question."

And she soon finds out that her attempts to put her marriage in the past tense are doomed. She informs Tony that she intends to begin divorce proceedings and will "aggressively pursue . . . an equitable distribution of our assets." But Tony has no intention of letting her go. He visits every prominent and highly recommended divorce attorney Carmela contacts, precluding them from representing her. When she finally does hire a willing attorney, he can't find an accountant who is unafraid to investigate Tony's finances.

Outmaneuvered by Tony, Carmela sets out to negotiate a mutually beneficial reconciliation with him. He's tired of living on his own, and wants to come home. Carmela is willing to let him, provided he meets her terms. She demands a promise that from now on there'll be no more gumads. His legalistic response doesn't definitively rule out future liaisons, but it's good enough to satisfy Carmela: "I swear to you on our children," he vows, "that my midlife crisis problems will no longer intrude on you anymore." Carmela also wants "something else in her life"—a career in real estate. She plans to build a house on speculation and needs $600,000 for a plot of land. Tony gulps, but agrees. The deal concluded, he moves back home. Over dinner with Carmela and A.J., he makes a champagne toast: "To the people I love. Nothing else matters."

The reconciliation of Tony and Carmela is of a piece with the series' uncompromisingly dark view of heterosexual relations and "family values." Love is a battlefield, as the eighties rocker Pat Benatar told us, but it's also a marketplace where men and women try to make the best deals for themselves. The men have the advantage, but women have some bargaining chips—mainly sex and their domestic labor, the things men need. Genuine love and desire may figure in the transaction, but they are inextricably bound up with economics.

Mafia wives are, of course, hardly the only women to prostitute themselves and their self-respect for financial security. The difference between the women at the Bada Bing strip club, who sell themselves by the hour, and Carmela Soprano, who does it for the suburban mansion, the credit cards, and the $600,000, has more to do with socioeconomic class than morality. Carmela is hardly unique in loving a man who abuses and betrays her but is a "good provider." Her situation illustrates the feminist argument that women collude in their own oppression to a greater extent and in more complex ways than do other dominated and oppressed groups.

But that doesn't mean Carmela is completely overmatched in her marital *lucha libre* with Tony. He needs her not only to take care of the home front but also to keep him tethered to some decency and normality, to make him believe he is not a "toxic person." She and their daughter, Meadow, are the best things in his life, and, as Dr. Melfi tells him, he will never leave her. This gives Carmela whatever power she has over her errant husband.

Signora Soprano may have her woes, but one thing she can count on is that Tony will never physically harm her. Other women in Sopranoland aren't so fortunate. The series is often shockingly frank about the brutalization of women by men. The list of dead and wounded includes Tracey, the twenty-year-old pregnant stripper beaten to death by Ralph Cifaretto ("She was just a whore," according to her killer); "lady shylock" Lorraine Calluzzo, shot to death while naked and on her hands and knees for failing to "kick up" money to a mob boss; Jennifer Melfi, raped in a parking garage by a young thug; and Adriana La Cerva, the fiancée of Christopher Moltisanti, battered by the man she loves and finally murdered after she confesses to him that she has been forced into informing for the FBI.

The Sopranos recognizes that we live in a world where equality between the genders is a chimera, and that women, with limited opportunities for freedom and autonomy, and faced with the prospect of male violence, must strike the best deals they can. Carmela at least recognizes her dilemma—she loves and needs a man who does her wrong, so how does she make the best of it? That may not be an "empowering" message, but it is a realistic one.

In the third season of *The Sopranos*, Tony meets a woman who is his equal, Gloria Trillo, a Mercedes-Benz saleswoman whom he encounters in Dr. Melfi's waiting room. Gloria doesn't need his money because she is successful in her own right. Unlike his previous gumads, she's smart, independent, and Italian. Tony is so taken by this sultry beauty that he doesn't stop to consider that maybe it's not a great idea to become involved with a fellow psychiatric patient. And for a while their affair makes him happy. The thirty-something Gloria is no young bimbo or *puttana*, but she is a sexually free spirit who'll make love with him in the reptile house at a zoo. During a session with Dr. Melfi, Tony tells his psychiatrist that Gloria makes him feel better than "your Prozac and therapy bullshit combined."

What Tony doesn't know is that Gloria is a severely depressed woman who attempted suicide after the breakup of her last relationship. Soon enough, she unleashes her pathology, her unpredictable and volatile moods, her extreme neediness. Tony confides to Melfi his fear that Gloria may be a "full-blown loopty-loo," but he's hooked on her and the drama of their affair and can't stay away. *"Amour fou,"* Melfi remarks.

And a crazy love it indeed is. One night, when Tony shows up late to dinner at her place, a seething Gloria flings the London broil she has cooked at him. Even worse, she threatens Tony's domestic life by arranging to meet Carmela and then calling her at home, ostensibly to talk about new cars. A furious Tony tells Gloria she has crossed the line, and he doesn't want to see her again. But when she later calls him, hysterically sobbing, he pays her a visit. They start arguing, and Tony tells her he's had enough and heads for the door. Gloria again threatens to tell Carmela about their affair.

That blunder detonates Tony's terrifying rage. He chases Gloria, overturning furniture, and throws her to the floor. When he hears her say, "Oh poor you," he realizes that Gloria's bottomless self-pity and vindictiveness are exactly the same as Livia's. "I didn't just meet you, I've known you all my life!" he cries. He has his hands around her throat, and as he throttles her she manages to whisper, "Kill me." Tony pulls back from the abyss, and flees, leaving her there on the floor.

In a series that has offered many moments of riveting drama, the showdown between Tony and Gloria stands out as one of the most emotionally explosive and most difficult to watch. But, horrified though

A WOP

A pound of spaghett' and a red-a bandan'
A stilet' and a corduroy suit;
Add garlic wat make for him stronga da
mus'
And a talent for black-a da boot!

Depictions of southern Italian men as brutish, even apelike, and suited only for menial work commonly appeared in mainstream publications during the peak years of immigration to the United States. (*Life*, 1911, Historical Pictures Service)

Coming to America: In Francis Ford Coppola's celebrated film saga, young Vito Andolini (Oreste Baldini, at left, in cap) gets his first glimpse of New York, where he will grow up to become Don Corleone, the mythic "Godfather" of organized crime. (Photofest)

Immigrant street life in New York's Little Italy, a scene replicated in many American cities in the early decades of the twentieth century. (Library of Congress)

Tony Camonte, the mobster played by Yiddish theater star Paul Muni (right) in Howard Hawks's 1932 *Scarface*, was based on Chicago gangland king Al Capone. As Camonte rises in the underworld, he becomes more American, leaving behind his greenhorn qualities—his accent, hand gestures, and cheap wardrobe. (Photofest)

Al Capone, the real "Scarface," shares a lighthearted moment with his attorneys during a 1931 federal grand jury hearing, shortly before he is indicted for income tax evasion. (© Bettmann / CORBIS)

As Rico "Little Caesar" Bandello, the Romanian-born Edward G. Robinson brought a brutish physicality and impatient energy to his portrayal of a small-time thug who rises to the heights of organized crime, only to lose it all, including his life. (Photofest)

The new medium of television brought reputed gangsters into American living rooms in 1950–51, when Senator Estes Kefauver's committee held hearings about a nationwide criminal conspiracy called the mafia. Movie theaters offered free broadcasts of the hearings for mob-curious Americans who didn't yet own TV sets. (Michael Rougier, Time and Life Pictures / Getty Images)

America's reputed top crime boss Frank Costello appeared before the Kefauver committee in 1951 (shown here before testifying). For the television broadcast, however, cameras showed only his hands—a theatrical touch that made Costello all the more compelling a TV character. (© Bettmann / CORBIS)

Joe Valachi, the low-ranking gangster whose public testimony before a Senate committee in 1962 introduced a new term—La Cosa Nostra—into the national discourse about Italian American organized crime (Central Press, Hulton Archive / Getty Images)

By the late 1960s, "The Mafia" was so powerful that it held New York City, including Lady Liberty herself, in its tentacles. Or so claimed this 1967 editorial cartoon from the tabloid *The Washington Star*. (Library of Congress)

Mangia, mangia: Kirk Douglas played a mafia patriarch in *The Brotherhood*. The film's resounding failure at the box office in 1968 almost prevented another movie about a Sicilian "godfather" from being made. (Photofest)

Scene from a marriage: Michael Corleone (Al Pacino) expects Kay Adams (Diane Keaton) to be a modern American wife and a traditional Sicilian spouse. She ultimately breaks free from this impossible bind, but her freedom comes at a tragically high cost. (Photofest)

Maerose Prizzi (Angelica Huston), a Brooklyn mafia daughter who out-schemes the murderous men of her family in the 1985 black comedy *Prizzi's Honor*. The manipulative Maerose makes her own destiny, and she's nobody's victim. (Photofest)

It's the good life: Karen Hill (Lorraine Bracco) enjoys a night out on the town with husband Henry (Ray Liotta) in Martin Scorsese's *Goodfellas*. Unlike Kay Corleone, bad-girl Karen loves being married to the mob. (Photofest)

The mafia wife as truth-teller: Jean Tempio (Annabella Sciorra) denounces the "men of honor" mystique in Abel Ferrara's *The Funeral*. (Photofest)

Lee Van Cleef (left) and Earl Holliman, as two hit men who are gay lovers, menace a mob moll (Jean Wallace) in *The Big Combo*. The 1955 film marked the first appearance of homosexuality in the gangster genre. (Photofest)

Oh, how I love you: The 1980s TV series *Wiseguy* hinted broadly at a crypto-gay relationship between its two antagonists, a mob boss (Ray Sharkey, right) and the undercover FBI agent (Ken Wahl) who pursued him. (Photofest)

Race matters: Tony Soprano (James Gandolfini) wages a vendetta against a black policeman (Charles Dutton) who had the nerve to give him a traffic ticket. (Photofest)

Family redefined, and relocated: Far from the mean streets of urban Little Italies, the Sopranos—Tony (James Gandolfini), Carmela (Edie Falco), and offspring A.J. (Robert Iler) and Meadow (Jamie-Lynn DiScala)—live large in suburban New Jersey. (Photofest)

When organizers of New York's Columbus Day Parade barred *Sopranos* stars Lorraine Bracco and Dominic Chianese from marching in 2002, Mayor Michael Bloomberg boycotted the parade and took the two actors to lunch in the Bronx Italian American neighborhood where Chianese grew up. (Andrew Savulich, New York *Daily News*)

Publicity-loving mob boss John Gotti during his salad days, before the feds finally sent the so-called Teflon Don to prison, where he died of cancer in 2002. Gotti's gang members, with their fondness for topless bars, steroids, and drugs, were more like Tony Soprano's rowdy goodfellas than Don Vito Corleone's sober "family" men. (Keith Meyers, Hulton Archive / Getty Images)

Former FBI agent Joseph "Donnie Brasco" Pistone (foreground, in sunglasses) with Salvatore "Bill" Bonanno, son of the late mob boss Joseph Bonanno. In 2004, the odd couple coauthored *The Good Guys*, a cops 'n Cosa Nostra novel. (Robert Sabu, New York *Daily News*)

we may be, we cannot turn away. Annabella Sciorra, the gifted but un-derutilized actress who played Gloria, says the character was perhaps the most challenging and rewarding role she has had since she made her screen debut in *True Love*, director Nancy Savoca's 1989 film about a young Italian American couple in the Bronx.

"I gave Gloria a similar background to Tony's—not mobwise, but psychologically," Sciorra says. "I think she was tormented by her mother. I think she's a mirror image of Tony's psyche. I always felt that she mirrored Tony psychologically. That's the way I played it. I gave her the same set of issues and problems—self-hatred, and not being able to forgive herself for whatever happened in her family, and [the fact that she was] tormented by a crazy family."[30]

Tony gets Gloria out of his life by having one of his goons threaten her with death if she ever attempts to contact him again. The threat works, and no more is heard from her. Then one night, as Tony and Carmela are going to bed, his wife tells him she heard that Gloria Trillo, "that nice sales lady," has committed suicide. The next day an upset Tony goes to the Mercedes dealership where Gloria worked, and a salesman informs him that Gloria hanged herself and didn't leave a note. "I got the impression she wasn't very lucky with men" is all he can offer Tony as a motive.

Furious and needing someone to blame, Tony storms into Dr. Melfi's office and demands, "Why the fuck didn't you help her?" His belligerence frightens her, but Melfi stands her ground. "I give my pa-tients everything I've got," she says. "She slipped through everyone's grasp." With that Tony calms down, and then reveals that he'd been projecting his own sense of guilt on Melfi. Gloria had reached out to him, he says, "and I wasn't there for her." Gloria's death is a reminder of what he fears most and doesn't want to believe about himself: that he is, as he puts it, "a toxic person."

Robert Viscusi, the specialist in Italian American studies quoted ear-lier, has written that Italian American males are typically depicted in popular culture as having "a penchant for violence and sexist relations with women."[31] The gangster genre consistently has reinforced that image, from the days of *Little Caesar* and *Scarface* to *The Sopranos*. A gun-toting Mediterranean man bossing around his wife and carrying on with his mistresses, or "molls" as mob women were quaintly called, is the archetypal image of the mafia hood.

As portrayed in pop culture, mobsters are about violence, easy money, and rebellion against straight society's rules. And sex. Sonny Corleone, more so in Puzo's novel than in Coppola's film, is basically a walking phallus. Puzo graphically (lovingly?) commits a lot of page time to Sonny's penis and its effect on women: "It was common knowledge that he was so generously endowed by nature that his martyred wife feared the marriage bed as unbelievers once feared the rack."[32] Prostitutes, upon viewing his "massive organ," would double their fees. Sonny's wife, Sandra, who says she "yelled bloody murder" the first time she saw "that pole of Sonny's," is grateful to God for her husband's infidelities. "When I heard he was doing the job on other girls I went to church and lit a candle."[33]

Sonny may be the best-endowed and studliest of fictional mafiosi, but as the movies, TV, and books have told us, men in the mob, being manly men, are chick magnets who juggle wives and gumads. Henry Hill has a gorgeous wife and two other women on the side. Tony Soprano has a vigorous sex life with a multicultural cast of girlfriends. His men—Paulie Walnuts, Silvio Dante, Ralph Cifaretto, Big Pussy—all have their gumads. Even septuagenarian Uncle Junior enjoys sex, especially performing cunnilingus on his girlfriend, Roberta. Gangsters flout conventional morality, and in their line of work they face the prospect of arrest and death every day. So infidelity both comes with the territory and compensates for the occupational hazards of mob life.

The purported sexual allure and potency of mobsters would seem to be inextricable from the general phallocentrism of southern Italian culture. In his study of Italian and Greek homoeroticism, *The Seduction of the Mediterranean*, British historian Robert Aldrich quotes from *La Pelle* (*The Skin*), Italian author Curzio Malaparte's novel about post–World War II Naples: "The true emblem of Italy is not the tricolor but the sexual organs, the male sexual organs. The patriotism of the Italian people is all there. Honour, morals, the Catholic religion, the cult of the family—all are there, in our sexual organs, which are worthy

of our ancient and glorious traditions of civilization."[34] Speaking of ancient tradition, one of the most famous images from the Roman city of
Pompeii is a wall painting of a rich merchant whose wealth is symbolized by his enormous sex organ, which he weighs in a balance scale.

But reality may differ from this image of mobsters as lusty outlaws
whose love-guns get as much, if not more, use as their lethal weapons.

"Mafiosi are almost asexual," according to Sicilian psychoanalyst
and professor Girolamo Lo Verso, who is "engrossed in the topic of how
seemingly potent dons and their ostensibly virile henchmen perform in
the sack." Lo Verso's conclusion: "badly, and very, very briefly."[35]

The professor claims that married mobsters mainly have "quickies"
with their wives just to make babies. But, according to him, they are no
more amorous with their other women.

"Mafiosi have whores and loose women," he says. "But lovers? No."
A real lover might make demands, and the mobster's supreme allegiance is to the criminal organization, not to any individual, much less
a mistress.

Mob life may, in fact, be attractive because it keeps women in their
place, as wives and whores, allowing men to spend most of their wak-
ing hours in their preferred company—each other. The homosociality
of organized crime enables men to escape the control of women. A
mob crew, notes psychoanalyst and author Glen O. Gabbard, is a "para-
military patriarchy" in which men, "most of them dominated by their
mothers all their lives, join together in a new family that promises to
liberate them from the yoke of maternal power. Lost in an abyss of
meaninglessness, stalked by the Grim Reaper at every turn and thirst-
ing for a purpose in their empty lives, these men turn to a powerful father who promises to take care of them."[36]

Some sociology must be added to Gabbard's psychoanalytic emphasis.

"The greatest potential conflict [within mafia groups] lay with
members of the other sex, and especially with mothers," observes Paul
Ginsborg, the British-born academic who is the leading authority on
contemporary Italy writing in English. "Women were traditionally ex-
cluded from the Mafia because they could not be expected necessarily
to subordinate kin ties to the needs of the organization."[37]

Mafiosi, Ginsborg affirms, are traditionalists when it comes to gender relations; they declare themselves to be "good Catholic patriarchs" who uphold a sex/gender regime in which daughters are virgins before marriage, divorce and adultery are frowned upon, and mothers are regarded as saints. "The womenfolk of mafiosi were symbols, and their propriety and effective protection boosted the reputation of a man of honor."[38]

But Jane and Peter Schneider, in *Reversible Destiny*, note that mafia groups (*cosche*) demand extreme loyalty and secrecy "even at the expense of the members' respective natal and conjugal families." Women, "although the guardians of these families, are no less constrained than men to internalize the priority of the metaphorical Family."[39]

And, if recent accounts from Italy are any indication, some women have internalized mafia values to the point where they themselves have become involved in family business. In July 2004, Sicilian police, in a crackdown on organized crime, arrested twenty-three persons, two of them women who were accused of heading a clan that operated near the city of Trapani. The women, both wives of mafiosi, ran a network of extortion rackets, according to the police.[40] Similar reports have emerged of women *camorriste* in Naples, a development *The Sopranos* acknowledged when Tony went on a business trip to that city expecting to deal with the aged mob boss Zi' Vittorio but discovered instead that it was the old man's daughter Annalisa who was in charge.

This does not mean, however, that women's liberation has come to Cosa Nostra. The women generally are mobsters by default, filling in for their imprisoned husbands or other male relatives. Southern Italian organized crime remains a male-dominated enterprise.

The Schneiders provide a vivid account of how Sicilian mafiosi symbolically and literally exclude women from their world. Mafia culture, the authors note, "denies and denigrates femininity . . . Through rituals, feasts, and hunting trips, the members shore up and continuously reassert a form of masculine identity that repels affection and dependency as womanly signs of weakness."[41]

Every mafia movie fan knows that food, its preparation and consumption in massive quantities, is a convention of the genre, from *The Godfather* to *Goodfellas* to *The Sopranos*. The Schneiders report how "food play" is central to male bonding among Sicilian mafiosi. Huge feasts, known as *grandi banchetti* or *grandi schiticchiate*, were major social occasions for Cosa Nostra members. Usually held in the countryside, these events were open only to males, who did all the cooking.

The Schneiders note that the mafiosi all had experience cooking for each other while in prison, which, for mafia movie devotees, inevitably evokes the memorable sequence in *Goodfellas* depicting the preparation of elaborate Italian meals by Henry Hill and his other incarcerated mob buddies. (Who can forget the *Goodfellas* guide to sautéing garlic: slice it paper-thin with a razor, so it dissolves in the heated olive oil.) At the Sicilian banquets, the men "revealed a striking ability to carry on without women by preparing each of the lavish, multicourse feasts entirely on their own."[42]

And when they had finished eating, "the revelers settled into an hour or more of hilarious, carnivalesque entertainment that parodied the absent sex."[43] The Schneiders provide an astonishing account of one such revel, where three mafiosi improvised priestly vestments out of tablecloths and conducted a profane mass, in which, at the end of each verse, instead of an amen, they would chant, *"Minchia!"* (the Sicilian slang term for penis). These "masses" often were elaborate parodies in which "some of the bonvivants performed erotic imitations of women doing a strip tease." One mafioso at such a bacchanalia "dressed up in pink silk women's underwear with lace trim, a pink satin nightgown and a hooded black satin cape. Plump oranges were used to give the illusion of breasts as he cavorted about."[44]

Mafia recruitment rituals and other traditions build solidarity among mafiosi, defining them by what they are not: women or homosexuals. The Schneiders cite the psychiatric transcript of an imprisoned mafioso who killed two other mobsters and attempted to kill a third. He claimed he committed the murders to "show himself and to others that he was the equal of the other men, 'one of the boys,' capable of manhood, and not one of 'them'—the women. Indeed the killings had helped him deal with his growing concern that he might be inclined toward 'pederasty,' by which he meant being sexually attracted to young men."[45]

Mafia dramas—and even films and TV shows in which Italian

American males are not criminals but are similarly volatile and violence-prone—often embody a covert homoeroticism. They invite the viewer to luxuriate in the power and sensuality of the Italian American male body—think of Tony Manero (John Travolta) in *Saturday Night Fever* preening before a mirror in his skimpy briefs, or swaggering Sonny Corleone (James Caan), his tight "guinea-T" clinging to his hairy chest. At the same time, they exorcise the specter of queerness by reinforcing traditional notions of proper manly behavior, as when Don Corleone slaps the sobbing singer Johnny Fontane for "crying like a woman."

In the mob comedy *Analyze This*, neurotic gangster Paul Vitti (Robert De Niro) agrees to undergo psychotherapy but warns his skittish shrink Dr. Ben Sobel (Billy Crystal) not to "turn me into a fag." For Paulie Walnuts, a captain in Tony Soprano's crew, being called a "cocksucker" is enough to incite him to homicidal fury. Richie Aprile worries that his son might be gay because he takes part in dance contests. And when Janice Soprano asks what difference it would make if he were, he punches her in the face. When she subsequently shoots him, women viewers cheered because she took out an abuser. I rooted for Janice because she also had blown away a lowlife who to me represented every violent homophobe.

The intertwined, symbiotic nature of misogyny and homophobia is a recurring motif on *The Sopranos*. Tony worries that seeing a therapist, and a woman at that, could violate his masculine image. When Furio Giunta finds young hoodlums Matt Bevilaqua and Sean Gismonte lounging around their apartment in their underwear, he remarks, in Italian, that they must suck each other's cocks. When Furio himself is shot in the leg and is in a doctor's examining room with his pants down, Tony teases him about his girly bikini underwear.

Uncle Junior is furious when word gets out that he is a cunnilingus aficionado because, as one wag remarks, "If someone will do that, he'll suck anything." (He breaks up with his indiscreet girlfriend Roberta by shoving a lemon meringue pie in her face—shades of Cagney and Clark in *Public Enemy*.) Both Tony and son A.J. speculate that the high school counselor David Wegner must be a "fag." Carmela, who will have an affair with Wegner, snaps at her husband, "What's with you, you think everybody's gay. Maybe *you're* gay!"

The mafia man's preoccupation with manhood and with masculine image seems almost a parody of the *maschilismo* of southern Italian culture. It also looks a lot like "the lady doth protest too much" writ large. Marriage and children assure his heterosexual public image, but the absence of women from mob society inevitably raises questions about homoerotic desire. In *The Godfather*, made men "go to the mattresses," that is, live communally in a single apartment, without women, during mob wars. Joseph Pistone observes that gangsters would much rather spend time in each other's company than with their wives or girlfriends. Wiseguys, as innumerable movies and TV dramas have shown us, engage in a lot of intimate physical contact, kissing and touching each other, sharing beds (like Charlie and Johnny Boy in *Mean Streets*) and otherwise behaving in ways that flout the Anglo-Saxon, John Wayne version of proper masculine behavior.

Though their carefully, even obsessively maintained masculine act relies on contempt for and objectification of women, the mobsters are mama's boys. Either they're locked in mortal combat with their mothers, like Tony trying to extract love from the unloving Livia, or, like Paulie Walnuts, their devotion is so fervent that its converse can only be the denigration of other women as whores because they can never be as good as Mamma. It is a "devotion tinged with worry about losing autonomy and restoring the defendency of childhood," observes media mobster analyst Glen O. Gabbard.

"Little boys identify with their mothers as well as their fathers," he notes. "The irony of a mobster with the name of 'Big Pussy' speaks to the feminine identification that the gang cannot deny yet cannot accept, either."[46] Big Pussy, who becomes an FBI informer, is a stand-in for the Big Mother, whose betrayal endangers the entire, all-male family. Tony symbolically eliminates the threat when he kills Big Pussy, one of his oldest and closest friends, but he cannot kill his actual toxic mother, Livia. "She is dead to me," he comments laconically after he realizes the full extent of her perfidy. But not even her actual demise liberates his psyche from "the mother of nightmares."

In the social mythology of the mob, there is an unbreachable barrier between the world of the "men of honor" and homosexuals who dishonor masculinity by being like women. But both the actual history of organized crime and its pop-culture representations belie the myth. Mobsters thrived on illicit enterprises such as gambling and prostitution, and in the pre–gay liberation days, they owned gay bars and bathhouses. Nick Tosches, in his biography of Dean Martin, reports that mobster Vito Genovese, "the most violent, most grasping, and most treacherous of his breed," owned drag queen bars and was married to a lesbian.[47] Gay folklore has long held that mafiosi put their sons and other male kin who were homosexual in charge of the gay bars they owned.

The Stonewall Inn, a Greenwich Village bar whose name is synonymous with gay emancipation because of the 1969 uprising that occurred on its premises and in the surrounding streets, was owned and operated by the mob. In the decades since the "Stonewall rebellion," there has been much speculation about why the police raided the bar on the evening of June 29. David Carter, in his 2004 book *Stonewall: The Riots That Sparked the Gay Revolution*, reports that the Stonewall was owned by "Fat" Tony Lauria, a gangster whose father was also a mob figure. Carter discovered that New York police targeted the bar because they believed mobsters were using it as the base of an extortion ring. Police officials also believed that Lauria and his associates were blackmailing patrons who worked at the New York Stock Exchange into stealing negotiable bonds, which mobsters purportedly sold through the bar.[48]

Gay gangsters actually do exist, but mob crews don't have antidiscrimination policies. Being homosexual in the mob can be a serious health hazard. John D'Amato, the acting boss of the New Jersey–based De Cavalcante family, was whacked when his confederates learned that he had a secret sex life. The married D'Amato had two girlfriends in addition to his wife, and he also went to sex clubs, where he sometimes had sex with men. (D'Amato's exploits would seem to undermine Professor Lo Verso's contention that mafiosi are "almost asexual.") The Jersey boss evidently was bisexual rather than gay, but any same-sex involvement was enough to warrant his death.

The mobster who shot D'Amato explained the hit when he became a government informer. Having a boss known to be less than 100 percent heterosexual would be "devastating to our *brigada*," the killer said, using an Italian word for a mob family. "Nobody's going to respect us if we have a gay homosexual boss sitting down discussing business with other families."[49]

The 2004 trial of Brooklyn mob boss Joseph Massino yielded another glimpse of sexual unorthodoxy in the supposedly queer-free culture of Cosa Nostra. Massino's attorney queried a mob turncoat about his relationship with a transvestite performer whose specialty was impersonating Cher. "Did you have a relationship with this person?" the attorney asked the informant, Frank Coppa.

"He was my accountant," the corpulent Coppa gruffly replied, insisting that it was another mobster, Ron "Monkey Man" Filocomo, who was involved with "Cher," a star performer at the Déjà Vu theater in Manhattan.[50]

A mob accountant who doubles as a Cher impersonator and is the lover of a hoodlum known as "Monkey Man"? As bizarre as that sounds, the story of Vito Arena tops it.

Arena was a convicted auto thief and a hit man for the Gambino crime family. The Gambinos knew that Arena was gay, but apparently he was such an efficient killer that they were willing to overlook his sexuality. In 1985, Arena was a star witness in the trial of eight Gambino members, including boss Paul Castellano, who was later killed by thugs loyal to John Gotti in a brazen hit outside a Manhattan restaurant. Arena had been serving a six-year sentence for auto robbery, and as a condition for his testimony, Arena demanded, and apparently received, special jailhouse favors, including Bruce Springsteen records, a facelift, and steak dinners. He also demanded that his male lover, who had been involved in some robberies, be allowed to join him in the same prison.

The "gay hit man," as Arena came to be known in the media, was relocated to Houston under the federal witness protection program, according to Houston police. In 1991 he was killed at age forty-seven when he tried to rob a record store. He had been living under the name "Victor Harris" and had been involved in numerous other robberies before he was shot to death by the store owner. There was no word whether he was out for cash or Springsteen CDs.[51]

The maschilismo of mob culture notwithstanding, why shouldn't there be homosexuality in the ranks of organized crime? Mafiosi conflate homosexuality and so-called feminine weakness and dependency (and in this they're hardly alone), but as mentioned earlier, the mob's all-male society and intense male bonding raises the specter of same-sex desire. And as the old gay liberation slogan declared, "We are everywhere."

The actual history of sexuality among Italian immigrants to America is, as is usually the case, much more complicated and compelling than the conventional wisdom. Richard Gambino's construct of *uomo di pazienza* and *donna di serietà*, indisputably heterosexual and committed to maintaining the family structure of the southern Italian poor and working class, only captures part of the story.

Historian George Chauncey provides some of the missing pieces in his groundbreaking 1994 book, *Gay New York: Gender, Urban Culture, and the Making of the Gay Male World, 1890–1940.* Chauncey's meticulous research, involving police and court records and other primary sources, unearthed a thriving homosexual subculture among Italian immigrants in New York City. "Fairies," the prevailing designation for homosexuals whose effeminacy was a public declaration of their orientation, constituted a colorful thread in the social fabric of Italian immigrant communities. Chauncey notes that Italian sections of Manhattan's Lower East Side had numerous saloons where fairies congregated. He reports than one Vito Lorenzo ran an establishment on Canal Street that the police charged was a "fairy place."[52]

These "obvious" homosexuals tended to seek sex partners not among their own ranks but among masculine same-sexers and heterosexual men. Straight Italian men, Chauncey found, interacted with "fairies" more readily than did Jewish immigrants, and were more likely to respond to their sexual advances. Chauncey cites a 1921 study of men arrested for homosexual behavior which noted that "at a time when the numbers of Italians and Jews in New York were roughly equal, almost twice as many Italians were arrested on homosexual charges. More significant is that turn-of-the-century investigators found a more institutionalized fairy subculture in Italian neighborhoods than in Jewish ones."[53]

Chauncey says three factors most likely accounted for the willingness of Italian men to engage in homosexual relations. The Catholic Church was so intent on condemning sexual "sin" between men and women that "it may implicitly have made sexual contact between men seem relatively harmless." One of Chauncey's interviewees, an elderly man who grew up in an Italian neighborhood, told him that homosexuality "just wasn't regarded as a mortal sin, it wasn't seen as that bad."

He also notes that while Jews left their villages for good with their family members, most Italian immigrants were single or married men unaccompanied by their families. "Italian men may have been more responsive to homosexual overtures than Jewish men in part simply because far fewer of them were living with their wives . . ."[54]

"Although many Italian men in New York also lived with their families and many others boarded with families, a large number of them lived in rooming houses, where they organized surrogate, all-male families with other Italian men," Chauncey writes. Italian men in large numbers participated in "bachelor subcultures," that is, "distinct but overlapping social spheres centered in the poolrooms and saloons where many workingmen spent their time, in the cellar clubrooms and streets where gangs of boys and young men were a ubiquitous presence, and in the lodging houses that crowded the Bowery and the waterfront."[55]

The hidden history George Chauncey unearthed conjures up possibilities Francis Ford Coppola and Mario Puzo never envisioned for *Godfather II*, with its painstakingly re-created scenes of New York's Little Italy during the 1920s—like a chubby-chasing fairy importuning portly Peter Clemenza under a gaslight at the corner of Hester and Mulberry Streets, or maybe a horny Tessio, unmarried and not especially interested in the virtuous Sicilian girls zealously guarded by their fathers, literally "going to the mattresses" with fellow hoodlums. Clemenza and Tessio would have to keep their same-sex dalliances on the down-low, however, since their boss Don Vito is a sexually straitlaced type who just wouldn't understand.

Homosexuality didn't appear in a gangster movie until 1955, in *The Big Combo*, directed by Joseph H. Lewis and written by Philip Yordan. Police Lieutenant Leonard Diamond (Cornel Wilde) has been told to end his surveillance of mob boss Mr. Brown because the investigation is costing too much and hasn't yielded any valuable information. Diamond decides to make one last attempt to uncover evidence on Brown by tailing his girlfriend, Susan, with whom he becomes obsessed. Brown's ethnicity is not specified, but he is played by the Italian American actor Richard Conte, who was known for his tough-guy roles. (Conte was the Corleone family rival Don Barzini in *The Godfather*.) Brown's predecessor, whom he killed, was a mob boss with the unmistakably Italian surname of Grazzi. Brown runs a gambling den in a mobbed-up part of town that Diamond refers to as "Little Mafia."

Brown also employs two hit men with the Italian-sounding surnames Fante and Mingo. Played by the well-known character actors Lee Van Cleef and Earl Holliman, the professional killers are lovers, and their relationship is depicted with surprising frankness for the era when the film was made. Fante and Mingo, in fact, seem to have the only sound relationship in *The Big Combo*. They are inseparable, they share a bedroom, and they treat each other with respect and consideration. They are also faithful to each other, even unto death. When Diamond begins to turn the screws on Brown, the mob boss decides his hit men have become a liability. In a double cross, he has them blown up with a bomb. Mingo survives, and, grieving for his lover and enraged at Brown, he helps the police to nab his boss.

Earl Holliman, who played Mingo, dispelled any doubts about the sexuality of the two hit men when he spoke after a screening of *The Big Combo* at the Third Annual Palm Springs Film Noir Festival in 2003. Discussing one scene he played with Lee Van Cleef, he remarked, "We shared a pair of pajamas, Lee's wearing the bottoms and I'm wearing the top to the pajamas and it's pretty obvious what's going on."

Gay gangsters didn't appear on-screen again until *Friends and Family*, a frothy farce released in 2003. This time the two lovers, bodyguards-cum-assassins named Danny and Steve, are totally uncloseted. Everyone knows they're a couple, and everyone's cool about it, including their boss Victor Patrizzi (veteran character actor Tony Lo Bianco), a benevolent kingpin accepting of "alternative lifestyles." The boss, in fact, plans to leave his criminal empire to Danny and Steve, since his own two heterosexual sons have no interest in the family business—they're more into fashion and cooking.

The plot, such as it is, is set in motion when a surprise visit from Steve's Midwestern parents threatens to blow their cover. It's not their son's sexuality that's the big secret; the parents know and accept. Steve is not "out" to his parents about his and his lover's occupations as mafia hit men. Steve has told his parents that he and Danny run a successful catering business. Further complicating matters, Steve's meddlesome mother wants him to throw a birthday banquet for his father, who, get this, is an FBI agent! Complications meant to be hilarious ensue; to maintain the ruse that they are caterers and not killers, Steve and Danny recruit their mobster cronies to pretend to be waiters working for their nonexistent gay catering company. But to convincingly play queer cater-waiters, the mobsters have to take "gay lessons" if the zany scheme is to work.

Friends and Family, made nearly fifty years after *The Big Combo* and after thirty-odd years of post-Stonewall gay activism, not surprisingly is much more candid about homosexuality than the 1955 film. But the earlier film has it all over its successor in artistry and taste. *Friends and Family* is a loud, chaotic, simpleminded mess, and its laughs are meager. Director Kristen Coury and scriptwriter Joseph Triebwasser didn't grasp the obvious: if the mafia is going to be treated in a comic fashion, the only workable tonal register is dark. The light and farcical tenor of *Friends and Family* actually renders the two lovers unappealing; when they try to extort a poor trembling schmo, we squirm instead of laugh. Scorsese or Chase could have made the scene mordantly funny, but Coury, in her misguided approach, renders it creepy and off-putting.

Other instances of gay representation in the gangster genre are few and far between. In Scorsese's *Mean Streets*, from 1973, criminals and queers collide when small-time mobster Michael Longo (Richard Romanus, currently seen as Jennifer Melfi's ex-husband on *The Sopranos*) and his friends Charlie Cappa (Harvey Keitel) and Johnny Boy Civello (Robert De Niro) share a ride with two gay men, one a stereotypical "screaming queen," the other a more sober type. The five are fleeing a bar where a mob-related shooting has occurred, and they all pile into Michael's car. Sammy, the queen, is crying hysterically over having witnessed the murder while his friend Benton tries to calm him.

"Sammy, get control of yourself," Benton says, while the straight men cringe in embarrassment. But Sammy is irrepressible. He sees some good-looking guys on the sidewalk and calls out to them. When told to behave, he snaps, "I won't, I won't!" Instead, he shouts, "They're all beautiful! I'll suck them all . . . I'll suck them all!" The scene is undeniably funny, and also surprising. The straight men, though discomfited by Sammy's carrying on, don't verbally abuse or bash him. Moreover, the two gay men are not strangers to the ostensibly heterosexual Michael, as Johnny Boy quickly realizes. "Friends of yours, Michael?" he dryly remarks.

On television, the late eighties–early nineties CBS series *Wiseguy* hinted broadly at a crypto-gay relationship between its two antagonists, a mob boss and the undercover FBI agent who pursues him. Vinnie Terranova, of the FBI's Organized Crime Task Force, sets out to win the trust of Sonny Steelgrave, a New Jersey crime chief. The two men bond over their history as former Golden Glove boxers, and Sonny takes on Vinnie as his protégé. When Vinnie protects his new mentor from a hit by rival gangsters, their rapport is solidified.

When Vinnie must bring Steelgrave to justice, he is tortured by self-disgust. Whereas the title character in *Donnie Brasco* feels only a twinge of regret when he turns in one of the mafiosi he has befriended, Terranova is devastated. "I turned friendship and loyalty into an obscene joke," he confesses to his brother, a Catholic priest. In the series's final episode, Vinnie is in group therapy for undercover cops.

The show was infused with homoerotic undertones. "The first half-season of 'Wiseguy' is a testosterone-drenched love story of aggressive men attracted to the manliness they recognize in each other," noted critic Joyce Millman in a *New York Times* feature timed to the release of the series on DVD. "Throughout the show," Millman observed, "feds and gangsters alike talk in a mock-flirtatious banter that hovers somewhere between an ironic adoption of gay posturing and a nervous assertion of heterosexuality. At Vinnie and Sonny's first meeting, Sonny sizes him up from beneath alluringly hooded eyelids and Vinnie sticks out his chin and sasses: 'What are you lookin' for, mister? Maybe I got some of what you want.' "[56]

When Terranova's true identity is exposed, Steelgrave flees. The two men wind up in a deserted movie theater, where their relationship is consummated, sort of—the obvious erotic attraction is displaced into fisticuffs. At the end of their long, punishing brawl, the two spent combatants share a bottle of liquor and reminisce about their fathers. Vinnie tells Sonny, "I want you to know there's a lot about who you are that I feel close to." The soundtrack fills with the strains of the Moody Blues kitsch-rock classic "Nights in White Satin," and the swollen eyes of the two men meet at the line "And I love you, oh, how I love you."

Love in a parked car is what Vito Spatafore has to offer, or, more precisely, early morning blow jobs. Spatafore, of the Spatafore Construction family, is a captain of the crew that used to be led by Ralph Cifaretto, Tony Soprano's major headache until Tony beat Ralph to death and had his body dismembered. The rotund Spatafore is an easygoing sort for a mobster; he even takes jokes about his weight in stride. But his affability notwithstanding, Vito is lethal. He whacked his own cousin, Jackie Aprile, Jr., by firing a bullet into the back of the aspiring young mobster's head. When his younger brother was put in a coma by a vicious nutcase known as Mustang Sally, Vito went to Tony and declared, "I want this cocksucker to bleed from his ass."

Finn DeTrolio might think it funny that Vito should use that epithet for Sally. Finn, the latest boyfriend of Meadow Soprano, decides to spend the summer in New York instead of at home in California, so Tony gets him a job on one of his construction sites. Finn actually does the job he's being paid for; the wiseguy idea of a day's work is sitting around kibitzing and playing cards. Mobsters make Finn uncomfortable, but he manages to cope—until the morning he arrives at work early and sees something he shouldn't.

He pulls up alongside a parked car that appears to have one passenger, a security guard, until up pops Vito, who had been orally servicing the obviously gratified guard. It's too late for Finn to avert his astonished gaze, as Vito makes eye contact with him. Later, the fat fellator approaches Finn and offers him tickets to a ballgame, as his guest. Freaked-out Finn doesn't know whether Vito's offer is an attempt to seduce him or a ruse that will lead to his being whacked. Or, as he later says to Meadow, "Maybe he wants to fuck me and then kill me." Meadow replies, somewhat illogically, that Vito wouldn't kill him because he, Vito, is a married man.

Finn, in a panic, plans to leave for California, but Meadow accuses him of wanting to run out on her. Finn reviews his options and then, certain that Vito would never whack Tony Soprano's son-in-law, suggests to Meadow that they get married. (Finn doesn't know that Vito killed Meadow's previous boyfriend, Jackie Aprile, Jr. But Jackie had proved himself a liability to the Soprano operation, while Finn is just a nice and somewhat wimpy middle-class college boy.) Meadow happily agrees to Finn's proposal and phones Carmela with the good news.

Gender relations and sexuality in the world of organized crime, and as depicted in the fictional representations of the Mafia myth, are rife with inconsistencies. Made men need and desire women, but they mistrust, fear, and even hate them. Traditional Italian family men, they demand fidelity from their wives while they assume cheating on their spouses as their prerogative. Women accept male dominance as a given, but they resist domination when they can, and sometimes they wield considerable power over their men. Mob wives and girlfriends suffer from their men's peccadilloes—"it's disgusting what you have to put up with," as one remarks in *Goodfellas*—but they also benefit from their husbands' crimes and are loath to leave their "good providers." Homosexuals are girlie-men whose existence is incompatible with organized crime's masculine ethos. But same-sex desire is always a possibility in all-male societies like Cosa Nostra, and if an actual homo proves his mettle as a killer, his deviance may be overlooked.

When it comes to gender and sexuality, the one definitive truth is that there are no definitive truths; these two realms, like the character of the mafioso himself, are riddled with mystery and unresolved, and irresolvable, contradiction.

7

Moulanyans, Medigahns, and Wonder Bread Wops: Race and Racism On-Screen and Off

The Negroes were considered of absolutely no account, of no force whatsoever.   —Mario Puzo, *The Godfather*

They recruit spics, they recruit niggers . . .
                                    —Frankie Pentangeli in *Godfather II*

I don't know if you know this or not, Sicilians were spawned by niggers.
                              —Cliff (Dennis Hopper) in *True Romance*

T o deal or not to deal? That's the question facing the assembled
heads of the nation's organized crime families in *The Godfather*.
Don Vito Corleone is adamantly against getting involved in the
narcotics trade, certain that such a move will bring down the full force
of law enforcement on their enterprises: "I believe this drug business—
is gonna destroy us in the years to come. I mean, it's not like gambling
or liquor—even women—which is something that most people want
nowadays, and is forbidden to them by the *pezzonovanti* of the Church.
Even the police departments that've helped us in the past with gambling and other things are gonna refuse to help us when it comes to
narcotics."

The other dons disagree; the money to be made is just too great to
resist, and anyway it's past the time when this burgeoning profit source
could be suppressed. But they are willing to put limits on drug dealing,
to control it.

"I don't want it near schools—I don't want it sold to children!" says Zaluchi, the don of Detroit. "That's an *infamia*. In my city, we would keep the traffic in the dark people—the colored. They're animals anyway, so let them lose their souls."

In the film, the dons accept their Detroit confrere's judgment and that's the end of it. In Mario Puzo's novel, they agree with Zaluchi that the drug trade cannot be stopped and must instead be controlled. But "as for his remarks about the coloreds, that was not even heard." The crime chiefs do not even regard blacks as worthy of mention. "The Negroes were considered of absolutely no account, of no force whatsoever. That they had allowed society to grind them into the dust proved them of no account and his mentioning them in any way proved that the Don of Detroit had a mind that always wavered toward irrelevancies."[1]

The contempt for blacks for supposedly allowing themselves to be oppressed is only one instance of the racial prejudice so common to mob dramas that it must be considered a trope of the genre. If not as essential as violence, sex, and *cucina*, race and racism nonetheless are recurring motifs that figure significantly in organized crime narratives.

In *Godfather II*, Frankie Pentangeli's brief against his hated rivals the Rosati brothers includes their willingness to hire nonwhites: "They recruit spics, they recruit niggers," he complains to Michael Corleone. Martin Scorsese's *Mean Streets* and *Goodfellas* both expose the racial attitudes of their Italian American protagonists. In the first film, Scorsese's breakthrough, Charlie Cappa (Harvey Keitel) is attracted to Diane, a beautiful black stripper. "Y'know . . . she's really good-looking . . . really good-looking," says Charlie in voice-over. "I've gotta say that again. She's really good-looking . . . but she's black . . . You can see that real plain." Then, after a brief pause, he says, "When you get down to it though, there's not much of a difference, is there?" As if waiting for an answer from someone, he asks again, "Well . . . is there?"

Although he is involved with Theresa, a young woman from his Little Italy neighborhood, he makes a date with Diane. But at the last minute, as he drives around the block where he is supposed to rendezvous with Diane, he gets cold feet. How could he possibly go out with a *melanzan'* (i.e., eggplant, a southern Italian term for a black)?

What would people in the neighborhood say? So he drives on, and stands her up. In another scene, Tony De Venziano (David Proval), who owns the bar where Charlie and his friends hang out, comments on a woman whose photograph Michael Longo (Richard Romanus) is admiring. "I know her," he says. He claims that he saw her "kissing a nigger." When Michael shoots him an uncomprehending look, Tony insists, "A nigger. A moulanyan. They were kissing. On the lips." A look of disgust crosses Michael's face as he holds the photo at arm's length.

In *Goodfellas*, Henry Hill (Ray Liotta) tries to calm his wife Karen's fears that he will be arrested and sent to prison. "You know who goes to jail?" he says to her. "Nigger stickup men, that's who. And they only get caught because they fall asleep in the getaway car." As if to vindicate Henry, Stacks Edwards (Samuel L. Jackson), a black man who takes part in the mob crew's multimillion-dollar Lufthansa airlines heist at Kennedy Airport, gets high and forgets to dispose of a truck used in the robbery. When the cops find the vehicle, Stacks pays for this error with his life—psycho mobster Tommy De Vito (Joe Pesci) shoots him in the back of the head.

Blacks become the scapegoats for the misdeeds and screw-ups of Italian mobsters on *The Sopranos*. Hit man Vito Spatafore whacks Jackie Aprile, Jr., but word is put out that the hapless young mob aspirant was shot by black drug dealers, "those jigs," as the boy's mother Rosie Aprile says. Both Tony Soprano and his cousin Tony Blundetto (Steve Buscemi) blame black males for their own personal failures in an episode aptly titled "Unidentified Black Males." Blundetto, injured while committing a murder, explains away his limp with the offhand comment, "Two black guys jumped me outside a bar."

Tony Soprano, who has always felt guilty that he didn't take part in the heist that sent his cousin to prison, always claims that he was attacked by two black males that night and had to go to the emergency room. But Dr. Melfi elicits the truth from Tony during a therapy session. He really hadn't been jumped by two black men. He had been arguing with his mother and suffered a panic attack, which caused him to pass out. He incurred his injuries when he fell and cut his head.

In an episode of the show's third season, Tony is stopped for a traffic offense by a black cop (Charles Dutton). Tony makes a disparaging remark about "affirmative action" to Carmela when he spots the cop in his rearview mirror. He offers a bribe if the officer will forget the ticket, and is incredulous when the angry lawman refuses. Tony turns to a corrupt Newark assemblyman to "fix" the ticket, but that's not enough for the vindictive mobster, who uses his influence with the pol to humiliate the officer by having him relieved of his duty.

In the fifth season, Tony's Uncle Junior has become increasingly addled. One night he leaves his home, in his pajamas, and goes wandering in his old Newark neighborhood, looking for his long-deceased brother Johnny. He comes to a familiar address—an old social club—but is thoroughly confused when he enters and happens upon a meeting of a black civic group. He tells the startled black men who approach him that he's looking for his brother. "Where's Johnny?" he keeps asking, becoming increasingly agitated. The blacks become impatient with this confused old white man until one realizes why the intruder has come to their door. "This used to be an Italian neighborhood," he remarks. The world has changed, and for the aged Junior, this is just one more reminder of that disturbing fact.

"A Hit Is a Hit," a superbly written (by Frank Renzulli and Joe Bosso) episode in the first season, is all about race, specifically the exploitation of black pop stars by the recording industry and Italian Americans' own conflicted racial attitudes.

Christopher Moltisanti and his fiancée Adriana La Cerva are out for a night on the town. They stop at a fast-food joint where all the other customers are black. Chris starts mouthing off when the wait for service begins to seem suspiciously long. "Hey, whose fuckin' welfare check you gotta cash to get a burger in here?" he demands.

An ultraslick, sharply dressed young black man approaches Christopher and Adriana. "Your woman looks embarrassed," he observes. Christopher calls him "Uncle Ben," but the man is unperturbed by the insult. Outside the restaurant, Adriana scolds Christopher: "What's with the attitude, Christopher? If it's not the blacks it's somebody else." Several stone-faced black men approach the couple, revealing that they work for the brother Christopher has insulted, Massive Genius (Bokeem Woodbine), a fabulously successful P. Diddy–like hip-hop entrepreneur. They invite Chris and Adriana to a party at their boss's mansion because "there's business to be done."

Both are impressed by Massive Genius's digs, and by his guest list, which includes Alec Baldwin and other celebrities. Christopher is especially taken with Massive G's heavy artillery, which he keeps in a locked case near his desk. As he shows off his weaponry to Christopher, he muses about the film mythology that matters as deeply to him as it does to his guest. *"The Godfather,"* he sighs. "I've seen that movie two hundred times." He also raves about *II* and has kind words for *III*, which he says was "misunderstood."

These pleasantries concluded, Massive G speaks of the business that is to be done. He is seeking financial justice for Little Jimmy Willis, a black rhythm and blues star from the 1950s who was ripped off by Herman "Hesh" Rabkin, a longtime associate of the Soprano organization. (Rabkin is modeled on an actual mobbed-up record producer, Roulette Records owner Morris Levy, notorious for exploiting African American artists like "Why Do Fools Fall in Love" singer and songwriter Frankie Lymon.) Massive G wants money for Willis's aged mother, and he asks Christopher to arrange a "sit-down" with Hesh so he can put his demand for "reparations" to the producer.

After the party an envious Christopher complains, "Moolies [from "moulanyans," blacks] got it goin' on." Massive G, who himself has a shady past, parties with movie stars and other A-list types, while the unglamorous Sopranos crew avoids publicity and has as its leader not a stylish hipster like Massive G but old Junior Soprano "in his moldy sweaters." Christopher finds this turn of events particularly galling because "our thing once ruled the music business." Even worse, this black upstart threatens his very identity. "We're the OGs [original gangsters], not them!" he complains to Adriana.

The sit-down takes place at Hesh's country estate, and this one tense scene distills decades of racial conflict and resentment. On one side are Massive G and his scowling associates, on the other, Hesh (played by Jerry Adler) and his mob partners, including Tony Soprano. Massive G begins the meeting by slyly toying with Hesh. "When you and Little Jimmy were partners on his hits, what parts did you write?" he asks. (Hesh's real-life prototype Morris Levy claimed cowriting credits on the hits Frankie Lymon composed, thus robbing Lymon of royalties due him.) Noticing the horses on Hesh's estate, he inquires, "You bought horses . . . what happened to Little Jimmy's royalties?"

"Little Jimmy bought horse," jokes one of Tony's boys. Jimmy, like his model Frankie Lymon, succumbed to heroin addiction.

Hesh bristles at Massive G's insinuations, claiming that his record company gave "a lot of Negro kids" their first break in the music business. But Massive G isn't impressed. He decries Jewish moguls in Hollywood, who he says were responsible for decades of racist film portrayals of blacks, adding that Jewish record producers were even worse. He tells Hesh his attorneys have done their research, and that "$400,000 would set the record straight."

It seems that Hesh has been outmaneuvered. He sits in his office, glancing at the photos on the wall of all the black artists who recorded for him, and, from his pensive expression, it appears he's feeling pangs of conscience. But he later calls Massive G and scornfully tells him, "Find some other schmuck to have your altruistic moment with." Massive G insists, but Tony warns him, "Don't press it." It turns out that Massive G sampled an old rhythm and blues hit produced by Hesh for one of his hip-hop jams and didn't pay for the rights. Massive G quickly calculates that litigation with Hesh would cost him more than $400,000, and his business sense trumps his quest for racial justice.

The same episode—one of the strongest in the entire series—also looks at racial identity from Tony's perspective. In therapy with Dr. Melfi, he confides his misgivings about becoming friendly with his neighbors, as both his psychiatrist and his wife have recommended. He complains that "the average white man" is boring and that he feels uncomfortable around these "medigahns" (a dialect pronunciation of "Americans"). He calls his suburban neighbors "mayonnaisers" and scorns the one Italian American among them, physician Bruce Cusamano, as a "Wonder Bread wop."

Puzzled, Melfi asks him, "Are you saying you're not white?" Tony acknowledges that yes, technically he is Caucasian. But to him "white" equals "medigahn," non-Italian. Tony's own racial subjectivity isn't black, but neither does he identify as "white." Only writers well acquainted with the peculiar racial identity drama of southern Italians could have crafted this dialogue. Renzulli and Bosso know that Anglo-Saxons considered southern Italian immigrants to be racially different from themselves, an in-between race, not black but not fully white, either. And that meant inferior. Italians responded either by seeking full acceptance as whites through assimilation, or, like Tony, by refusing to relinquish what they considered their distinct cultural identity, even while they pursued the American dream of material success.

"A Hit Is a Hit" makes one of the series' boldest "sympathy for the devil" gambits by portraying Tony Soprano, whose way of life is entirely atypical of Italian Americans, as an Italian American everyman. He is more down-to-earth, more genuine, more *autentico* than the respectable, noncriminal "Wonder Bread wops" and their "medigahn" friends, with their insider stock trading and disdain for the Murano glass in the Soprano mansion. The motif of the Sopranos clan as more roots-conscious than the assimilated Italians reappears throughout the series, particularly in the fifth season, when Carmela angrily confronts her status-seeking mother over the latter's supposed ethnic self-hatred.

Tony Soprano, despite his racism, is not averse to doing business with African Americans when it suits him. When black protesters picket Massarone Brothers Construction for its hiring practices, Tony accepts payment from Mr. Massarone to "fix" the problem. What Massarone doesn't know is that the whole thing is a setup, and that Tony is splitting the money with the minister who leads the protests. Tony and two associates also cut a deal with Maurice, a former black militant and community activist who has become so disenchanted that he is willing to be the front man for a housing rehabilitation scam run by Italian gangsters. That both black men are willing to sell out their followers for financial gain is consistent with the show's jaundiced view of capitalist America, where everyone has his price and there's no such thing as dirty money.

A Bronx Tale, the 1993 film adapted by Chazz Palmintieri from his semiautobiographical play of the same name, and directed by Robert De Niro, condemns racism and organized crime. Palmintieri plays Sonny, a neighborhood mob boss in the eponymous borough, and De Niro is Lorenzo, a bus driver trying to deter his impressionable son from falling under Sonny's influence.

The film opens in the early 1960s, when Calogero (Francis Capra) is a nine-year-old living in the Italian American Belmont section of the Bronx. He happens to see mob boss Sonny shoot a man in what appears to be a parking dispute. When the cops try to convince Calogero to point the finger at the shooter, the boy, who evidently has learned the rules of *omertà*, keeps his mouth shut. Sonny wants to repay the favor by offering Calogero's father, Lorenzo (De Niro), some easy work and extra cash. But Lorenzo is a proud man who scorns the Sonnys of the world, and he rejects the offer. To this working-class hero, the real tough guy is the man who gets up every day and works to support his family, as he instructs his son.

But the smooth-talking and charismatic Sonny takes a liking to Calogero, and soon has him working the local bar earning tips and running errands. Lorenzo discovers this and warns Sonny, "Stay away from my son!" in a confrontation that stops just short of violence.

The film's action jumps forward to the late sixties, when Calogero—who has started calling himself "C"—is a teenager. Calogero (now played by Lillo Brancato) has become a part of Sonny's inner circle. But Lorenzo refuses to cede his paternal rights to Sonny, and the two men are still warring for the youth's soul.

Now, on the verge of manhood, C faces a moral crisis. He has been hanging with other young Italian American males who are a bunch of losers, bigots who attack black kids as they ride their bikes through the neighborhood, and gangster wannabes who mindlessly admire the unproductive and violent lives of their heroes. They also regurgitate the adults' benighted racial attitudes. When C objects to the attack on black kids who are just riding their bikes through "their" (the Italians') neighborhood, another boy repeats his father's comment, "That's how it starts," that is, the dreaded black incursion.

C is intelligent and sensitive enough to look askance at their motives and behavior, but he can't make a clean break with them; he hasn't yet the maturity to subordinate parochial neighborhood allegiances to a higher morality. His dilemma is only heightened when he meets and falls for young black girl, Jane (Taral Hicks), while his loser friends are at the same time stirring up an interracial feud involving her brother.

C's father, for all his decency, disapproves of his son's budding romance with Jane, asking him why he can't go out with "a nice Italian girl." But Sonny, his gangster surrogate father, encourages Calogero to ignore Lorenzo's and his community's attitudes, and instead to follow his heart. Sonny's disdain for convention is liberating for the boy, while his father's attitudes confine him. Some of the wisdom Sonny imparts to C is just coldhearted mafia cynicism—"It's better to be feared than loved," "You should do what you want because nobody cares about you anyway." But in this matter at least, Sonny is a better teacher than Lorenzo.

Sonny, in fact, literally saves C's life when he prevents him from joining a bunch of his loser friends in a racist attack that backfires, with disastrous results for the Italian youths, who end up burned to death by the incendiary device they'd intended to hurl at a gathering of black youths. Viewing the charred corpses of their would-be attackers, one black youth remarks, "They look better that way."

The complexity of Sonny's character is one of the film's most original touches. Though Sonny makes his living outside the law and rules his neighborhood by instilling fear, he can also be wise and generous. He is even a somewhat poignant figure, lonely and lacking love in his life. He doesn't even have genuine friends. His men fear and respect him, but any regard they might have for him is due to the fact that they depend on him for their livelihood. He has no family of his own, hence his attachment to another man's son. He sees C for the last time in his bar. Sonny's face lights up when he spots the young man. As he waves to C, he meets his death—shot point-blank by the son of a man he had killed at the beginning of the film.

Robert De Niro contributes a solid and understated performance as Lorenzo Anello, a blue-collar Sicilian American of unyielding integrity who struggles to support his family and protect his son from the lure of easy and illicit money. But it's De Niro's direction that really impresses. His years of working with gifted directors, particularly his old friend and collaborator Martin Scorsese, paid off: A Bronx Tale is well paced, its pivotal moments expertly staged and dramatically compelling, and he elicits strong performances from his young stars Brancato and Hicks. The scenes between C and Jane in the first flush of puppy love have a sweetness and the halting, tentative rhythms of two kids from disparate backgrounds getting to know each other. (Jane is intrigued by C's exotic-sounding first name, Calogero, and he proudly explains its Sicilian origins.) De Niro demonstrates a strong, sympathetic, and unsentimental feel for the multiethnic working-class milieu of the Bronx in the 1960s, and he evocatively uses period music, both African American and Italian American.

A *Bronx Tale* is a singular entry in the mob movie canon in that it honors the genre's conventions—there's the remorseless violence and much ethnic color, with characters named Frankie Coffeecake and Eddie Mush—while exuding an atypical "moral power," as child psychologist Robert Coles notes.[2] The film is unique in its depiction of racism and the mafia cult of male violence as intertwined social evils that represent a terrible waste of human potential. "There's nothing sadder in life than wasted talent" is Lorenzo's favorite saying, which C has taken to heart. With his story of a Bronx teenager torn between opposing father figures Palmintieri successfully combines two genres, the bildungsroman and the gangster movie, while bringing to the latter unusual complexity and moral gravity.

The film's antiracism theme derives from Palmintieri's own experiences growing up in the working-class, Italian American Belmont neighborhood in the Bronx, the same community that was home to rock singer-songwriter Dion "The Wanderer" DiMucci. When I met Palmintieri in the summer of 2002, he told me that although it was widely assumed that the film's interracial love affair was Robert De Niro's contribution to the screenplay, it was actually based on his own relationship with a young black woman.

Yeah, a lot of people think it was De Niro's idea, because obviously Bob has dated black women. [De Niro's current wife, Grace Hightower, is African American, as was his first, Diahnne Abbott, and he had twins with ex-model and actress Toukie Smith.] But no, that was always in the script, back when *A Bronx Tale* was a play. I dated a black girl and I fell in love with her. Well, you think you're in love when you're sixteen years old. We went together for some months and we just drifted apart. Obviously, the pressure was pretty tough. But we cared about each other. I was never prejudiced toward anyone. I could never understand that in my neighborhood. There was hatred for black people, and there was no hatred on my part. It bothered me. But being in the middle of it, as Calogero was, I always had to dance with both sides, because these were my guys. I grew up with them. I found that to be interesting. That's why I had to write about it.[3]

For sheer off-the-wall strangeness, it'd be hard to beat *Ghost Dog: The Way of the Samurai*, director Jim Jarmusch's wildly recombinant 1999 comedy-drama that blends multiple genres: gangster, martial arts, and blaxploitation, all to a hip-hop soundtrack created by RZA of the rap group Wu-Tang Clan. The title character, played by Forrest Whitaker, is an African American mafia hit man who has adopted the spiritual and philosophical stance of a samurai. Ghost Dog devotedly carries out assassinations for his boss Louie (John Tormey), a midlevel mafioso who years earlier had earned the black man's loyalty by rescuing him from a beating by racist thugs. Louie and Ghost Dog never meet in person, communicating only by carrier pigeons.

Things start to unravel when mafia don Vargo (Henry Silva) orders the murder of one of his men because he is having sex with his daughter, Louise (Tricia Vessey). Ghost Dog successfully carries out the hit, but there is an unintended consequence: Louise witnesses the murder. Vargo is furious, and he and his right-hand man Sonny Valerio (Cliff Gorman) put a contract out on Ghost Dog. Because Louie was ultimately responsible for the hit, he fears for his life. So, to protect him, Ghost Dog swings into action, and, wielding his gun like a sword, he begins to track down the men threatening him and his boss.

The mobsters in *Ghost Dog* are like no others ever to shoot up a screen. Powerful? Cunning? Charismatic? Fuhgedaboudit. Talk about *il declino del padrino*—these pathetic old men embody the mob's ignominious decline. Lonely and broke, they can barely make the rent on their shabby "social club," and when they can't, they're forced to hold their sit-downs in a Chinese restaurant. They don't seem to be involved in any of the typical mob enterprises, or much of anything besides deciding whom to kill next. That's when they're not sitting in front of the TV like zombies watching Betty Boop and Woody Woodpecker cartoons.

Compared to this gang's don, wizened old Don Corrado Prizzi in *Prizzi's Honor* was a vigorous young buck. Vargo at times seems barely alive, more a wheezing revenant than a flesh-and-blood human. When he speaks, weird non sequiturs flow from his mouth, in what seems a parody of the mafioso's penchant for elliptical communication. And when he and his crew step outside, an obnoxious kid throws objects at them from a window.

Ghost Dog confronts urban racial politics head-on and with off-center wit. In one scene, the mobsters discuss Ghost Dog's name, noting its similarity to many rapper monikers. Sonny Valerio announces that his favorite rapper is Public Enemy's Flavor Flav, and quotes his lyrics. Sonny particularly likes Flav's "Cold Lampin' With Flavor" ("Ya eatin' death 'cause ya like gittin' dirt from da graveyard") and he does an arthritic little dance as he raps along to it in front of his bathroom mirror. It's a mind-bending moment—Cliff Gorman, a Jewish actor best known for playing an effeminate gay man in *The Boys in the Band*, impersonating an Italian American gangster with a jones for black hip-hop—and it's hard to believe that Jarmusch didn't intend his audience to make all those associations.

The mobsters mock "Indians and niggers" for their colorful nicknames, while they answer to monikers like "Big Angie" and "Sammy the Snake." A frail Chinese man disables a black mugger with some kung fu moves. Ghost Dog's closest friend is Raymond, a Haitian ice cream vendor (played by the African actor Isaac De Bankolé) who speaks no English, and Ghost Dog speaks no Creole, yet they understand each other perfectly. Is this just one of director Jarmusch's typically offbeat notes, or is their wordless communication a "black thing" that whites wouldn't understand, a mystical bond issuing from their shared Africanness? *Ghost Dog* plays up the mutability of racial and ethnic identity—hip-hop-loving mafiosi, African American samurai—but here Jarmusch seems to be engaging in some sentimental racial essentialism.

Running throughout this often very funny yet disturbing film (the graphic violence is no laughing matter) is a theme of degeneration. The mafiosi are living fossils, with no ostensible reason for existing other than to whack people. Ghost Dog himself is devoted to the samurai's warrior code, but he is cognizant of the near-impossibility of adhering to it in contemporary society. Speaking of himself and Louie, Ghost Dog the urban samurai remarks, "We're from different ancient tribes and now we're both almost extinct. But sometimes you got to stick to the ancient ways, the old school ways." But, Ghost Dog, the old ways just don't work any more.

Race and racial conflict are central to a number of films about Italians and blacks that, while not gangland dramas, are set in the same urban milieu, usually blue-collar New York City. These include Spike Lee's provocative *Do the Right Thing* (1989) and *Jungle Fever* (1991), and Raymond De Felitta's warmhearted (but not softheaded) *Two-Family House* (2000).

Spike Lee made both films in the wake of several brutal racist assaults by Italian Americans on African Americans—the 1986 attack on several black men in the Howard Beach section of Queens, which resulted in the death of one of them, and the 1989 murder of Yusuf Hawkins, an African American teenager, in Bensonhurst, a predominantly Italian section of Brooklyn.[4] Lee channeled his anger over these crimes into explorations of race, racism, and interethnic conflict, with a particular stress on black–Italian relations. Both films are intermittently powerful, offering piercing and discomfiting insights into the attitudes and behavior of New York's various contentious tribes. But both are marred by Lee's chronic, overbearing tendentiousness and lack of narrative focus.

Not all Italian American commentators would agree. The cultural critic Pasquale Verdicchio claims that both *Jungle Fever* and *Do the Right Thing* dramatize "differences between groups in order to highlight similarities . . . Further, Spike Lee's representations of ethnic conflict constitute a critique of 'white' ideology by exposing the mechanisms through which 'whiteness' instrumentalizes ethnic conflict to its benefit."[5]

Verdicchio argues that both films "use Italian immigrants as a sounding board to address issues of ethnic inclusion/exclusion, solidarity, difference, and similarity." Italian immigrants, however, do not appear in Lee's films; second- and third-generation Italian Americans do. Lee, says Verdicchio, "casts Italians as different, but not so different, from Blacks, because in the end they too cannot achieve full acceptance." This, Verdicchio observes, "re-establishes the Italians' ties with the typifications assigned them in their homeland and as immigrants, and thereby highlights their marginality."[6]

Verdicchio means that Spike Lee's depictions of Italian Americans as not quite white evoke the historical denigration of the Mezzogiorno by nineteenth-century northern Italian theorists of racial degeneration, and, once southern Italians began to emigrate to America, their subsequent racist mistreatment by WASP nativists.

He also cites "the tension that plays on the similarities between the two groups." In both films, "characters take on each other's movements, expressions, etc., as part of the process of ethnic masking. Gold chains, hand movements, verbal and physical communication, none are the dominion of one or the other group; Italians act Black, and African Americans act Italian."[7]

In *Do the Right Thing*, Mookie, the pizza delivery man (played by Lee, who is always far less assured in front of the camera than behind it), confronts Pino (John Turturro), the son of Sal (Danny Aiello), the pizzeria's owner. Mookie reminds the bigoted Pino that his favorite athletes and performers, such as Michael Jordan and Prince, are all black. (Lee could have had Pino retort that Prince is half-Italian, as *Rolling Stone* magazine reported in 1981,[8] which might have taken the two characters' dispute in some more interesting directions.) Mookie needles Pino about his own racial identity: "Your hair is kinkier than mine. What does that mean? You know what they say about dark Italians." Comments Verdicchio: "This hits the mark directly, not in the sense that Pino wishes he were Black, but that, in fact, Pino's subjectivity (as a Southern Italian) is Black identified. Pino is historically black."[9]

This assertion is nonsense. It's an irony of history that Pino, a dark-skinned, kinky-haired Brooklynite whose family hailed from Sicily, an island on Africa's doorstep, should be an antiblack racist. But Pino's subjectivity is Italian, which he conceives as white, or "white identified." Lee himself clearly views Italians as white folks, even as embodiments of white supremacy.

In 1989, when the film was released, *The New York Times* published a colloquy on its "issues and images." The article presented the opinions of a group of distinguished commentators that included blacks, Jews, and an Anglo-Saxon, but not a single Italian American.[10] (Some things never change: the *Times*, in all its rapturous praise for *The Sopranos*, has never addressed in any serious fashion the views of those Italian Americans who dislike the show.) Henry Louis Gates, Jr., the prominent African American intellectual, discusses the film's denouement, in which black rioters torch Sal's pizzeria after police kill a black man inside the restaurant. As the camera pans across the photo gallery of famous Italian Americans on the pizzeria's wall—De Niro, Pacino, Sinatra, DiMaggio—the portraits are devoured by flames.

Gates says: "Sal is the keeper of the Western canon. He's the person who decides who the all-time greatest hits are on the wall. And this becomes the gate to be stormed."[11] Gates here endorses demagoguery: Lee holds that the overworked owner of a small, downscale pizza parlor, a man who could have joined the white flight from a once-Italian, now black neighborhood but who instead continues to work there, is emblematic of the oppressive white power structure that kills innocent black men. So it's understandable that a mob would destroy his and his family's livelihood.

Lee doesn't idealize his black characters—and in fact the Italian American social critic Michael Parenti accuses him of perpetuating stereotypes of black men. Lee's character Mookie, says Parenti, "is a walking racist stereotype, a goof-off young Black male who is unable to hold a steady job."[12] He is also a less-than-attentive father to his son, as he is reminded at high decibels by Tina, the boy's Latina mother (Rosie Perez in one of her earliest film roles). When Mookie hears her speak to his son in Spanish, he demands that she use only English, as "it's bad enough his name is Hector."

Just about everybody in the film—Italian, black, Latino, Korean, Irish—is something of a bigot. But Lee has singled out Italians for particular animus. Besides the portrayal of Sal and his pizzeria as an embodiment of the Western canon, there are the different fates Lee doles out to him and to a Korean merchant. The Korean doesn't exactly see blacks as fellow people of color—to him they're all potential shoplifters. Moreover, the Koreans are newcomers to the neighborhood, unlike Sal, who has worked there for decades and is well known by the community. As he remarks about his black customers, "These people grew up on my food." But, unlike Sal's pizzeria, the Korean's business is spared by the mob because he sides with them and renounces whiteness, proclaiming, "Me black me black, me no white."

Lee returned to the terrain of black and Italian relations in *Jungle Fever* (1991), this time focusing on an ill-fated affair between Flipper Purify, a married African American architect (Wesley Snipes), and Angie Tucci, his Italian American secretary (Annabella Sciorra). The black characters, including Flipper's friends, react negatively to his involvement with a "white" woman; when they learn that she's an Italian from Bensonhurst they're even more dismayed. Angie's family is hardly more understanding. When her father Mike (played by Frank Vincent, whose numerous gangster roles include Billy Batts in *Goodfellas* and Phil Leotardo in *The Sopranos*) learns of the affair, he beats her and throws her out of the house.

Critic Pasquale Verdicchio claims that *Jungle Fever* is "even more explicit in its presentation of Italian racial ambiguity" than *Do the Right Thing*. Verdicchio notes that Vinnie, one of the Bensonhurst Italians, dresses in black, wears gold chains, drives a Cadillac, and listens to rap. But with the exception of rap fandom, all the traits Verdicchio cites have been part of urban Italian American culture as long as I can remember. (Verdicchio was born and raised in Italy, not in Italo-America.) That they are shared—and not only by blacks and Italians, but also by another major New York ethnic population, Latinos—says more about cross-cultural affinities in America's most ethnically diverse city than it does about Italian "racial ambiguity."

The film comes closer to supporting Verdicchio's point when Frankie, one of the Bensonhurst paisans, responds to a taunt that his mother must be black: "My mother's not black, she's just dark. There are dark Italians. Hey, I'm as white as anybody in here."[13] This moment, however, like Pino's overt racism, demonstrates another irony of history, the social and psychological investment (southern) Italians have made in whiteness, despite their history of having been racialized as less than fully "white," and despite the evidence of their mixed blood in their facial phenotypes, complexion, and hair texture.

Giorgio Bertellini, in an observation similar to Verdicchio's but more carefully considered, notes that although the film's title and narrative depict the relationship between Snipes's and Sciorra's characters as "the result of a libidinal attraction between two 'different' races rather than a romantic encounter between two human beings," it is remarkable that "the film does not refer to the Italian American characters, especially to Angela's father and brothers, as perfectly integrated or fully assimilated White citizens. Their racial distinctiveness, apparently less obvious if compared to Flipper's own neighborhood, is there to be seen."[14]

But the film contradicts both Verdicchio and Bertellini in one key scene. Flipper and Angie are having a conversation, or rather, Flipper is lecturing her, about the reasons a white woman like her wants to get fucked by a black man like him. She needs a respite from bland whiteness, a literal infusion of color. She's envious of his beautiful black skin because she, being melanin-deficient, at best can only acquire a light suntan. Flipper, arrogant and condescending, speaks to Angie as if she were a blond, blue-eyed Heidi instead of the dark-haired, dark-eyed, and olive-skinned southern Italian sitting next to him.

There's no indication that Spike Lee intends Flipper's obtuseness to be ironic. It is, in fact, the director's own blind spot. At the time of release, Lee was reported to have described white women as "muglies" who get involved with black men solely out of sexual curiosity. White women pursue black men because black men "know how to f—k," as Lee told *Newsweek*.[15] (And white racism is based on "fear of the Big Black Dick," as he told another publication.) So to him the issue of interracial relationships is predetermined from the start: white women who get involved with black men are in thrall to the myth of the black sexual superman. It is, and can only be, "jungle fever."

Angelo Mazzocco, an Italian American academic, notes that Lee's stance "is an affront to the dignity of white American women, for it implies that these women are lust-driven sexual objects void of discretion and humanity."[16] Mazzocco also deftly skewers Lee's invidious portrayals of Italian Americans:

> In Lee's scheme of things, the Italian mothers of Bensonhurst are all dead, killed (the movie implies) by the overwhelming sexism prevalent in their homes; the fathers are tyrannical, patriarchal clowns ready to savage their children at the least provocation; the sons are a slothful, violent lot who forever sputter anti-black epithets; the daughters are overly protected, frivolous things who, when not cooking for the voracious, sexist male members of their families, fantasize about the black man's sexual prowess. By contrast, the residents of Harlem are rational, productive members of the community who resort to violence only when engulfed by the vortex of drug addiction. The women of Harlem are compassionate and sensible, and they would be exemplary wives and mothers were it not for the "white bitches" who rob them of their men.[17]

Racism, Mazzocco wrote, is a "social cancer" whose "resolution is urgent and incumbent on every American institution, including the cinema." But "the one-sided, sloganeering approach of *Jungle Fever* cannot help to fight racism because the film's own logic is itself racist.[18]

Mazzocco's trenchant criticism of *Jungle Fever* appeared in *Voices in Italian Americana (VIA)*, a small-circulation academic journal, so his views, as well as those of other Italian Americans critical of the film, never intruded on the hosanna chorus of praise for the film from critics and journalists, who for the most part have been in Lee's corner from the start of his career. From the beginning Lee came on as an insurgent black filmmaker, an angry, socially aware auteur willing to tackle the big issues—racism, interethnic strife, sexism, color consciousness among African Americans—which Hollywood either routinely ignored or trivialized. Yet the hype obscured the truth about Lee: with the exception of a few films—his documentary *Four Little Girls* and *Malcolm X*—his reach has always exceeded his grasp. Lee's mastery of the film medium can't conceal the intellectual shallowness and confusion, the tendency to substitute posturing and attitude for ideas, which has marred even his best work and overpowered most of his later efforts.

Both the pro-Lee Verdicchio and the critical Mazzocco overlook the key element in the portrayals of Italian Americans in *Do the Right Thing* and *Jungle Fever*: ambivalence. Lee has a love-hate relationship with this ethnic group, having seen them at their best and their worst, the latter largely defined by Lee as their racism. Most of the Italians in *Jungle Fever* are dumb, brutal, and racist. But Angie Tucci bears the same last name as one of Lee's closest childhood friends, and she and Paulie Carbone (John Turturro) are two of the most decent characters in the film. By contrast, Flipper, the African American hero, is a shallow, self-centered buppie. And when Flipper tells Angie that she was just curious about sex with black men and didn't have any genuine feelings for him, she replies, "Don't tell me how I feel." The line— improvised by Sciorra—cracks the stifling schematicism of the film, if only for one isolated moment.

Annabella Sciorra had never spoken on the record about her experiences making *Jungle Fever* until we met for an interview at her Manhattan apartment in the fall of 2002. She was aware of media reports, including a story in *The Village Voice*, that there had been conflict between her and her director on the set of *Jungle Fever*. She had also heard about Lee's widely reported remarks disparaging white women. "Spike has a really strong attraction to Italian Americans," Sciorra says.

> I think he also came to his maturity as a student at New York University [where Lee studied filmmaking], watching a lot of Scorsese and De Niro, and I think he tried to emulate that. When I saw *Mo' Better Blues* [made between *Do the Right Thing* and *Jungle Fever*], I thought, Oh, wow! He's gone after a style that's really reminiscent of Scorsese, with all the improvisation and all that.
>
> The race issue . . . I'm hesitant to talk about it because it's such a deep issue to me. It runs really, really deep for me. It really came to a boiling point doing *Jungle Fever*. I felt that my character Angie really fell for this guy. I never once thought that it was about [sexual] curiosity. When the movie came out, I wasn't here. I was in Seattle shooting another movie, so I missed a lot of the discussion. I only heard about it. I didn't

know why *The Village Voice* was having some big discussion about me and Spike and that we had some big argument or we had some big fights—which we *didn't*!

But Sciorra and Lee definitely did have differing interpretations of the Angie–Flipper relationship.

Why would somebody sleep with somebody just because of curiosity about color? I didn't understand it. That's what the movie was supposed to be about, but I didn't know that. So I didn't approach it that way. It wasn't that I tried to actively go against what Spike wanted, but I just didn't understand that that was what he was going for. My life experiences didn't bring me to that, so I didn't see it in the script. Maybe it was there and I didn't see it. I just really thought that she fell for this man because he was educated.

I would love to talk to Spike about it now. I wonder what was happening at that time that we both didn't understand about each other.

From Sciorra's recollections, it appears that Lee was intent on making *Jungle Fever* a racial polemic. She recalls that he had wanted her to take her costar Wesley Snipes to an Italian street festival in Brooklyn, apparently expecting that the sight of the mixed couple would incite an ugly racist response from the Italians. "We never ended up doing it," Sciorra says, "but I don't think it would have been anything like what he [Lee] thought."

A scene that made it into the finished film gave further evidence that Lee intended to portray Italians in the most unflattering light. Angie and Flipper visit the San Gennaro festival in Little Italy, New York's oldest Italian American fete. "We're at San Gennaro and there's a guy selling something, behind a banquette, and they have a close-up of his point of view. Basically, he's just looking at the camera, but he has a very suspicious sort of look." Sciorra says that the sequence was edited to make it appear that the vendor was looking askance at this interracial couple, "and that's not what he was reacting to."

Sciorra adds that "a lot of weird stuff that happened" during the film's production.

Like, the candy store that we shot in, where John Turturro's character Paulie worked. Apparently the guy who owned the candy store was selling it, and that's how they [Lee's production company] got to use it. They had to redo it and everything. He [the owner] had some problems in the neighborhood. I don't know what the problems were exactly, but I came to find this out afterward, because they shot it on Avenue M [in Brooklyn], where I grew up. Somebody in the neighborhood had, I don't know what, thrown rocks through the window or something. There was some real estate issue that had nothing to do with the movie, had nothing to do with anything, and they [the media] made it into a racial issue. It was on the cover of the [New York] Post and the [New York Daily] News that they were shooting Jungle Fever in this neighborhood and the people in the neighborhood were Italian (which is not true, it's a predominantly Irish-German-Jewish area), and it was the Italians in the neighborhood who didn't want the black people there.

I was like, "Wait a minute. This is not what's happening . . . There's no racial problem in the neighborhood. They're not mad at us because we're here shooting a movie." I'm not gonna deny that there probably were Italian Americans who felt like, "She shouldn't be doing that movie. Why is she doing that movie where she has sex with a black man?" I'm not gonna deny that. I don't know those people, but I'm sure they exist. I don't know how it got started. I don't know if it was a press thing that got out of hand or if it was somebody trying to create some drama around a situation that didn't exist, to give some hype. But it was unfair.

Near the end of Jungle Fever, after Flipper and Angie have ended their relationship, Angie goes home to Bensonhurst, carrying her suitcase, and her father welcomes her back. Sciorra says the idea for the reconciliation came from Joe Pesci, who originally was supposed to play Mike Tucci but quit the film before shooting began. Sciorra and Pesci met for the first time some ten years after *Jungle Fever*.

> He said to me, "You know I was supposed to be your father in *Jungle Fever*." I said, "Yeah." He said, "You know why I dropped out?" I said, "Well, I heard from Spike what the reason was, but I would love to hear it from you." But it was the same reason. Joe felt that even if he would beat me up and throw me out of the house, and disown me, he felt that there should be some sort of reconciliation, that after all, it was his daughter and that he would have to accept her back because culturally that's what he would do as an Italian. That's what he felt, and Spike said, "Okay."
>
> But Joe wanted a guarantee that that scene would be in the movie and Spike wouldn't give him that guarantee, which is a very hard thing. You can't give an actor a guarantee that some moment's going to be in a movie. You have a studio behind you, also. It's a very difficult thing. I don't think any actor gets that kind of say. But that's why he dropped out of the movie.
>
> I have nothing bad to say about Spike Lee, because Spike gave me all my moments. They're all in there. Everything I wanted to do with that character is in the movie, so in the end, Spike saw what I was doing and put it in the movie—and he didn't have to. But John [Turturro] also helped me a lot with my character and with being on the set. I was asked to improvise a lot, and I would say stuff that wasn't acceptable for that situation, but I just felt that Angie was smarter than maybe Spike thought she was. I felt like Angie had more information. If I'm an Italian American woman from Brooklyn, and she's an Italian American woman from Brooklyn—okay, I'm an actress, she's working as an assistant or a temp—but why wouldn't she have that same information? So, if you put me in a situation where I'm improvising, I'm going to let her have that information. But I guess I didn't understand where he was going and I guess he didn't understand where I was going until after it was all over and done. But like I said, it's all there. All my moments were there.[19]

With *Summer of Sam* (1999), Spike Lee's love/hate attitude toward Italian Americans hardened into an uninflected hostility. *Do the Right Thing* and *Jungle Fever* showed Italians "at their paranoiac, loathsome worst," according to critic John Gennari, but "those caricatures have . . . been surpassed by the Bronx primitives" of *Summer of Sam*.[20] The film is also the only one of the director's three movies about Italian Americans to portray mobsters as dominant figures in their communities, neighborhood "protectors," and dispensers of vigilante "justice."

Summer of Sam, which has no major black characters, explores the impact of the "Son of Sam" murders on the residents of a Bronx Italian American neighborhood, including a mob boss and his crew. *Sam* is populated with little else but grotesque stereotypes of Italian Americans; the community Lee depicts consists mainly of sexually compulsive men and slutty women, young wives victimized by their lothario husbands, mob bosses, and their bigoted and moronic street thugs.

The project began atypically for Lee in that he planned neither to write nor to direct it. His interest was piqued by an early draft of a script by Victor Colicchio and Michael Imperioli, the brilliant young actor best known for his work on *The Sopranos*.

"The reason for me doing this film is because I love the script," Lee said in 1999. "It's a great story, simple as that. Michael Imperioli and Victor Colicchio handed me the script. At first I was going to executive produce it. Then I changed my mind and did a re-write of it."[21]

However much of Imperioli and Colicchio's material made it into the finished film, Lee is the auteur of *Summer of Sam*, and it is infused with his vision and sensibility. He, then, bears responsibility for the monolithically ugly depictions of Italian Americans, as well as for the film's numerous other artistic failings—its excessive length (nearly two and a half hours), the showy and undigested mélange of cinematic techniques, and overall narrative incoherence.

For several months in 1976 and during the summer of 1977, a serial killer named David Berkowitz, who dubbed himself the Son of Sam, terrorized a Bronx neighborhood, shooting to death six young men and women and seriously wounding another seven. (He also struck in Queens and Brooklyn.) The deranged Berkowitz claimed a neighbor named Sam Carr transmitted the order to commit the killings through his dog. Lee presents the murders as the catalyst for simmering im-

pulses waiting to erupt in the Bronx Italian community, whose members, driven by fear and paranoia, turn on one another.

The film's main characters—or rather types, since none is a fully realized, credible human being—are an unhappily married couple, Vinny
and Dionna (John Leguizamo and Mira Sorvino), and a punk rocker,
Ritchie (Adrien Brody), an old friend of Vinny's. Ritchie has returned to
the nabe after a year in Manhattan and, to the consternation of his old
pals, he's changed from the borough boy they knew into a punk, with
spiky hair and a faux British accent. Since "different" equals "suspicious" in this neighborhood, the locals suspect that Ritchie is the Son
of Sam, an unlikely assumption considering a serial killer would hardly
choose to stand out the way Ritchie does.

The police, frustrated by their inability to catch the killer, request
the assistance of Luigi (Ben Gazzara), the local mob boss, and he orders his crew to find the Son of Sam. Led by Joe T (the excellent
Michael Rispoli), who sells drugs for Luigi, the thugs pick up their
baseball bats and go into vigilante mode, all in the name of protecting
the neighborhood. They draw up a list of suspects that comprises all
the weirdos and outsiders in the neighborhood. Ritchie, with his blond
Mohawk, becomes a prime suspect. Ritchie works part-time as a gay
hustler, for reasons never explained, but he has a girlfriend, the neighborhood *puttana*, Ruby (Jennifer Esposito), and the two outcasts form
a rock band, Late-Term Abortion.

The vigilantes persuade Vinny, formerly Ritchie's best friend, to en-
trap the punk rocker. Vinny, high on drugs, sets up Ritchie, luring him
into the street where Joe T and his hoodlums beat him bloody. They're
about to drag him off to Luigi, but Ritchie's stepfather fortuitously
steps forward—brandishing a pistol—to tell the mob that the police
have arrested the real killer. As the vigilantes back off, Ritchie's mother
and Ruby tend to his injuries, while a guilt-stricken Vinny lurches off
down the street.

Lee lards this slim story with lots of flashy but extraneous detail, including a three-minute music video, multiple film stocks, and various
other cinematic effects. The overly busy production design, however,
can't camouflage the crudity of his directorial sensibility. The film is
awash in caricatures of Italian Americans. These paisans are devoted to

their families, loyal to their mob boss, tortured by religiously induced sexual guilt, bigoted, and ever-ready to crack skulls with their baseball bats. Vinny, a horny hairdresser, is afflicted by the Madonna/whore complex. Since he can't expect his sweet wife, Dionna, to engage in oral and anal sex, he pursues other women and goes to sex clubs. Joe T and his boys are loud brutes, insensate bigots given to cursing and fighting.

And of course, these Italians have to be racist. In one scene Dionna gets out of her car and announces to Vinny that she wants to have sex with a black man with a huge penis. She is taunting him, and we know why: for an Italian guy, nothing could be more repulsive, more unforgivable than his wife making the beast with two backs with a moulanyan. But Vinnie hasn't made any racist remarks or otherwise indicated that he hates blacks. For Lee, it's simply a given that a character named Vinny would be a racist.

One scene says it all about the director's view of his characters. The young Italian guys are hanging out in a cul-de-sac in their neighborhood; right next to the dead-end sign is an Italian flag. Get it? These wops are such losers.

If another director had set *Summer of Sam* in a black or Latino community and had depicted the residents in similarly negative fashion, the liberal intelligentsia rightly would have denounced it as sheer bigotry and hate-mongering. But when Spike Lee—a multimillionaire who has made commercials for Nike, a corporation notorious for its Asian sweatshops—savages a working-class community that happens to be Italian American, there's barely a peep of criticism.

As *New York Times* columnist Clyde Haberman observed, "What do you think would happen if a white director went to Harlem and shot a film portraying blacks almost exclusively as gangsters, dopers, and sex-obsessed stupes? How long would it take before Al Sharpton or [NAACP head] Kweisi Mfume put protestors outside movie theaters? One minute or two? Yet show Italian-Americans in that kind of harsh and unfair light—as the black director Spike Lee does relentlessly in his new film, 'Summer of Sam'—and all you hear is some low-level grumbling."[22]

Michael Rispoli, who played Joe T in *Summer of Sam*, defends the film. "I've liked Spike's movies. I don't always agree with him, but I like to work with him as a filmmaker," he says. "It was a great experience working with him. He let us improvise a lot, maybe too much. It was a very satisfying experience." He claims Lee's depiction of a Bronx neighborhood on the verge of a collective nervous breakdown was accurate: "People were scared out their minds, there was a monster out there, and nobody knew what to expect." The script, he adds, "reflected what Victor Colicchio saw happening in his neighborhood, the fear and paranoia."

Rispoli sidesteps the question of whether *Summer of Sam* stereotypes Italian Americans. "The actor's job is to do the script," he says. "You can always say I don't want to be a part of this script, it's too stereotypical, but it depends on how much money you've got in the bank."

Rispoli says he turned down the lead role in a John Gotti biopic, but the film got made anyway. "I specifically don't go in for characters if I think they're detrimental to the Italian image. But if you're gonna tell a story and you're gonna tell it right, and it takes place in 1977, in the city, and this is the way it is, then why not tell that story, and hope for the best."[23]

The actor supports his historical accuracy argument with an analogy to another period film, *Two-Family House*, director Raymond De Felitta's acclaimed 2000 feature set in a working-class Italian American neighborhood in Staten Island during the 1950s. Rispoli played the film's lead character, Buddy Visalo, a likable working stiff with dreams of being a singer in his own saloon. Visalo purchases the run-down eponymous structure in pursuit of his dream, but first he must evict its remaining tenants, an Irish alcoholic and his young, pregnant wife.

When the wife, Mary Neary (Kelly Macdonald), gives birth to a brown-skinned baby, racism rears its ugly head. And when Buddy falls in love with her and the affair becomes common knowledge, his distraught wife Estelle (Katherine Narducci) berates him for going with a "nigger-lover." The ethnic slurs "mick" and "wop" are also freely used in the film. Feeling guilty about having evicted Mary, Buddy sets her up in an apartment above an Italian salumeria [pork store and deli]. Buddy isn't even aware of his true intentions, but the less than grateful Mary guesses them, and blasts him and all Italians: "You're all a race of pimps!"

Some objected to this language, Rispoli notes, just as others criticized the portrayal of blue-collar Italian Americans in *Summer of Sam*. "But that's the way people felt. It was the fifties."

The uninhibited use of racial and ethnic slurs might be off-putting to some viewers, but the language would hardly shock anyone familiar with the work of Martin Scorsese or Spike Lee. The difference between De Felitta's film and *Summer of Sam*, however, is that while De Felitta portrays his characters as prejudiced, he doesn't treat them as contemptible losers, worthy only of derision. He instead presents their attitudes as expressions of fear, insecurity, and insularity. Moreover, he shows that intolerance isn't somehow hardwired in Italian Americans, as Spike Lee seems to believe. Buddy Visalo, a good and decent man, is quite capable of rising above the parochial biases of his community; at the film's conclusion, he is living with Mary and her mixed-race son, whom he has adopted, in the Buddy's Tavern of his dreams.

Raymond De Felitta says he strove to portray the attitudes of white ethnic working-class New Yorkers of the 1950s with accuracy, without editorializing or imposing the (purportedly) more enlightened views of our era on the material.

> Well, you know, racism is a word now that means something that it didn't mean fifty years ago—which is not to say that racism didn't exist. But I always felt that the important thing about the racism in my movie was that its perniciousness was so casual. It didn't mark you as a racist to call someone a moulanyan or even a nigger. It was the street language of the day, and it was the way a lot of these guys were brought up. They were brought up in tough environments. And in tough environments, as we see in world history over and over again, people get beat up on, and then they beat up on the next one down. But however the food chain works, black people were at an enormous disadvantage—the greatest disadvantage of everyone—so everybody beat up on them.
>
> People were brought up—Italian, Irish, whatever they

were—all of them feeling that they were superior to black people—who were born here. That was just the ugly truth. Did it
mean they hated black people? I don't think they hated black
people. I don't think they were racist in the way that we now
think of it. I think it just meant that they knew they were in a
better position socially, that they had the advantage.

And there were a lot of Italians with dark skin and curly hair.
So that right away makes them not look like everybody else who
was already here, and makes them look more like the most
disadvantaged people who were already here. So they [Italians]
were probably even more defensive on that level. But their ability to stick together also probably promoted so much group
thought and what we now think of as racism. But racism is
racism no matter how you cut it.

I just think, though, that given how we now think of it, we
tend to misunderstand a lot of things in the past. For me, this is
a scary remaking of history, because I think that one of the great
disservices that can be done—and I had to face this in getting
the movie made—is to prettify the truth. I had very supportive
producers, but every so often somebody would say, "Do we have
to use such language? Do we have to use the n-word, do we
have to call him a Mick?" I thought, we can change it, but that
wouldn't serve the history of [the 1950s]. And I felt, if you don't
do this honestly, the story will still make sense, but you'd miss
what matters in the difference between those times and ours.[24]

"There is no easy way to set the Mafia apart from the general culture it
operates within."[25]

Italian critic Alessandro Camon's observation that mafiosi swim in
the same cultural tide as their noncriminal brethren applies not only to
beliefs and practices about sex and gender. The racist attitudes of gangsters portrayed in films discussed in this chapter are not peculiar to
them. They unfortunately reflect not only the sentiments of fictional
and actual gangsters but also some of the less salutary aspects of Italian
American communities, including a suspicion of outsiders bred in the

conditions of the Mezzogiorno, and antiblack racism, a product of the complex history of relations between African Americans and Italian Americans.

Southern Italian immigrants and blacks from the rural American South began to arrive in Northern U.S. cities at roughly the same time, the late nineteenth and early twentieth centuries. Both were poor, marginalized peoples desperate to improve their lot. Both groups were engaged in many of the same blue-collar occupations and trades, as laborers, barbers, small shopkeepers. And Italians and blacks were despised by WASP America as primitive, uncivilized, and prone to violent crime.

"The Italians in America had to bear the Full Monty of American racist contempt," says academic and author Robert Viscusi.

They were categorized as Negroes, basically, and they got treated the same way that black people got treated after the fall of Reconstruction. In fact, the importation of Italians and the fall of Reconstruction are simultaneous events—not entirely by accident. Because the Italians were brought in partly as a way of keeping the black people's wages low. Italians would work for practically nothing. So there was a kind of a sword between the Italians and the African-Americans from square one—and it's still there, hasn't disappeared by any stretch. The Italians were treated with contempt by the rich and also by the rest of the poor—the Irish and the African-Americans resented them. Rich people treated them with the same delicacy that they treated black people.[26]

The southern Italian immigrants had felt the sting of racism in their own country, before they ever landed in America. "The *milanesi* will tell you, '*Da Roma in giù cominicia l'Africa*' [Africa starts south of Rome]," as Robert Viscusi has noted. "Northern Italians fear the South, regarding it as the source of various ills and weaknesses that racial myth associates with Africans and Semitic tribes. The stigma associated with southern Italians has followed them to the United States . . ."[27]

"An invidious comparison was always made between [southern Italians and] fair-skinned and allegedly more industrious and law-abiding northern Italians, called 'Teutonic Italians' by Henry Cabot Lodge," observes historian Robert Orsi.[28]

"The history of Southern Italy, the region from which most Italian immigrants [to the United States] originate, is steeped in an ambiguous relationship with the rest of the peninsula," notes Pasquale Verdicchio. Northern Italian theorists like Cesare Lombroso, Enrico Ferri, and Alfredo Niceforo "established the racial inferiority of southern Italians through cranial measurements and other pseudoscientific criteria."[29]

Politicians in northern Italy adopted these racist notions, dismissing southern Italians as dark-skinned and barbaric, and not even Christian: "The ancient term of abuse for them was 'Turks.' "[30]

Notions of southern Italian inferiority were used to justify the annexation of the South by the Piedmont-based national government established under the Risorgimento in the 1860s. The people of the Mezzogiorno did not identify with the newborn Italian nation-state, seeing it as a distant oppressor that imposed harsh taxation on them. Their main loyalties were to their families and villages. When southerners resisted repression by the new Italian government and the newly established national army, they were labeled as bandits, brigands.

Resistance to northern rule lasted for decades, "during which typifications of Southerners as Africans, Indians, cannibals, etc. became even more rooted. These assignations were, of course, used in derogatory terms meant to associate Southerners with other equally despised peoples." This racial rhetoric served to justify not only military intervention in southern Italy but also colonial annexations in Africa: "The chronological coincidences between the repression of southern rebellions and the invasion of African lands such as Eritrea are not to be overlooked."[31]

Southern Italians fled their homeland by the millions, seeking to escape not only *la miseria* (poverty) but also political disenfranchisement and outright repression, as well as conscription into the Italian military and forced participation in Italy's colonial wars. When they arrived in the United States, they found themselves in a racial limbo-land, their role in America's peculiar racial drama ambiguous.

Robert Orsi says it is a fact "largely ignored by historians" that "Italian American history began in racially inflected circumstances every-where in the United States." Native-born, Anglo-Saxon Americans wondered, "Were the olive-skinned newcomers white or black, the only two possibilities in the domestic racial taxonomy?" Orsi adopts historian John Higham's term, "in-betweenness," to describe the status of south-ern Italians during the early years of immigration to America. He cites "four factors, rooted in specific social conditions in Italy and the United States," which converged "to constitute the dilemma of inbetweenness for the immigrants and their children." These were the racist terms used by northern Italians to distinguish themselves from southerners, the adoption of this racist discourse by American WASPs, the simulta-neous arrival in North American cities of other darker skinned peoples, and the determination of southern Italian immigrants to make new and dignified lives for themselves in their adopted country.[32]

"In certain regions of the Jim Crow South, Italians occupied a racial middle ground within the otherwise unforgiving binary case system of white-over-black,"[33] observes Matthew Frye Jacobson in *Whiteness of a Different Color*, his study of racial identity formation among European immigrants to the United States. Italian American historian Rudolph Vecoli has noted, "In the years of massive immigration, the racial clas-sification of Italians was in doubt. Many Anglo-Americans questioned that these swarthy sons of sunny Italy were really white. Employers and labor leaders referred to them as 'black labor,' while the color line was invoked to keep them out of certain neighborhoods, schools, and or-ganizations."[34]

White privilege has been a constant in America since colonial days, but whiteness itself has been contested, and has gone "through a series of historical vicissitudes."[35] That the whiteness of southern Italians was subject to dispute is exemplified by a 1922 miscegenation case in Al-abama (cited in Chapter 1) involving an African American man and a Sicilian immigrant woman. Jim Rollins had been convicted for un-lawful sexual contact with a white woman, but the conviction was overturned by a higher court because the woman, Edith Labue, was Sicilian, and Sicilians, according to the court, were not conclusively white.

Jacobson adds that the ruling was not peculiar to courts in Alabama, but rather was part of "a broader pattern of racial thinking throughout the United States between the mid-nineteenth century and the mid-twentieth century."[36] This time period roughly coincides with the arrival of southern Italian immigrants to America and their assimilation into American society as whites.

The intertwined histories of Italians and blacks in America have been marked from the start by competition and conflict. Italian immigrants "moved into established black neighborhoods at the turn of the century in Philadelphia, St. Louis, Cleveland, and Greenwich Village, among other places; fifty years later, African Americans were displacing Italians in these same locations," Orsi relates.[37] Italians also went into occupations that blacks had dominated, such as barbering, restaurant work, masonry and other construction, and garbage collecting, in many instances displacing and excluding blacks.

Conflict became more common after the Depression era and World War II, as the two peoples competed with each other for "jobs, housing, and neighborhood power and presence."[38] Relations further worsened as the two largely urban groups found themselves jostling for economic and political power during the 1960s and '70s in the declining industrial cities of the North and Northeast. Conservative Italian Americans like Philadelphia mayor Frank Rizzo, a former police officer, and self-appointed community defender-cum-vigilante Anthony Imperiale in Newark, New Jersey, came to embody antiblack backlash; their hard-line, often racist "law and order" politics was applauded by many whites and loathed by blacks. During the 1980s, assaults on blacks who ventured into Italian American neighborhoods horrified New York City and helped to elect its first African American mayor, David Dinkins.

But surprising as it may seem given this dire history, Italian Americans and African Americans have enjoyed close and cooperative relationships.

"Innocent of the racial code in this 'free country,' newly arrived immigrants often worked with and lived among African Americans," notes Italian American historian Rudolph Vecoli.[39]

"It was not just that Italians did not look white to certain social arbiters," according to Matthew Frye Jacobson, "but that they did not act white. In New Orleans Italian immigrants were stigmatized in the post–Civil War period because they accepted economic niches (farm labor and small tenancy, for instance) marked as 'black' by local custom, and because they lived and worked comfortably among blacks."[40]

Music was a central arena in which blacks and Italians encountered and cooperated with each other. In Louisiana, the state that gave birth to jazz, many Italians refused "to join in the effort to suppress Louisiana Blacks." The Louisiana Italians "largely ignored the calls to racial hatred."[41] Ethnohistorian Garry Boulard has observed that "while the Italian Americans and Louisiana's Blacks shared economic, social, and political similarities, their cultural identities were even more firmly intertwined."[42]

This was probably most fully evident in the two groups' "social and entertainment rituals, particularly regarding music." At Italian-owned jazz clubs in New Orleans, such as Matranga's, Joe Segretta's, Tonti's Social Club, and Lala's Big 25, "inevitably both Black and Italian musicians were featured performers." Openly flouting racial segregation, "both Black and Italian musicians played together in informal settings, copying each other's work, blending the musical strains of their respective African and Mediterranean origins."[43]

Louis Prima, the Sicilian American trumpeter and singer, exemplified the progressive approach of Italian American musicians regarding racial matters:

> His appearances before Black audiences, the jam sessions with noted Black musicians, his unwillingness to appear in segregated and racially tense Southern cities, all underlined Prima's private racial values, values which were steeped in the historic tradition of Black and Italian cooperation in New Orleans. Because they shared the same economic deprivation and cultural hostility from the White establishment, Blacks and Italians developed a general relationship of mutual support, survival, and political outlook.[44]

Louis Armstrong, the New Orleans native and jazz virtuoso and one of the greatest artists America has produced, began his career in Matranga's, a Crescent City nightclub owned by a Sicilian mafia family.

Henry Matranga, who ran the club, "treated everybody fine," according to Armstrong, "and the colored people who patronized his tonk loved him very much."[45] Matranga was by no means the only mobbed-up club owner in the history of jazz. Notorious gangsters like Vito Genovese and Lucky Luciano also ran nightspots where leading jazz and pop artists performed. In his 1980 book *Wait until Dark: Jazz and the Underworld, 1880–1940*,[46] historian Ronald L. Morris chronicled the intimate connections between music and mafia in New Orleans, what Nick Tosches has called "the symbiosis between show business and *la bisiness*."[47]

During the 1920s and '30s, in both the Deep South and in Northern cities, mobsters and musicians enjoyed working relationships that were mutually beneficial. Sicilian and Jewish gangsters hired jazz musicians, black and white, to play in their establishments, and generally paid them well and provided good working conditions. (Italian and Jewish mobsters loved the jazz played in their clubs—Al Capone and his brothers were hardcore fans who lavishly tipped their favorite players, like pianist Earl "Fatha" Hines. Their Irish and Anglo-Saxon counterparts, on the other hand, didn't much care for "hot" music.) By hiring racially mixed bands and welcoming an integrated clientele, the mobsters even made a contribution to social justice. Of the Roaring Twenties gangsters, Morris says,

> They may have been avaricious to some degree, but by fighting for small measures of social justice—through hiring practices, integrational policies, a softened attitude toward women and young people generally, and the feeling of avoiding moral condemnation of others—they made an effort to improve patron pleasures in as safe and respectful an atmosphere as possible . . . The opportunities and salaries and attention lavished upon jazz artists, who were all the while being provided with a dignified setting in which to perform (at least compared to the past), freed from concern about racial interference, were new departures that brought a share of wealth and fame in its train.[48]

Black jazz musicians and Italian and Jewish gangsters found they had some other things in common besides a love for jazz. They admired each other's flashy sartorial style and ultramasculine self-presentation, each other's "butch realness," as a later generation would call this stylized gender performance. Both liked living large—gambling, booze, reefer, and women were shared favorite pastimes. But as Morris observes, the affinities went even deeper: "Themselves fleeing persecution yet without traditional American bigotry towards blacks, Jews and Sicilians were squeezed into living side by side, or in adjacent neighborhoods, combating identical challenges to their cultural integrity and physical well-being. Jews, blacks, and Italians were all unable to penetrate significant segments of the American economy and faced exclusion from the chieftains of industry and finance."[49]

Mob-owned and -operated clubs and cabarets began to wane in the 1930s, less because of the hardship of the Depression (mobsters preferred liquid cash over credit, so many had abundant financial reserves) than because of political pressure from antigangster urban reformists. Their own bad business decisions—many "quit simply taking risks and became complacent about the night club business"—also helped sound the death knell for jazz clubs. The musicians, most of them black, suffered the most from the breakup and dissolution of the mob club scene. Beginning around 1930, "only the most versatile, durable and nattily-dressed black orchestras and bands would survive."[50]

For more than a century, the Mardi Gras celebrations of New Orleans have featured parades of black men garbed as American Indians. Wearing braided wigs and fantastically colorful and eleborate costumes, the Mardi Gras Indians, as they are known, dance through crowds of revelers, beating tambourines and singing chantlike songs that have influenced the city's jazz and rhythm and blues. These performers traditionally hold their own parade, separate from the main Mardi Gras celebrations, on March 19, which Sicilians and other southern Italians celebrate as St. Joseph's Day.

In 2004, *New York Times* correspondent Jon Pareles interviewed one of the leaders of the Mardi Gras Indians, eighty-one-year-old Tootie Montana, who recalled the past close relationship between blacks and Italians. Montana noted that blacks also celebrated St.

Joseph's Day, because " 'the Italians and us were like this,' Mr. Montana said, holding two fingers close together."[51]

The African American/Italian American jazz connection thrived even after the music migrated from New Orleans to Chicago and the Northeast. And although African Americans indisputably have been the leading innovators in every epoch of the music's history, Italian Americans have made and continue to make important contributions.

George Wallington, a Sicilian-born musician whose birth name was Giacinto Figlia, was one of the original beboppers, having been the first pianist to perform with trumpeter Dizzy Gillespie and saxophonist Charlie Parker in the 1940s, at such New York boîtes as the Three Deuces and the Onyx Club.[52]

Joe Lovano, the Cleveland-born Sicilian American saxophonist who is a leading figure in contemporary jazz, has had a lifelong relationship with black music and black musicians. A gifted composer and bandleader as well as a superb instrumentalist, Lovano has developed a distinctively personal jazz style based on the language created by the music's mainly African American innovators and infused with his own ethnic sensibility. He has written and recorded compositions with titles such as "Bread and Wine" and "Miss Etna," and on his 2002 album *Viva Caruso* he crafted inspired jazz reinterpretations of Italian songs associated with the great tenor.

Lovano says his first teacher was his father, Tony "Big T" Lovano, also a saxophonist. And the lessons weren't only musical. Lovano senior, who had a substantial regional reputation in the Midwest, regularly worked with African American musicians, both local and nationally known players. "My dad was really involved with the African American musicians in Cleveland," Lovano told me in 1995. "He had a real open and beautiful attitude about combinations of peoples. He always had mixed groups . . ."[53]

During the 1960s racial upheavals in Cleveland, Tony Lovano started playing in white-owned, suburban supper clubs because a number of the inner city nightspots he had worked in were destroyed during riots. Lovano says that his father would "explode" at white club owners who balked at his black musicians, fearing they would attract black patrons. "He'd say, 'Look, you hire me, I play with the best musicians in town, and you don't tell me who to play with.' "[54]

Lovano is today's most prominent Italian American jazz artist, but there have been many others. A partial roll call of them includes pianists Chick Corea and Lennie Tristano; singer-pianist Buddy Greco; clarinetist Buddy DeFranco; the brothers Pete and Conte Candoli, both trumpeters; drummer Louis Bellson (Luigi Balassoni); saxophonists Flip Phillips (Joseph Filipelli), Jimmy Giuffre, Sal Nistico, Vido Musso, Frank Vignola, and Charlie Ventura; violinist Joe Venuti; and guitarists Pat Martino, Joe Pass (Giuseppe Passalaqua), Bucky Pizzarelli and his son John, and Al DiMeola. Eddie Lang (Salvatore Massaro), who made his mark in the 1930s, is regarded as the father of jazz guitar playing. Louis Prima, before he became a pop entertainer, was a fine, Armstrong-influenced jazz trumpeter.

But notwithstanding the camaraderie and collaboration among African American and Italian American musicians, the latter enjoyed a privileged position early on in the history of jazz. The first jazz group to make a recording was not an African American outfit but the white Original Dixieland Jazz Band, led by the Sicilian American trumpeter Dominick "Nick" La Rocca.[55] The band's "Darktown Strutters Ball" was a smash hit in 1917, selling an unheard-of million copies. La Rocca wrote one of their other hits, "Tiger Rag," known to generations of football fans as "Hold That Tiger."

The ODJB reached its peak popularity in 1919, early enough in jazz history to have influenced Louis Armstrong, who was an admirer of La Rocca's playing. Their music, however, has not stood the test of time. *Lost Chords*, a collection of recordings made by white jazz artists between 1915 and 1945, issued in conjunction with Richard M. Sudhalter's book of the same name,[56] includes several selections by La Rocca's band, and by today's standards, they sound hopelessly corny. It's some kind of injustice that the Original Dixieland Jazz Band got to be the first recorded jazz band and enjoyed considerable success, while legendary black cornetist Buddy Bolden, generally considered the father of jazz, never made a record, and died indigent in a mental institution.

The pattern of mutual support and cooperation between African Americans and Italian Americans began to unravel as Italians, "once they became aware of the terrible price to be paid for being 'black' . . .

hastened to distance themselves from African Americans and to be accepted as white."[57] Their racial subjectivity had never been "historically Black," contrary to Pasquale Verdicchio's claim, and they were eager to dispel the "racial ambiguity" attributed to them by WASP nativists. The Mezzogiorno immigrants were "determined to become 'cristiani,' their word for 'human beings' . . . They were going to shed the mark of the 'Turk' at last." In America "the mark of the Turk was color," so they, and even more their children and grandchildren, realized that the path to their advancement lay in "differentiating themselves from 'the dark-skinned other.' "[58]

Italian Americans employed various strategies to draw the line between themselves and blacks. They told themselves myths, which they came to believe, such as that Italian Americans had stronger families than blacks and therefore never accepted "welfare." This, of course, is not true. My own maternal grandfather, for example, received public assistance when he became disabled by illness and my family was unable to support him. He even had an African American social worker, assigned by the government.

Richard Gambino claims in *Blood of My Blood* that "mutual misunderstanding" has often characterized relations between the two groups, expressed in "differences perceived in music, body language, attitudes toward welfare, in family patterns, sexual behavior, and neighborhood characteristics."[59]

But too often Italian Americans "perceived" differences in order to establish their superiority to blacks and other dark-skinned minorities such as Puerto Ricans. Those perceived differences have fueled animosities that have exploded into open racial conflict, such as the battles over neighborhood and school integration that have been waged in New York and other major American cities such as Chicago, Philadelphia, Boston, and Newark.

Gil Fagiani experienced these interethnic clashes when he lived in New York's East Harlem during the late 1960s. An Italian American whose professional and personal life brought him in close contact with Puerto Ricans and blacks, he had a unique perspective on relations among East Harlem's various tribes. His experience of the neighborhood as a very young man, not much more than a youth, involved radical politics and heroin addiction, racism and organized crime. Today he is a social worker who directs a residential program for alcoholics, as well as a poet, essayist, and community activist. (In 1992 he and I were among the cofounders of Italian Americans for a Multicultural United States, a left-wing advocacy group opposed to that year's celebrations of the five hundredth anniversary of Christopher Columbus's "discovery" of America. IAMUS lasted until the late 1990s as an educational and activist organization of progressive Italian Americans.)

Italian East Harlem at the time I lived there in the late sixties had shrunk considerably from its peak . . . but there was still a certain vibrancy to the area [Gil recalls]. I was working for an antipoverty agency so I was very involved with the Puerto Rican community, as well as with African Americans. From the time I began my work, I had always heard about the gangster elements in the Italian American community. One of my first memories is that of a storefront that was part of my agency having its windows shot out because Italian mobsters felt it was encroaching on their turf.

One day I was walking on 116th Street with a couple of Puerto Rican guys, toward the Delightful Coffee Shop, which is still there. These guys said they couldn't go in there because it was a mafia place. At the time I wasn't sure how to take that, whether they were just stereotyping or whether their comments were a product of ethnic conflict in the neighborhood. Later I found out there was a lot of truth in what they were saying. That a lot of people who were involved in different levels of crime, some of it organized, did hang out there, including the Red Wings, a famous Italian street gang that was sort of a training operation for future wiseguys.

Gil has numerous painful memories of conflicts between Italians and Puerto Ricans.

Around 1967 I lost my moorings and began to use drugs heavily, and I became strung out on heroin. I saw things from a different perspective, as someone in need of narcotics . . . The Italians had a ferocious reputation, even among the tough elements in the Puerto Rican community. One day in '67 or '68 I was hanging out in a park, and some Puerto Rican guys came running saying, "The Italians are coming, the Italians are coming!" It struck me as a bit ludicrous because I was Italian, but not many people knew it. I was completely immersed in the Puerto Rican community. [He married a Puerto Rican woman from East Harlem, whose brother was married to a Sicilian.] I was moving very slowly, while everybody else was just stampeding out of that park. I took my time. Then this limousine went by and somebody in it started firing into the park. I remember diving to the ground as bullets were pinging off the cement. Later I learned that this reputation for ferociousness in the Italian American community had been earned by these kinds of incidents.

A lot of Italian Americans, not all, but quite a few, had rotten attitudes toward the Puerto Ricans, blaming them for destroying Harlem and specifically blaming the Puerto Rican drug addicts, which is a tremendous irony, because the heroin wholesalers on Pleasant Avenue were Italians, and they were dealing heroin throughout city. It was one of the city's biggest drug markets.

Despite the famous *Godfather* scene in which the dons agree to sell narcotics only in black neighborhoods, Gil says in East Harlem, Italian Americans sold and used drugs. He says "the closest I ever came to dying" was "when I was really strung out, in bad shape, and there were rumors that people were overdosing from the heroin being sold on 115th Street. In the macabre world of drug addicts, there's no better advertisement than people overdosing from heroin because of its purity. So I went to a building on 115th Street, right across from Our Lady of Mt. Carmel [the cathedral that was the spiritual center of East Harlem Italian Catholicism], knocked on the door, and two Italian guys sold me some bags. I was going to go to Woodstock, and I wanted some dope to bring with me."

Gil went to a rooftop at 104th Street to shoot the dope, and he says that as soon as he put the needle in his arm, "I knew I was going to go down." Gil overdosed and nearly died. (He never did make it to the party at Max Yasgur's farm.) "They [the Italians who sold him the dope] must have been directly connected to the Pleasant Avenue wholesalers to have such pure heroin." Gil recalls the heroin operation on Pleasant Avenue as being "sort of a cottage industry . . . there was a network of Italian social clubs, and a lot of these clubs were involved in the heroin trade, hundreds of people, men and women. Lots of young guys were making huge profits as drug couriers, carrying 'packages.' "

Gil says he heard all the stories about how wiseguys protected the neighborhood, making sure no disorganized crime intruded on Italian turf. But "the other people in the community who weren't Italian didn't feel safer, they felt threatened, and it was a corrosive thing. I saw it myself. You'd see in this area, which was a poor neighborhood, you'd see very fancy cars, double-parked, and you knew what people were up to. It was brazen. You had people of color getting arrested on bullshit charges and you had other people committing very serious crimes able to flaunt them and get away with it."[60]

But several decades before Gil Fagiani lived there, Italian Harlem boasted a progressive political leader who adamantly opposed racism and ethnic prejudice, and strove to build a coalition of the area's different communities. Vito Marcantonio, who represented East Harlem in the U.S. Congress for fourteen years between 1935 and 1950, was a tenacious advocate for labor rights, civil liberties, and a noninterventionist foreign policy. The son of southern Italian immigrants, he also led the American Labor Party, an important third party in U.S. political history.

Congressman Marcantonio stood up for Italians against WASP bigots, some of whom, like the virulently racist Mississippi senator Theodore Bilbo, openly referred to Italians as "dagoes." But Marcantonio was also a committed antiracist who would intervene to prevent racial clashes in his district, and didn't shy from challenging Italian Americans.

When fights erupted between black and Italian students at Benjamin Franklin High School in September 1945, Marcantonio and his mentor, educator Leonard Covello, persuaded Frank Sinatra to speak to students at a school assembly. Marcantonio signed and authorized the distribution in Italian East Harlem of a leaflet that proclaimed, "The same people who hate us . . . who discriminate against us also hate the Negro people, the Jews, the Catholics, the foreign born. They hate everyone who wants America to be free for all the people." Going even further, Marcantonio explicitly linked the fates of Italian Americans and African Americans when, at a meeting at Benjamin Franklin, he declared, "We of Italian origin know the meaning of discrimination. Consequently we refuse to impose discrimination on other people."[61]

During Marcantonio's fourteen years in public office, he faced concerted opposition from enemies ranging from anti-immigrant, racist conservatives, especially Southern politicians, more mainstream political figures and organizations, and the Roman Catholic Archdiocese of New York. "Marc," as he was popularly known among his supporters, also had to navigate among the disparate elements of East Harlem, including pro-Mussolini Italian Americans in the period before World War II. (Marcantonio was unequivocally anti-Fascist, if sometimes reticent about his anti-Fascism.) Because "Italian Harlem was a major Mafia center, especially in the East 116th Street social clubs and cafes," he also had to arrive at a modus vivendi with the various mob groups in his district.[62]

Marcantonio was not an anti-mafia crusader; in fact his relationship with gangsters fell somewhere between a détente and an alliance. East Harlem mob figures gave "discreet but substantial assistance to his campaigns," and it was rumored that his bodyguards came from the ranks of La Cosa Nostra.[63] Marcantonio's attitude and behavior toward mobsters was typical of Italian East Harlemites, who, hostile to the outside world they felt was opposed to them, condoned such illegal activities as gambling and even racketeering. It was smart politics, too, because the Congressman already had enough enemies without risking the opposition of a powerful force known for its willingness to use violence against its antagonists.

A towering figure like Vito Marcantonio, urban populist, coalition builder, and multiculturalist *avant la lettre*, should be much better known than he is. And in 1986, producer Martin Bregman announced plans for a film biography of the East Harlem leader, to star Al Pacino.

The Congressman's life, which spanned the peak years of Italian immigration, the New Deal, World War II, the start of the cold war, and McCarthyism, could have made a great movie. But for reasons never disclosed, the film was not made. Instead, a year later Paramount announced that Pacino would star in an upcoming third installment of *The Godfather*.[64]

Southern Italian immigrants to the United States definitely suffered stigma and outright discrimination, but is it true that they were categorized and treated like blacks, as Robert Viscusi and other Italian American scholars assert, or that they were a people "in between" white and black?

Not according to Thomas Guglielmo, whose 2003 study of Chicago Italian Americans, *White on Arrival*, announces its position with its title. Guglielmo, a professor at the University of Notre Dame, maintains that Italian Americans' embrace of white racial identity was not simply an attitude adjustment to the realities of American racism. It was possible because law and custom did define them as Caucasian. Though many southern Italian immigrants experienced racial prejudice, they were nonetheless viewed as white, and they enjoyed the privileges whiteness bestowed.

Guglielmo distinguishes race from color, which seems counterintuitive given that we generally regard color as the visible marker of race. His case for this distinction notes that from the mid-nineteenth to mid-twentieth centuries, there were two primary ways of discussing and structuring race, the first being color, as when people spoke of the black race, the white race, the yellow race. But Guglielmo uses "color" as a social category and not a physical description, noting that some "white" Italians could "be darker than 'black' Americans." Race, during the same time period, could refer to many disparate groupings, whether large categories like Nordics and Mediterraneans or smaller ones, such as northern and southern Italians.[65]

The distinction between race and color was never absolute, but despite its "discursive messiness," it "was crystal clear when it came to resources and rewards. In other words, while Italians suffered greatly for their putative *racial* undesirability as Italians, South Italians, and so forth, they still benefited in countless ways from their privileged color status as *whites*."

Italian immigrants paradoxically were both brutalized by race and protected by whiteness; they had an "anomalous social position as racial outsiders and color insiders."[66]

Guglielmo acknowledges that "for decades, a wide range of individuals and institutions deeply racialized Italian immigrants and their children—criminalizing them mercilessly, restricting them from immigrating to the United States in large numbers, ostracizing them in various neighborhoods, and denying them jobs on occasion." He also describes the racial aspect of press coverage of organized crime in Chicago: "Both the type and quantity of crime coverage marked Italians unmistakably as racially distinct and problematic in a variety of ways. First, the mere appearance of Italians' constant criminal activity strongly suggested, even if it was rarely stated, that they were somehow *hereditarily* drawn to crime."

Crime stories "also marked Italians as racially distinct and problematic by continually stressing their dark skin" while "many commentators further racialized Italian criminals by describing them as savage—and sometimes simian—beasts more akin to animals than human beings."[67]

But Guglielmo insists that even those most hostile to Italians "never challenged Italian whiteness in any sustained or systematic way," and this color status "made an immense difference in every Chicago Italian's life—whether they realized it or not, whether they identified as white or not." Their whiteness "alone made some things possible— such as the ability to immigrate to the United States and naturalize as citizens—and other things immeasurably easier, such as buying a home, finding a job, joining a union, and attending a quality school."

World War II witnessed "the increasing collapse of race and color categories." At the turn of the century and into the early decades of the twentieth, the U.S. naturalization application had asked immigrants to provide both their race and color and expected different answers for each. For example, Italians were often listed as southern or northern Italian for race and white for color. By the beginning of World War II, however, "Italians, as well as many other groups . . . began offering the same answer for the race and color questions: white."

In the early 1940s, the U.S. government revised immigration forms, making it no longer possible for applicants "to fill in the race question with answers like 'Irish,' 'Hebrew,' or 'South Italian.'" Race and color categories, formerly separate, were "melded." The melding of these categories became conventional wisdom and practice. "This simplifying of race/color discourse encouraged Italian Americans to see themselves racially as white. With races like 'Italian' fast becoming 'ethnic' or 'nationality groups . . . many Italian Americans must have felt they had little other choice."[68]

Guglielmo sometimes overstates his case for the undisputed whiteness of Italians, and at other times he hedges a bit, as when he notes that they were "relatively" secure in their white status. From Guglielmo's own account of anti-Italian prejudice in Chicago, it's evident that Italians often were deemed less "white" than other groups of European origin, and that the presumed protection of whiteness was not always available to them. What is indisputable is that Italians were not subject to a racial caste system, nor to systematic, legally sanctioned discrimination and disenfranchisement, which clearly gave them an advantage over blacks. They were able to fully embrace white identity, to the point of using it as a weapon against black assertion. As Guglielmo sadly notes, Chicago Italian Americans were some of the most vocal supporters of residential segregation, wanting to keep blacks out of "their" neighborhoods. Some were even leaders of movements to evict the few blacks who had moved into Italian-dominated areas. This blatant racism has by no means been limited to Chicago Italians.

If Guglielmo has contested the "in-betweenness" argument, the notion of southern Italian racial ambiguity nevertheless persists in popular culture. "You know what they say about dark Italians," as Mookie insinuates in Do the Right Thing.

Quentin Tarantino, for whom racial provocation is a stock-in-trade, served up a large helping in his script for True Romance, a 1993 film directed by Tony Scott. In one scene, Vincenzo Coccotti, a Sicilian American mob boss (played by, of all people, the manifestly non-Mediterranean Christopher Walken), tortures Cliff Worley (Dennis Hopper) to get him to reveal the whereabouts of his son, who has run off with a suitcase full of mafia cocaine. Cliff's not going to give up his son, and he knows that will cost him his life, but in the meantime he's going to have some fun taunting his torturer. "I don't know if you know this or not, Sicilians were spawned by niggers," he says. Seeing the incredulous reaction of Coccotti and his henchmen, Cliff launches into a bizarre and fanciful rant about the purported racial origins of Sicilians:

> It's a fact. Sicilians have nigger blood pumping through their hearts . . . You see, hundreds of years ago the Moors conquered Sicily. And Moors are niggers. Way back then, Sicilians were like the wops in northern Italy. Blond hair, blue eyes. But once the Moors moved in there, they changed the whole country. They did so much fuckin' with the Sicilian women, they changed the bloodline forever, from blond hair and blue eyes to black hair and dark skin. I find it absolutely amazing to think that to this day hundreds of years later, Sicilians still carry that nigger gene . . . Your ancestors were niggers. Your great, great, great, great grandmother was fucked by a nigger, and had a half nigger kid. That is a fact. Now tell me, am I lyin'?

Needless to say, the Sicilian mobsters do not find Cliff's history lesson particularly instructive.

In *Zebrahead*, a 1992 drama about interracial romance among students at a racially and ethnically diverse Detroit high school, two young men, Zack, a Jewish kid with an affinity for black culture, and Dee, an African American teen, defy racial barriers and become close friends. When Zack begins dating Dee's cousin Nikki, his white friends assume he's seeing her because of sexual curiosity about black women (another case of "jungle fever"), while her black friends can't understand why she's interested in him. In one scene, the African American girls talk about dating white boys. When they get around to Italians, confusion ensues, as the girls cannot agree on whether Italians truly are white. One declares, "Not really."

Robert Casillo makes the interesting observation that "a putative Italian savagery may also be seen in films that have nothing to do with gangsters, boxers, or ethnic settings. Dark-skinned Italian-Americans have often been cast in films and on television as Indians and Arabs, two of the traditionally demonic 'enemies' of Western civilization."[69] Rudolph Valentino, born in Naples, became famous starring in *The Sheik* as an Arab who exudes a seductive but decadent sexuality. Frank DeKova was an Italian American character actor who often played American Indians in movies and on such TV shows as the 1960s sit-com *F Troop*, where he regularly appeared as Chief Wild Eagle.

One Italian American, however, took Indian impersonation to such extreme lengths that for Americans of all backgrounds, he was the essential Indian, the embodiment of Native America.

Iron Eyes Cody appeared in the "Keep America Beautiful" television ads broadcast in the early 1970s, coinciding with the emergence of the environmental movement and the first Earth Day celebration. His image was unforgettable: while careless Americans littered the country's lakes and forests, he turned toward us with a sorrowful expression, a tear trickling down his cheek.

By the time he made those ads, he was already a veteran Hollywood actor who had appeared in many films since the 1930s, from the Bob Hope comedy *The Paleface* to *A Man Called Horse*, as well as having played numerous, often uncredited small roles as an Indian in westerns. At the time of his death in 1999, he had appeared in more than one hundred films. He even has his own star on Hollywood Boulevard's Walk of Fame.

But Iron Eyes, supposedly of Cherokee/Cree descent, was actually a second-generation Sicilian American from Louisiana. Angela Aleiss, a postdoctoral student at UCLA, began to research Cody's background in the 1990s, after reading his ghostwritten autobiography, *Iron Eyes: My Life as a Hollywood Indian*.[70] There were too many facts that did not seem to add up, and she began to investigate. Aleiss learned that it had long been rumored in Hollywood that Iron Eyes was not really an Indian. He claimed to be from Oklahoma, but elsewhere he had given Texas as his birthplace.

Iron Eyes had a younger brother, Frank, and Aleiss traced his background. Frank's widow had said his birthplace was Texas, but his Social Security application gave it as Gueydan, Louisiana. Aleiss spoke to a librarian in Gueydan who told her that Frank had indeed been Iron Eyes

Cody's brother. When she contacted a local paper, she learned that area residents had known for decades that Cody had been born there. He was born into a Sicilian immigrant family and his real name was Espera DeCorti.

Aleiss wrote the story of Iron Eyes Cody's true origins for the *New Orleans Times-Picayune* in 1996. She told her readers that Cody's "true heritage lies within the state's [Louisiana's] southwestern parish of Vermilion and its records of probates, deeds and baptisms."

She located an eighty-year-old woman named May Abshire, who was Iron Eyes' half-sister. Abshire told her that their mother had been Francesca Salpietra, "a short woman with long black hair and dark skin who grew up in Sicily among a family of winegrowers. Her traditional parents arranged her marriage to Antonio DeCorti, an Italian immigrant awaiting his bride-to-be in New Orleans."

Iron Eyes' mother arrived in Louisiana in 1902, a decade after the notorious 1891 lynching of eleven Sicilian immigrants in New Orleans. "Widespread tensions erupted between the city's Italian and Irish residents, and by the turn of the century, New Orleans greeted its immigrant arrivals with suspicion and hostility."

"We were known as 'Dagoes' . . . when we got there," Abshire recalls her mother telling the children.

Abshire told Aleiss that the DeCortis soon left New Orleans to work in Louisiana's sugarcane fields, where Sicilian immigrants commonly replaced black slave labor.

Iron Eyes was born on April 3, 1904, in the small town of Kaplan, not far from Gueydan. Baptismal records at Holy Rosary Catholic Church show that he was christened "Espera." He was the second of four children; Joseph William was the eldest and his sister Victoria Delores and brother Frank Henry were the younger siblings.

Francesca and Antonio DeCorti barely made ends meet with their small grocery store in Gueydan. May Abshire told Aleiss that in 1909, Antonio had a run-in with the notorious Black Hand Society, an organized crime group that preyed on Italian immigrants. He fled to Texas and never returned. Francesca subsequently married Alton Abshire, a native Louisianan, and bore five more children, including May.

May told Aleiss that even as a boy her half-brother would dress up as an Indian and lead neighborhood boys in outdoor games. "He always said he wanted to be an Indian," Abshire recalled. "If he could find something that looked Indian, he'd put it on."

After their father Antonio's death in 1924, the three DeCorti brothers journeyed to California to start a new life. They changed their names to Cody, and Iron Eyes "turned 100 percent Indian," as May puts it. "He had his mind all the time on movies," she said.

Aleiss observed, "For Iron Eyes, Hollywood became a comfortable escape from his unsettling past. He easily sympathized with an oppressed people and knew firsthand of hardship and persecution. He pledged his life to Native American causes, married an Indian woman (Bertha Parker), adopted two Indian boys (Robert and Arthur), and seldom left home without his beaded moccasins, buckskin jacket and braided wig."

In 1995, Native Americans in Southern California honored Iron Eyes for his long-standing contributions to Indian causes. They recognized that he was not an Indian, but his charitable deeds were deemed more important than his true heritage. That same year, Aleiss contacted Iron Eyes by telephone, and he denied his Louisiana origins. "You can't prove it," he told Aleiss, adding, "All I know is that I'm just another Indian." But as Aleiss noted, "Iron Eyes' Indian guise, his Hollywood fame, was an escape from an early life of hardship and despair. Ultimately, he created his own Native American identity."[71]

Cody told reporters that Aleiss's revelations were not true, but he refused to provide any documentation about his origins over the next three years, until his death in January 1999. Aleiss repeatedly asked him to send her something that would prove his Indian origins, but he never did.

After her article appeared, Aleiss contacted an old friend of Cody's, Charles Alley, the father-in-law of film director Ron Howard. Alley, who had known Cody since 1938, assured Aleiss that her version was true. The Internet Movie Data Base, an authoritative online source for information about films and television, identifies Iron Eyes Cody as Espera DeCorti, born in Louisiana.

An episode of *The Sopranos* dealing with Native American opposition to Columbus Day, titled "Christopher" and written by Michael

Imperioli and Maria Laurino, has the character of mobster Ralph Cifaretto threatening to expose that Iron Eyes was really an actor of Sicilian ancestry. The script, bizarrely enough, erroneously denies the
claim. If *The Sopranos* blew a chance to explore this strange and amazing tale of Italian American self-reinvention, surely there is a movie to
be made about Espera "Iron Eyes Cody" DeCorti, a man who as an
Italian could have claimed a white identity, but instead chose to "pass"
as a member of a people who had endured much worse than his own.

The anthropologist Micaela di Leonardo observes that Italian Americans she interviewed in California for her doctoral dissertation (published in 1984 as *Varieties of Ethnic Experience*) often had an intense
and unique "love/hate" relationship with blacks, as well as with other
racial minorities.[72] Robert Orsi, alluding to racial assaults in the New
York neighborhoods of Howard Beach, Gravesend, and Bensonhurst,
notes, "Even the expressions of rage that have been evoked recently by
a series of tragic events in northeastern cities disclose undercurrents of
attraction, disappointment, and mutual implication. These two peoples
have had to deal with each other for a century, sometimes for better,
sometimes for worse."[73]

One of the worst episodes in the Italian American/African American encounter began on August 23, 1989, in the Bensonhurst section
of Brooklyn, when some thirty young men, mostly Italian Americans,
confronted four black youths looking to buy a used car, fatally shooting
one of them, seventeen-year-old Yusuf Hawkins. Mafia gangsters often
like to pose as defenders of "the neighborhood" from dangerous outsiders, and it turned out that several of the Italians who confronted
Hawkins and his friends in Bensonhurst, including the one who actually shot the black youth, were either mafia wannabes or low-level mob
associates.

Sixteen years after Hawkins was gunned down, a mob turncoat admitted that he had instigated the killing. Joseph D'Angelo, testifying for
the prosecution in the 2005 federal racketeering trial of John A. "Junior" Gotti, the son of the deceased Teflon Don, said he summoned the
gang of young men that attacked Hawkins and his friends in Benson-

hurst. D'Angelo, then a twenty-year-old self-described protégé of Salvatore "Sammy the Bull" Gravano, said he heard rumors that a group of black and Latino youths was coming to Bensonhurst, where he ran a store. He said he called a friend, Joseph "Joey Babes" Serrano, who brought his own friends to confront the supposedly threatening outsiders. One of these friends was Joseph Fama, who was later convicted of killing Hawkins and sentenced to thirty years in prison. D'Angelo also admitted lying to the police about his involvement in the hate crime. "We were supposed to lie. As part of the mob that's what we do. That's what they teach you, not to help the police, ever," he said. He additionally admitted pressuring an eyewitness to the killing to not talk to the police.[74]

If young thugs instigated and carried out the crime, the race hatred that motivated them hardly was theirs alone. The killing and its aftermath exposed to the world's gaze the appalling racism festering in Bensonhurst. When the African American activist minister Al Sharpton led a protest march through the neighborhood, residents disgraced themselves by cursing at and mooning the marchers, and brandishing watermelons as racial taunts. (That last touch was truly surreal, as Italians, both in Italy and in America, are inveterate watermelon eaters.) A contingent of gays and lesbians participated in the march, which elicited homophobic epithets from some of the young Bensonhurst males, while others mimed homosexual acts, a startling bit of street theater.[75]

The intense media coverage during the weeks after the murder of Hawkins and the protest cast Bensonhurst in a harshly negative light, as a neighborhood dominated by violent racist boors. Sad to say, too many of the area's residents did their best to live up to the media portrayals. Others took a defensive, often self-pitying tone, claiming theirs was a decent neighborhood, and that what happened that August night on Bay Ridge Avenue was an "isolated incident" that had been "blown out of proportion" (a gay Italian American from Bensonhurst used exactly those words when I interviewed him for a magazine article not long after the murder).

One newspaper, however, the venerable liberal weekly *The Village Voice*, went beyond the widespread condemnations of Bensonhurst as an irredeemably racist enclave to investigate the roots of bigotry in one of New York's "remaining white homelands." Nelson George, an African American journalist, noted that New York white ethnics are literally losing ground to "the tribes of black, brown, and yellow peoples," and they respond by "running away or watching ruefully as their European enclaves turn into Third World villages."

George's thoughtful, sympathetic article was infused with the "undercurrents of attraction, disappointment, and mutual implication" Robert Orsi cites. He urged his readers to "imagine the anxiety of a working-class Italian teen in Bensonhurst, getting bum-rushed culturally if not physically every day of his life."

"Where are their dynamic role models?" George asked, noting, "The most written-about Italian American in this city is not a politician, athlete, or pop star, but that man John Gotti."

George noted that although mobster Gotti "conforms to a stereotype that's bedeviled Italian Americans since *The Untouchables*," for many young working-class Italian youths "Gotti's turf control, both of Howard Beach [Queens] and his nefarious empire, is a welcome proof of potency."

"Who is addressing their high dropout rate and rising criminality?" George added. Though the murder of Yusuf Hawkins and "the everyday anti–Third World bias" of Bensonhurst youth are inexcusable, the "untreated racial hostility that burst free in Bensonhurst . . . was generated by a nagging, evil insecurity . . ."[76]

Two other *Voice* correspondents, Mark Bauman and Samme Chittum, spent several months prior to the racial murder interviewing "wiseguy wannabes" in Bensonhurst. Their article, published with George's and several others the week after the incident, portrayed an aimless bunch of neighborhood youths, "Bensonhurst's hardcore," who hang out on street corners getting into trouble. Most of them long for jobs with city government agencies, but feel they have little chance of getting them. Others, however, strive for positions "in 'La Cosa Nostra,' one of New York's oldest and most respected firms." Only a few will eventually become wiseguys, according to the reporters, but "none of them . . . will grow up untouched by the antiquated style and casual violence foisted on them by almost a century of Mafia tradition."

These youths, "fortified by their faith in the Godfather myth," feel the "nagging, evil insecurity" Nelson George described, and they take it upon themselves to be their neighborhood's protectors and avengers, armed with baseball bats, beer bottles, and, as Yusuf Hawkins and his friends discovered, more lethal weapons.[77]

Jerome Krase, a Brooklyn-born sociologist who is of Sicilian descent on his mother's side, recalls growing up in Brooklyn in the 1950s, at a time when "the mafia, the 80th Precinct, and the Grand Avenue 'Boys' were the neighborhood's first lines of defense against the imperial growth of black Bedford Stuyvesant and their teenage gangs—the 'Bishops' and the 'Chaplins.' " Reflecting on the Bensonhurst events, Krase observes that "each group in the city has a unique history before they got here, but once here they fall into the same pattern of intergroup hostility, the volume and violence level of which rises and falls like the tide."[78]

Although "the reputation of Italian Americans and Italian-American neighborhood groups as vocal opponents of racial integration is not undeserved," why, Krase wonders, are Italians perceived as being so much more biased than other ethnic groups? Because working-class Italian Americans tend to live in urban areas in the path of nonwhite, minority group expansion, "they are also the most likely to experience interracial and inter-ethnic conflict on a local level between themselves and other ethnic minorities." The "cultural propensity of Italians toward residential stability has resulted in their being, in many cases, the last white ethnic group in changing urban communities."[79]

Gil Fagiani has his own *Bronx Tale* of racism and racial violence. His family has deep roots in the predominantly Italian American neighborhood of Belmont; his father was baptized in a church at 187th Street and Arthur Avenue. Though he and his family moved away when he was five years old, other relatives remained, and he frequently visited the old neighborhood during the 1970s. It was there, at the intersection where the church stood, that he says he witnessed "one of most shameful things, to me as an Italian American that I have ever observed. I went to a feast [Italian street festival] one year and there was this carload of young Italian American toughs driving around and they stopped the car when they saw some blacks and Puerto Ricans and got out and beat them up, literally beat them bloody."

Several years earlier, Fagiani was enrolled in a drug rehabilitation program in the Bronx. After a twenty-four-hour marathon meeting, the group members celebrated with an outing to the Bronx Zoo.

> We had gone in a bus, there must have been about thirty of us. And on the way back, instead of taking Fordham Road, we went directly through the Italian American community. It was like a utopian moment. We were a mixed group, mostly black and Puerto Rican, but maybe about 20 percent of us were white. We had our arms around each other and we were singing songs, and we were going down 187th Street and all of a sudden the bottles started flying, and it was a really scary scene. Some of the guys I was with wanted to get out and fight these Italian guys. But I saw windows opening, and I was worried that the next thing coming at us would be rifles.
>
> The police blamed *us* for driving through the area—"Why the fuck did you come through this community?" they said.

The violence, says Fagiani, "was a very frightened, tribal response to us just driving down the street."

> But it's one thing to experience these things on an individual level, as I did, and another to see the larger picture. Italian American communities were some of the last to join the white flight. In the Bronx, which I know intimately, there were a lot of destructive trends. The Bronx was burning. The Irish neighborhoods had broken up, the Jewish neighborhoods had broken up. The Italians stayed. And they were pitted against these huge structural trends that were going on—the abandonment of buildings [by landlords], the lack of services, the organized arson—all of that. They were on the frontlines. They were desperate.
>
> And not to make excuses for them, because they could have gone some other route, perhaps tried to form alliances with other groups, but there was a lot of chaos and anarchy during that period. It's not like there were all these organized progressive forces in the Puerto Rican and African American communities, either. There was a lot of chaos. So the Italians were at the

edge of it, and they acted in a really tribal way. People had these visions of society totally breaking down, and one of responses to that is tribalism.[80]

Jerome Krase notes that no ethnic group has been "immune to this plague" of tribal conflict and violence. When researching newspaper accounts of interethnic violence in which Italian Americans were not involved, he came across incidents of strife between blacks and Koreans, blacks and other Asian groups, blacks and Jews, Jews and Hispanics, as well as intra-Caribbean and intra-Hispanic clashes.

Krase believes the reason for the media focus on Italian Americans as epitomizing white racial bigotry is "the reluctance of most Italian-American organizations and their leaders to honestly address the problem of racial and ethnic bias." In most cases, "Italian-American spokespersons have tended to deny the extent or degree of the problem or to make defensive statements when bias incidents in the community occur. This has resulted in an even greater focus on the community because it projects an appearance of lack of remorse or sympathy for victims of bias-related violence."[81]

Joseph Sciorra, a folklorist and professor at the City University of New York, and the brother of actress Annabella Sciorra, excoriates Italian American leadership in an essay, "Italians Against Racism," included in an important but overlooked 2003 anthology provocatively titled *Are Italians White?*[82]

Sciorra frames his powerful and disturbing essay with an account of his participation in one of the protest marches through Bensonhurst. He held a homemade sign that read ITALIANS AGAINST RACISM. Its use of the plural, he dryly notes, was "a simple expression of hope." Before the march was over, a handful of like-minded persons joined him. But the experience was frightening and horrific, as marchers endured vile, racist taunts and faced the threat of violence. Sciorra himself was singled out for special abuse by "laughing, cursing, and spitting" onlookers, who clearly regarded him as a "race traitor, the internal threat to the prevailing local rhetoric."

As disgusted and saddened as he was by the behavior of neighborhood residents, by their "grotesque performance of collective hate,"

Sciorra also was "deeply distressed by the excruciating silence emanating from the self-proclaimed leaders of the Italian American community."

> The city witnessed the utter lack of leadership as cautious politicians, out-of-touch academics, and aloof *prominenti* were invisible and ultimately ineffective in participating in the public discourse surrounding the unfolding events. I desperately searched for, but did not find, an Italian American of public stature who stepped forward in those early tense days to make an unequivocal repudiation of racism and violence, and to speak out against its manifestation in Bensonhurst . . . A clear and authoritative Italian American voice was absent from the public sphere where the city's citizens could turn for understanding, resolution, and healing. The so-called leadership was struck by deep denial and paralysis.

Sciorra notes that some Bensonhurst Italians behaved decently. One woman and her daughter came to the aid of the dying Yusuf Hawkins. Another woman joined a group of local residents who confronted some of the arrested suspects outside the police station on the night of the killing, and was reported to have shouted, "You should be ashamed . . . You're a disgrace."[83]

There were a few other such occurrences not mentioned by Sciorra. A group of Italian American women visited Yusuf Hawkins's mother to express sympathy and support for the bereaved woman. Frank Barbaro, at the time a New York State legislator, brought representatives of the Italian American and African American communities together and organized a Coalition on Intergroup Harmony. But such actions, though laudable, were rare, and they could not dispel the image of Bensonhurst as a racist community, whose members, in the face of the outrage and sorrow of so many New Yorkers, chose to engage in what Robert Viscusi has called "an unforgettable dumb show of bigotry."[84]

Race and racism figure prominently in the Mafia myth, and, as we have seen, these tropes are grounded both in the reality of Italian American organized crime and in the historical encounter between Italian immigrants and African Americans.

Does this mean that *The Godfather*, and by extension the Mafia myth itself, is racist? Do Italians and other Euro-Americans love *The Godfather* and other mob classics because these films play to their fantasies of racial purity and racist exclusion?

The first two *Godfather* films were released in the early 1970s, when "white racial and ethnic purity was being seriously threatened by nonwhite peoples."[85] In American cities, blacks and whites frequently found themselves on opposing sides in clashes over residential and school segregation, school busing, employment discrimination, and police tactics. During the same era, Latino activist movements, such as the New York Puerto Rican militant group the Young Lords, and the National Council of La Raza, a mainstream organization for Southwestern Chicanos, also emerged, articulating a new ethnic consciousness and political agendas.

Vera Dika, in an essay included in a collection of critical writings on *The Godfather*, insists that the film "must be seen as a significant fantasy, one that embodies the wish for an all-white militant group, one that exists to the exclusion of all other races and ethnic Americans . . . the wish here is for a time when organized crime could be controlled by one ethnic group, and is dramatized in the film by the active exclusion of African Americans, Puerto Ricans, and other ethnic groups in an antiseptic dream of racial and ethnic purity."[86]

There undoubtedly are some Italian Americans foolish and bigoted enough to see mafiosi, actual and fictional, as ethnic champions and neighborhood defenders holding the line against threatening nonwhites. But if *The Godfather* represents a "significant fantasy," it is not the exclusive property of Italian Americans. The *Godfather* films, *Goodfellas*, and other mob movies, like the 1983 *Scarface* (with Cuban gangsters played by the Italian Americans Al Pacino and Robert Loggia) and now *The Sopranos*, have a devoted following among African American, Latino, and other non-Italian American audiences. Massive Genius's comment to Christopher Moltisanti in an episode of *The Sopranos* that he'd probably seen the first *Godfather* two hundred times, no doubt elicited knowing laughter from the show's many African American fans.

Black and Latino artists and entertainers have expropriated mafia imagery and themes since the 1970s. James Brown christened himself the Godfather of Soul, and leading salsa musician Willie Colón titled an album *Cosa Nuestra*, the LP cover featuring photos of him decked out like a mafioso. In the 1980s, African American and Latino rappers began to incorporate mafia imagery and references into their music and image. Films like *The Godfather*, *Goodfellas*, and *Scarface* were major influences on the development of gangsta rap.

Gangsta rap grew out of a fascination with the lifestyle lived by organized crime's biggest names. Kool G. Rap's 1988 hit "Road to the Riches" featured the couplet "He likes to eat hearty, party / Be like John Gotti, and drive a Maserati." Since then other rappers have paid lyrical tribute to the late New York mafioso, including the Fun Lovin' Criminals and Too Short. New Orleans–based hip-hop producer Master P has in his stable of rappers the group Gambino Family, one of whose members calls himself Gotti, as well as the solo artist Lil' Italy. Were he still alive, the "Dapper Don" might be amazed that he has spawned hip-hop progeny Big Gotti, Don Gotti, Juan Gotti, Bazooka Joe Gotti, Yo Gotti, and the gangsta rap producer Irv Gotti.

In 2004, raunchy rapper Lil' Kim released a CD titled *La Bella Mafia*. Her video for one of the tracks, "Came Back for You," featured a guest appearance by Victoria Gotti, the daughter of the deceased don who earned her own celebrity as a schlock novelist and star of her own reality television series. "Shout out to my girl Victoria Gotti and the whole Gotti family, stay up," Kim says at the beginning of the song.

New York rappers Nas, Mobb Deep, and Murder Inc. blend observations about black gangs and their criminal activity with images and lingo from mob movies like *Scarface* and *The Godfather*. Other gangsta rappers to emerge in the late 1990s include Scarface and the group Three 6 Mafia.

Most of these mafia-infatuated performers adopt the imagery and lingo just to create commercially viable personae; as the mafioso played by John Turturro in Spike Lee's film *She Hate Me* remarks, the gangsta rappers are just acting. But sometimes the worlds of "gangsta" and real-life gangsterism coincide.

Irving Lorenzo, a Latino from Hollis, Queens (the same neighborhood that gave the world Run-D.M.C. and LL Cool J) was a DJ with a local following until he crossed the East River into Manhattan and established himself as a record producer. His label, Murder Inc., home to million-selling hip-hop artists Ja Rule and Ashanti, "parlayed the thug life into a multimillion-dollar business that set trends in popular culture for youth across America."[87]

Early in Lorenzo's career as a producer, a rapper gave him the nickname "Gotti" in homage to the mob boss. Since then he has gone by the name Irv Gotti. Besides adopting a mobster persona, he gave his record label an organized crime image, with a Web site punctuated with the sound of gunfire, images of bullets penetrating the Murder Inc. logo, and pictures of rappers dressed up as 1940s-style mobsters. But according to federal investigators, the company's mobbed-up image is more than just marketing. In 2003, FBI agents raided Murder Inc.'s midtown Manhattan offices, seizing computers and documents. By late 2004 the company, now a subsidiary of Universal Music Group, the largest music company in the world, was the target of a federal probe into drugs, murder, and money laundering in the rap industry. The feds alleged that "Irv Gotti" was partners with an actual gangster, Kenneth (Supreme) McGriff, "a drug baron who helped fuel the deadly crack epidemic of the 1980s."[88]

Why, if the Mafia myth is racist, would young blacks and Latinos find something inspiring and worthy of emulation in it?

Snoop Dogg (Calvin Broadus), one of hip-hop's most popular and colorful figures, has frequently gone to the well of mafia imagery for inspiration. His "Downtown Assassins" blends fictional and historical representations of La Cosa Nostra, and links himself with them. "There's four major gangs that run the city of G's [gangstas] / the Violators, the Gambinos, the Corleones and me." On his 1996 track, "Tha Doggfather," he boasts, "I put down more hits than mafioso made / And Lucky Luciano 'bout to sing soprano."

The rapper, interviewed for a 2002 *Newsweek* article about Al Pacino, enthused about his love for the Italian American actor and his gangster films, especially *Scarface*.

"I watch 'Scarface' about once a month," said Snoop Dogg, who "sees the movie as a metaphor for every minority's struggle against the system." "I think any brother watching it can identify with what the main man is going through," he said. "And when you throw in Pacino—who hop-hop got *mad* love for since 'The Godfather'—I mean, you've got to love it. Pacino keeps it hard-core and real gangsta in all his films. I go see them all just for that Pacino flava."[89]

Snoop Dogg is not alone in finding a metaphor "for every minority's struggle against the system" in mob movies and Italian gangsterism. Capone n' Noreaga are a popular rap duo from Queens who grew up in the borough's housing projects, enduring rough childhoods and numerous run-ins with the law. Capone (Kiam Holley) and Noreaga (Victor Santiago) met in 1992 while serving kitchen duty together at a correctional facility. Upon their release they decided to team up as rappers.

In an interview for the Web site *Artistdirect.com*, Capone said, "Though I don't wanna go out like the mobster Al Capone, I like how he operated. If he was alive today, he would probably appreciate our song 'Blood Money,' because it talks about getting paid any way a brotha can. He was a criminal, but he had a lot of strong qualities, and listeners gotta remember the fact that I can get with his positive side without following the negative. He was a leader and an organizer. 'Illegal Life' [another Capone n' Noreaga track] talks about things that could have happened during Capone's rule."

The affinity of black and Latino hip-hop artists for gangster personas, themes, and imagery demonstrates that they also see "a welcome proof of potency" in the Mafia myth. They're well aware that Italian gangsters, on-screen and in life, can be racist, but they take what they want and need from the mythology and ignore the bigotry. Their fascination with mob narrative and its tropes validates Chris Messenger's observation that the genre "is not coextensive with Italian American narrative but is rather an offshoot from it, hybridized by the experience of many ethnic and/or oppressed groups that are suspicious of the law."[90]

There's another aspect of the gangster/gangsta kinship to consider: the Italian mafioso has his counterpart in African American culture. The pimp or the "mack daddy" is a rap archetype, and this figure "functions like the Mafia don in Italian-American culture," that is, as "a cipher that helps critique mainstream capitalism while also affirming it in a most extreme fashion."[91] The "brotha getting paid any way he can" is like the Italian mobster making his daily bread in defiance of society's laws and conventions.

Gangsta rap has been criticized for celebrating the violence, misogyny, and homophobia of actual organized crime. Some African American commentators, noting that most of the consumers who buy gangsta rap recordings are white, accuse the genre's artists of engaging in a contemporary form of minstrelsy. They charge that gangsta rap, like the minstrel shows and blackface performances of the early twentieth century, serves up caricatures of African Americans for the delectation of whites. The charge is remarkably similar to the antidefamationist argument that artists like David Chase and Martin Scorsese entertain non-Italian audiences with degrading stereotypes of Italian Americans as mafia criminals.

But while some Italian Americans fume about mafia stereotypes, most pop-culture consumers find the Corleones, the Sopranos, and various other fictional wiseguys colorful and entertaining, familiar figures who pose no real threat to anyone but each other. Contrast that with the often hysterical denunciation of gangsta rap by conservatives, white and black, for the threat it purportedly poses to America's impressionable youth. There have been no calls for Congressional investigations into the harmful effects of mafia movies and TV shows, as has been the case with gangsta rap.

There is, however, one important difference. No one has accused David Chase, Martin Scorsese, or Francis Ford Coppola of living the mob life they have depicted in their art. The investigation of Irv Gotti's Murder Inc. record label, and before that, the troubles of Death Row Records, whose notoriously violence-prone CEO, Marion "Suge" Knight, served five years in prison, demonstrate that the world of gangsta rap is not entirely divorced from actual gangsterism.

Around the same time that American gangsta rappers were beginning to season their rhymes with mafia "flava," an Italian performer used rap to condemn gangsterism. Francesco Di Gesù, better known as Frankie Hi NRG, jump-started the Italian rap scene in 1992 with "Fight da Faida" (Fight the Feud). With its half-Italian, half-English re-

292 / AN OFFER WE CAN'T REFUSE

frain urging resistance to mafia clans and their blood feuds, "Fight da Faida" became the most re-released and most popular *rap italiano* track of the 1990s. At a time when most Italian rappers were slavishly imitating American artists and styles, Di Gesù, born in Turin to Sicilian parents, demonstrated with his clever internal rhymes that the Italian language was well suited to rap. "Fight da Faida" even included a section in which a woman chanted a *filastrocca*, a rhyming Sicilian verse form with affinities to rap.

In sharp contrast to the celebration of Italian American mafioso stereotypes in gangsta rap, "Fight da Faida" deplored the brutality and far-reaching corruption of organized crime, and bravely urged Italians to "launch a decisive offensive . . . against the mafia clans."[92]

Frankie Hi NRG wasn't the only Italian to employ rap in the service of social criticism and political protest. The Neapolitan band Almamegretta had a hit in Italy in 1993 with "Figli di Annibale" (Children of Hannibal), an antiracist rap that attributed the dark skin and hair of many southern Italians to their having descended from the Carthaginian general who "crossed the Alps with ninety thousand African men." (Imagine how that might go over in Bensonhurst, blasted over a sound system at the Feast of Saint Rosalia.) During the 1990s, other Italian rappers, such as the groups 99 Posse, Sud Sound System, and Articolo 31, made recordings that delivered trenchant commentary about Italian society. But social consciousness began to fade from Italian rap in the new millennium, as the music increasingly adopted the gettin' paid/gettin' laid clichés of its American forebear.

Race, racism, and organized crime long have been entangled in American history and in popular culture: Little Italy hoodlum Charlie Cappa standing up his black date, Frank Pentangeli ranting about "spics and niggers" getting a piece of "our thing," the mob dons of *The Godfather* decreeing that dope can only be sold to "the colored," Tony Soprano getting his rocks off by humiliating a black police officer. The racial attitudes and racist behavior depicted in mob dramas didn't just emerge from their scriptwriters' imaginations. They are grounded in history, both Italian and American.

The Southern Italian immigrants, from whose ranks came the Cosa

Nostra gangsters, themselves had been subject to racism. They arrived as a people who had been marked as racial inferiors in the land of their birth, a stigma that followed them to their new home, where it bedeviled them for decades. In one of history's bitter ironies, some of them— as they gained social capital, including the privileges accruing to whiteness—inflicted prejudice and discrimination on other, darker skinned and more disadvantaged people. Yet another irony—and much Italian American history falls into the ironic register—the purported predilection towards crime of the southerners was viewed as evidence of their racial inferiority. But in America, Italian American gangsters, real and fictional, have served as enforcers of racial boundaries and perpetrators of racist violence.

The complicated story of Italian American engagement with African Americans and other nonwhites is one of conflict and cooperation, mutual distrust and mutual attraction. Popular culture portrays the conflict and the distrust more often than the cooperation and attraction; it's a rare film like A Bronx Tale that explores both sides of the dialectic.

The great African American intellectual and activist W.E.B. Du Bois declared that the problem of the twentieth century is the problem of the color line. The location of olive on the spectrum of the color line has been unstable, shifting over time from a hue deemed too close to the dark end to a darker shade of white.

The Italian American gangsters of film, television, and literature can seem to be not-quite-white people. That's because the genre has racialized them, as far back as Scarface, with its primitive, even ape-like, protagonist. Sometimes racialization takes the form of an ethnic exoticism that plays up "colorful" qualities that distinguish Italians from more assimilated Euro-Americans. At other times, the genre's tropes of savage violence, boorish behavior, and conspiratorial scheming suggest an invidious racial stereotype.

The novel that has served as the template for mob narrative— Puzo's Godfather—consistently depicts Sicilians in racial terms, though most commentators have failed to notice. Besides portraying them as a culturally distinct group with a predilection for cunning and violence, he also uses color to emphasize their difference, their "otherness." Carmela Corleone holds Kay's white hand "in her two brown ones,"

Michael's Sicilian bride Apollonia has skin of an "exquisite dark creaminess," and Michael's complexion is "a clear olive-brown." Puzo portrays the Corleones (and Sicilians in general) as Mediterranean colored folks who have endured both oppression in their homeland and prejudice in America. But the novel, even more than the films, candidly depicts the Corleones' own racism (and that of their underworld associates) towards American blacks.

Racism is hardly peripheral to the Mafia myth, but neither is it central. As we have seen, the mythology fascinates and inspires nonwhite performers, such as Snoop Dogg and other African American and Latino hip-hop artists who "got mad love" for Al Pacino. Besides rappers, filmmakers like the Hughes Brothers (*Menace II Society*), Mario Van Peebles (*New Jack City*), and music mogul–turned-director Damon Dash (*State Property*) have served up ultraviolent tales of black criminality that, to varying degrees, partake of the Mafia myth.

The myth can also inspire actual crime, as in the case of Irv "Gotti" Lorenzo's Murder Inc. record company, which, if prosecutors are correct, was a front for illicit activities, just as Vito Corleone's Genco Olive Oil Company was the legit face of his underworld empire. For impatient, aggressive, and sometimes talented men from urban ghettos, whether they are the poor quarters of Palermo or the housing projects of New York City, the Mafia mythology continues to exert its seductive, deadly appeal.

8

Cultural Holocaust or National Myth?:
The Politics of Antidefamation

When Italian Americans are depicted in television, in films, and in fictional literature, they are almost always cast as vicious hoodlums, childish buffoons, or both.   —Richard Gambino, *Blood of My Blood*

While the stereotype of the Italian mobster certainly is prevalent, it is hardly the cutting edge of racism. Some stereotypes have higher consequences than others.

    —Libero della Piana, "Are Italians the New Anti-Racist Front?"

The gangster's life gets all the movie and TV attention because it's the most narrative-friendly, charismatic version of our particular cultural capital. This is the homage the rest of America pays to Italian-American magnificence: You've made us mythic.

    —Bill Tonelli, "A 'Sopranos' Secret: Given the Choice, We'd All Be Mobsters"

New York City's annual Columbus Day Parade, held the second Monday of October since 1929, is typically an innocuous celebration of Italian American ethnicity, a day for celebrities, high school marching bands, and local politicians to strut down Fifth Avenue in a three-hour salute to one of the city's largest, if dwindling, ethnic communities.

The last time the parade generated any serious buzz was when Sophia Loren was its grand marshal in 1998. That was until 2002, when, for the first time in anyone's memory, the mayor of New York decided not to make the traditional appearance at the event. That year Michael R. Bloomberg "skipped the event out of pique," specifically, his annoyance that the parade's organizers went to court to bar him from marching with his two guests, actors from the HBO mob drama *The Sopranos*.[1]

Bloomberg had invited Dominic "Uncle Junior" Chianese and Lorraine "Dr. Jennifer Melfi" Bracco to join him in the parade, much to the annoyance of the celebration's organizers, the Columbus Citizens Foundation. The mayor had neglected to ask them if it was okay to bring the two actors, which rankled. But even if he had requested permission he would have been turned down, because the parade organizers believed *The Sopranos* denigrates Italians.

Lawrence Auriana, president of the Columbus Citizens Foundation, and, according to *The New York Times*, a "Wall Street money manager," sued in federal district court to prevent Bloomberg from marching with Chianese and Bracco. The mayor said he didn't invite the actors because he's a *Sopranos* fan—he claimed never to have seen the show—but because they contributed to New York City causes and charities. Bloomberg gave Auriana and the Columbus Citizens the equivalent of a mayoral *vaffanculo*, saying if they didn't want him to march with his friends he'd sit out the parade with them. He, Chianese, and Bracco celebrated Columbus Day by having lunch at an Italian restaurant in the Bronx.

Chianese believed his and Bracco's exclusion stemmed from an incident in the 1999 Columbus Day Parade. He was in the parade, on the float of HeartShare, a New York nonprofit that provides social services to children and families. "I was on the float, wearing their [HeartShare's] T-shirt," Chianese recalled. "But also on the float with me were a couple of guys who were imitating De Niro and Joe Pesci, wearing chains and looking like mobsters. I found out later that the parade organizers resented that these guys were acting like this. I understood that. What did mobsters have to do with the parade? I think that carried over to three years later when I was denied access to the parade because I was in *The Sopranos*."

Chianese apparently was not aware that in 2000 and 2001 the

Columbus Citizens had barred *Sopranos* cast members from the parade.[2]

"It's their parade, it's a private parade, and you want to have Italian pride, so you're not going to have mobsters up there. That's why I understood it. I can see why they wouldn't want anyone representing mobsters. But Lorraine and I weren't representing mobsters.

"I felt hurt because I would have liked to have been in the parade, I'm proud of being Italian," Chianese added. But instead, "I had lunch with the mayor, in my old neighborhood in the Bronx. The mayor presented me with my grandfather's papers and the passenger list [from the ship that *nonno* Chianese took to arrive in the United States]. I had tears in my eyes. It was a beautiful day."[3]

Robert De Niro has long been an Italian American icon. But to the Order of the Sons of Italy in America (OSIA), the actor is nothing but a celebrity hit man whose entire career has been devoted to assassinating the reputation of Italians and Italian Americans. When the OSIA (which bills itself as the largest and oldest national organization for Italian Americans) heard in August 2004 that the Italian government planned to confer honorary Italian citizenship on De Niro, they wrote to Italy's prime minister Silvio Berlusconi, urging him to cancel his government's plans.

The OSIA complained that De Niro, whose paternal great-grandparents immigrated to America from a village in the southern region of Molise, had made a career of playing gangsters ever since he portrayed the young Vito Corleone in *Godfather II* in 1974. (The OSIA somehow overlooked his flashy role as small-time Little Italy hoodlum Johnny Boy Civello in Scorsese's *Mean Streets*, released a year before the second *Godfather* film.)

"He has done nothing to promote Italian culture in the United States," the OSIA charged. "Instead, OSIA and its members hold him and his movies responsible for considerably damaging the collective reputations of both Italians and Italian Americans."

The letter also claimed that by honoring De Niro, the Italian government was insulting millions of Italian Americans, who purportedly have been outraged by the actor's "distorted and unbalanced portrayal of people of Italian heritage."

The Sons of Italy's long-standing grudge against De Niro was reignited by his participation in *Shark Tale*, an animated feature film for young viewers made by DreamWorks, the production company founded by filmmaker Steven Spielberg, recording industry mogul David Geffen, and former Disney executive Jeffrey Katzenberg. In the aquatic comedy De Niro provides the voice of Don Lino, a great white shark and boss of the reef. Two *Sopranos* stars also voice lead roles. Michael Imperioli is Frankie, Lino's oldest son and a hothead piscine counterpart of Christopher Moltisanti, and Vincent "Big Pussy" Pastore is Luca, Don Lino's octopus underboss.

In January 2004, the OSIA and several other Italian American organizations got wind of DreamWorks' plans to release *Shark Tale* in October, and went into battle mode. They cobbled together the National Coalition Against Racial, Religious and Ethnic Stereotyping (CARRES), a paper organization of some twenty Italian American groups, with token non-Italian representation provided by one Polish American and two Arab American organizations. CARRES, upset about the film's shark mafiosi, with their Italian names and their use of terms like "fuhgeddaboudit" and "capeesh," asked DreamWorks to "change the gangsters' last names in *Shark Tale* to ones that do not call to mind a specific ethnic group and to remove all script elements that identify them as Italian."

The CARRES crowd was particularly outraged that the movie was aimed at young audiences, whose impressionable intellects supposedly would be harmed by the pernicious images of underwater wiseguys. "It is the first children's mafia movie," said Dona de Sanctis, a CARRES spokesperson and a director of the OSIA. "They are passing this stereotyping on to the next generation . . . This man [Spielberg] is going to make millions of dollars with a film that is going to introduce unflattering and untrue stereotypes of Italian-Americans as gangsters to millions of children."[4]

CARRES began an e-mail pressure campaign against the film and even lobbied to have the Motion Picture Association of America (MPAA) change the film's rating from PG to PG-13 or R. And all for naught, as it turned out. *Shark Tale*, released in October 2004, was a hit, making more than $49 million in its opening weekend and going on to gross $160 million in the United States.

The campaigns against De Niro and *Shark Tale*, besides being ineffectual, were laughable. The OSIA's notion that millions of Italian Americans are furious at Robert De Niro is downright delusional, as they have been among his most ardent fans since he first appeared on-screen. (The fact that the actor is only one-quarter Italian, which was reported early on in his career, has never lessened Italian American affection for him.) Moreover, it's nonsense to claim that De Niro has "made a career" of playing gangsters with Italian names. Of his approximately seventy films, he has played only a half-dozen mob parts, including those in the comedies *Shark Tale* and *Analyze This* and its sequel, *Analyze That*. Most of the roles in his four-decade career have not even been Italian or Italian American characters.

The criticism upset De Niro, who had been delighted by the Italian government's decision to honor him. He offered a confused and not particularly articulate rejoinder to the antidefamation organizations. "The characters that I played are real—they are real. So they have as much right to be portrayed as any other characters," De Niro said while in Italy to promote DreamWorks' oceanic fantasia.[5]

The actor took out most of his pique on Italy. In the fall of 2004 he blew off appointments with Italian officials and failed to show up for his own Tribeca Film Festival in Rome. (De Niro had created the festival in New York to help revive the spirits and economic fortunes of his Tribeca neighborhood in downtown Manhattan, after the terrorist attacks of September 11, 2001.) By December, however, he was mending fences. He opened, in Rome, the first exhibition in Italy of paintings by his father, the late Robert De Niro, Sr., a renowned New York artist. At the gala inauguration of the exhibit he charmed the many Italian officials and celebrities who attended. The Milan-based newspaper *Corriere della Sera* reported that plans to award De Niro honorary Italian citizenship were back on track.

If the self-appointed guardians of Italian American honor had it in for De Niro, Italians saw the controversy differently. The three-thousand-plus residents of Ferrazzano, the village that De Niro's great-

grandparents left in the late nineteenth century, "are among his greatest fans and are adamant that he should be formally made an Italian."⁶
Every August since 1994, the village, now populated by well-off professionals and white-collar workers, has turned out for a weeklong festival
of De Niro films.

"We're proud of De Niro because he is the best actor in the world
and comes from Ferrazzano," said Mariassunta Baranello, organizer of
the festival. "Our history has good and bad bits. You cannot just deny
the past. And after all, it is only cinema."⁷

Italian American advocates and organizations have protested depictions
of their ethnic kin as gangsters since *Scarface* was released in the
1930s. Their indignation has waxed and waned with the tides of popular culture's production of mob-themed entertainment. In the 1950s it
was the long-running TV crime show *The Untouchables* that incited
their ire; in the late 1960s it was Mario Puzo's *Godfather* novel, and, in
the following decade, the *Godfather* films and the imitations they
spawned. Besides the Sons of Italy, other organizations, such as the
National Italian American Foundation (NIAF) and UNICO, have decried movies like *Prizzi's Honor*, *The Untouchables*, and *Goodfellas*. But
nothing in recent memory has fired up the antidefamation troops as
much as *The Sopranos*.

To them, "The HBO network and its series *The Sopranos* are guilty
of defaming and assassinating the cultural character of Italian Americans by using their religion, customs, and values in a violent and im-
moral context that damages the image and reputations of an estimated
20 million Americans of Italian descent," according to a press release
issued in 2000 by NIAF and a half-dozen other organizations.

At a New York City forum held by NIAF in 2001, Joseph V. Scelsa,
an official with the City University of New York and a prominent Italian American figure, argued that *The Sopranos* and other movies and
TV shows about gangsters represent a "cultural holocaust" for young
Italian Americans. The show's popularity conclusively demonstrates
that Americans hate Italians, say others. "They"—influential elite types
in the media and academia who purportedly demonstrate "politically

correct" deference to other ethnic, racial, and social minorities—would never applaud similarly grotesque portrayals of blacks or Jews, according to many Italian American critics of *The Sopranos*.

Sopranos haters have denounced the show in public forums like the NIAF conference, organized letter-writing campaigns, held protests outside HBO's corporate offices in Manhattan, and proposed resolutions in state legislatures decrying the series. They've also launched frequent and frequently scurrilous ad hominem attacks on David Chase as a "self-loathing" Italian American wracked by Oedipal angst. (How else could he have created that horrible mother Livia Soprano, who isn't like any Italian American mamma who ever lived!)

The *Sopranos* brouhaha has raised a number of thorny issues that merit serious consideration but generally are ignored or dismissed in the popular discourse about the series. These include the self-image of Italian Americans (a century after the immigrants began to arrive in the United States, some of their descendants apparently believe WASP America still hates them, and still feel vulnerable to bias), the persistence of the gangster as an exemplar of Italian American ethnicity, and the role of pop culture in disseminating particular images of ethnic minorities and the power of those minorities to influence how they are portrayed.

The *Sopranos* controversy also involves class distinctions among Italian Americans. Some of those most opposed to the show are corporate CEOs and successful professionals who serve on the boards of organizations like NIAF. They, having made it to the upper-middle and upper classes, resent the persistence of the gangster image, particularly its association with all things prole. Ambivalence also colors Italian American responses to *The Sopranos* as some who enjoy, even love the show nonetheless are disturbed by its perpetuation of an image they find offensive and onerous.

And what is the real-world impact of ethnic stereotyping? Does the mafia stereotype really harm Italian Americans? How is it like, and not like, racism? Given that Italian Americans are not oppressed in any sense as Italian Americans, don't all the protests about *The Sopranos* have the ring of special pleading, and, worse, of a tunnel vision that ignores far more serious forms of bias and stigma?

Some Italian Americans go so far as to describe the show as a dire threat to an entire culture. "Clearly, Tony Soprano & Co. must be destroyed—in the court of public opinion. Like their Roman forebears, Italian-Americans must draw a line in the sand if they are to rescue a heritage that has been hijacked by the likes of David Chase, creator of 'The Sopranos,' " wrote Rosario Iaconis in an op-ed piece that appeared in *Newsday*. Iaconis is director of the Italic Institute of America, a Queens-based organization that promotes Italian culture and language.

"As self-loathing Italian-Americans go, Chase has parlayed his life-long Oedipal angst into the most blatantly anti-Italian program in the history of television," thundered Iaconis. "Along the way, he has attracted an army of accomplices and enablers," including such prominent Italian American fans of the series as Rudy Giuliani, former New Jersey senator Robert Torricelli, former New York senator Al D'Amato, and Andrew Cuomo, who have "all done their bits to promote Chase's Big Lie."

> Why have so many journalists, politicos and educators embraced such a repellent, hurtful stereotype—particularly one they would find reprehensible if applied to Jews, Asians or Hispanics? Are the scions of Italy a race of the damned? When Italians are cut, do they not bleed? Or is it simply a case of *schadenfreude* gone wild?
>
> Aided and abetted by "The Sopranos," Italophobia is rapidly becoming the defining intolerance of the new millennium. Everyone wants a piece of the action—from the literati to the glitterati to the lumpen proletariat—because they have come to believe that Italo-Americans are indeed the lowest of the lowbrow.[8]

The Columbus Citizens' Lawrence Auriana echoes Iaconis's view of *The Sopranos* as a form of class war against Italian Americans. "The program is a bad caricature of our culture," he says. "It's not only that it's about criminals and organized crime. It characterizes us as a base, uneducated group."[9]

Paul Basile, a columnist for the Chicago-based monthly journal *Fra*

Noi ("Among Us"), acknowledges that *The Sopranos* is an artful production. But that just makes him hate it even more. "Apologists for *The Sopranos* will argue that the show is well done, but in my estimation, that makes it all the more reprehensible," he writes.

> A destructive message presented in a well-crafted package makes that message all the more seductive and potent. The films of Nazi propagandist Leni Riefenstahl are considered by many critics to be cinematic masterpieces, but she will never be allowed to enter the pantheon of film gods because she used her talents to foist Adolf Hitler on the German people.
>
> Apologists for *The Sopranos* will hide behind the Constitution, claiming that it is protected by the First Amendment, but that debases one of our most precious rights. The Nazis are allowed to march in Skokie and the Klan to rally in Georgia thanks to the First Amendment. But the First Amendment doesn't make what they have to say good or decent or true, it only protects their right to say it.

Basile goes on to liken *The Sopranos* to a powerfully seductive but deadly drug, from which the public, Italian and non-Italian, presumably must be protected.

> Why do so many Italian Americans love *The Sopranos*? For the same reason that non-Italian Americans love it. Americans have long adored their outlaws, from the days of Jesse James to the present. And when you combine that enduring national obsession with a walloping dose of Italian passion, the result is almost narcotic. Quite honestly, if *The Sopranos* were the only show in town to traffic in such dangerous substance, I'd be more sanguine. But the fact is that just about every time you see Italian American characters on the big or small screen, they're fighting the mob, fleeing the mob, or being the mob.
>
> Apologists for *The Sopranos* argue the show's detractors should relax. To them, I say, "Do the math." A mere one in 20,000 Italian Americans is currently involved in organized

304 / AN OFFER WE CAN'T REFUSE

crime. When Hollywood gives me 19,999 decent-to-heroic Italian Americans for every Mafioso it serves up, that's when I'll relax.[10]

Contrarian culture critic Camille Paglia thinks that members of the intelligentsia love *The Sopranos* because it permits them to displace their bad faith about race and racism onto Italian Americans, who can be defamed without any significant repercussions.

In a 2001 lecture on the topic of "Tony Soprano, the Media and Popular Culture," Paglia said:

> My personal opinion is that the haute-bourgeoisie in New York and the critics who praise [*The Sopranos*] so much have a tremendous problem in their own city and with race. They are extremely segregated; they're full of liberal notions about multiculturalism, affirmative action, but the actual life of the bourgeoisie, those people in the media, is completely white, completely. Go to any party in New York, it is all white.
>
> So I think there's a heavy guilt trip that they have; and the whole thing about *The Sopranos* is a cryptic version of dealing with race issues in this country. They could never authentically, directly deal with African Americans in the way that they've dealt with *The Sopranos*. The fact that it shows that Italian Americans are literally the last group that people are free to libel means that all Italian Americans have to start banding together and realizing that.

Paglia charges that multiculturalism in education has resulted in the downgrading of the great cultural achievements of the Mediterranean world, leaving only crude stereotypes of Italians.

> The canon that used to be taught in schools that descends from Mediterranean culture, from Greece through Italy down through the Middle Ages and to the rebirth of Greco-Roman humanism and so on with the Renaissance, that is gone, in terms of the culture as a whole. And as a consequence, the only

thing that's left is this constant replay of those libelous images of Italian Americans on *The Sopranos*.[11]

The show is bad enough in itself, say its critics, but even worse, it has had a ripple effect in popular culture, inspiring more mafia mania.

In mafia mythology, music and mobsters are almost as inseparable as gangsters and their gumads. The Corleones waltz to Italian composer Nino Rota's indelible *Godfather* theme, Charlie in *Mean Streets* gets drunk while the rock and roll novelty "Rubber Biscuits" plays on a bar jukebox, Henry Hill's cocaine-fueled frenzy in *Goodfellas* is set to the ping-ponging rhythms of the Rolling Stones' "Monkey Man." Then there are the compilations of Italian and Italian American songs that have been heard on the soundtracks of mob movies and TV shows, such as Jerry Vale's popular *Mob Hits* and *Peppers and Eggs*, from *The Sopranos*, not to mention Uncle Junior singing the Neapolitan *canzone* "Core 'ngrato" on an episode of the show.

But the producers of *La Musica della Mafia: Il Canto di Malavita* took the tradition one step further. The album, released in 2002, consisted not of numbers that have been associated with mobsters in the movies and on television but actual folk songs written and performed by 'Ndrangheta gangsters from the southern Italian region of Calabria.

The Sons of Italy's Dona de Sanctis trashed the album as a crass attempt to cash in on the notoriety of *The Sopranos*. She observed that members of 'Ndrangheta were "vultures who preyed on the Calabrian people for centuries" and that the songs shouldn't be commercialized.

"What I find so despicable is that they used authentic instruments of southern Italy," de Sanctis told the New York *Daily News*. "They use the Jew's harp. They have authentic rhythms, such as the tarantella, and Calabrese dialect. They use all of these cultural assets to sell the Mafia. This is like using Michelangelo's 'Pietà' to sell topless dancers."[12]

The 'Ndrangheta, a fearsome criminal syndicate, does indeed have a culture, and the songs are an expression of their violent, pitiless world. And why wouldn't they use "the authentic instruments of southern Italy" and play "authentic rhythms," since they are southern Italian musicians? Should they instead use Casio keyboards and drum machines? Her Pietà and topless dancers analogy is beyond absurd; distasteful or not, *La Musica della Mafia* is an authentic expression of a particular Italian subculture, not some devious attempt to conflate southern Italian folk music and criminality. What de Sanctis objects to is the fact that the album exists at all.

Other Italian Americans appreciate, even love *The Sopranos*, but bristle at what they see as the dismissal of their concerns about stereotyping by the show's admirers.

Marie Cocco, a nationally syndicated liberal political columnist, confided to her readers that she's "awfully fond" of Tony and Carmela Soprano. "Like much of America, I'm all tied up in their peculiar style of family bonding," she wrote in a 2002 column. She finds herself "drawn in by Tony's confused efforts to do the right thing" and intrigued by

> Carmela's social striving, despite her ambivalence about the source of the nouveau riches that finance her climb . . .
> But you can love "The Sopranos" and still loathe the way legitimate gripes about Italian-American stereotyping are dismissed. They're cast aside by everyone associated with the smash HBO show. By its legions of Italian-American fans— some of whom log on to HBO's chat rooms to wax nostalgic about such topics as those bygone Sunday dinners. They are disregarded by the mainstream media, which scoff at complaints about ubiquitous portrayals of Italian-Americans as scheming gangsters and serial adulterers.

Noting how establishment newspapers such as *The New York Times* and *The Wall Street Journal* have dismissed such concerns as "overblown" and "unjustified," Cocco observed. "If you do not believe it is still acceptable to malign Italian-Americans, try to imagine critics for such publications casting aside, with open contempt, the concerns of other ethnic groups. Bet you can't."[13]

Frank Pugliese, a playwright (*Aven'U Boys*), screenwriter (his credits include the acclaimed HBO drama *Shot in the Heart*), and former artistic director of the New York theater company Naked Angels, sounds a similar note.

CULTURAL HOLOCAUST OR NATIONAL MYTH? / 307

I think the actual page-by-page writing [on *The Sopranos*] is really impressive. The acting is some of the best acting on TV. If it were one show out of about twenty shows that are about Italian Americans, I wouldn't mind it so much. But when the show—and this concerns me about Italians and non-Italians doing it—when the show is used to define my background, I have to say, "No." I'm very unhappy with it, and I reject it. It's not the case. So I react strongly. Don't use that show to tell me what I'm about. It's not. So that's how I feel about it. I don't know how much that's the show's fault. It's kind of all our fault.[14]

Pugliese here is ascribing responsibility to the Italian Americans who are the main creators of mob entertainment and perpetrators of the Italian gangster image. But others prefer to assign blame to an ill-defined "they," a sinister media cabal that delights in impugning Italian Americans while regarding other racial and ethnic minorities as off-limits.

The Italic Institute's Don Fiore, in a posting to H-ITAM, an online list serve, or e-mail exchange, of Italian American academics and activists, wrote, "It would never be permitted to happen, but imagine that someone was undaunted enough to create a TV series called *The Shapiros*, which featured the corrupt dealings of a family of Jewish financiers. Or a show about a family of bomb-planting Islamic terrorists. Or African American welfare queens. Or Hispanic drug dealers."

Fiore overlooks how these supposedly protected groups have been and continue to be stereotyped. How about the near-invisibility of Latinos in popular culture, except when they appear as Mexican gardeners, gang members, or drug dealers? What about the overwhelmingly negative depictions of Arabs as remorseless terrorists, which predated September 11, 2001, and continue unabated? The Fox TV network series *24* in early 2005 antagonized Arab antidefamation organizations with a storyline about a family of Arab terrorists led by a mother who made Livia Soprano look like June Cleaver.

If there are more varied and fewer stereotypical images of African Americans in popular culture, that isn't because politically correct white liberals in the media wouldn't dare abrade black sensibilities;

it's due to the concerted, decades-long political struggle blacks have fought against demeaning, racist depictions.

And as far as Jews are concerned, has Fiore seen how they frequently are portrayed on *The Sopranos*—as mafia associates and corrupt, mafia-aligned politicians? Or on Larry David's HBO comedy series *Curb Your Enthusiasm*, with characters calling each other "Jewface" and being neurotic, devious, and pushy—in other words, acting stereotypically? David even made a Holocaust joke that played on a linguistic confusion between "survivor" and a participant in the TV reality series *Survivor*. The Italian American David Chase has as much right to depict a depressed, philandering, and sometimes murderous mafia paterfamilias as the Jewish Larry David has to make edgy jokes that some Jews no doubt find offensive.

Both Fiore and his Italic Institute colleague Rosario Iaconis seem blind to the differences between an irksome stereotype and racist mythology, and to the real-world consequences of both.

If the antidefamationists think gangster stereotyping has such noxious effects on Italians, perhaps they might consider how the exploitation of white fears of blacks and black criminality has influenced, or rather poisoned, American politics. Richard Nixon devised his notorious "Southern strategy" to woo white men away from the Democratic Party by playing on their resentment of the gains blacks had made through the civil rights struggle. During the 1988 presidential race between George Bush, Sr., and Massachusetts governor Michael Dukakis, GOP hatchet man Lee Atwater seized on Willie Horton, a black prisoner who committed a rape while he was furloughed from the Massachusetts penal system. Atwater, wrote political commentator Harvey Wasserman, "filled the airwaves with brutally racist black-and-white ads meant to make Horton and Dukakis seem blood-related. The poisonous stench helped send the Democrats into a tail spin."[15]

Throughout the 2004 presidential campaign the Republican Party waged a jihad against homosexual Americans, portraying George W. Bush as the leader who would save the nation from the horrors of same-sex marriage and other sodomitic affronts to "traditional values." Bush even went so far as to propose amending the Constitution to prohibit gay men and lesbians from marrying their partners.

In this context, Rosario Iaconis's claim that "Italophobia is rapidly becoming the defining intolerance of the new millennium" is not only self-pitying and preposterous; it is also shockingly obtuse.

If any single person represents the Italian American establishment, it would be Kenneth Ciongoli, a neurosurgeon who is the national vice chairman and a former president of NIAF. Ciongoli shares Fiore's and Iaconis's outrage over gangster stereotypes, as well as their unwarranted self-pity and political obtuseness.

"We're a polite people. We don't want to tread on anyone else's trauma," Ciongoli told me during a lengthly telephone interview. "We're not automatically victims. We hate victimology. But the cultural elite or the liberal cabal that creates this image of us has to be taken on head-on. We've not been willing to do that. Right now we're just throwing darts at an amorphous board. No one's in danger of catching any, because we haven't really aimed them. We don't want to name Jewish people, we don't want to name black people, but both of those peoples have maligned us far more than we've maligned them—if we've ever maligned them."

"If" we've ever maligned them?

Here in New York, a state with large Italian American and African American populations, politically progressive Italians like me have been embarrassed and infuriated for years not only by the base behavior of street corner racists in Bensonhurst and Howard Beach, but also by the rhetoric of certain prominent Italian Americans, including elected officials.

Rudolph Giuliani, dubbed "America's Mayor" after September 11, 2001, acted for most of his eight years in office as if he were only white New York's mayor. He consistently played to his base among white ethnics, including Italian Americans, while treating the city's black and Latino communities with condescension at best but more often with outright hostility. He refused to meet with African American community leaders, claiming he needn't bother because they were opposed to his policies. Jimmy Breslin, the eminent newspaper columnist and author, remarked that contempt for people of color was a hallmark of Giuliani's administration.

During Giuliani's tenure, acts of brutality by New York cops against young blacks and Latinos occurred with disturbing frequency, the most horrific being the torture of Abner Louima, a Haitian immigrant. Police officer Justin Volpe falsely arrested Louima after an altercation in Brooklyn, and, in the precinct house, jammed a wooden stick so violently into Louima's rectum that the Haitian needed several surgeries to repair the damage to his bladder and intestines.

Giuliani's typical response to criticism of his police force's tactics was to smear the cops' victims. In March 2000, after an undercover officer shot to death Patrick Dorismond, a young African American who worked as a Times Square security guard, Giuliani responded to public outrage by releasing the sealed records of the deceased man's arrest as a juvenile. His family filed a wrongful-death suit against the city, citing Giuliani's release of the criminal records "as part of a pattern of smearing people hurt by the police." The city paid $2.25 million to settle the suit.[16]

Former Republican U.S. senator Alphonse D'Amato no longer represents New York State, but he remains a presence in politics and the media. In 1991, D'Amato distinguished himself by declaring on a radio program that New York City's African American mayor, David Dinkins, should go to Africa "and stay there."[17] In 1986, when the senator was asked about a low-income housing project in his state, he reportedly commented, "We didn't do too well with the animal vote, did we? Isn't it the animals who live in these projects? They're not our people."[18]

During New York State budget battles in 1995, Republican senate majority leader Joseph Bruno declared, "the blacks, the Hispanics" are "the people that got their hands out. They are the ones fighting for welfare."[19]

Bob Grant, born Robert Gigante, was one of the earliest and most successful right-wing radio "shock jocks," a belligerent reactionary who regularly serves up red meat racism to his white listeners. On his New York–based program he once said, "We have in our nation, not hundreds of thousands but millions of sub-humanoids—savages, who really would feel more at home careening along the sands of the Kalahari, or the dry deserts of eastern Kenya—people who for whatever reason have not become civilized."[20]

Grant has frequently expressed his belief in the "scientific" form of racism called eugenics, and often promotes what he calls the Bob Grant Mandatory Sterilization Program. (Guess whom he wants to keep from reproducing.) Besides delivering such sickening Nazi-like rhetoric, Grant often uses southern Italian dialect expressions like *sfaccim* (devil's sperm) to slur his favorite bêtes noires, blacks and other nonwhites, liberals, and gays.

Grant, who has been befouling the airwaves for decades, is by no means speaking into some echo chamber of right-wing extremism. The man has a sizable following, particularly among his fellow ethnics. The New Jersey resident counts "many fans among the state's sizable chunk of increasingly conservative Italian-American voters. Also fueling Grant's popularity in this racially tense state is his unabashed racism," as Doug Ireland reported in *The Nation*.[21]

Perhaps Ken Ciongoli, who lives in Vermont, is unaware of these and other instances of Italian Americans maligning blacks and other minorities. But those of us who live in New York and other major urban areas of the North and Northeast recognize them for what they are: unvarnished expressions of bigotry that poison political discourse and foster ill will between groups in our diverse society. These attacks, combined with lethal racist violence in places like Bensonhurst, also create an impression of Italian Americans as some of the most militant enemies of people of color.

As for "naming" Jewish people, Ciongoli doubtless is referring to Hollywood producers and studio executives, a favorite target of bigots of all stripes, whether they're black nationalists like New York academic Leonard Jeffries, with his crackpot notions about humanist "sun people" (blacks) and oppressive "ice people" (whites, especially Jews), or conservative Italian Americans like, say, Kenneth Ciongoli. In the case of the latter, the sneaky allusion to Jews is a rhetorical ploy to evade the inconvenient fact that it's largely Italian American artists who make movies and TV shows about the mob. Ciongoli must think some scheming Hebrews took the creator of *The Sopranos* by the arm and whispered seductively, "David, boychick, ve vant you make a TV show that'll assassinate the cultural character of the wops . . . there's good money in it for you if you do."

Kenneth Ciongoli, meet William Donohue, president of the

Catholic League for Religious and Civil Rights, who proclaimed on national TV, "Hollywood is controlled by secular Jews who hate Christianity in general and Catholicism in particular. It's not a secret, OK? And I'm not afraid to say it."[22]

Libero della Piana, a syndicated journalist, made the stunningly obvious (though not to Iaconis, Fiore, and Ciongoli) observation that "while the stereotype of the Italian mobster certainly is prevalent, it is hardly the cutting edge of racism. Some stereotypes have higher consequences than others."

Della Piana is in a unique position to know the truth of this, as he is the son of an Italian American father and an African American mother. In a column titled "Are Italians the New Anti-Racist Front?" he examined the National Coalition Against Racial, Religious and Ethnic Stereotyping (CARRES) and its campaign against *Shark Tale*. "As a son of Italian American and Black American parents I wondered whether CARRES represented a new anti-racist consciousness in the Italian community. Or are Italian American organizations just irked by being stuck with the mafia label? Are Italian American organizations just against stereotypes, or are they against racism at all levels of society?"

Based on CARRES's record to date, della Piana sadly concluded that the former is the case—this purported coalition is concerned solely with what it considers to be defamatory images of Italian Americans. "Italian immigrants to this country suffered a long history of discrimination, exclusion and violence," he wrote. "There is also a long history of Italian Americans committed to interracial unity and inclusiveness. But most of the Italian American community left their darker immigrant brethren behind when they gained political clout, economic success and acceptance in white society."

Italians Americans today "are not stopped by the police because of their skin color or prevented from flying because of their last names. Racial profiling is however the ongoing reality for people of color today," he observed. "The failure to address racism also breeds a lack of trust," he added. The NAACP, the National Council of La Raza, and the Anti-Defamation League all refused to join CARRES because of its narrow focus on ethnic stereotypes, although two Arab American organizations concerned with the image of Arabs in the media and popular culture did join.[23]

If it is obvious that Italian Americans are by no means the most sinned against of all ethnic groups, the antidefamationist complaints are correct in one respect: African Americans and Latinos, as well as social minorities like gays, do have a greater purchase on liberal and leftist sympathies than do Italian Americans.

"It's a curious fate to be an 'unprotected' ethnic minority where all bets are off in contemporary politically correct discourse," as Chris Messenger, a professor of English at the University of Illinois in Chicago, notes in his 2002 study, *"The Godfather" and American Culture*.[24]

And it's also true, as noted in Chapter 1, that non-Italians sometimes feel free to play fast and loose with Italian American stereotypes—in advertising, political campaigns, journalism—which they might refrain from doing to other ethnic, racial, or social minorities.

Furthermore, there have been some truly tasteless attempts to cash in on the popularity of *The Sopranos*, few more so than a Public Broadcasting Service (PBS) documentary shown in early 2004, "The Medici: Godfathers of the Renaissance." The documentary, promoted as "historical," portrayed the Medici family that ruled the city-state of Florence as fifteenth-century mafiosi. Even worse were the so-called lesson plans for teachers and students posted at the PBS Web site. They featured "rapsheets" of the Medicis, as well as a list of their "capos" and their "hits." Since the mafia did not exist during the time of the Medicis, "it is hard to escape the conclusion that the label appears here only because the Medici were Italian."[25]

But those Italian Americans who are so worked up over gangster stereotypes, so caught up in yes, their victimology, never seem to consider why Italian American stereotyping elicits less concern than racism, anti-Semitism, or homophobia. Racial minorities, Jews, and gays get more sympathy because they experience far more bias, stigma, and outright discrimination than do Italians.

"I worry when these Italian American groups try to claim victimhood and use it as a hammer to drive home their agenda," notes veteran journalist George Anastasia. "I understand their argument, I just don't agree with it. Maybe my grandfather and your grandfather experienced discrimination because their names ended in vowels. I look around today and I don't see it."[26]

Moreover, if some seem insensitive to complaints about mob stereotypes, it is often because they recognize not only that these images generally are created by Italian Americans themselves—which differentiates them from derogatory portrayals of other minorities—but that they are also avidly consumed by Italian Americans.

Not all who dislike *The Sopranos* couch their arguments in Kenneth Ciongoli's brand of aggressive philistinism or invidiously slight other minorities.

Ben Lawton, born in the United States and raised in northern Italy, is a professor of film and Italian studies at Purdue University who also moderates H-ITAM, the listserv of the American Italian Historical Association. When it comes to *The Sopranos*, H-ITAM serves as a cyberspace battlefield where academics and activists have been engaged in a long-running and often ferocious war of words over the series. In a lengthy posting to the list serve, Lawton contrasted Coppola's and Scorsese's depictions of organized crime with David Chase's *Sopranos*, and found the latter wanting.

"It seems to me that perhaps the most fundamental difference between Coppola and Scorsese on the one hand, and Chase on the other, is that the former have a deep love for all that is positive in their heritage and, by extension, an intense resentment and perhaps even hatred for those Italian Americans who have harmed Italian Americans directly and indirectly over the years, that is, not just of the Mafia as such, but of the Mafioso mentality (*Mean Streets*)."

Lawton argues that whereas "Coppola and Scorsese are openly and avowedly proud of their Italian/American heritage," David Chase "seems embarrassed to be of Italian American extraction. He seems to despise the Italian Americans who tell him that they are hurt by his program. He certainly does not wish to engage in any kind of dialog with them."

The Sopranos, according to Lawton, depicts all its Italian American characters (with the possible exception of Carmela) "in a manner that is deliberately demeaning.

"Coppola's godfather was called 'Corleone,' or Lion Heart," Lawton observes. "Chase's godfather is called 'Soprano.' We all know how a man becomes a soprano." Lawton sees in the depiction of Tony Soprano, who faints at the sight of Italian deli meat, a parallel to the cas- trati, the male singers gelded at puberty so they would retain their boy soprano voices. Tony has been castrated by his creator, David Chase, and Lawton disapproves: "What kind of 'capo' faints at the sight of sausage? What kind of 'capo' sees a shrink, and a female one at that? What happened to the masculine code of omertà? . . . I don't claim to know anything about the Mafia except what I have read. But, from what I have read, it is my sense that these are (or were) serious people . . . they were anything but buffoons."

Lawton, incredibly enough, dislikes *The Sopranos* because it por- trays gangsters negatively! Why, real gangsters were serious people! They didn't have names like "Big Pussy"—no, they had much more dignified monikers like "the Chin," "Tony Ducks," or "Joe Pig" (all ac- tual nicknames of real mobsters). Lawton's critique entirely misses the point: today's mobsters, the greedy, anarchic, mindlessly brutal, and inept thugs depicted on *The Sopranos*, deserve to be satirized, to be "dissed." Whatever admirable qualities some earlier gangsters might have had—their nurturing of jazz is one that comes to mind— have been lost in Tony Soprano's generation. That the decline would be the subject of Chase's show was evident from the very first episode.

"If there is any group of Italian Americans who might have a right to protest representation in the series, it's the tiny number of contempo- rary Italian American gangsters," says Fred Gardaphé.[27]

Lawton at least concedes that his knowledge of "the Mafia" is sec- ondhand, drawn solely from his reading. George Anastasia, however, knows the topic from a much closer vantage point. He has covered Ital- ian American organized crime for more than twenty years as a reporter for *The Philadelphia Inquirer*, and is the author of several books about the mob, including the highly regarded *Blood and Honor*.[28]

"The noble men of honor, if they existed at all, disappeared two generations ago with the death of Carlo Gambino in New York and the assassination of Angelo Bruno in Philadelphia," he observes. "They were the prototypes for Don Corleone." Such men "came to this country, struggled as immigrants, found their opportunities limited, and chose organized crime as a way of life. The choice is not one that should be applauded, but given the circumstances in which they found themselves as young men, it is at least understandable."[29]

Today's mob, however, is a degenerate version of the old, immigrant-era crime groups, and Chase, according to Anastasia, gets it exactly right in his portrayal of the Soprano organization. "*The Sopranos* accurately captures the turmoil and disorganization that have brought about the demise of the American Mafia. The reasons, cultural and generational, are clearly a part of the story line." Anastasia says the show's themes, including Tony Soprano's struggles to keep his crew in line and his nostalgia for the old days, "could come right from the transcripts of court testimony I have heard or secretly recorded conversations I have listened to."[30]

Robert Viscusi, director of the Wolfe Institute for the Humanities at Brooklyn College and the president of the Italian American Writers Association (IAWA), has little patience for the argument, made by Lawton and others, that *The Sopranos* lacks the gravitas of *The Godfather*. Viscusi recalls:

> For thirty years, the big Italian American organizations were complaining about *The Godfather*—none of them more substantially than the National Italian American Foundation, which actually published a book in 1997 called *Beyond "The Godfather."* [Kenneth Ciongoli and the novelist and critic Jay Parini coedited the book, a collection of writings on Italian American identity and culture.]
>
> I was at a conference that they [NIAF] held in 2001 at the [New York] Hilton, talking about *The Sopranos*, and Camille Paglia, that great expert, got up and compared *The Sopranos* negatively with *The Godfather*, because in *The Godfather* the gangsters are shown with dignity, and blah-blah-blah.
>
> And this now has become received doctrine. Everybody says now, "Oh, *The Godfather* was good, this is terrible." This shows you what fascists they may really be. Because the thing about *The Sopranos* that makes it attractive to people like you and me, is that it's a deconstruction of the fascist Italian gangster. It shows you this big nightmare bully, the fascist, and there he is

peeing in his pants and fainting at the sight of a slice of salami. And then, of course, there's the wonderful joke of his name— the soprano! Nobody ever seems to talk about that. He's a so- prano, no matter how much he beats on his chest.

Tony Soprano—as everybody can plainly see—is an Ameri- can, right down to the tips of his toes. It's a profoundly Ameri- can story. That's why everybody likes it. It's not just about Italians. That is what strikes me as the pathological ethnocen- trism of Italian Americans. That they think that this is "just about us." But it isn't. And yet when some recognize these sto- ries as metaphors for whatever—capitalism, assimilation—they get highly indignant and say, "Well, why does our experience have to be used?"

But [continues Viscusi, working up to a full head of steam,] it's not only us! Have they seen any movies about African Amer- icans lately? Have they seen any movies about Jewish Ameri- cans, Latino-Americans, Okies, Southern Americans, people in the suburbs of Chicago? There's an endless list. Those people in [Jewish-American film director] Todd Solondz's movies are not Italians. Some of them are Jews; some of them are other things. To me so much of this belies a kind of hatred of culture and a will to ignorance that is absolutely staggering. And an incredible arrogance. Like only things that people say about us are worth even listening to. I've heard so many people say, "Only to an Italian," but that's not true.[31]

Viscusi's point about the hatred for culture, the philistinism of anti- defamationists, hits home. Case study: Kenneth Ciongoli's analysis of the works of Martin Scorsese.

"I get upset with Martin Scorsese," Ciongoli complained to me.

He seems to have a genius recognized by his peers in Holly- wood, but he doesn't seem to be able to use that genius in any way except violence. For example, Barry Levinson gave the Jew- ish people *Avalon*, [Bill] Cosby gave the African Americans *The Cosby Show*. Where's our *Cosby Show*? If anything, we are *The*

Cosby Show. So, where's Martin Scorsese, where's Francis Ford Coppola? Perhaps it's not economically viable for them and that's the reason, but it doesn't seem to bother Barry Levinson or even Steven Spielberg. What really upsets me about Scorsese is the way he always links our food. Someone will chop a head off and then they're eating some kind of pasta. He does that constantly. He even included his mother in it, which I thought was unbelievable.[32]

Ciongoli would never have made it as a film critic. There are no moments such as he describes in any of Scorsese's films. Perhaps he's thinking of the darkly comic scene in *Goodfellas* where Henry Hill, Tommy De Vito, and Jimmy Conway drop in on Tommy's mom on their way to dispose of the body of Billy Batts, the made man Tommy unwisely assaulted in a bar. His mother, played by the always delightful Catherine Scorsese, of course gives them something to eat, and proudly shows off one of her hilariously bad paintings. While the goodfellas are enjoying Mamma De Vito's hospitality and artwork, poor Billy Batts, locked in the trunk of Henry's car, is writhing in his death throes.

Scorsese used his mother in a number of his films—*Mean Streets, Goodfellas, Cape Fear,* and *Casino* among them—for good reason. She was a natural, a warm, engaging, funny presence, and I for one always looked forward to her appearances in her son's movies. I like to imagine what the famously feisty and outspoken Mrs. Scorsese, who died in 1997, would have to say in response to Ciongoli's comments about her son.

Ciongoli and other like-minded Italian American advocates basically are demanding "positive images" of themselves and positive role models for young Italian Americans, just as other minority groups have done. It's an understandable inclination, but such demands can be the enemy of art. Michael Bronski, a cultural critic who writes mainly about homosexuality and American society and culture, says that many gays and lesbians evaluate pop-cultural productions by the criterion "Is it good for the gays?," echoing the famous Jewish version.

"The question itself is the product of a survivalist impulse," Bronski notes. "Given the overwhelming prevalence of queer hatred in the

world (not to mention general confusion and ambivalence over homosexuality), worrying about whether a book or movie was 'good for the
gays'—whether it would engender more dislike or even suspicion of
homosexuality—is, in many ways, a reasonable response."[33] But, Bronski cautions, "One problem of using the 'Is it good for the gays' argument is that it is not equipped to account for nuance, shading, or even
irony and literary seriousness."

Setting aside the survival issue—Italian Americans, unlike gays and
lesbians, face no threats to their legal status, social autonomy, or physical safety—the same can be said for Italian American responses to *The
Sopranos*.

Drea De Matteo, who memorably portrayed the doomed Adriana
La Cerva on *The Sopranos*, says as much, but more bluntly. "The Italians who thought *The Sopranos* portrayed dumb Italians are themselves
the Italians making us look stupid," De Matteo told *New York* magazine. "If they just think 'mob . . . violence . . . bad' and can't see the
show as a literary piece, that shows how simplistic and narrow-minded
they are. It's the emotional violence on that show that's really more significant. The people who complain about this, what they really should
do, is take a couple of literature classes, a couple of classic-film classes,
and shut their mouths."[34]

Dominic Chianese, though gentler to the antidefamationists than
De Matteo, expresses a similar view.

> I feel that if writers choose to write about it [organized crime],
> they have a perfect right to do that, because of our Constitu-
> tion. On that basis I don't think there should be any censorship.
> Yet at the same time I feel the Italians, as a community, if we
> are a community of ideals and ethnic pride, we want to hold on
> to the fact that we're good and proud people, and that we con-
> tribute to the world in a positive way. We're givers, we're lovers,
> educators, artists, we're all these things, so I can understand
> wanting to protect all that, and I certainly protect it as an in-
> dividual.
>
> I tell people I can play a mobster because I am an actor, but
> I'm also an Italian who wants to bring something to the world,

through literature, music, art. I just feel we have to think more like Europeans [who Chianese says are more sophisticated about culture than Americans]. We don't seem to realize that we have a great culture, so that talking about gangsters, it's a little drop of ink into an ocean, and a drop of ink is not going to hurt us because that same drop of ink is in every culture. I understand it [the antidefamation point of view] but I don't think we should get so uptight about it.[35]

Or as crime reporter George Anastasia puts it, "Are we, as Italian Americans, so insecure about our position in society that we believe a television show could somehow negate all the accomplishments over the centuries that can be attributed to Italians and Italian Americans?"[36]

Human nature involves duality, dramatic tension [Chianese continues]. Within us all I think is the feeling that things are not right in the world, the world is not peaceful. We all know that as human beings, there's something dark in all of us. We surprise ourselves sometimes with our anger, our ability to hate. The storytelling we have [on *The Sopranos*] is all based on dramatic tension, good versus evil, and how we strive for happy endings. We strive for that even though we know life isn't like that. What really drives us human beings in the wrong direction is the prevalence of fear in our lives, and how fear makes us closed, intolerant, narrow-minded, and provincial. It takes a lot of guts to open up to cooperation, peace, tolerance, and all the things that can work if we get to a higher level of evolution.[37]

Chianese adds that Italian Americans upset about *The Sopranos* should concentrate on creating and supporting other films and TV shows about themselves, instead of "wasting time, money, and print" protesting what David Chase and his writers create.

Annabella Sciorra recalls that

when *The Sopranos* first came on, I received some messages from people who wanted to protest, who wanted an Italian American actress to protest the show, and I didn't even have

HBO. I got HBO so I could watch it, like a couple of episodes, and I thought, "This is great! This is great! I don't care that they're in the mafia"—what is the mafia, anyway? I don't even know what that means. What does that mean anymore? To all those people I have to say, go write your own scripts. Go write about something that's not that [organized crime]. Write about some great Italian Americans who haven't been written about— it would be great if their stories were told.[38]

Chianese, speaking of actors who have played gangsters, Pacino, De Niro, Gandolfini, Turturro, and himself, says:

We're artists, and our job is to hold a mirror up to nature. I feel proud to be playing a part like Uncle Junior. Because I'm show-ing that a member of the mafia is a human being. Well, that's true, everybody knows that. David Chase's genius is in his por-trayal of Tony Soprano, who as a boy in a mafia family finds out that life is miserable because of this environment—so it's a metaphor for life. The story of the mafia, or of cowboys and In-dians, is just to get our attention. What's really important is what makes a human being in any civilized society productive, or what makes him or her nonproductive. Greed for money, lust for power, which is in all of us. In every culture there are people who are out to gain money and power and doing so will cause problems. You can't deny it. So how do you deal with it? It's re-ally a lesson in life.[39]

It's understandable that actors like De Matteo, Sciorra, and Chi-anese would be protective of *The Sopranos*, since the show has pro-vided them with the best roles of their careers. Nor is it surprising that they would reject charges that by performing on *The Sopranos* or in other mob movies and TV shows they're helping to perpetuate negative images of people of their ethnicity. As talented artists, these Italian American actors recognize schlock—derivative, stereotypical, and de-meaning material—when they see it, and they have no desire to put their talent at the service of junk.

But sometimes economic necessity does influence their choices.

"Actors, they gotta work—'scuse me, they gotta work! They gotta eat! They gotta pay the rent!" says Chazz Palmintieri. The actor, who has played his share of mob roles, has his own criteria for which ones he'll take. "I try to do parts, if I play a mafia guy, where he's somewhat redeemable and somewhat human—not just a buffoon. You can't name a mafia guy I've played who was a *total* buffoon!" He cites as an example Cheech, the character he played in Woody Allen's *Bullets Over Broadway*. Palmintieri's performance as a gangster with a genius for playwriting was a perfectly calibrated blend of underworld menace and artistic self-absorption and ruthlessness, and he was nominated for an Academy Award for Best Supporting Actor.

In the hit mob comedy *Analyze This*, Palmintieri is Primo Sidone, a rival to Robert De Niro's Frank Vitti. He has several hilarious moments in the film, the funniest being his recitation of the various mob nicknames he's used during his criminal career. But Palmintieri didn't play the character for laughs. "I was the straight man for Billy Crystal and Bob [De Niro], which was fine," he says. "Both of them are brilliant comedians. So, to me, it was just playing it straight, playing it real. In all my roles, I play it real and play it straight. Never go for the laugh. Let the laugh happen through the character."

Despite the claims of the show's detractors, the mobsters on *The Sopranos* are not stereotypical figures, a fact the cast members recognize and appreciate. David Chase and his writers "respect their creations enough not to broad-brush them with insipid gangland stereotypes," as Ian Rothkerch put it for *Salon.com*. "The wiseguys might wear pinky rings and pinstripes, but they're also full of quirky neuroses and colorful vocabularies." Not only is the writing strong, "the series boasts a pitch-perfect ensemble cast of actors who give their dissolute characters an uncommon honesty and humanity."[40]

In a roundtable discussion on *Salon*, several *Sopranos* cast members spoke about the uncommonly high quality of the show's writing.

"When I read it [the script], to be honest, I didn't see how great it was," recalled John Ventimiglia, who plays Artie Bucco, owner of the mob-backed Nuovo Vesuvio restaurant. "I think part of that was conditioning with me. You were talking about typecasting before and as an Italian actor, I get handed a lot of crap—stereotypical stuff about the mob and all that business. I never read a good one before this. When my agents handed it to me, I automatically said, 'Oh, here we go. Another comedy about the mob.' I thought twice about going in."

"As far as being caricatures, I don't think anyone on *The Sopranos* is a caricature in any way, shape or form," said Steven Schirripa, who plays Bobby "Baccala" Bacillieri, Uncle Junior's aide-de-camp and minder.

"First of all, keeping it from becoming a caricature is the writer's job. I can make anything real as long as the writing's there," observed Federico "Furio Giunta" Castelluccio.[41]

But sometimes the writing isn't "there," and the parts are skin-deep and stereotypical, even demeaning.

There is a scene in director Raymond De Felitta's *Two-Family House* in which Michael Rispoli, as Buddy Visalo, is accused of acting "like a monkey" by his sourpuss wife, Estelle, when she finds him and a friend lip-synching and dancing to a tune on the jukebox.

When I asked Rispoli whether he felt that Italian American actors sometimes are put in the position of being performing monkeys, he laughed and said, "I say all the time, when the organ grinder plays you gotta dance like a monkey." Rispoli continued:

> I'll tell you how it is for me. I'm obviously stereotyped. I'm blue collar, generally inner city. I've played Irish and Polish, but mostly Italian. I've played Boston Italians, Chicago Italians, and New York Italians. I'm not a star, I don't call the shots. So when they say they need somebody like this, they want to get a certain something from me. When I did *While You Were Sleeping* I was kind of a goofball, a gavone, not too bright. [Rispoli played Joey Fusco, a boorish but well-meaning guy who makes futile romantic overtures to Lucy Moderatz, the film's main character, played by Sandra Bullock.]
>
> Listen, commedia dell'arte is a beautiful art form. So here we are so many years later and there are still commedia-type characters one plays. So I played that in that film. It was a hit. Then I was asked to do that all the time and I didn't want to. But I was called in for it all the time.

Rispoli said he tried to give these clichéd parts some nuance, but casting directors didn't want nuance. "They'd say, 'Be more Italian,' meaning, be goofier.

"Based on the way I look, the way I walk and talk and sound, I don't have the same opportunities" as other not-so-ethnic actors, Rispoli added. "Nobody's ever going to hire me to play a Connecticut prep school teacher. I would love to some day.

"I don't mind being a goofball for the right project, if it's well written. If you don't feel connected to the material somehow it's miserable. All I know is that if they need an Italian guy they call me up. Sometimes they need an Italian guy and they say [about him], 'We already know what he can do.' "[42]

"I'm more offended and embarrassed by the portrayals of Ray Romano's mother and father on the hit sitcom *Everybody Loves Raymond* than I am by anything David Chase has offered," observes George Anastasia, in an essay whose title proclaims his esteem for Chase's series: "If Shakespeare Were Alive Today, He'd Be Writing for *The Sopranos*."[43]

"Whenever the Bard needed passion, pathos, humor . . . whenever he needed characters who reached out and grabbed life with all their hearts, both their hands, and any other appendage that worked, he told a story about Italians. When he wanted morose and brooding, we got *Hamlet* . . ."[44] To those Italian Americans offended by *The Sopranos*, Anastasia counsels, "Change the channel." Those who think the show reinforces defamatory images of Italian Americans should remember that "only bigots and idiots buy into stereotypes and I don't think we need to waste a lot of time and energy worrying about them. They also believe all Jews are rich and all African Americans lazy . . ."[45]

Anastasia's counsel is wasted on NIAF's Kenneth Ciongoli, who is convinced of the deleterious effects of *The Sopranos* and other mob stories on Italian Americans. These works have, according to Ciongoli, "taken a significant percentage of our people and given them an image of themselves that simply is not only not true, it's detrimental to their success and advancement in every possible way."

Ciongoli, who agrees with Joseph Scelsa's characterization of the various expressions of the Mafia myth as a "cultural holocaust" for Italian Americans, points a finger at a supposedly anti-Italian cultural elite.

"I'm talking about filmmakers, about *The New York Times, The Washington Post.* On the other hand, our own have done it, too. They assimilate to this culture. They assimilate to the intellectual—if they are that, I hate to give them this appellation—'elite,' and then they proselytize their views, which happen to be against us. Those of us who feel differently haven't percolated to the top yet.

"*The New York Times* is clearly anti-Italian," he insists. "They think we are philistine, reactionary, right-wing—as opposed to them being on the left. They see us as their enemy even when they haven't called it that way. But I think we should take 'em on head-on. I think it's the only thing they'll respond to."

So what is to be done?

"Making a stink and going and picketing *The New York Times* and saying, 'You are anti-Italian,' the way perhaps the Jewish people or certainly the blacks would do, is antithetical to our culture," Ciongoli replies. "But perhaps that's what has to happen. I don't know that it ever will happen, because for example, NIAF's board is full of CEOs of many hundred-million-dollar corporations. Those guys aren't gonna picket anybody."[46]

Ciongoli doesn't say how *The New York Times* is anti-Italian, other than the fact that its critics consistently have praised *The Sopranos,* nor does he specify exactly how it and other mob dramas are detrimental to the success and advancement of Italian Americans. One could argue that because of the dominance of gangster images, many Italian Americans, particularly the young, know little else about their culture and heritage. But who bears responsibility for that? *The New York Times?* David Chase? Martin Scorsese? Frank Pugliese comes closer to the truth when he says it's all our fault, meaning we Italian Americans, and not just our artists.

During our conversation it became clear to me that Ciongoli is outraged because he has so thoroughly assimilated to the white American mainstream that any image of Italian Americans as less than middle-class respectable, any and all depictions of them as wild, flamboyant, unassimilated, constitute a personal affront.

The anthropologist Micaela di Leonardo agrees that socioeconomic self-interest fuels the anger of the well-placed, successful types she calls "ethnic brokers."

Certainly people are more sensitive if it is important for their economic well-being to appear morally upright and totally unconnected to criminality. But nobody really thinks Italian Americans are connected to organized crime anymore. [Well, maybe.]

In most parts of the country, Italian Americans mirror the general class distribution, and many of them have been socially mobile, and most of them don't give a shit [about the gangster image]. But there is the ethnic broker. It's the business of ethnic brokers to give a shit, whether you're black or Jewish or Italian American, because it's *your* economic connection.

But it doesn't mean that it's actually hurting Italian Americans as a whole—and I don't think it is. Where you've got a situation where the population is not able to achieve social mobility—or hasn't done so—as for example, the vast mass of black Americans—yes, you have a black middle class, but it's not very big. And then you have this kind of gangster-rap drug-dealer, pimp phenomenon, which plenty of black Americans have participated in and made a living off of. But as a cultural phenomenon, it's really bad news for a lot of working-class black Americans. It makes it harder for them to achieve social mobility because of the way in which white Americans then relate to them. But I just don't think that's true for Italian Americans.

Frankly, I'm not that interested in protesting it [gangster stereotyping] at all. Because, for me, the importance of symbolic politics is whether or not it translates into political economy. And it just doesn't. It has not for twenty years for Italian Americans. I taught at Yale for six years and I watched the proportion of Italian American undergraduates grow by leaps and bounds, not unconnected to Bartlett Giamatti, the first Italian American university president. So, there's been a real postwar phenomenon of making it for a big chunk of the Italian American population.[47]

"These people who are concerned over these negative depictions of their groups, they should put out positive depictions. I believe in you deal with negative speech by more speech," argues James B. Jacobs, a professor of constitutional law at New York University who directs the university's Center for Research on Crime and Justice. Jacobs has also served on the New York State Organized Crime Task Force.

"Italian Americans are very well represented in legitimate professions and businesses and arts and sciences in America. I don't think *The Sopranos* is really harming the status of Italian Americans," he says. He has Italian American students who are interested in anti–organized crime initiatives, and he coauthored a book, *Busting the Mob: United States v. Cosa Nostra*, with one of them.[48]

> But I'm not Italian American myself. Maybe some people would be more sensitive to it than I. But again, I just think the way to deal with it is to emphasize the positive and not worry so much. People enjoy these depictions of the mafia, and in a funny way, I don't think it seems to spill over on Italian Americans. They're like "the Mafia," you know. They have their own special niche in American culture. People really enjoy watching this stuff. It's very popular, very compelling. These people have great personalities and they're interesting and maybe they do things that people would like to do or flirt with doing but are afraid to do. So, they live vicariously through these groups.[49]

Rebecca Scarpati, a psychotherapist and the daughter of Dominic Chianese, says she kept her children, two boys and a girl, from watching their grandfather's show because of the graphic sexuality and violence on *The Sopranos*.

"Sex and violence on the show can be very raw and very ugly, and I don't believe these are images children should see. The show is for adults," she says. Scarpati also felt that her kids were too young to appreciate the irony in the show's depiction of sexuality and the sexual objectification of women.

But she bristles at the notion that Italian American artists shouldn't create programs like *The Sopranos*.

328 / AN OFFER WE CAN'T REFUSE

That to me is a form of prejudice. Why can't Italian American writers write about their experience, whatever it is? Who owns the experience of being an Italian American? No one owns that experience. So if David Chase writes about this social milieu because for whatever reason it resonates with him, and they're fully fleshed-out characters, much more so than so many literary and film and TV characters who aren't Italian, how can that be a bad thing? It just so happens that they're in the mafia.

But the mafia is a very dramatic situation. It's people at war. No one is going to stop doing cop shows, or making war movies. But to me it doesn't epitomize the Italian American experience at all.

Scarpati likens the furor over *The Sopranos* to the criticism Alice Walker received that her novel *The Color Purple*, with its violent, spouse-abusing character called Mister, damaged the image of African American men. "You don't get that if you're a white writer and you have a [character who is a] wife beater. No one worries that it's representing all white men as wife beaters. So David Chase is writing about this culture, but it doesn't mean that all Italians are mafiosi."[50]

Bill Tonelli, a former editor at *Rolling Stone* and *Esquire*, now a freelance writer and the editor of *The Italian American Reader* (William Morrow), was so irked by the attacks on *The Sopranos* and by the rhetoric of antidefamation activists that he penned an op-ed essay for *The New York Times* attacking the antidefamationist position.

. . . The Mafia stereotype sticks because Italians are good at turning all their impulses, good or evil, into highly organized, fiercely efficient enterprises. If you have any doubt, consider the Roman Empire, or the Roman Catholic Church or the Giuliani administration. The early gangsters took a motley collection of squalid vices and victimless crimes—the desire, during Prohibition, for alcohol; gambling and the money-lending required to sustain it; prostitution—and turned it into an empire. Did they not make a lot of a little? Do you think it was easy to organize all those restless criminal spirits into such a well-oiled, tightly functioning machine?

. . . The gangster's life gets all the movie and TV attention because it's the most narrative-friendly, charismatic version of our particular cultural capital. This is the homage the rest of America pays to Italian-American magnificence: You've made us mythic. Maybe somewhere there are still adults who identify with the cowboy heroes of yore, but for the most part the public gun duel in the dusty street has been replaced by two stealthy bullets in the back of the head . . .

Of course, the reality is that Italians have pretty much gotten out of the crime business; we stopped producing good gangsters around the time we stopped producing good middleweights, and for the same socio-economic reasons . . .

As always, today's most ambitious criminals come from the world's poorest, toughest precincts, notably Russia, if the newspapers can be believed. But none of the relevant parties—not the screenwriters, not the F.B.I.—feels comfortable or conversant enough with these alien new gangsters to abandon their beloved Italian racketeers. Nobody's ready to give up on them, not even we who putatively suffer from the stereotypes. Thanks to the movies, the image of the cowboy endured at least a century longer than the cowboys themselves. Our mobsters may never go away.[51]

Tonelli told me that heated discussions about *The Sopranos* on the H-ITAM list serve prompted him to write the *Times* essay.

I felt that Italian Americans had somehow managed to come through all of that kind of pathology [anti-Italian prejudice and discrimination] unscathed, and they were as stubborn, as stoic, and as mule-like as they were thirty years ago. They would seethe—I would seethe, sometimes, even—but quietly. Through some pridefulness or whatever, you would never want these people to see that they hurt your feelings, or that they hurt you, or you felt damaged, or that you felt that you had a complaint.

Then suddenly it was a kind of ethnic victimization that I started to see manifest itself. That's really what drove me crazy:

"Oh, we're being damaged, we're being destroyed. There's the Italian American holocaust. This is cultural genocide."[52]

Micaela di Leonardo maintains that the anti-*Sopranos* furor has been instigated and sustained by the Italian American elite, but Tonelli stresses the role of those Italian Americans who haven't achieved great success in American society, in driving the antidefamationist train.

"I began to see all these guys who were kind of disillusioned and disappointed in their lives and looked around and said, 'Why didn't I get further or why didn't I get more money or why didn't I have more influence, why don't more people listen to me?' I think for these guys, it's very convenient to say, 'Well, the answer is something over which I have no control. It's that Americans hate Italians, and that's why I've been victimized by this and I've been held back and this insurmountable obstacle has been thrown in my path.' "

Rather than hate Italians, Americans, Tonelli believes,

are actually deeply envious of Italians, and are envious of being a part of that stream of culture and history . . . To quote myself, in the piece in the *Times*, "To be Italian, I felt, was the most fun you could have and still be white." That you could be passionate, you could be loud, you could be maybe a little dangerous, you could definitely have some anti-authority traits as a group and as a culture. You don't want to take it too far. You don't want to be Puerto Rican, you don't want to be black, you don't want to be poor, you don't want to be the underclass, you don't want to be part of some permanent despised minority. But as an Italian, you somehow bridge that. You're seen as being passionate, loud, flamboyant, but also one of the descendants of the race that essentially built civilization—that is, a certain strain of civilization.

I've found that they [antidefamationists] save their most potent venom for anybody they perceive to have access to mainstream media. There was a young guy who did a story for *The New York Times* about a casting call for *The Sopranos* in Jersey.

The turnout vastly, exponentially, exceeded what they expected. They had to have security and they ended up seeing just the smallest fraction of these people—the casting people did—because it was like a mob. It was like an army turned out for this thing, and this guy wrote a story about it that ran on the front page of the *Times*.

Well, these old guys in the e-mail discussion room—not the scholars, but the activists—they tore this guy to shreds. They accused him of selling out his heritage, of selling out his parents, his grandparents. They said every bad, lethal thing they could possibly say because he wrote this story. And the undercurrent in all these attacks was that he had sold his soul to get into *The New York Times*.

This is an accusation that these guys would throw at me, or at anybody else, that if you have any kind of access to mainstream media like *The New York Times*, like a book publisher, like HBO, like a movie deal or anything like that it's clear you are an Uncle Tom, you're a Benedict Arnold, you sold out your ethnicity, because *The New York Times* for some reason requires Italian Americans to be presented in a certain way or HBO or the military-industrial complex or whatever's running things requires Italian Americans to be defamed. It serves some purpose. They don't actually say what purpose, but they know it serves some purpose.[53]

Frank De Caro, a gay Italian American journalist and television personality who grew up in suburban New Jersey, has observed that

The Sopranos is like a McMansion of pathos built on a foundation of comedy, much like real life . . . Its characters—the Prozac-popping mobster, his hooligan son, his "spiritually thirsty" wife and his London broil–flinging *comare*—may not be admirable, but they're stewed in genuine marinara. They're not role models, but they capture the suburban Italian-American experience better than any other show—or film—I've ever seen. And they use curse words I'd only ever heard my grandmother say . . . When Christopher used a certain Italian slang word for the female anatomy [*pucchiacca*] in the episode about the movie business, I know of several Italian Americans who fell off their couches laughing. It was the kind of thing I never thought I'd hear on national television.

Tony Soprano and company may be a little overdone—the men's jewelry too flashy, the women's hair too big—but they're never, ever boring.

I heartily disagree with critics who say the show perpetuates negative stereotypes. *The Sopranos* gives us a wide assortment of characters, from lower-class thugs to upper-middle-class professionals with country club memberships . . .

The show has done the impossible: It has made it cool to be from New Jersey. In my case, it also has been an excuse to re-embrace my heritage. There is a scene where Tony takes his daughter, Meadow, into a church and makes her look at its beauty. He reminds her that her relatives may not have designed the church, but they had the artistry to build it. Seeing something as well built as *The Sopranos* makes me just as proud of the Italians who craft such gripping television.[54]

De Caro appreciates *The Sopranos* for its true-to-life portrait of the suburban Italian American world he knew. Robert Viscusi, however, hails the show for its political stance. Viscusi deplores what he regards as the depoliticized nature of Italian American discourse about *The Sopranos* and the mafia image in general. To talk entirely in terms of "is this good for the Italians?" or to decry such characters as Vito Corleone and Tony Soprano as out-and-out malefactors who besmirch the image of Italian Americans is to miss the point.

"Is Zeus good or bad? What kind of a question is that?" Viscusi demands.

This is beyond good and evil. That's the thing that these small-minded accountants and policemen who run these anti-mafia image programs never seem to quite understand. This is not a catechism devil that you're talking about here. This is something way beyond that! Part of the problem with all this is the ruthless repression of politics in Italian American discourse, and if you don't talk about politics, you can't talk about this [Italian American identity and culture] because that's what it is. It's not image. We're not selling shoes. It's politics. It's profound cultural politics—that is to say, politics that works through culture.

You can't really understand it without talking politics. And not Democratic-Republican, electoral-in-Union-County kind of politics. But historical politics. In the case of Italians, fascism and antifascism, imperialism and anti-imperialism. These are terms that a lot of Americans can't bring themselves to use. They're afraid . . . they're more afraid that someone's going to call them a Marxist than they are that somebody's going to call them queer![55]

Familiarity with the political history of Italy and Italian Americans is necessary to understanding how the mafioso or the fascist, for example, came to live so large in the Italian American imaginary. Both serve as a rebuke to the image of the Italian as an ignorant peasant, a loser, and a coward. (Popular joke when I was a child: "What's the shortest book in the world? *Italian War Heroes*.") Italian fascism claimed that it would restore the power and glory of Imperial Rome. Not only Italians in Italy bought this bill of goods. Many Italian Americans who experienced the traumas of immigration and a hostile reception in their new homeland saw Mussolini and his regime, with its imperial pretensions and grandiose iconography, as an antidote to the slights and privations they had endured.

The mafioso enjoyed similar cachet in working-class Italian American communities because he likewise presented an image of power and self-sufficiency, of someone who would not be ground down by the "medigahns" but who would *fare l'America* (literally, make or do America, as the immigrants used to say) on his own terms.

But, of course, both were false and destructive solutions to real problems of poverty, underdevelopment, and powerlessness. And though Mussolini tried to suppress the Sicilian mafia organizations,

334 / AN OFFER WE CAN'T REFUSE

fascism and mafia gangsterism had much in common, both being male-dominated, violent, authoritarian, and oppressive. This is what Viscusi is getting at when he says *The Sopranos* deconstructs "the fascist Italian gangster . . . this big nightmare bully." Tony Soprano isn't just a louche thug, nor is he an ethnic stereotype concocted by a supposedly self-loathing Italian American. He is the product of history and politics, of political economy, forged in the Mezzogiorno and transformed—and, one hopes, ultimately made extinct—in America.

When asked whether he agrees that the persistent mafia image has had a damaging effect on Italian Americans, Viscusi replies:

> I don't think that we are singled out for worse treatment than other people. Otherwise why would it be that we are financially so successful? We've done very well in this country. I never really hear that from these people [the antidefamationists]. All I ever hear is whining and moaning.
>
> I don't think that it has all these deleterious effects—or let me put it another way. The question is what are the effects and what is one to do about them? There are people who say the impact is Holocaust-like. Other people say, "The way to deal with this is to protest. File a lawsuit." My relatives in Italy say, "There are five fingers on a hand. You need them all." So, I think some people should file lawsuits, if their temperaments run that way, fine. But it's not the only thing to do. For plenty of people it would be a waste of time, and I'm one of those people. My approach has been rather to look for the elements in Italian American culture that I find gratifying and that I would care to pass on to my students or to my children.[56]

Journalist and author Maria Laurino published an essay in *The* (supposedly Italian-hating) *New York Times* claiming that the image of Italian Americans on television has not evolved to account for their movement into the professions and the middle class. She argued that TV keeps Italian Americans locked in a time warp, where all paisans are working-class and uneducated.[57]

"But it isn't true!" exclaims Viscusi. "What's the name of the fellow who hosts *The Tonight Show*? Jay Leno! He's Italian. Maria Laurino doesn't mention that, and neither does anyone else who goes in for this kind of particularism. It's just not so. I'm not saying that there's no prejudice against us. I'm not saying that there's no classism against us. I'm not saying there's no regionalism against us. But what I am saying is that it isn't nearly as bad as they make it out to be."

Laurino, however, did make a strong case that popular culture, finding it "increasingly difficult to portray the ways in which ancestral roots affect identity and shape the character of third-, fourth- and fifth-generation hyphenated Americans . . . relegates ethnicity to working-class stories boasting crude language and Old World gestures."[58] She concluded that *The Sopranos*, though decried as stereotypical, is just about the only show that depicts contemporary middle-class Italian Americans dealing with present-day issues and problems.

Viscusi echoes the comments of Dominic Chianese, Annabella Sciorra, and others that instead of dedicating so much time and energy to denouncing *The Sopranos*, Italian American advocates and activists can and should "engage in self-representation and support representation of Italian Americans that does not conform to these silhouettes [mob images]."

"Italian-Americans, in general, have been very slow to do that," he says.

I can tell you from bitter experience—because I've been out there promoting things of this sort for a long time now with the Italian American Writers Association. It's very hard to get people—Italian American judges and doctors and lawyers and whatnot—to buy those books.

The fact that these people don't have the enlightened self-interest to support the illustrations of themselves that they say they would like to see, but rather put all of their money and time and energy and effort into protesting this other stuff . . . They give life to this stuff that it wouldn't necessarily have, that they could give to something else. They have options, and to use one of my favorite clichés, "It's better to light a candle than to curse the dark." There's too much of that, as far as I'm concerned, in Italian Americans. Too much cursing of the dark and too little lighting of candles.

I don't say that they shouldn't protest. I just think that there are implications to protesting that they don't always think about. And among those implications, one of the main ones is, what could you be doing with the time other than this? What could you be doing with your organization's money other than this, instead of having one of these big festivities and hiring a big room in a hotel to talk about David Chase all afternoon? Why not talk about [Italian American novelist and essayist] Helen Barolini all afternoon, who wrote an absolutely incredible book, *Umbertina*, about the history of Italian American women. That would be so much more sensible.[59]

Italian American critics of *The Sopranos* have accused David Chase of treating them and their concerns with contempt, mainly because he has not engaged in dialogue with them. That's not to say that he has ignored their protests or hasn't considered the issues they raise. In an interview with the film director Peter Bogdanovich, he spoke not only about the accusations of ethnic defamation, but also about Italian American culture and achievement, and his own sense of himself as an Italian American.[60]

I have serious disagreements with the Italian antidefamation people . . . Every once and a while we deal with it [on the show, as in the Columbus Day episode and in the episode that features a dinnertime discussion of ethnic stereotypes and the mafia image by Jennifer Melfi and her family].

I think the Italian American experience is an advertisement for America, for the democratic experience. It's hard for me to think of a group who has come from so little who've done so well. I'm talking about southern Italy; I'm not talking about the Tuscans or about the Romans. We're talking about people from southern Italy who came over here in the early part of the twentieth century who were illiterate. They knew less than people coming across the border from Mexico who can read, okay?

They have done spectacularly well, I think, in America. If you have so little self-esteem at this point that these movies bother you I have to wonder why. Also because this Italian mob thing has become for whatever reasons a national myth. So to be picking it apart and saying this is a shame on the Italians . . . for some reason the whole of America has taken this story onto themselves. What is it about us that has allowed that to happen? Is it because we kill people? We can see plenty of killings and vulgarity. That has nothing to do with it. And in the end I think if your self-esteem is that shallow, and you have a problem with the fact that this tiny minority called gangsters makes it tough for the rest of us, I think you should take your case to them. I don't think it'll happen, but I think that's what you should do.

Chase has revealed that the *Sopranos* episode in which Tony tells his daughter, Meadow, that his grandfather and other Italian laborers built a Catholic church was inspired by an incident in his own life. As an adult, he learned that his grandfather and grandfather's brothers had constructed churches in Newark. When Bogdanovich asked how it might have affected him if he had known this when he was growing up, Chase replied, "I might have had more self-esteem."

This off-hand but revealing remark is the key to understanding Chase's attitude toward his ethnicity. Lack of self-esteem, or a mix of shame and defensive pride, is not uncommon among descendants of those who, as Chase says, came to this country with so little. Shame, in fact, has been a leitmotif in Italian American life from the moment the immigrants started families in America. For the first generation born here, becoming American meant "learning how to be ashamed of our parents," as East Harlem educator Leonard Covello writes in his memoir *The Heart Is the Teacher*.[61] Giving up the Italian language, or rather the southern Italian dialects of the immigrants, was for that generation the first step in distancing themselves from their backgrounds.

The ethnic cheerleading and even chauvinism of the antidefamation groups notwithstanding, shame and embarrassment about and alienation from what Robert Viscusi calls "our complicated and difficult" heritage have affected subsequent generations of Italian Americans: shame about their origins in poverty and underdevelopment; shame about looking and behaving differently from "real" Americans, the WASPs; shame about being, or being perceived as, blue-collar, in a nation where everyone is supposed to be a comfortably middle-class consumer of capitalism's bounty; shame about having polysyllabic, vowel-laden last names that the medigahns couldn't pronounce. (David Chase's own southern Italian grandmother might not have been ashamed of her family's name, De Cesare, but she believed it would be a hindrance to her kin's assimilation to American life, and changed it to Chase.)

And shame about being associated with criminality.

The *contadini* (landless or land-poor farm workers), fishermen, and manual laborers who made up much of the southern Italian immigrant population were not only poor and unlettered. They came to America bearing the stigma imposed by northern Italian theorists of racial degeneracy, who had deemed them inferior by dint of biology (or rather, positivist pseudoscience) and culture.

Northern Italy did not regard the people of the Mezzogiorno as heirs to the Renaissance, as sons and daughters of Michelangelo, Dante, and Leonardo. Racial theorists saw them as more akin to peoples the northerners regarded as savage and inferior—Turks, Arabs, Africans. WASP nativists, attracted to notions of racial superiority and degeneracy, eagerly adopted and perpetuated the made-in-Italy stigma. David Chase, then, is not self-loathing, as his Italian American critics contend: he's ambivalent about his background, like many of us. That ambivalence informs *The Sopranos*, complicating its *italianità* so that it can't be characterized simplistically as a matter of "positive" or "negative" images.

One of the things of which Chase is proud is Italian food. In the Bogdanovich interview, he said, "I remember there was Italian food in my house, in my cousin's house, and at a few restaurants. Now you can walk down a street in Utah and find trattorias and buffalo mozzarella. I think it's great. I'm actually very proud of the fact that this cuisine is probably the preeminent cuisine in America right now."

This is no trivial thing, as *cucina*, the artful preparation of and communal consumption of food, is central to Italian and Italian American culture, signifying conviviality, pleasure, solidarity, and social identity. Even the most ardent critics of *The Sopranos* can't deny that the show gets this right, often hilariously so, whether it's Carmela offering up "last's night's *sfogliatella*" for breakfast, or chef Artie Bucco creating luscious delicacies in the kitchen of his Nuovo Vesuvio restaurant, or Father Phil rhapsodizing over the "melted moozadell' " in Carmela's baked ziti. Italian food, or rather, its absence, can even provoke domestic discord, as when a temporarily pasta-deprived A.J. Soprano incredulously objects, "What? No fuckin' ziti?"

"Family. Redefined." was the tagline of an HBO ad campaign for *The Sopranos*, and for once we got truth in advertising. David Chase's series broke new ground in its treatment of both Italian American families and Cosa Nostra "families." The latter type, represented by the criminal organizations run by Tony Soprano and his rivals, is a long way down the evolutionary scale from the Corleones. Instead of Don Vito's and Michael's well-oiled and invincible machine, the mob clans on *The Sopranos* are disorganized and in decline, casualties of both law enforcement and their own avarice, stupidity, and bloodlust.

Pop culture and academia have long portrayed the Italian American family as a tradition-based institution that offers physical and emotional nurturance, support, and cooperation—think *Moonstruck* or Richard Gambino's *l'ordine della famiglia* as described in his influential study *Blood of My Blood*. Popular culture and academic scholarship both emphasize the resilience of the southern Italian immigrant family and its values. It is undeniable that the family structure was crucial to the survival of the people of the Mezzogiorno, both in Italy and in America. But there is a dark side, too, that needs to be acknowledged, if we are to fully understand Italian American history.

For the immigrants and their descendants, the family could also be an arena of conflict, pain, and alienation. Its demands could fuel resentment and rebellion, as members, particularly but not solely women and children, were forced to subordinate their individual needs and desires to the interests of the family unit. Men could be authoritarian patriarchs, especially if in the larger world they were exploited and powerless. Italian American women often faced a double burden, of being responsible for maintaining the home while also, because of economic necessity, being forced to work outside of it. Family life could be especially difficult for nonconforming members, including independent-minded daughters and gay sons, like me.

These realities rarely are acknowledged by the ethnic activists and antidefamation organizations, but they are as much a part of the history of Italian American family life as the more positive dimensions.

Mario Puzo and Francis Ford Coppola may not have had firsthand knowledge of organized crime, but both intimately knew Italian American families, and their Corleones represent, in a heightened, near-operatic fashion, the light and the dark sides, the love and loyalty, the deceit and betrayal, of Italian American domestic life. The Sopranos goes heavier on the dysfunction, as befits the era and the nouveau riche milieu.

Antidefamationists who fail to see that The Sopranos is, as Drea De Matteo says, a "literary piece," miss how it resembles a nineteenth-century family novel as much as an organized crime story. Tolstoy's famous observation in Anna Karenina—"All happy families resemble one another; every unhappy family is unhappy in its own fashion"—fits Tony's famiglia as neatly as one of his sharkskin suits clings to his burly physique.

During a dream sequence in an episode of the series' fifth season, Tony tells his high school coach Mr. Molinaro, "My family wasn't like other families." The Soprano clan—philandering mobster Johnny Boy, sour Livia, and their children, Tony, Janice, and Barbara—was one of Tolstoy's unhappy families, and its members certainly were unhappy in their own fashion. Their existence was always precarious because of the illicit source of their livelihood, which exacerbated the troubled, even pathological relationships between both parents, the parents and their children, and between the children.

When the show explores the domestic sphere, whether it's Tony's family of origin or the one he has made with Carmela, it questions what a family is and scrutinizes the relationships within it, while also situating the family within the larger social worlds of upper-middle-class suburbia and the tribal subculture known as "the Mafia."

If Rosario Iaconis's claim that David Chase's "lifelong Oedipal angst" underlies The Sopranos isn't credible, Chase has confirmed that the conflict between a mother and her son was the starting point for the series. In the interview with Peter Bogdanovich, Chase revealed that

> the original story was about a gangster who has a very difficult mother who is not a typical mob mother. I had read about this mob grandmother in Philadelphia, the head of the mob in Philadelphia at that time, apparently she was quite a contender and a very difficult woman.

> So I was interested in doing this mother-son thing having to do with the gangster [having to] get psychotherapy because of his problems with his mother. Gang war is declared. His mother is angry at him for neglecting her. The therapist, because she has a window into his mind and is listening to all this stuff about his mother, says, "I think your mother may be the one who's behind this gang war." That was the original idea.

But Chase has infused the show with some elements of his own family drama. "I think the way the characters interact with each other, if you take the mob out of it, especially the way the members of the family interact with each other" recalls his upbringing, except that "there was no cursing in my family.

"My mother and father are not John and Livia Soprano by any stretch of the imagination," Chase said. But his mother was "negative and downbeat," and this personality trait of hers was an inspiration for Livia.

Italian American antidefamation activists and organizations claim they fight to protect the image and honor of Italian Americans. But here's an ironic possibility to consider: Are their protests against the mafia image tainted by class snobbery toward some of their ethnic kin? NIAF's Kenneth Ciongoli says his organization's board of directors is full of corporate CEOs and successful professionals, like himself, a neurosurgeon. It's not surprising that Italian Americans at that socioeconomic level would be rankled by the persistent pop-culture image of the mafia gangster. As Micaela di Leonardo has observed, it's the business of "ethnic brokers" to care most strongly about these things.

But some Italian Americans perceive an unconscious class bias against them and their culture in the antidefamation protests. Johnny De Carlo, a self-described "goomba" from New Jersey, expressed this point of view in a lengthy posting to the H-ITAM list serve. His prose doesn't have the polish or sophistication of the professors who also post there, but his argument is worth quoting at length.

> Italian-Americans that live in the New York–New Jersey area are often described as goombas or paizans or guidos, and that doesn't mean they are gangsters or "Sopranos." I will speak in the first person because I am a goomba. I watch *The Sopranos*, sure, and I love gangster movies like *Mean Streets* and *Goodfellas*. They are great entertainment, and I love them even more so because they are starring Italians and take place in my neighborhoods . . .
>
> *The Sopranos* is true to life and hits close to home. I happen to live in New Jersey and am Italian, and I dress and eat and listen to the same music as a lot of those Sopranos. To be able to relate to that is very cool, and many goombas like me can relate to it. Does that mean that I am a killer or a cheater or a stealer? No. Even if I happen to know a wiseguy or someone half-connected does that make me a bad person? No.

(Steven R. Schirripa uses the term "goomba" the same way as De Carlo, to denote "a certain kind of Italian-American, probably born on the East Coast—New York, New Jersey, Boston, Rhode Island—probably third generation from the old country." "He's not a gangster," says Schirripa, a professed goomba. "He's not a wiseguy or a made man, or a goodfella or a member of The Family—but he knows these guys, or guys like that, and some of them know him.")[62]

De Carlo continued: "Pro-Italian groups who slam *The Sopranos* and other Italian-American portrayals need to lighten up and understand that every single Italian-American mob movie fan doesn't sit there saying 'wow I'd cut off my best friend's head just like Tony Soprano did in a heartbeat if he pissed me off like that.'"

The proud goomba believes that the disdain of "Harvard-educated" Italian Americans for people like him and his working-class friends is similar to the animus successful, conservative African Americans purportedly bear toward "young black men on the streets blasting Snoop Dogg and slapping high fives to each other while pulling up their jeans."

De Carlo concluded his posting:

Not everyone has to be a doctor or a lawyer. That's why I take offense when Italian activists say that Italian-Americans are portrayed as fat, gold chain wearing gangsters. The gangster part of it is the part that steals and kills. The goomba part is the part that wears the gold chains and eats a lot of spaghetti . . .

Every single description [of Italian Americans in popular culture] may fit on one person, or maybe just a few will fit. And if none fit at all, but your family hails from the same old country, then God bless and enjoy your life. What is the point in sitting there worrying or protesting things? I say to everyone of every ethnic group: lighten up and live. Whether you are Jewish, Irish, black, green, or whatever, be proud and do what makes you happy. Worry about wars and disease and other horrible things, not about ethnic stereotypes.

9

Conclusion: *Addio*, Godfather?

The Mafia myth is deeply entrenched in the mind of America as an enduring and remarkably resilient narrative, one of the longest-running shows in pop-culture history.

Sicilian and other Italian crime groups began to operate in America at the turn of the past century, but their pop-culture incarnations didn't burst on the scene until the 1930s, in gangland dramas like *Scarface* and *Little Caesar*. Movie audiences were thrilled, shocked, and titillated by the bloody exploits of Rico Bandello, Tony Camonte, and other celluloid hoodlums. Depression-era audiences identified with their battles against established authority, even though they inevitably were punished for their transgressions, usually by dying in a "hail of bullets."

Italian gangsters were less visible in popular culture during the 1940s, when Nazis and other monsters, usually supernatural, became Hollywood's designated bad guys. But they reemerged in the 1950s and '60s, in popular television series such as *The Untouchables* and movies like *Capone*. During those decades, well-publicized government investigations of organized crime told Americans that the gangsters they had been watching in the movies and on television were fictional representations of real-life criminal conspirators who posed a grave threat to the nation.

The mafia gangster truly became a mythic figure in the late 1960s, with the publication of Mario Puzo's novel *The Godfather*, and in the early 1970s, with the release of the first two *Godfather* films. *The Godfather*, in both its literary and cinematic incarnations, sold the public the fiction of a vast, centralized, and enormously powerful criminal organization run by Sicilians and their American-born offspring.

These dark, dangerous men made offers that could not be refused, sent their enemies to sleep with the fishes, and loved their families enough to kill for them. They captivated audiences in America, and later the world, becoming cultural archetypes who represented more than just crime. Puzo and Coppola—followed by Scorsese and later David Chase—pumped the mob genre full of metaphoric lead, making it tell tales of ethnicity and assimilation, of capitalism and corruption, and of families and how they could be both nurturing and toxic.

Since the 1970s, the Mafia myth has saturated the entertainment media, spawning numerous spin-offs and even parodies. Mediterranean mobsters not only appear in movies and television series, but also crop up in animated feature films and children's cartoon shows, in TV commercials, video games, and on Web sites. Mafia imagery and themes influence other pop-culture genres, including hip-hop, with rap performers who strike "gangsta" poses and rhyme about criminal exploits, real and imaginary.

No one knows for certain the true origins of the term "mafia," but its original usage was as a collective appellation for the organized crime groups that emerged in Sicily in the mid- to late nineteenth century. In America, criminal organizations established by Sicilian and other southern Italian immigrants came to be popularly known as "the Mafia," and continue to be so, even though the idea that there exists such a single criminal entity, so assiduously promoted by law enforcement agencies, the media, and the entertainment industry, has been debunked.

Today the "Mafia" label also gets slapped indiscriminately on crime organizations of varying ethnicities—Russian, Mexican, Chinese, Colombian—and even on noncriminal affiliations. The Kennedy family and its associates were dubbed the "Irish Mafia," Elvis Presley and his good buddies were the "Memphis Mafia," an informal network of homosexual executives in the entertainment industry is known as the "Gay" or "Lavender Mafia."[1]

Though "mafia" has passed into general parlance, connoting more than its original meaning, it retains particular significance for Italian Americans. The conventions and clichés of the Mafia myth not only define a genre; they have to a large degree defined Italian Americans, both to non-Italians and even to Italian Americans themselves, as some of the latter have seized on these depictions to derive a sense of ethnic identity. "The Mafia" is now the paradigmatic pop-culture expression of Italian American ethnicity, despite the fact that gangsters never constituted more than a tiny percentage of the massive southern Italian immigration to America.

It's often said that Italian mobster films constitute a popular entertainment genre, that they are the westerns of today, the prevailing national myth. "The urban cowboy is the mafioso, the guy in a limousine shooting up a lot of people on St. Valentine's Day," says Gay Talese.[2] The distinguished author of *Honor Thy Father* misrepresents that mob milestone—the St. Valentine's Day victims were lined up in a garage and shotgunned, execution-style—but his basic point is unassailable.

Many Italian Americans and their sympathizers, however, have little patience for this argument. To them the Mafia myth simply tarnishes the image of Italian Americans while imparting unwarranted glamour to the life of organized crime.

Movies like *Goodfellas* and TV shows like *The Sopranos*, their artistic merits notwithstanding, have fostered a skewed image of one ethnic group's complex historical experience. (Truth be told, the mob image would not be so widespread and persistent were it not for the artistic excellence of the best mafia movies and TV shows.) Italian American advocates are justified in objecting to seeing their heritage reduced to unflattering pop-culture clichés. I have often been annoyed and offended by the persistent, near-monolithic depiction of people of my ethnicity as violent criminals or vulgar proles who lack education, finesse, and any aspirations other than to provide for their families.

"Italian" is equated with "mafia" so frequently that any aspect of culture involving Italy or Italians is seen through the lens of the Mafia myth, as in the 2004 Public Broadcasting Service documentary on the Medicis that portrayed the Florentine dynasty as a Renaissance organized crime family.

American news media gave considerable play in June 2005 to a study that found that young Italian men were less macho and homophobic than their American counterparts. Researchers from the University of Missouri surveyed college-educated men in Rome and Palermo, asking them about their attitudes towards women and gays.

The Italians turned out to be far less sexist and more comfortable about homosexuality than the Americans the researchers had questioned.

Though the survey undermined persistent images of Italian males as hypermacho Don Juans who dominate women and bash gays, one paper, the right-wing tabloid *New York Post*, used the findings as an opportunity to reinforce mob stereotypes. The *Post* made the study the front-page story of its New York Pulse lifestyle section, with a headline proclaiming: "Revise Guys: Bada Bing! Italian men not so macho after all."[3] The cover featured a photo not of Italian men but of the lead male cast members of *The Sopranos*, with cartoon thought-balloons over each actor's head saying witty things like, "It's nice the way Paulie's hand feels on my shoulder" and "Look at this posture! Thanks, ballet lessons." Whereas PBS turned the Medicis into mobsters, *New York Post*, mindlessly exploiting the Mafia myth, transformed educated young *palermitani* and *romani* into the Italian American gangsters of a TV television drama.

This association is by no means limited to United States media. A critic with the British Broadcasting Corporation, in his rave review of the Neapolitan music group Enzo Avitabile and Bottari, described the *bottari*, a squad of percussionists, as "a bunch of goodfellas." Avitabile, a veteran of the Italian music scene who is an outspoken leftist, denounces Naples's *camorra* organized crime groups on one of the tracks from the very CD the BBC reviewer praises.[4] The reviewer's offhand characterization of Avitabile's musicians reflects an all-too-common tendency of journalists to make unwarranted references to organized crime when they are writing about Italians or Italian Americans.

Italian American advocates are also justified in pointing out a double standard when it comes to the stereotyping of Italian Americans and other groups, particularly racial minorities, who have far greater purchase on the sympathies of good liberal people than do Italians. As *The New York Times'* Clyde Haberman observed, had a white director portrayed black residents of Harlem as drug- and sex-crazed louts and gangsters—which is exactly how Spike Lee depicted a working-class Italian American community in his egregious *Summer of Sam*—the outrage would have been immediate and unequivocal.

Moreover, non–Italian American media figures and cultural commentators—particularly those most enraptured by *The Sopranos*—sometimes are dismissive of Italian resentment over stereotyping. As syndicated columnist Marie Cocco noted, "you can love 'The Sopranos' and still loathe the way legitimate gripes about Italian-American stereotyping are dismissed."

What Italian Americans find objectionable can vary from paisan to paisan. Veteran crime reporter George Anastasia says he's more offended by the overbearing Italian American mother on the TV sitcom *Everybody Loves Raymond* than he is by *The Sopranos*.

The long-running series starring adenoidal comic Ray Romano gave antidefamationists something to complain about in its final season, when Marie Barone, played by Doris Roberts, morphed from a hybrid of Italian and Jewish maternal stereotypes to Vito Corleone in drag.

Marie, the Long Island matron forever baking lasagna and meddling in her kin's lives, had always been the power center of the Barone family. She used food, love, and approval—and threats to withdraw all three—to rule over her irascible husband, her two grown sons and their wives, and just about anyone else who entered her orbit. She dispensed favors as a mob boss would—to control their recipients and ensure their loyalty. So when, in one of the show's last episodes, her long-suffering relatives angrily object to her machinations, she retorts, "You know how much these favors would cost you on the streets?" And, like any mob boss, Marie is the keeper of family secrets, which she threatens to disclose when her power is challenged.

By likening the Barone family struggles to those of a mafia clan, *Everybody Loves Raymond* invoked a central trope of the Mafia myth: the intertwining of family and "family." Godmother Marie may well have been the *Raymond* writers' homage to Mario Puzo, who said he based his don partly on his own formidable mother.

I would add the dumb stud Joey Tribbiani, played by the part-Italian actor Matt LeBlanc on the NBC sitcom *Friends* and on its dreadful spin-off *Joey*, which also wastes the talent of ex-*Sopranos* star Drea De Matteo.

The National Italian American Foundation, which has been waging a perpetual indignation campaign against mafia movies in general and

The Sopranos in particular, deemed LeBlanc worthy of its Entertainment Achievement Award. They presented him with this honor in 1999 despite the fact that LeBlanc's Joey Tribbiani is a one-note and truly stereotypical character, unlike the complex and compelling Tony Soprano, created by two genuinely gifted Italian American artists, David Chase and James Gandolfini. NIAF's preference for LeBlanc/Joey attests to Robert Viscusi's observation that the antidefamation groups are driven by "hatred of culture and a will to ignorance that is absolutely staggering."

Two so-called "reality" programs are even worse offenders. *The Family*, a (thankfully) defunct ABC-TV series launched in 2003, relocated the ten members of a blue-collar, Italian American family from New Jersey to Palm Beach, Florida, "playground to the famous and ultra-rich," where they competed with one another for $1 million.

The Family, described by one critic in *USA Today* as a "tacky debacle," reveled in regional, class, and ethnic insults. The show's premiere episode delighted "in ridiculing the family's heritage, from the snobbish dismissal of their preference for Italian food (set to old-world music), to the on-air logo that echoes the logo for *The Godfather*."[5]

In 2004 the Arts and Entertainment cable network aired a new reality series titled *Growing Up Gotti* that presented a purportedly unscripted look at the life of Victoria Gotti, daughter of the late mob boss John Gotti and a single mother who is raising her three sons by imprisoned mobster Carmine Agnello.

New York Times television critic Alessandra Stanley observed that the series's star, an "improbable Mediterranean blonde" who "looks like Donatella Versace and dresses like Jessica Rabbit," seemed like a real-life Carmela Soprano. "Ms. Gotti is a Carmela kind of domestic diva," Stanley noted. " 'Don't even start,' she hollers at one of her sons in the deep, flat voice perfected by the wife of the HBO crime boss Tony Soprano. Her boys all look and sound the same—like Anthony Jr. on 'The Sopranos' . . ."

La Gotti, however, claims that she finds the HBO series offensive and does not watch it. For one thing, she believes it does not accurately portray Italian American women like her. But she's not above milking her own family's notoriety. After a blind date goes awry, she tells the man's driver, "I'll give you a thousand dollars if you take him to a ditch somewhere and roll him in." Gotti's TV series is, in fact, "just the latest in a series of Victoria Gotti mobsploitation moves." Ms. Gotti, who has published several schlock novels and writes a column for the supermarket tabloid the *Star*, "has turned her father's crime family connections into her own thing: a Cosa Mia."[6]

The don's daughter pays her father the respect she obviously feels he's owed. (Gotti, however, was no family-loving Don Corleone. As posthumously released prison recordings revealed, he frequently reviled his kin in language more suitable for enemies about to be whacked.) Her Long Island mansion is filled with oil portraits and framed photographs of John Gotti. When her sons John, Carmine Jr., and Frank get on her last nerve, she invokes him as if he were a Roman household god and only his intervention could discipline her hair gel–addicted brats.

Growing Up Gotti proved a hit for the Arts and Entertainment Network; unlike *The Family*, which ended after nine episodes, Gotti's show returned for a second season in early 2005. But both shows demonstrate a truth that seems to confound antidefamation activists: some Italian Americans are ready and willing to perpetuate unflattering and even belittling images of themselves.

If the mafia image is a kind of minstrelsy, as anthropologist Micaela di Leonardo claims, a stylized performance that exaggerates certain ethnic tropes to the point of caricature, Italian Americans have done their part to keep the minstrel show running. Victoria Gotti at least is being herself on her show, or the version of herself she wants the world to see. The *cafone* clan on *The Family*, however, willingly played the demeaning roles assigned them by the show's producers.

But a caveat is necessary: though it can seem that Italian Americans choose to perform as latter-day versions of the organ grinder's monkey, as Michael Rispoli says, the entertainment industry usually calls the tune.

Over the past eight decades, Italian American ethnicity has been portrayed in increasingly narrow terms, starting with types rooted in some degree of social reality (the poor immigrant, the Prohibition bootlegger), which through repetition became clichés, which hardened into reductive stereotypes that have attained the status of ethnic archetypes—the Mafia gangster, the blue-collar boor, the dumb but lovable stud.

The weight of all this (mis)representation does impede the creation and mass-marketing of alternative images. John Turturro's experience with *Mac*, his 1993 film based on the life of his immigrant father and uncles, is instructive. As he notes, it wouldn't have taken him five years to raise the money for his film about law-abiding and industrious Italians had he instead portrayed the three brothers as gangsters.

Italian Americans, then, do have reason to question the way we often are portrayed in popular culture. But it's also true that the more overheated critics of *The Sopranos* and similar entertainments desperately need a reality check. Irksome as they may be, images of Italian American organized crime do not reflect or reinforce the exclusion of Italian Americans from the opportunities of U.S. society, as has been the case with the racial stereotyping inflicted on African Americans and other nonwhite minorities.

Dr. Joseph Scelsa of the City University of New York calls mafia stereotyping a "holocaust" for Italian Americans. But if anything in the Italian experience can be likened to the catastrophe suffered by European Jews, it would be the grinding poverty, oppression, and political disenfranchisement that, in the late nineteenth and early twentieth centuries, drove millions of southern Italians to emigrate. It would be more accurate, however, to compare those conditions to serfdom, not genocide.

It is indisputable that the southern Italians who fled Italy to escape *la miseria* experienced bias and discrimination in the United States. Elite and popular opinion regarded the impoverished and culturally distinct newcomers as unlikely to assimilate into a majority Anglo-Saxon nation, and even considered them a separate and inferior race with an inherent propensity to violent crime.

But for the descendants of the immigrants, America largely has been a success story. It may have taken them longer to attain upward mobility than it did for the Irish and Jews, but the evidence of their successful pursuit of the American dream is incontestable. Italian

Americans may be offended by *The Sopranos* and they may justifiably question why popular culture, rather than reflect the complex reality of their lives, continues to deal in the currency of outdated stereotypes. (Italian Americans hardly are alone in this regard.) But it is not credible to claim that the Mafia myth has blocked the progress or irreparably damaged the self-esteem of millions of Americans of Italian descent.

Ethnic stereotyping does not impinge on Italian American lives as destructively as racism and other forms of bias that carry more real-world consequences, such as antigay prejudice. If Italian American antidefamation organizations are so convinced that gangster stereotypes are injurious, they ought to make common cause with other groups opposed to racism and prejudice, something the Italian American establishment consistently has been reluctant to do. It's not acceptable to object only to unflattering images of Italians.

Much of the criticism of shows like *The Sopranos* comes from mainstream or conservative groups whose calls for positive images of Italian Americans mask a penchant for ideological conformity. They would suppress not only mafia gangster movies and TV shows but also critical dialogue within Italo-America about issues like racism. Organizations such as the National Italian American Foundation and the Order of the Sons of Italy in America never seem to muster the *forza* and *coraggio* to challenge their ethnic kin when they victimize others, even when, like the racist demonstrators in Bensonhurst, Brooklyn, they justify their intolerance as an expression of ethnic community values.

In 1992, Italian American leftists, including myself, founded an ad hoc group, Italian Americans for a Multicultural United States (IAMUS), to oppose that year's Columbus Quincentennial celebrations. Our founding statement declared that Columbus, who enslaved indigenous peoples in the Americas, was no Italian American hero, and that our history offered examples of men and women who were far more deserving of icon status.

We subsequently were denounced as "nigger-lovers" (several of our members had appeared on *Like It Is*, the ABC-TV public affairs program hosted by African American journalist Gil Noble), "Reds," and "fifth columnists" out to convert our paisans to Marxism-Leninism. One hate letter we received insisted that "Italian Americans do not support multiculturalism," an unintentionally ironic assertion, given that the places from which so many Italian Americans originate—Sicily and Naples—were some of the world's earliest multicultural societies.

Our critics were far more outraged by our suggestion that Christopher Columbus didn't deserve to be an Italian American icon than they were by the murder of Yusuf Hawkins. (Some of them argued that by criticizing Columbus we were attacking Italian Americans themselves.) Why, we wondered, do conservative Italian Americans think that fictional mobsters are more detrimental to the image of our people than racist thugs and their apologists?

Some left-wing Italian Americans, however, maintain that mob movies and TV shows serve a conservative political agenda. Political scientist Michael Parenti, in his book *Make-Believe Media*, argues that the Mafia myth deflects the attention of the public from the far more extensive corruption within the corporate and political elites that make up the American ruling class. *New York Times* columnist Maureen Dowd hints at the same point when she describes the Bush family as "the WASP Corleones."

But when it comes to popular entertainment, whom would audiences rather spend time with—colorful Italian Americans, with their outsized passions and appetites, or upper crust Episcopalians? Moreover, the more sophisticated mob stories, such as *The Godfather* and *The Sopranos*, do depict Italian American organized crime as part of a much larger corruption reaching to America's corporate boardrooms and government offices.

The most ardent critics of mafia movies and TV shows might take comfort in the following possibility. *The Sopranos*, despite its enormous popularity, could represent the last gasp of the genre. Indeed, the decline of the American mafia is a central theme of the show. The gangster genre is, after all, rooted in a social reality that is largely a thing of the past: the experience of poor immigrants from southern Italy and their subsequent status as working-class urbanites, usually from New York or New Jersey.

Television producer Tom Fontana (*Oz*, *Homicide*) grew up Sicilian American in Buffalo, New York, a city with a reputation as a center of organized crime activity. He thinks the time will come when the Mafia myth is no longer sustained by actual Italian American organized crime. It just hasn't happened yet.

"It'll be interesting to see [the Mafia myth] in fifty years—because now it's a myth that we're still part of," he says.

It's not like the Old West, which is now so in the history that the mythology is mythology, and has to be reinvented by every generation. In fifty years, it'll be interesting when there are no Italian mobsters or organized crime, how it'll be depicted then, because then it truly will be history. Right now, it's still out there. There's still enough of it to keep the myth alive.

I am less embarrassed by the film or television portrayals of mobsters than I am of the real guys. Here's an example. September 11 happens, the world is in mourning, the tragedy—I lost a lot of friends who were firefighters, people I went to high school with. And the mob steals the scrap from the World Trade Center. Some fucking asshole says, "You know what? We can make some money off the World Trade Center."

Now that's not something I made up as a writer. David Chase did not make that up. Mario Puzo did not make that up. A real Italian guy sat somewhere in New Jersey and said, "I got this big idea. We can turn this tragedy to our profit." So, is reality less harsh than the film version? I don't think so. If I wrote that in a movie, does someone have the right to attack me and say, "You're showing the bad side [of Italian Americans]"? It's the truth.[7]

Playwright and screenwriter Frank Pugliese deplores the persistence of the Mafia myth. "C'mon, it's time for us to step out of this," he says. "There are Italian American people doing amazing things in writing, art, and music. We don't have to be stuck in this badda-bing thing!"

He believes, however, that the mob genre may very well outlive Italian American organized crime.

I think it's going to have a long life. Because the more unreal it gets, the longer the life will be. It really will become just a show we watch. The real life might be Italian Americans in New Jersey just trying to figure out what to do because they lost all their pension money in Enron. That's probably a real Italian American story. What are we gonna do with our college fund when that pension fund is cut in half? But that's not gonna be the story that we all play . . . we're all gonna play whatever Tony Soprano's doing next week. Because it's not real, I think it's easier to sustain, in a way.[8]

Unreality pervades some recent iterations of the Mafia myth: the underwater underworld of *Shark Tale*, the mafioso pigeons called the Goodfeathers on the *Animaniacs* TV cartoon series, an episode of the PBS television cartoon series *Arthur* that featured a mob called the Altos, and the interactive theater piece *Mob Hits: The Show*, a long-running New York attraction. Some may object to seeing criminals turned into cute and cuddly figures of fun. But given the longevity of the Italian gangster as a pop archetype, it was inevitable that he would eventually appear in comic and parodic guises.

And when compared to far more threatening real-world miscreants—say theocratic gangsters like Osama bin Laden and his crew of Islamist bad boys, or domestic right-wing terrorists like Oklahoma City bomber Timothy McVeigh—gangsters, with their intra- and interfamily feuds, seem almost quaint, as familiar and reassuring in their familiarity as the Frankenstein monster lumbering about the castle or Dracula intoning "I do not drink . . . wine." The misdeeds of our old friends Don Vito and Tony Soprano are on a human, not apocalyptic scale, unlike an Islamist with a dirty bomb that could wipe out thousands.

For now, the entertainment industry keeps turning out mob movies and television series. But recent expressions of the Mafia myth don't bode well for the future of the gangster genre. Films like *This Thing of Ours*, *Wannabes*, *Mail Order Bride*, and *Friends and Family* tend to bolster the argument that the genre is nearly exhausted.

Mail Order Bride (2003) and *Friends and Family* (2001) were mob comedies that died at the box office. *Bride*, according to *The New York*

Times, was "a strained, incoherent farce, that if it accomplishes anything positive, it will be to drive another nail into the coffin of that exhausted subgenre, the mob comedy."[9] *Friends and Family*, the virtually humorless comedy about two gay gangsters who are open about their sexuality but closeted (to their families) about their line of work, had a brief run on the gay film festival circuit but failed to attract a larger audience.

Wannabes, from 2000, was yet another version of the standard fable of young men who break out of their dead-end lives by becoming criminals. Angelo, a Bensonhurst boy, and some friends take up bookmaking, and they eventually come to the attention of Santo, the local mob boss, played by Joe Viterelli, best known as "Jelly," Robert De Niro's aide-de-camp in *Analyze This*.

The film, written by William DeMeo, who also plays Angelo, added nothing new or surprising to the mob genre. "There isn't a single image or vocal inflection in 'Wannabes' . . . that isn't familiar from 'The Sopranos' or from countless movies about the mob. All the familiar stereotypes are on hand," noted *New York Times* critic Stephen Holden.[10]

This Thing of Ours, released in 2003, had the dubious distinction of being a vanity project by an actual mobster, Danny Provenzano, the grandnephew of the notorious mobbed-up Teamster boss Anthony "Tony Pro" Provenzano. Danny incorporated details from his own criminal career—including beatings and kidnappings—into his screenplay.

Provenzano starred as Nick Santini, a made man who convinces "the family" to bankroll an Internet extortion scheme he has devised with some of his pals. Given the pedigree of the director-screenwriter-star, it was reasonable to expect that *This Thing of Ours* would have the ring of authenticity, of mob life seen from the inside. But Provenzano's film, "a loosely knit collection of anecdotes," exudes the stale air of undigested influences: "For all of his personal familiarity with the material, Mr. Provenzano has turned out a movie that largely owes its tone and style to other movies."[11]

The auteur manqué at least was spared the pain of a dismal opening night. Provenzano was unable to attend the premiere of *This Thing of Ours* because right before it opened in theaters he took up residence in a New Jersey prison, having pleaded guilty to charges of racketeering and tax evasion in connection with the printing business he ran. (*Printing?* What kind of a legit gig is that for a wiseguy?) Provenzano's adventures in filmland might have inspired a great *Sopranos* episode, had not David Chase already given us "The Legend of Tennessee Moltisanti," in which Christopher tries and fails to turn his life in the mob into a movie script.

The future of television mob dramas doesn't look very promising, either. Ever since *The Sopranos* captivated viewers in 1999, broadcast television executives have been searching for a series that might match some of the HBO series's quality and appeal.

Their quest, alas, has proved futile. NBC's *Kingpin*, about a young and ambitious drug lord conceived as a Hispanic Michael Corleone (his first name was, in fact, Miguel), failed to generate much interest during its six-week run in 2003. *Line of Fire*, an ABC series from the same year, featured a smart and well-spoken gangster named Jonah Malloy, who ran a Hibernian crime syndicate in Virginia. That show also was canceled after one season. One TV critic's assessment of *Line of Fire* captured not only the central problem of that failed series but the potential pitfall that any attempt to create a compelling gangland drama must avoid. "It's only fair to admit that with rare exceptions— *The Godfather, The Sopranos* and a handful of others—I have no interest in Mob stories," wrote Robert Bianco of *USA Today*. "It is certainly possible to shape a great drama out of the inner workings of a crime syndicate, as *The Sopranos* proves. But shows like *Line of Fire* seem to spring from the assumption that the subject is of overwhelming interest all by itself."[12]

If a well-written and well-acted film or TV series, of similar quality to *The Sopranos*, indeed is possible, the question remains, what would it be about? David Chase recognized that no one wanted to see yet another story about a mob crew from Brooklyn, so the only place left to go was into the characters' domestic and interior lives. Now that he's brilliantly done that, what's left to say?

Throughout this book I have argued that the current era in mafia history is that of the *declino del padrino*. This excellent and elegant coinage by Vittorio Zucconi, of the Italian newspaper *La Repubblica*, refers to the decline of Italian American organized crime, brought about by external factors—primarily vigorous law enforcement, the RICO statute having proved an invaluable tool for mob-busting—and by organized crime's increasing disorganization, lack of discipline, drug use, and internecine wars. The socioeconomics of Italo-America also have played a major role in the decline; as Italian Americans increasingly left the nation's Little Italys to move into business and the professions, the old street culture that sustained mafia families began to die out.

All this does seem to confirm criminologist James B. Jacobs's contention that "Cosa Nostra's survival into the next millennium, in anything like its twentieth century form, can be seriously doubted."[13]

But although the halcyon days of Italian American organized crime, of "the Mafia," are definitely past, it may be premature to write its obituary. News accounts from the first half-decade of the new millennium reveal that there's still some life left in the wheezing old corpus. Some mob organizations, in fact, have proved adaptable to new realities.

In January 2005 federal prosecutors in Brooklyn brought indictments against several purported members of the Gambino crime family, as well as a telephone company executive from Missouri, for organizing "one of the largest fraud schemes in United States history." The Gambino members, one of whom was the son of John Gotti's *consigliere*, plotted to defraud millions of consumers by placing unauthorized charges on their telephone bills and credit cards.

The case, noted *The New York Times*, was significant because it highlighted "how mobsters long associated with bookmaking, loan-sharking and other traditional underworld operations have begun embracing technological advances and pursuing far more sophisticated schemes in the Internet age."[14]

New Yorkers probably hate the Metropolitan Transit Authority, the entity that runs the city's subway, buses, and commuter trains, more than any government agency besides the IRS. City residents already furious over repeated fare hikes and unreliable service found another reason to loathe the MTA when it was revealed in September 2004 that the agency had become a cash cow for the mob.

The MTA paid more than $10 million in salary and bonuses to real estate developer Frederick J. Contini to turn a vacant thirty-two-story office building in Lower Manhattan into its new headquarters. The agency's critics deemed the project, which went more than $300 million over budget, a fiasco. Then federal prosecutors disclosed that the extremely well compensated Contini had long-standing ties to two mob groups, the so-called Gambino and Genovese families. He had even entered a secret guilty plea to other racketeering charges earlier in 2004.

According to the federal indictments, Contini siphoned off more than $10 million from the work on the MTA headquarters through inflated bills, extortion, and kickbacks on demolition, fireproofing, asbestos, and elevator contracts. Contini was charged along with two reputed mobsters, one the brother-in-law of mob turncoat Sammy "the Bull" Gravano and a union business agent.

Here's how Contini and his mob confreres ripped off the MTA and taxpayers. Contini would permit mobbed-up subcontractors for various projects to hire lower-paid, non-union labor, while billing at the union rate, which was often 100 percent more than the non-union rate. Contini sometimes took his piece of the action as a kickback, at other times the subcontractors kept all the extra cash. Besides the overbilling scheme, Contini also helped his mob buddies out with no-show jobs.

"The indictment shows a significant level of [organized crime] involvement . . . in an important public project," said an assistant U.S. attorney. "In this case, millions of dollars that could have otherwise been saved went into the pockets of criminals."

Contini himself sounds like somebody Tony Soprano might know and do business with. He lived in what *The New York Times* called "a palatial home" in suburban New Jersey, which he unfortunately was forced to sell to pay his mounting legal bills. He also owned a Manhattan nightclub called Chaos, and the Blue Elephant, a restaurant.

The developer also has one of those legendary volatile tempers, like Christopher Moltisanti or Joe Pesci's goodfella, Tommy De Vito. As if his MTA problems weren't enough, Contini was convicted for slashing a bar patron across the face and neck with the broken stem of a wineglass in 2002. The man's wounds required sixty stitches to close.[15]

The classic 1954 film *On the Waterfront* exposed organized crime's control of New York's docks. Directed by Elia Kazan and starring a young Marlon Brando, *On the Waterfront* shone a spotlight on the corruption of trade unionism by the mob, and on the struggle of oppressed dockworkers for work and dignity. The story dramatized actual conditions and occurrences on the docks, and its main characters were based on real people. Brando's Terry Malloy was modeled after whistleblowing longshoreman Anthony De Vincenzo, and the wiseguy union boss Johnny Friendly, played by Lee J. Cobb, was based on Albert Anastasia, the notorious gangster who himself was executed in a Manhattan barbershop.

Nearly fifty years after the film's release, and after a "prosecutorial full-court press" against the mob and its maritime corruption, gangsters still maintain a hold on the waterfront and its workers, despite their having been driven out of many of their other traditional rackets.[16] In 2002 the Brooklyn U.S. attorney announced the indictments of crime boss Vincent "the Chin" Gigante, his son, and six other alleged wiseguys on criminal charges related to the docks.

Between 2002 and 2004, federal prosecutors kicked serious mafia butt, indicting, convicting, and imprisoning major mob leaders, including Joseph Massino of Queens, described by the feds and the media as the last of the mafia dons still at large. Mob groups are having a hard time recruiting new talent to replace old, dead, or imprisoned members. Few of the remaining leaders demonstrate anything resembling the sagacity and self-control of the old-time bosses.

But New York mafia groups, though reeling from all the arrests and betrayals from within, evidently aren't extinct yet. Veteran Cosa Nostra observers say that while "other bands of ethnic criminals come and go . . . the old Mafia persists."[17]

The various court cases involving New York organized crime defendants show that Cosa Nostra's business model—"turning fear into money"[18]—has proved remarkably resilient, according to prosecutors. Despite the many successful prosecutions of gangsters since the 1980s, "the mob continues to impose a tax of sorts across the region with its grip on legitimate businesses ranging from neighborhood coin laundries to the unions and companies on the New York waterfront."

The command structure of mafia groups, which permits leadership succession, has a lot to do with their durability, say prosecutors. If the feds are correct on this point, ambitious hoodlums will come forward to replace the Joe Massinos and other incarcerated or dead bosses. New leaders will appear as long as the mob's long-established illicit economy remains intact, even if scaled down, since moneymaking is the raison d'être of organized crime.

Former FBI undercover agent Joseph "Donnie Brasco" Pistone boasts that he "dealt a serious and damaging blow to the American Mafia." But, he adds,

> I was not naïve enough then, nor am I now, to believe that we came anywhere near to destroying the mob and ending organized crime. It is true that the Mafia today is not nearly as strong or far-reaching as it was only two or three decades ago, that its top bosses are all dead or in jail, that more turncoats are breaking their vows of *omertà* than ever before, that "disorganized crime" is more like it, given the sorry state of mob leadership. But that doesn't mean the Mafia is dead and buried. Far from it.[19]

Pistone, of course, has a vested interest in his "It's Alive!" scenario; organized crime remains his meal ticket decades after he left the FBI. He went from being a successful undercover agent to working as a consultant to law enforcement agencies, a lecturer, and an all-around mob expert. He coproduced the 1997 film based on his exploits as Donnie Brasco as well as the short-lived television series *Falcone*. He also has written or cowritten several books about "the Mafia." Most were nonfiction, but in 2004, Pistone teamed up with Salvatore "Bill" Bonanno, son of the late mob boss Joseph Bonanno and the protagonist of Gay Talese's nonfiction book *Honor Thy Father*, to coauthor a cops 'n' Cosa Nostra novel, *The Good Guys*.

His self-interest notwithstanding, it's hard to argue with Pistone when he declares, "As long as there is money to be made illicitly and with minimal investment, there will be wiseguys ready and willing to make the score."[20]

The Sopranos makes the same point when, in its premiere episode,

Tony and crew watch a TV interview with an ex-mobster "turned government informer and bestselling author" who claims there'll always be a market for what the mob has to sell, things like drugs, pornography, and credit.

But even acknowledging that there remains a mob economy, with gangsters ready to provide goods and services that some people want, Cosa Nostra as business enterprise and a culture may very well have been doomed by the unprecedented betrayal of Joseph Massino, the Queens-based crime boss dubbed "the last don" by the media.

Massino became the first mafia chief to betray this thing of theirs when he secretly recorded his prison conversations with another gangster in late 2004. Having been convicted in July 2004 on federal murder and racketeering charges, Massino faced new murder charges that could have resulted in his facing the death penalty.[21] As part of his cooperation with the feds, he told them about a plot by Vincent "Vinny Gorgeous" Basciano to kill a federal prosecutor. Massino then, in two separate conversations, discussed the plan with Basciano inside the Metropolitan Detention Center, a federal jail in Brooklyn where both men were imprisoned.

Massino's cooperation with the government was "all the more extraordinary" because he was known to be "an Old World stalwart who clung to the fading values of honor and *omertà*, the Mafia's code of silence."[22]

Some law enforcement figures believe that Massino's violation of the protocols of *omertà* means that the mafia in America is doomed. If Massino can sell out, there is little incentive for mob soldiers lower down the pecking order to remain loyal.

"The mafia as we know it is effectively over," according to Ronald Goldstock, a former head of New York's organized crime task force. "If people in the lower orders didn't know that their bosses would sell them out, then they know it now."[23]

When the news emerged in early 2005 that Massino had been informing on his associates, there were reports of a major crisis in other organized crime groups, with some veteran gangsters reported to have fled New York.[24]

But even this milestone in gangland history was overshadowed by the arrests, in March 2005, of two retired New York City detectives, Louis Eppolito and Steven Caracappa, on charges that they had been moonlighting as hit men for the mob. Federal prosecutors said the two, who had been partners on the force, had carried out one execution on their own and helped out with at least seven others. They also were implicated in a failed plot to kill mob turncoat Sammy "the Bull" Gravano. The feds additionally brought drug dealing and money laundering charges against the pair.

Federal agents busted Eppolito and Caracappa while they were dining at an Italian restaurant in Las Vegas. Eppolito, after retiring from the police force in 1990, pursued a film career, playing bit parts in *Goodfellas*, *Bullets Over Broadway*, and other crime and action movies. Unlike screenwriter manqué Christopher Moltisanti on *The Sopranos*, Eppolito did write a movie, a straight-to-DVD film, *Turn of Faith*. (The 2001 crime drama starred veteran film and stage actor Charles Durning, boxer Ray "Boom Boom" Mancini, and Tony Sirico of *The Sopranos*.) But the disgraced detective's fictional chef d'oeuvre has got to be *Mafia Cop: The Story of an Honest Cop Whose Family Was in the Mob*.

In this autobiography—published in 1992, well after he and Caracappa allegedly had begun to moonlight for the Lucchese "family"—Eppolito acknowledged that his father and uncle had been made members of the Gambino crime organization. He claimed, however, that he had turned away from the gangster life and had honorably and honestly served the New York Police Department.

Caracappa, who worked in "a sensitive organized crime homicide unit," provided federal investigators the smoking gun they needed, in the form of a computer printout that revealed he had searched for information about a Nicholas Guido, who was killed in 1986. Caracappa allegedly had given the information to another mobster, who wanted to whack a Gambino associate named Nicholas Guido. It turned out, however, that Caracappa had fingered the wrong Guido, a law-abiding telephone installer.[25] The mistaken-identity victim was shot to death while sitting in a car outside his Brooklyn home on Christmas Day.

Eppolito and Caracappa evidently feel no shame or remorse for their alleged crimes (the two have pleaded not guilty to the charges against them), since they intend to profit from their role in what may well be "the worst scandal in NYPD history."[26] The New York *Daily News* reported that while behind bars, the disgraced cops were trying to negotiate a movie deal with Universal Pictures.

"I hope it's better than *Turn of Faith*," one law enforcement source quipped.[27]

Then, just a few days after the arrests of Eppolito and Caracappa, came yet another bombshell. Federal agents busted thirty-two New York mobsters, including the reputed head of the Gambino organization, based on the investigations of an Italian American undercover FBI agent who, like Joe "Donnie Brasco" Pistone, had deceived his mob associates so expertly that they were on the verge of making him a made man.

Both the Eppolito-Caracappa and Brasco Redux stories served to remind that New York remains "the center of the Mafia universe and home to five of its crime families."[28] The cases also further reinforced the symbiotic relationship between organized crime and the entertainment industry. As the *Daily News* observed, "Both tales assumed a Hollywood patina: the FBI agent was right out of 'Donnie Brasco,' while one of the two detectives had a bit part in 'Goodfellas.' "[29] In his autobiography Eppolito says Robert De Niro asked him for authentic tips on the mob.

As the spate of organized crime cases in recent years makes evident, the well of potential gangster storylines hasn't been exhausted yet. No doubt some filmmaker or TV producer will dramatize Joe Massino's rise and downfall, with perhaps Paul Sorvino or Armand Assante as the *omertà*-busting don. Regardless of whether Eppolito and Caracappa get their movie deal, there's sure to be a cinematic or small-screen recounting of their exploits. (But if they are convicted, their victims' relatives can sue them under a law that prohibits felons from profiting from their crimes.) I see Vin Diesel as Eppolito, a dark-complexioned ex-bodybuilder who in his prime was as bulked up as the action movie star. All Diesel would need is a Brooklyn accent, a curly wig, and a bushy seventies style mustache such as Eppolito wore during the disco era.

"New Mafia" scams, like the looting of New York's Metropolitan

Transit Authority and the Internet credit card ripoffs, also might in-spire future films, or at the very least a few episodes of *Law and Order*. And why not? The antidefamationists notwithstanding, the gangster genre is too good to give up on, too rich with dramatic possibilities. David Chase's version of the Mafia myth doesn't have to be the final installment.

But if the genre is to retain any vitality and relevance, it will have to move beyond the "Old Mafia" narratives rooted in the vanishing street-corner culture of blue-collar, urban Italian American neighbor-hoods. American artists—filmmakers, television producers, authors—might heed the example of the martyred Sicilian prosecutor Giovanni Falcone and follow the money. By tracing mafia cash flows, Falcone penetrated a web of corruption entangling mafiosi with legitimate businesses, public institutions, and officials at the highest levels of government.

The theme of organized crime thriving in a symbiotic relationship with respectable individuals and mainstream institutions was brilliantly explicated in *Godfather II*. In that film, the mobbed-up Senator Pat Geary excoriates Michael Corleone in explicitly anti-Italian terms. Vito's son calmly and coldly replies, "Senator, we're part of the same corruption." Cosa Nostra will and should remain a subject for popular art as long as the upper- and underworlds are partners in crime.

In Italy, the Sicilian mafia is a phenomenon whose business is inter-twined with the political economy and governance of a nation, and is not only a problem of Sicily or the Mezzogiorno. The staggering corrup-tion of the Italian political class is well known, as epitomized by the *Tangentopoli* (Bribe City) scandals of the early 1990s. The subsequent *Mani Pulite* (Clean Hands) prosecutorial investigations uncovered a vast network of corruption involving businessmen and politicians. The scandals toppled two giants of the Italian political system, former prime minister and Socialist Party leader Bettino Craxi, accused of hav-ing illegally amassed a vast fortune, and Giulio Andreotti, the leader of the Christian Democrats, who was accused of collusion with the mafia and complicity in murder.

In Sicily, any public servants "brave or foolhardy enough to try to see the rule of law enforced"[30] have found themselves under fierce at-

tack from mafiosi, who haven't hesitated to murder high-ranking officials. The successful anti-mafia prosecutions brought by magistrates
Giovanni Falcone and Paolo Borsellino resulted in their assassinations
in 1992. Public outrage over their murders forced the Italian state,
which had been largely indifferent to organized crime's depredations, to
crack down.

But despite greater vigilance by law enforcement, organized crime
remains a grave problem for Italy. In 2004 a horrific war among rival
camorre (criminal gangs) broke out in several working-class districts in
Naples, claiming many lives, including those of innocent bystanders
and passersby. In Sicily, mafia killings have declined and major mafiosi
have been brought to justice. But, as one prominent magistrate pointed
out, organized crime remains "ready to strike anyone serving the Italian
state."[31]

The Italian state itself remains vulnerable to penetration by the
mafia and individuals aligned with it. "The mafia has relationships with
representatives of the institutions and of civil society," announced the
prosecutor's office in Palermo in October 2004, when it indicted no less
a figure than the president of the Sicilian Region, Salvatore Cuffaro,
along with the entrepreneur Michele Aiello, and two other high-ranking
regional government officials, one from the carabinieri (a branch of the
national police force), another from the Customs Service.

The indictments described "contacts among men of politics, businessmen, and ties to Cosa Nostra."[32] Cuffaro, a member of Forza Italia,
the political party of right-wing Prime Minister Silvio Berlusconi, was
accused of leaking to mafiosi the findings of police investigations of organized crime.

The extent of mafia control of legitimate commercial activity in
Palermo was revealed in January 2005 in a double-barreled blast of media reports. A documentary on the national RAI-TV network reported
that 80 percent of Sicilian businesses pay the *pizzo*, or protection
money, to Cosa Nostra.

The newspaper *La Repubblica* reported that police had gotten hold
of an accounts book that detailed illegal protection payments for the
Vucciria area of Palermo. The ledger revealed for the first time the
rules and regulations that dictate who must pay *pizzo*. It showed that

mafia groups impose a graded tariff on businesses—small shops must fork over 500 to 1,000 euros per quarter, upscale shops such as jewelers pay 2,500 to 3,000 euros, and big shops pay 5,000 euros. Shopkeepers with family members in prison are exempt, as are those with relatives in the police force. Those who suffer a bereavement are let off a single quarterly payment. New shops setting up in the area are obliged to make a hefty down payment. Mafiosi coming into the Vucciria area from outside have to pay 3 percent of their take to the local bosses.

Regional President Cuffaro, under indictment for mafia connections, objected vociferously to the RAI-TV report, claiming that only 5 to 10 percent of shopkeepers pay for mafia protection. But the ledger, confiscated from a mobster arrested in Palermo, provided "line-by-line, street-by-street evidence of Mafia extortion."[33] Both the RAI report and the ledger confirm the finding of Italian sociologist Diego Gambetta that the main business of the mafia is the provision of private protection—both from unorganized crime and from the mafia itself.[34]

Given the pervasiveness of organized crime in Italy and its ties to the worlds of politics and business, it's no surprise that movies and television dramas about the mafia are a long-standing tradition. *La piovra* ("The Octopus"), a popular 1984 TV series, starred the internationally known actor Michele Placido as a police official fighting a "new mafia," based in Sicily but with a global reach, and enormously rich from international drug trafficking.

More recently, the RAI-TV network presented the highly popular and much-acclaimed "Inspector Montalbano" series, adapted from the bestselling novels of Sicilian author Andrea Camilleri about Salvo Montalbano, an unorthodox, left-wing, and cuisine-obsessed police commissioner from the fictive town of Vigàta. Camilleri's novels and the TV adaptations present a sardonic vision of Sicily, where mafiosi continue to exert their destructive influence on politics and daily life.

Compared to American filmmakers who simply recycle the mob genre's clichés, Italian directors keep the genre fresh by grounding it in politically engaged critiques of the social conditions that permit the mafia to flourish. Two of the best of these recent works are dramatizations of actual events in Sicily. *I cento passi* ("The Hundred Steps," from 2000) tells the story of Peppino Impastato, the disaffected son of a Cosa Nostra family who was murdered in the 1970s by gangsters because of his anti-mafia activism; while *Placido Rizzotto* (2000) depicts the life of the title character, a trade union leader killed by the mafia in 1948. Both films, despite their heroes' violent deaths, eschew pessimism and despair; they end by promising that the struggle these courageous men waged against the mafia must and will continue.

Two films by Neapolitan directors released in 2001 that are polar opposites in style and tone depict the *camorra* as a scourge that blighted the lives of both its members and its victims. *Luna rossa*, written and directed by Antonio Capuano, presents the Cammarano clan as present-day Neapolitan incarnations of Agamemnon and his children Orestes and Electra.

At the start of the film, the bloodthirsty Cammaranos have dealt a rival clan a deadly blow, but their victory is hollow, as they are eventually consumed by their own violence and moral rot. The aging Godfather Tony keeps a caged black panther in his bedroom, as well as an oil painting of two horses copulating. Killing and fucking are the Cammaranos' chief pursuits, which they do with ruthless abandon. Besides whacking rivals, they also eliminate each other. Amerigo, Tony's son, murders his father by breaking the old man's neck. The Cammaranos' sexual perversity includes incest, as the family matriarch Irene seeks to bed her sullen son Oreste, who slashes himself with razors in rage and frustration over his being a member of such a monstrous family.

The film goes increasingly over the top, as the body count rises and the various sexual intrigues and power plays unfold. In an extravagant dream sequence, Oreste wanders naked through a Greek temple. The film, with its vision of the *camorra* as unredeemably evil, eventually becomes an unmodulated scream, but for much of its running time it is a compelling and often frightening plunge into a moral abyss.

Tornando a casa couldn't be more different. Whereas Capuano's film is stridently theatrical, Vincenzo Marra's is a quiet, modest work indebted to such neorealist classics as Luchino Visconti's *La terra trema*. As in that 1948 film set in a Sicilian fishing village, writer-director Marra hired real *pescatori*, from the island of Procida, as the protagonists of his somber and moving drama of a Neapolitan fishing boat crew.

The crew, which includes a young North African, has been fishing illegally in the waters south of Sicily, where the catches are more plentiful. After nearly being captured by North African authorities, they return to the port town of Pozzuoli, near Naples. But the *camorra*, which controls the waterfront, regards them as competition and will not permit them to work in the area.

The men are forced to make the dangerous trip south again, to North African waters. On the Tunisian coast, one of the young Italians joins the North African crew member, whom he has befriended, and disappears into a crowd of desperately poor Arabs who also struggle for survival. The film concludes with this image of solidarity among the Mediterranean poor and displaced, who live marginal lives due to oppressive structures, whether organized crime syndicates or authoritarian governments.

Not all Italian films about organized crime are so sober-sided. *Tano da Morire* (1997), an outlandish mafia spoof complete with musical numbers, was directed by a woman, Roberta Torre, a northern Italian who relocated to Sicily and married a Sicilian filmmaker, Daniele Cipri.

Tano satirizes not only the mafia cult of violence but also the covertly homoerotic bonding of the "men of honor." The movie culminates in a scene set in La Vucciria, the famous Palermo marketplace, in which local women perform a rap number mocking Tano Guarrasi, a minor mafioso murdered in his butcher shop. One stout *palermitana*, in a moment of inspiration, grabs a long *cucuzza* squash, which she uses as a pretend microphone while she lip-synchs to the rap lyrics.

Tano da Morire and its follow-up, *Sud Side Stori* (2000), are both indebted to the work of Torre's husband, Daniele Cipri, and his partner Franco Maresco, filmmakers who became notorious in Italy for outrageous, darkly comic movies such as *Toto Who Lived Twice* and their *Cinico TV* videos. Cipri and Maresco's stock-in-trade is an all-out satiric assault on Sicilian institutions and culture, including the Catholic Church and the mafia. In 1998, *Toto*, which depicted mafiosi as biblical characters, became the first movie banned by Italy's censorship commission in more than twenty years; the censors declared it blasphemous, "an attack on sacred values and mankind." In one scene, an angel has sex with a chicken.[35]

Roberta Torre's 2002 film *Angela* broke with the style of her two previous films and with the conventions of the mob genre in its straightforward, dramatic treatment of the life of a woman in the mafia. The title character, played by Italian stage actress Donatella Finocchiaro (Torre generally uses nonprofessionals in her films), works in a shoe store that also serves as a front for her mafioso husband Saro's drug business. Angela, beautiful and much younger than Saro, feels genuine affection for him, and he loves her. She helps out with the drug trade, stuffing packets of white powder into shoeboxes and even delivering them to Saro's customers. She abides by her husband's rigid code, but she also chafes at her subordinate position in the male-dominated mafia culture.

Everything is going well—the local cops are paid off, there's peace with other mafia clans, and business is thriving—when Angela risks everything by falling in love with Masino, a handsome young mafioso who comes to work for Saro. Angela and Masino at first try to resist their mutual attraction, but one night, while Saro is away, they consummate their passion.

When the police raid the shoe store and arrest Saro's gang, their affair is revealed. The cops have taped some incriminating phone calls between Angela and Masino, and they try to use the tapes to get her to inform on her husband and his associates. She refuses to cooperate, and ends up completely isolated and vulnerable—her husband can't forgive her, Masino disappears, and she's in the hands of the law.

Torre tells Angela's story in a stark, no-nonsense style that represents a radical change from the broad and at times cartoonish *Tano* and *Sud Side Stori*. She avoids melodramatic mafia clichés, and instead dispassionately depicts a social milieu in which cocaine dealers and hit men pose as respectable business people, and where families are bound together more by intimidation than by love.

Le conseguenze dell'amore (*The Consequences of Love*, 2004), by the Neapolitan director Paolo Sorrentino, depicts mafiosi "not as deranged gangsters but sophisticated technocrats."[36] This quietly devastating work, quite unlike any previous mob movie, centers not on the mafiosi but on one of their victims, Titta Di Girolamo, a fifty-year-old former stockbroker from the southern Italian city of Salerno.

Di Girolamo (played by the excellent Toni Servillo) once lost a substantial amount of mafia money in a bad investment. But rather than kill him, the gangsters sentenced him to life imprisonment, in an anonymous hotel in a Swiss city. Forced to become a mafia money launderer, each week he awaits the delivery of a suitcase full of cash, which he must deliver to a bank.

Exiled to a cold, foreign place, Di Girolamo maintains an emotional detachment as chilly as the Swiss weather. He can barely tolerate even the most undemanding social interaction; offering a polite response to another hotel guest's greeting requires a great effort. Separated from his wife, he tries to maintain a relationship with his three teenage children by telephone, but only his sullen daughter will speak with him, and just barely. His father regards him as a criminal and won't have anything to do with him.

But this taciturn, aloof man seethes with anguish and desperation, which he medicates with heroin. Too controlled to abandon himself to addiction, he manages his heroin use as rigidly as he distances himself from humanity: he injects only once a week. His life has been reduced to this static routine—wait for the dirty money to be dropped off at his hotel, deposit it in the bank, shoot dope—until he becomes enamored of the hotel's beautiful barmaid Sofia (played by Olivia Magnani, granddaughter of Anna). His feelings for Sofia not only thaw his gelid reserve, they also lead him to defy the mafiosi who have stolen his life. But for the trapped Titta, this act of existential rebellion can have no happy ending, and the consequences of love prove fatal.

Director Sorrentino deplores the tendency of American filmmakers to make movies from the mob's point of view, a strategy that has produced such compelling outlaws as Vito Corleone and Tony Soprano. "I love Scorsese's and Coppola's films," Sorrentino told the British paper *The Guardian*. "They're great portraits, but they fell in love with mafiosi. They have mythologised organised crime."

Sorrentino's mafiosi are businessmen, calculating and ruthlessly efficient, but never flamboyant or "colorful." (Sorrentino ironically establishes their "professionalism" in a memorable sequence in which they interrogate Di Girolamo in an empty hotel auditorium where a medical conference is being held, the mafiosi seated at a banquette previously occupied by prostate cancer specialists.) When crossed, they don't burst into operatic rages—they don't even raise their voices—but always remain eminently reasonable, even when committing murder. And this makes them all the more terrifying.

In the United States, *The Sopranos* has come closest to the Italian critique of organized crime as embedded in the structures of mainstream society. Chase's series has the novelistic richness and complexity, the psychological insight and social criticism of the best Italian films and television series. If there is a future for the mob genre in America, it will not be in claptrap like *This Thing of Ours* or *Wannabes*, which simply regurgitate familiar tropes and clichés. It instead will lie in the kind of formally inventive, politically engaged, and outraged treatments of organized crime at which Italians excel. In other words, American mob narrative will have to become more European.

Sicily, interestingly enough, has had its own counterparts to Italian American antidefamation activists, in those islanders who have adopted the mantle of *sicilianismo*, a defensive strategy of ethnocultural identity politics. The exponents of *sicilianismo* have accused antimafia activists of unfairly tarnishing all of Sicily in their campaign against Cosa Nostra. This criticism, however, is rarely extended to works of popular culture that seriously examine the workings of organized crime, and the nexus of mafia, capitalism, and politics.

The Mafia myth will endure until pop-culture consumers decide they've had enough of it, and that eventuality isn't on the horizon. But what of Italian American stories that fall outside the parameters of the mob genre—what is their future? The mob genre has largely defined Italian Americans in pop culture, not only to the world but to themselves. As veteran organized crime reporter and *Goodfellas* author Nicholas Pileggi stated, "If you're Italian American and looking for a clue to your background and to the world your parents came from, the whole history of organized crime is an interesting source."[37]

But Italian American does not equal mafia. "Mob narrative is not coextensive with Italian American narrative but is rather an offshoot from it."[38]

"It's an important element of Italian American history, no question," says Robert Viscusi. "But it's not, in itself, a way of studying that history. In other words, it's a cultural epiphenomenon that you can't take as an authority on anything."[39]

What, then, would constitute Italian American narrative in the current era?

The late eminent Palestinian American intellectual Edward Said, speaking at a conference of the Italian American Writers Association (IAWA) in 2001, posed a fundamental question: If you discard reductive caricatures and stereotypes, what do you put in their place? Italian Americans who object to distorted portrayals need to think about what sorts of alternative depictions they want to promote. And that means a discussion of what it means to be Italian American, a century after the great migration and after decades of assimilation.

For other American ethnic minorities, particularly African Americans and Jews, literature has been essential to the exploration, and even the creation, of identity. The intellectual rigor and imaginative fecundity of black and Jewish writing has had an impact well beyond those communities; American culture would be immeasurably poorer without the works of Bellow and Baldwin, Morrison and Roth, Ellison and Miller.

Gay Talese, in a famous—some would say infamous—1993 essay in *The New York Times Book Review*, asked, "Where Are the Italian American Novelists?"

Italian Americans haven't produced much literature, other than [Pietro Di Donato's 1939 proletarian novel] *Christ in Concrete* and Puzo's novels, Talese claimed. He offered as explanation the purported lack of encouragement for literary ambitions, or even reading and education, in working-class Italian American households.

How was it possible that of the estimated 20 million Americans with Italian roots—a group that among my generation produced such heralded Americans as the painter Frank Stella, the architect Robert Venturi and hosts of film directors, educators, financiers, and scientists—that this group was so *underrepresented* in the ranks of well-known creative American writers? Were there no Italian-American Arthur Millers and Saul Bellows, James

Baldwins and Toni Morrisons, Mary McCarthys and Mary Gor-
dons, writing about their ethnic experiences?[40]

"We do not have an Italian literature in the sense that Southern
Italians are written about," claims Talese's cousin, Nicholas Pileggi.
"The Irish have a real literature. You could spend the rest of your life
reading Irish literature and never read the same book twice, but that's
not true of the Italians. It's mostly an oral tradition."[41]

It's not true [retorts Robert Viscusi]. Of course there's a literature—there's fifty literatures. There's Neapolitan literature,
there's Sicilian literature, there's all kinds of dialect literature.
Every region of Italy has its own dialect literature. There is
also—and I know this is a dirty word to use around Italian
American writers—such a thing as history. Now, you don't necessarily find it in the comics, and you don't necessarily find it in
movies, and you certainly don't find it in books about the mob.
To try to understand Italian American history with books about
the mob is like trying to understand American history by reading
books about Legs Diamond.

I mean, it's related, but you can't imagine somebody studying American history without knowing something about Thomas
Jefferson, Abraham Lincoln, and Teddy Roosevelt and George
Washington and Franklin Roosevelt and the Lend-Lease Act
and the Smoot-Hawley Bill and the antitrust laws.

Italian history has plenty of that kind of thing. However, you
don't learn it in an American school. So if you want to pontifi-
cate about it, in public, you have to go to the library. And it
seems to me that people who say things like this have not gone
to the library. It's an easy way out. You can learn a lot of things
about the Vietnam War by reading *Doonesbury*, but it can't be
your only source.[42]

Italian American writers, in fact, began creating imaginative, auto-
biographical, and critical literature early in the twentieth century. They
include Pietro Di Donato, whose *Christ in Concrete* was made into a

film by blacklisted director Edward Dmytryk, the acclaimed biographer Frances Winwar (Francesca Vinceguerra), the novelist and short-story writer John Fante, novelist Mari Tomasi, and the playwright and novelist Dorothy Calvetti Bryant.

In the decades since World War II, distinguished work has come from the novelists Helen Barolini (*Umbertina*), Rita Ciresi (*Blue Italian*), and Carole Maso (*Ghost Dance*); novelist and poet Gilbert Sorrentino; essayists and critics Frank Lentricchia, Robert Viscusi (who has also written an award-winning novel, *Astoria*), Barbara Grizzuti Harrison, Fred Gardaphé, Maria Laurino, Anthony Valerio, and Camille Paglia; and the poets Lawrence Ferlinghetti, John Ciardi, Gregory Corso, Diane di Prima, Jay Parini, Maria Mazziotti Gillan, Daniela Gioseffi, Dana Gioia, Felix Stefanile, and Joseph Tusiani.

Gay Talese, a pioneer of the "new journalism" that emerged in the 1960s, wrote the nonfiction novel *Honor Thy Father*, about mobster Joe Bonanno and his son Bill, and *Unto the Sons*, an epic recounting of southern Italian immigration to America centered on the lives of Talese's own forebears.

Don DeLillo, the great postmodernist whose novels such as *White Noise* and *Libra* have established him as one of contemporary fiction's most influential figures, eschewed ethnic themes until *Underworld* (1997). That sprawling novel employed an Italian American protagonist, who like DeLillo grew up in the Belmont section of the Bronx, to tell a wider story of the "intersection of personal and public experience" in five decades of American life.[43]

Talese, DeLillo, and the other writers I have cited are among the best-known creative forces in Italo-America, but there are many others, writing books and essays, publishing poetry in chapbooks or small-press and academic journals, making documentary films and writing plays.

Italian American narrative, in whatever genre, has always been preoccupied with politics, culture, identity, and gender/sexuality. Yet, despite these bona fides, it generally was not included under the American Studies rubric. The work of Italian American writers often was undervalued because it was simply not perceived, not by academia or by the publishing industry and critics. Italian American critics themselves have had to establish the significance of Italian narrative in American culture.

"The question then, for Talese, should have been not so much 'where are the novelists?' but 'why are the novelists ignored?' " writes Anthony Julian Tamburri, one of the current leading figures in Italian American criticism.[44]

Italian American writing is too often still denied the cultural currency it deserves.

"A few years ago, a friend submitted a novel about [law-abiding] working-class Italian-Americans to a New York publisher and found an Italian-American editor there who loved it," Fred Misurella recalled in a 2002 opinion column for the *Christian Science Monitor*. "But alas, the novel, though very good, was never published. Not 'enough blood and guts,' a more senior editor said."

Misurella's friend, unable to find a publisher for his novel, broke it into short stories, which he published in literary magazines. His friend's experience attests to a vexing issue facing Italian American writers. "Editors, influenced by Hollywood, popular taste, or their own bias, expect goons in action in Italian-American stories. The writer with a thoughtful, literary turn of mind is unlikely to find a sympathetic audience among them."[45]

That's not to say that there is no market for nonmob fiction by and about Italian Americans. Corporate attorney–turned-novelist Lisa Scottoline sometimes features Italian American characters and story lines in her popular legal thrillers. But the best-known and bestselling contemporary Italian American writer is Adriana Trigiani, author of a series of novels based on her atypical upbringing in the Virginia mountain town of Big Stone Gap. Her novels—*Big Stone Gap*, *Big Cherry Holler*, *Milk Glass Moon*, and *Queens of the Big Time*, along with *Lucia, Lucia*, which is set in New York—have won her a dedicated following among Italian Americans, particularly women.

Trigiani, the daughter of immigrants from the Puglia region of southern Italy, moved to New York when she was in her twenties, where she worked in television, scripting documentaries and writing for *The Cosby Show*. Her novels are by no means great literature, but they are infused with *italianità*—besides featuring Italian American characters and themes, some even include family recipes. But despite Trigiani's popularity—or is it because of it?—her work is largely ignored by critics in the field of Italian American studies.

Gay Talese and others have noted that Italian American filmmakers have achieved greater recognition and commercial success than have novelists and other fiction writers. For the most part, however, their Italian American films have been mob stories. The most successful movie about Italian Americans who aren't criminals remains *Moonstruck*, written by an Irish American, John Patrick Shanley, and directed by a Canadian Episcopalian, Norman Jewison. The romantic comedy, for which Cher won a Best Actress Oscar in 1988, earned some $85 million at the box office.

But other nonmobster Italian American films have barely registered with moviegoers. Stanley Tucci's *Big Night* (1997), a well-crafted tale of two immigrant brothers trying to make a go of their authentic Italian restaurant in the 1950s, was a hit with critics, but it earned $12 million, a piddling sum by Hollywood standards but enough to qualify it as an indie hit. John Turturro's *Mac*, Nancy Savoca's *Household Saints*, and Ray De Felitta's *Two-Family House*, however, all made $1 million or less. Even Chazz Palmintieri's well-reviewed *A Bronx Tale* topped out at about $18 million. Compare these figures to the hundreds of millions made by the *Godfather* films, or to the viewership for *The Sopranos*, which routinely exceeds the Nielsen numbers of broadcast television programs.

Chooch, a 2004 comedy, illustrated the difficulties of making and selling Italian American films that are not gangland dramas and that have broad box-office appeal. Joey Summa, Carmine Famiglietti, and Gino Cafarelli, from Queens, New York, wanted to capture the life and culture of their working-class ethnic neighborhood before it disappeared.

A movie producer, Steve Loglisci, had heard of the struggling trio's work, their one-act plays presented in out-of-the-way houses, and was a fan of their popular novelty tune, "HaYa Doin'?," which the Yankees adopted as a motivational anthem. (They had another New York area hit with "The 12 Days of Guido Christmas.") The friends told Loglisci "about the disappearing Italian neighborhoods of New York, about the need to do something unrelated to the mob—about this great Italian neighborhood in Queens, Corona Heights . . . Before long, and with $1 million in backing, they were shooting a broad comedy called 'Chooch,' a term derived from the Italian word for donkey. Roughly translated, it means lovable screw-up."[46]

Chooch, released in August 2004, tells the story of Dino Condito (Carmine Famiglietti), a Queens paisan who lets down his softball team by striking out in the bottom of the ninth inning against Hoboken, earning him the nickname "the Chooch." His cousin, improbably named Jubilene (Joey Summa), which sounds more like a female country singer than a New York Italian American, cashes in his savings from his first Holy Communion so he and the Chooch can enjoy a vacation in Cancún. When the cousins land in Mexico, they're abducted by a pair of thugs—something to do with a missing bag of money—and are left in the desert at the mercy of Mexican soldiers. Dino's Queens buddies, and his pet dachshund, eventually save the two cousins.

Chooch didn't impress the critics. "It's nice that two stand-up comics from Queens can make a movie about their neighborhood and some wacky fictional adventures. Nice, but that doesn't mean the film is worth anyone's time besides those of their families, friends, neighbors and the nice man from Connecticut who let them use his restaurant," wrote Anita Gates in *The New York Times*.[47] David Blaylock of *The Village Voice* commented, "Devoid of *Sopranos* stereotypes, the film charms with its p.c. portrayal of Italian Americans, yet the depiction of Mexicans veers toward the offensive."[48]

Not only critics were underwhelmed but audiences as well. *Chooch* earned a mere $31,000 at the box office, losing nearly all of producer Loglisci's modest investment.

The failure of *Chooch* and of other far superior nonmobster movies raises the question: Is there a market for Italian American stories in which the characters are none of the types that audiences have come to enjoy and expect?

"Among the creatures of film, syndication, and video who will not die are The Fonz of *Happy Days*, a macho Latin-lover type; Tony

Manero of *Saturday Night Fever*, a less intelligent Latin-lover type; Rocky Balboa, a brute; and Puzo's cast of colorful mafiosi," laments New York–based writer George Guida.[49] Noting that most Italian American stereotypes are male, Guida asks, "Do we need to reconstruct the public identity of the Italian-American man?" and answers in the affirmative.

Such reconstruction, however, must avoid the impulse to generate "positive images" to replace tired stereotypes. "I think the danger is then trying to sanitize those people so that they aren't as interesting," says television producer Tom Fontana. "Whenever you're trying to say, 'There's the good Italian,' the good Italian's an inherently dull Italian. Any character's only interesting because of both his flaws and his virtues. If you separate one from the other, then you don't have a well-defined character. So it's tricky. It's definitely tricky."

Fontana has avoided this trap by creating complex and surprising Italian American characters, some of them gangsters, as on his HBO prison series *Oz*, others not, such as the Giardellos on his previous show, the NBC network cop drama *Homicide*. Mike Giardello, a Baltimore police lieutenant, and his son Al, an FBI agent, were of mixed Italian American and African American ethnicity, a television first. Giardello *padre* was played by Yaphet Kotto; Giancarlo Esposito, who is actually black and Italian, played Al.

> They say that the great plays happen in time of national upheaval [Fontana notes]. Shakespeare wrote in a time, the Elizabethan era, when there was shit flying all over the place. The Greek playwrights wrote in times of enormous turmoil. Maybe my [baby-boomer] generation has had it too easy. I've had a good life. I know there are people who've had fucked-up parents or all kinds of shit happen to them, but I think basically our parents were trying to get us to a place where we were comfortable and we were happy.
>
> So what happens is that the problems that an Italian American writer would write about that aren't life and death in the mob become psychological and social—relationships, divorce, parents, children, so that it becomes more like everything, like

all the other kinds of writing that's out there. Because we're not in jeopardy as a group the way we were fifty years ago or sixty years ago or seventy-five years ago. We're not in jeopardy anymore with that kind of operatic-sized problems that the immigrants had to deal with. We're basically an hour-long family drama now.[50]

For one Italian American writer, that one-hour family drama is *The Sopranos*, and beyond that, there's nothing in Italo-America worth paying attention to or preserving. Maria Russo, a contributor to *Salon*, used her review of Maria Laurino's book *Were You Always an Italian?* as the jumping-off point for a harsh and remarkably ill-informed assessment of Italian American culture.

"It seems like a good time to be Italian-American," she begins. "*The Sopranos* has managed to make baked ziti and big hair seem cool, and among the *paesani* spirits are high . . . Seemingly out of nowhere, *The Sopranos* has added a level of complexity and emotional depth to the mob-story genre, and I admit that each time I see the show's sophisticated little gem of an introduction, with its long scroll of mostly Italian-American names, I feel something happy surge through me."[51]

But Russo distrusts her own inclination to slip into "a warm bath of ethnic pride" because "Italian-American culture is a mixed bag, full of goodies but also full of some truly rotten stuff." There is the "proud picture of Italian-Americans' family devotion, work ethic, resourcefulness and achievements against the odds," but also racism, xenophobia, low educational expectations, and "an emotional immaturity masquerading as 'passion.'"

Being Italian American, she says, "is a social and economic dead end for some, while for those with a firmer foothold in the middle class it's a psychological trap, a vague longing for connection to an immigrant culture that no longer exists and a motherland that has moved on."

Russo, like Bill Tonelli, sees the mob genre as "the most vital expression of Italian-American culture." It has attained that status because it takes "this kind of harsh, prosaic, limited third-generation immigrant life . . . these inarticulate, yearning palookas, and adds a veneer of glamour and excitement to their struggles. In a way, the very success of the Mafia-movie genre has caused Italian-Americans to strike a secret, perhaps unconscious bargain: The movies deliver a version of their ordinary life—the pasta, the Sinatra, the ever-present relatives—but with the thrill of always-impending violence and piles of money."

Despite her authoritative-sounding pronouncements, Russo doesn't really see Italian Americans. She views her coethnics in the most reductive, insulting, and yes, stereotypical terms, denying the existence of other Italian Americans who, like her, are educated and articulate, but unlike her, have a conception of *italianità* that flouts the caricatures she conjures up.

For Russo, *The Sopranos* represents the last gasp of Italian American culture, not just *il declino del padrino*, and from her perspective, that's a good thing.

A "revitalization" of Italian American culture is unlikely because there is

> very little feeding this particular ethnicity machine and no incentive for Italian-Americans to marry each other and produce kids who will consider being Italian-American a major part of who they are.
>
> In all the jubilation about the success of *The Sopranos*, it can't be lost on people that the show is recording the last days of the mob as we know it. It's also, therefore, a long, slow elegy for an Italian-American sense of identity that's bound to fade away as well. As I finished Laurino's book I realized . . . that the ultimate success of Italian-American culture will be its disappearance.

That last sentence is shocking, as Russo no doubt intended. A writer who had said the same thing about African American or Jewish American culture would be deemed racist or anti-Semitic, and rightly so. Russo conceives Italian American culture as static and frozen in time, somewhere in the mid-twentieth century, and incapable of dynamism or growth. And by conflating Italian American and mafia, she reveals not only her ignorance of what's actually happening in

Italo-America but also a lack of imagination and intellectual curiosity. Blinded by stereotypes, Russo sees no possibilities for culture beyond the dominant representations.

Her snobbery toward working-class Italian Americans, those she derides as "inarticulate, yearning palookas," means that someone like Johnny De Carlo, the self-professed proud "goomba," can't be anything but an embarrassing anachronism. No doubt she eagerly awaits his disappearance, along with his tracksuits, paunch, and neatly groomed hair. But his manifesto, as delivered in this book's previous chapter, makes it clear that he and his fellow goombas have no intention of going anywhere, except maybe to the neighborhood salumeria and the occasional "guy bar."

Italian Americans in general aren't ready to leave the stage of history and disappear into white America. As the United States census of 2000 revealed, Americans of Italian descent reverse the tendency of other groups of European origin to identify themselves as American rather than as members of a specific ethnic group or ancestral heritage. Rather than diminishing, individuals reporting Italian heritage actually increased 7 percent when compared to 1990 figures.[52]

It's not that Russo is entirely off base. Italian Americans do have a high rate of out-marriage, many do not know or care anything about contemporary Italy, and some do engage in a deplorable and self-defeating tribalism. But her vision is a partial and skewed one that by no means constitutes the full picture of contemporary Italo-America.

What Russo offers is a version of the "twilight of ethnicity" concept associated with the Italian American sociologist Richard Alba, who held that ethnicity is purely historical, tied to immigration and the first generation of Italian Americans, and recedes as the descendants of the immigrants become assimilated Americans.[53]

Some commentators maintain that much contemporary Italian American ethnicity is "symbolic," that is, "based on an identification with, and a 'feeling' for the heritage of a group or, more specifically, elements that have been 'abstracted' from the traditional cultural pattern like dietary items or folk art." This version of ethnicity has become more evident as Italian Americans increasingly move into the middle and upper middle classes.

But being Italian American seems to have implications beyond the symbolic. Italian American ethnicity "still appears to carry over into everyday life, generating some tensions with mainstream culture (e.g., coming to terms with ethnic familism and lingering prejudice). It can have instrumental, as well as expressive significance, in later generations." It is not entirely voluntary but instead "remains a category of social structure and a label, with attendant generalizations, imposed by others."[54]

These externally imposed generalizations are, of course, those of the Mafia myth and the related stereotype of the earthy but unintelligent and boorish prole. But what of the aspects of culture and identity embraced by Italian Americans themselves? Out of what ingredients do today's Italian Americans create their *italianità*?

Like many third-generation Americans of Italian descent, I grew up in a home where *italianità* was no distant memory but a lived experience. My parents pretty much stopped speaking their parents' dialects when they and other "old-timers" died off, keeping only curse words and various homey expressions like *Madonna mia, cappadost, stonato*.

But our ethnicity survived in daily life, in the foods my mother prepared, in the music she and my father loved (besides the Italian American icons Sinatra, Bennett, and Jimmy Roselli, my parents enjoyed Italian singers like Sergio Franchi and Caterina Valente), in the way we celebrated Christmas and other holidays, in the Italian immigrant parish where we attended Mass, in the importance we attached to familial and other face-to-face relationships, and in my parents' and other relatives' expressed mistrust of and alienation from mainstream, white-bread American culture. We called ourselves Italian, not Italian American, and most of our close relationships were with other paisans.

We watched TV shows like *Leave It to Beaver* and *Father Knows Best*, but they might as well have been science fiction, so fantastic and far removed from our own lives were these images of middle-class America.

Did I sometimes chafe at the bonds of ethnic and familial culture? Certainly, and especially as I became an angry and rebellious adolescent. But if I moved away from Italo-America, it was a short-lived separation, as I began to think seriously about my heritage while I was in my mid-twenties. I realized how much I'd been shaped by southern Italian history and culture, and I wanted to make sense of this rich but sometimes confusing and troubling legacy.

For me, Italian American identity entails coming to grips not only with the experience of my grandparents' and parents' generations, but also with Italy. First, I began to seriously study the Italian language. (Like many third-generation Italian Americans, I mainly knew the dialect words and expressions I'd picked up in my and my relatives' homes.) I had ample opportunity to practice what I learned on my travels to Italy, which became an annual pleasure. In my choice of Italian itineraries, I invert the racist northern Italian slogan about Africa beginning south of Rome; for me, that's where Italy starts. Not in Tuscany, so beloved by British travel writers and tourists, nor in Piedmont or Lombardy. But in Lazio, Campania, Calabria, and especially Sicily.

In those places, I felt all aspects of myself—ethnic heritage, sexuality, politics, cultural interests, and aesthetic sensibilities—come together, and at times also clash. In southern Italy I saw where the stuff of my ethnic identity came from, and came to understand myself better by understanding the ways in which I am like my Italian friends and how I am different from them.

My Italian experiences are also the reason I can never romanticize mafiosi as colorful outlaws and devoted family men. In Sicily, I felt the mafia's baleful presence in the soldiers guarding the homes of magistrates and driving through the streets of Palermo in military jeeps, in the roadside shrine on the stretch of highway where Giovanni Falcone and his entourage were blown up, and in my visit to the anti-mafia foundation established by Falcone's family.

My Sicilian friends told me what it was like to live in a place where criminal syndicates operated with near-impunity. One said his father had always refused to take him and his sisters to a famous amusement park because "bad men" owned it; another witnessed a murder on a city street in broad daylight when he was a child. Once, when several of us were at a street fair in Catania, the main city in eastern Sicily, a friend insisted we leave because he sensed tension in the crowd, which he attributed to the presence of rival clan members.

But the oddest encounter with the mafia as a fact of daily life came when I myself was mistaken for a "man of honor." My partner, Robert, and I, with six Sicilian friends, arrived at a seafood trattoria in the mafia-dominated coastal town of Castellammare del Golfo. As we entered the nearly empty restaurant late that summer afternoon, the fear and anxiety of the proprietor and his family were unmistakable. (A friend confirmed the accuracy of my perception.) I wondered what their reaction might have been had they known the eight strangers were not mafiosi but gay men.

These experiences made me understand better than any of the books I'd read or the films I'd seen why my grandparents had left this spectacularly beautiful island that I had come to love.

That I can "return" to Italy to enrich my *italianità*, and to construct an ethnic identity out of materials I select, depends, I know, upon a certain degree of privilege. But so what? Given where I came from, my modest roots in working-class Italo-America, I'll be damned if I'm going to feel guilty because I can afford (thanks to American Express Sign and Travel) airfare to Italy, decent accommodations, and good meals. It does mean, however, that beyond the givens of my name, Mediterranean phenotype, and upbringing, my ethnicity is chosen, constructed.

But it seems pointless to me whether it is "functional" or "expressive" or "symbolic," because it is all those things, depending upon time, place, and circumstance.

Like so many Americans of varying backgrounds, I have longed for a consistent and fulfilling identity in a society where consumer capitalist ideology generates needs and desires and declares money to be the absolute law. Self-conscious, middle-class, and university-educated people may more cogently articulate this longing, but others also feel it. Johnny De Carlo's defense of goombas and their culture embodies a resistance to cultural homogenization and to the exalting of consumer capitalist values over humanistic ones.

(But it's important to remember that a preoccupation with identity can have its downside. Identity-based politics can be parochial and limiting, at worst a form of tribalism, whether the tribe is defined in terms of race, ethnicity, sexuality, or some other social category. Whatever benefits a group may derive from such politics, it is crucial to maintain a conception of the public good that transcends particularism.)

Some Italian Americans may be living in Richard Alba's twilight of ethnicity, in which *italianità* is nothing more than a surname or a preference for Italian food. But for many others—including me—Italian American ethnicity continues to evolve, and is not fixed or tied to any one decade.

Stuart Hall, the British-Jamaican scholar who is a preeminent cultural theorist, observes that identity "is not something which already exists, transcending place, time, history and culture." Identities, he states, are "subject to the continual play of history, culture and power."

Hall maintains that identities, "far from being grounded in a mere 'recovery' of the past, which is waiting to be found, and which, when found, will secure our sense of ourselves into eternity," are actually the names "we give to the different ways we are positioned by, and position ourselves within, the narratives of the past."[55]

Joseph Sciorra, folklorist and a director of cultural programs at the City University of New York's John D. Calandra Italian American Institute, conceives Italian American identity in Hall's terms, as protean and fluid. Sciorra's Web site, *Italian Rap* (www.italianrap.com), is, he says, "part of an ongoing effort to develop a sense of *italianità* informed by history and vernacular culture that stands in opposition to ethnic chauvinism, racism, sexism, or homophobia."

Sciorra dedicates the Web site to "all you historians and writers, you painters, you healers, ecstatic dancers of *la pizzica tarantata*, sons and daughters of Artemesia Gentileschi and Louis Prima, you women warriors and Neapolitan Rastas, you piece workers and day laborers of poetry and prose, devotees of *La Madonna Nera*, you po-mo neo-*streghe*, you *nuovi briganti* leading the cultural insurrection for fresh ideas, a reinvented community, and a new vision of who we are and what we can become."

But as important as it is to pursue new visions, one cannot lose sight of the past, which has intrinsic significance. Rudolph Vecoli of the University of Minnesota, one the deans of Italian American his-

toriography, writes that Italian American history is "an epic story of a diaspora, the story of the tragedies and triumphs of millions, the story of
generations struggling to reconcile the old and the new. It is neither
grander, nor meaner than the story of other migrant peoples, *but it is
our story.*"

But the Italian American experience also has broader significance.
Americans of Italian background, Vecoli notes, have "collectively comprised a considerable segment of the American population; there is no
sphere of life in which our presence has not been manifest. To delete
that experience is to omit a big slice of American history." Vecoli insists
that Italian Americans belong in any national conversation about "our
sources of diversity and of unity."[56]

Honest, critical dialogue among Italian Americans is as important
as participating in that national conversation. Not defensive posturing
or ethnic cheerleading, but an exchange that confronts difficult questions and is unafraid of dialectics, because "without contraries [there]
is no progression."[57] Earlier in Italian American history, when the Italian language was still widely spoken, there was no shortage of critical
discourse and internal critique. Nor had Italian Americans forgotten
the social inequities and the political repression that had driven so
many Italians to emigrate from the Mezzogiorno.

The waning of this tradition of lively dialectical critique has rendered Italian American public discourse ineffectual on such vital matters as racism, as the most prominent Italian American voices during
the racial crises in Bensonhurst and other New York neighborhoods
were not those of intellectuals or advocacy groups but of street-corner
bigots. It has also meant that the response to mafia stereotyping all too
often has been simplistic, knee-jerk, and tainted by an invidious attitude toward other ethnic or social minorities.

Italian American educators, artists, and activists are working to
remedy this situation. Robert Viscusi founded the Italian American
Writers Association in the wake of the Bensonhurst tragedy to foster
discursive power and promote critical dialogue. Fred Gardaphé, another Italian American visionary, wants to create university-based think
tanks to solidify Italian American studies and bring to the discipline
"the rigor and power of African American and Jewish culture."

Gardaphé envisions establishing these centers "in cities where there were mob families"—New York, Chicago, San Francisco, Los Angeles, New Orleans, Las Vegas, and Kansas City. "The idea is to replace the mob with academia," he says. He focuses on these cities because the academic centers "need to be where Italian Americans are; you can't do this where there is no community."

What he's proposing is daunting and perhaps quixotic—in effect he wants colleges and universities to compensate for the failures of Italian American families and institutions to transmit cultural heritage to successive generations. But his is also an admirable and necessary project, because the lack of cultural transmission has meant that too many young Italian Americans know themselves only through skewed pop-culture images. They know all about Vito Corleone but not Vito Marcantonio, John Gotti but not John Fante.

As a young man in Chicago, Gardaphé was exposed to and tempted by mob life, but he says he found his way "out of the streets" through academia. He is convinced that there will be "a post-mafia renaissance in Italian American culture . . . You have to see what Italian American writers are producing these days, and there's a lot out there."

Some of "what's out there," in writing and other creative activity, includes organizations like the Italian American Writers Association; the feminist cultural collective Malia; academic centers such as the Calandra Italian American Institute at the City University of New York; Casa Italiana of New York University; and Gardaphé's Italian American Studies program at the State University of New York at Stony Brook on Long Island; and publications such as *Voices in Italian Americana*, *Fra Noi*, and the *Italian American Review*.

New, critical interpretations of Italian American history and culture are coming from organizations such as the American Italian Historical Association; and from academics such as Luisa Del Giudice, director of the Italian Oral History Institute in Los Angeles; folklorist and cultural programmer Joseph Sciorra; literary critics Robert Viscusi, Anthony Julian Tamburri, and Louise De Salvo; the historians Philip V. Cannistraro, Salvatore Salerno, Jennifer Guglielmo, Robert Orsi, Donna Gabaccia, and many others.

Michael Imperioli and his wife, Victoria, a theatrical designer, brought some *italianità* to New York's off-Broadway scene in 2004 when they founded Studio Dante in Manhattan. In a tiny but beautiful space (designed by Mrs. Imperioli) modeled on an Italian opera house, Studio Dante presents realist urban dramas, often with Italian American themes and performers. Its production *Baptism by Fire*, a new play by John D'Appolito about the troubled relationship between an Italian American father and his son, starred Vince Curatola, better known as New York mob boss Johnny Sack on *The Sopranos*; the theater's second production, *Ponies*, featured Imperioli and John "Artie Bucco" Ventimiglia.

Studio Dante also presents work that flouts the usual popcult images of Italian Americans, such as *Twisted Head*, a one-man show written and performed by actor-screenwriter Carl Capotorto (*Mac*, *The Sopranos*) about growing up Sicilian American and gay in the Bronx.

The Guild of Italian American Actors, a revitalized version of the New York–based Italian Actors Union founded in 1937, established the GIAA Ensemble Artists Repertory Theater Company, Inc. (GEAR), in January 2004. GEAR focuses on readings and performances of plays by Italians and Italian Americans, regardless of subject matter.

The guild aims to promote "a positive image of Italian Americans and Italians in the media," but the organization echoes Chazz Palmintieri's comment that "actors gotta eat," and recognizes that performers of Italian background may sometimes need to portray "negative types" in order to work in the entertainment industry. GIAA warns antidefamationists that "criticism directed at GIAA actors by well meaning but otherwise misguided Italian Americans will not be tolerated by GIAA. Such people/groups will better serve our mutual goal of promoting positive images of Italian Americans by joining with us to assist writers with good scripts in obtaining financing for their positive image projects rather than singling out individual actors for criticism."

Rudolph Vecoli observed that Italian American history began with "an epic story of a diaspora," the great migration from southern Italy. Josephine Gattuso Hendin, a critic and novelist who teaches literature at New York University, speaks of a second diaspora, "from post-World-War-II urban Little Italys throughout America."

The first "transposed Italian lives into the new world; the second preserved *italianità* by a process of appropriation or reinterpretation. Both journeys produced narratives of cultural collision and change."[58]

Gattuso Hendin says that recent Italian American writing, work produced since the second diaspora, "constitutes an emerging ethnic aesthetic which . . . revolutionizes our thinking about current art with a powerful return to realism about the continuities of history, and to symbolism in dealing with the complexity of individual experience."

This new Italian American literature, grounded in both the realistic and the symbolic, could provide source material for mass-audience, pop-culture media such as film and television. I for one would love to see a talented Italian American auteur adapt *A Fine Place*, Nicholas Montemarano's quietly powerful novel about the impact of an atrocious racial crime—the killing of a black teenager—on a young Italian American who had been a reluctant perpetrator, and on his troubled family.[59]

Montemarano's is not an uplifting, "positive" novel about Italian Americans. It is a pain-filled, disturbing work, but also a wise and compassionate one. Ezra Pound famously proclaimed that "artists are the antennae of the race," and Montemarano lives up to that dictum by transmitting truths that institutions and individuals who claim to speak for Italian Americans are unwilling to face.

Literature need not be the only source for new Italian American stories; they also will come from the way Italian Americans live today. Two newspaper accounts offer rich raw material just waiting to be transformed into art.

East New York, a section of Brooklyn, had been a working-class Italian American neighborhood for many decades. But more recently, it has been home to other immigrant communities, Latinos and Caribbean blacks. The area also has suffered from many of the ills affecting poor communities, including crime, violence, and homelessness. A *New York Times* story provided a moving account of how one former resident, Mary Calderone Brill, returned to the neighborhood after nearly forty years and established a bond with Gerald and Shirley Hazel, elderly black immigrants from Guyana who were the current residents of her childhood home, the modest wood and brick house that her immigrant father Salvatore Calderone had built in the 1920s.[60]

As Mary Calderone Brill and her grandson Jake Mooney, the *Times* reporter, converse with the Hazels, the Italian past and the Guyanese present converge in a dialogue of shared attitudes and aspirations. Mary, Gerald, and Shirley recognize their commonalities; at one point, Gerald Hazel says to Mary, "You know what you remind me of? Back home. This is how we grew up back home."

Unlike East New York, the Queens neighborhood of Middle Village remains home to a large Italian American community. There, in January 2005, a purported hate crime occurred in which both the perpetrators and the victim were Italian Americans. Daniel Romano, twenty, had long scandalized residents of his working-class neighborhood with his outlandish appearance—his blue bouffant hairdo, black clothing and fingernails, and the large crucifix he wears upside down. Local residents teased him for dressing like a "Goth kid," a freak in "a community with small homes, neat lawns and populated with many Roman Catholics."

But Romano is in actuality a professed Satanist, and his religious beliefs apparently offended two local teenagers, Paul C. Rotondi and Frank M. Scarpinito, who attacked him with a metal club and an ice scraper. When the youths were arrested, they were charged with hate crimes, which carry harsher penalties. (Such charges are usually brought when an attack involves a victim's ethnicity, religion, or sexual orientation.) George J. Farrugia, an assistant district attorney, said the defendants believed that Daniel Romano worshiped Satan and "over the last month and a half, they have had it in for this kid . . ."

Romano told *The New York Times* that he was raised Catholic but is now a Satanist. "My allegiance is to Satan and I hate Christianity, Judaism and Islam, but I don't hurt anyone," he said. "I take out my anger in mosh pits and S-and-M clubs. I think it's ironic that the Christians got violent with the Satanist." Daniel's mother, a practicing Catholic, said that although her boy worships the devil, he's a good kid who "doesn't hurt nobody."[61]

Spike Lee's *Summer of Sam* featured an improbable Italian American character who was an outcast in his neighborhood, but Romano's story is the real thing, a bizarrely fascinating account of a misfit's rebellion against his ethnic community. Though my own adolescent revolt never involved Satan worship, I can relate.

The image of Italian Americans in popular culture will continue to be a contested one, shaped by the Mafia myth but also by resistance to it. Images will be generated from the grassroots and by the economics of the entertainment industry. Clichéd and stereotypical images will continue to be made and marketed, because pop culture always has dealt in marketable tropes and clichés, and not only of Italian Americans.

The sassy and indomitable black woman, the scary underclass black male, the spitfire Latina, the amusing campy homosexual (and his obverse, the kinky sexual outlaw), the Asian martial arts genius and the techie nerd—these and other stereotypes abound. They flatten, even distort the realities of complex lives. But then popular culture rarely deals with race and ethnicity with the insight, subtlety, and originality that advocates demand. This means that the entertainment media may very well continue to depict Italian Americans as mobsters, boors, and buffoons, and as people obsessed with food and family.

But consider another possibility. Italian Americans owe their high visibility in American popular culture in large measure to the very gangster image so many deplore. If the mafioso as cultural archetype were to become extinct, might Italian Americans themselves drop off the radar screen? Today the lead roles in the continuing American drama of immigration, discrimination, and assimilation are played by Latinos and Asians. As their stories increasingly are told, descendants of the European immigrants, including Italians, may discover that they've become irrelevant. In other words, the demise of the Mafia myth just might mean the end of the Italian American as a protagonist in American popular culture.

Some, like the writer Maria Russo, may welcome this development. But I prefer to side with Fred Gardaphé, Josephine Gattuso Hendin, Robert Viscusi, Stuart Hall, and all those who insist that ethnic identity and art need not—indeed, must not—be grounded in nostalgia for the past and immutably fixed in time. Ethnicity remains a riveting, complicated drama of American life, and popular art that illuminates its workings still is needed. Whether we Italian Americans continue to produce mobsters, fictional or actual, the Mafia myth cannot be the last word about our lives and culture. Italian America still has many more stories to tell.

Notes

INTRODUCTION

1. George De Stefano, "UnGoodfellas," *Nation*, February 7, 2000.
2. Bill Carter, "Fewer Whacks, But a Bigger Hit," *New York Times*, December 15, 2002.
3. Ellen Willis, "Our Mobsters, Ourselves," *Nation*, April 2, 2001.
4. Stephen Holden, "Sympathetic Brutes in a Pop Masterpiece," *New York Times*, June 6, 1999.
5. Sarah Boxer, "Therapists Go Crazy for One in Sopranos," *New York Times*, December 29, 2001.
6. "Dress Like Tony," *Newsday*, March 11, 2003.
7. Jeff Giles, "Al Pacino Says He Did Not Enjoy His Early Success," *Newsweek*, June 3, 2002.
8. "Gotti," like his idol and namesake, may find himself living not so large in a federal prison. In January 2005 he was indicted on federal charges of laundering profits from drugs sold by his friend, Kenneth "Supreme" McGriff, through his record company.
9. Clyde Haberman, "A Stereotype Hollywood Can't Refuse," *New York Times*, July 30, 1999.
10. George De Stefano, "Family Lies," *Film Comment*, August 1987, 23.
11. Robert Warshow, *The Immediate Experience: Movies, Comics, Theatre and Other Aspects of Popular Culture* (New York: Atheneum, 1971).
12. Ethel Spector Person, "Knowledge and Authority: The Godfather Fantasy," *Journal of the American Psychoanalytic Association* 49, no. 4. (Fall 2001).
13. Daniel Bell, *The End of Ideology* (Cambridge, Mass.: Harvard University Press, 1988).
14. Charles Strum, "Even a Mobster Needs Someone to Talk To," *New York Times*, January 3, 1999.
15. Terry Golway, "Italian Americans Are Making It Clear That They Are Fed Up with the Culture's Cartoon-Like Treatment of Their Lives," *America*, March 27, 1999, 6.

16. "The Sopranos and Other Stereotypes: How Harmful Are They?" NIAF Round-table, May 15, 2001.
17. Tom Robbins, "The Mob Was the City's Watchdog," *Village Voice*, March 28, 2003.
18. Lizzie Francke, "A Labor of Love," *Guardian*, December 30, 1993.
19. Felicia Lee, "Italian American Stories Without Bullets," *New York Times*, April 22, 2001.
20. Clyde Haberman, "Where's Ivan (The Terrible) Sopranoff?" *New York Times*, June 12, 2002.

1. ITALIANS TO ITALIAN AMERICANS: ESCAPING THE "SOUTHERN PROBLEM"
1. Sandra Mortola Gilbert, "Mafioso," in Regina Barreca, ed., *A Sitdown with "The Sopranos"* (New York: Palgrave Macmillan, 2002).
2. Mario Puzo, *The Godfather Papers . . . and Other Confessions* (Greenwich, Conn.: Fawcett Crest, 1972), 182.
3. Ibid.
4. David A. J. Richards, *Italian American: The Racializing of an Ethnic Identity* (New York: New York University Press, 1999), 98–99.
5. Ibid., 99–100.
6. Richard Gambino, *Blood of My Blood* (New York: Anchor/Doubleday, 1974), 63.
7. Antonio Gramsci, *The Southern Question* (West Lafayette, Ind.: Bordighera, 1995), 20.
8. Gambino, *Blood of My Blood*, 70.
9. Antonio Gramsci, *Selections from the Prison Notebooks* (New York: International Publishers, 1971).
10. Richards, *Italian American*, 107.
11. Gambino, *Blood of My Blood*, 42.
12. Richards, *Italian American*, 112.
13. Jerre Mangione and Ben Morreale, *La Storia* (New York: HarperCollins, 1992), 102.
14. Ibid., 103.
15. Gambino, *Blood of My Blood*, 85.
16. Puzo, *Godfather Papers*, 183.
17. Mangione and Morreale, *La Storia*, 105–106.
18. Puzo, *Godfather Papers*, 183.
19. Mangione and Morreale, *La Storia*, 340–341.
20. Ibid.
21. Salvatore J. La Gumina, ed., *Wop! A Documentary History of Anti-Italian Discrimination in the United States* (San Francisco: Straight Arrow Books, 1973), 28.
22. Ibid., 41.
23. Ibid., 142.

24. Ibid., 135, 136.
25. Ibid., 67.
26. Ibid., 140.
27. Ibid., 15.
28. Matthew Frye Jacobson, *Whiteness of a Different Color: European Immigrants and the Alchemy of Race* (Cambridge, Mass.: Harvard University Press, 1998), 57.
29. Ibid.
30. Ibid., 4.
31. Gay Talese, *Unto the Sons* (New York: Knopf, 1992), 462.
32. Ibid.
33. Ibid., 463.
34. Gambino, *Blood of My Blood*, 3.
35. Robert A. Orsi, *The Madonna of 115th Street* (New Haven, Conn.: Yale University Press, 1985), xix.
36. Ibid., xix, 21.
37. Ibid., 78.
38. Ibid., 82.
39. Ibid., 82–83.
40. Ibid., 84.
41. Katherine Narducci, telephone interview by the author, July 5, 2002.
42. Orsi, *Madonna of 115th Street*, 98–99.
43. Ibid., 103–104.
44. Narducci, telephone interview by author.
45. Leonard Shecter and William Phillips, *On The Pad* (New York: Berkley Medallion Books, 1973), 196, 284.
46. Orsi, *Madonna of 115th Street*, 128.
47. Ibid., 128–129.
48. Ibid., 104.
49. La Gumina, *Wop!*, 16.
50. George De Stefano, "Family Lies," *Film Comment*, August 1987.
51. The rumor was decisively debunked by Kitty Kelley, in *His Way*, her 1986 biography of Sinatra. Kelley, no admirer of Sinatra, also refuted Puzo's implication that Sinatra's gangster pals got him released from his contract with Tommy Dorsey by threatening the bandleader's life.
52. La Gumina, *Wop!*, 18.
53. Gambino, *Blood of My Blood*, 305.
54. Mangione and Morreale, *La Storia*, 405.
55. Howard Kurtz, "Cuomo Hails Story Rebutting Rumors of Crime Ties," *Washington Post*, October 28, 1987.
56. Gay Talese, telephone interview by the author, March 2003.
57. Ibid.
58. "Political Profiling of Italian-Americans an Alarming Trend," OSIA Press Release, October 17, 2002.

2. THE MAFIA: MEDITERRANEAN MENACE, AMERICAN MYTH

1. "Kefauver's Mafia Exposé," *Washington Post*, March 1, 1999.
2. Jerre Mangione and Ben Morreale, *La Storia* (New York: HarperCollins, 1992), 261.
3. Daniel Bell, *The End of Ideology* (Cambridge, Mass.: Harvard University Press, 1988), 141.
4. Mangione and Morreale, *La Storia*, 254.
5. Stephen Fox, *Blood and Power: Organized Crime in Twentieth Century America* (New York: Penguin, 1989), 342.
6. Ibid., 342–343.
7. Nick Tosches, *Dino: Living High in the Dirty Business of Dreams* (New York: Dell, 1992), 365–366.
8. Mangione and Morreale, *La Storia*, 347.
9. Alexander Stille, *Excellent Cadavers* (New York: Pantheon, 1992), 14–15.
10. Diego Gambetta, *The Sicilian Mafia: The Business of Private Protection* (Cambridge, Mass.: Harvard University Press, 1993), 84.
11. Ibid., 145.
12. Anton Blok, *The Mafia of a Sicilian Village, 1860–1960* (New York: Harper and Row, 1974).
13. Gambetta, *Sicilian Mafia*, 1.
14. Ibid., 2, 3.
15. Ibid., 3.
16. Ibid., 7.
17. Paul Ginsborg, *Italy and Its Discontents* (New York: Palgrave Macmillan, 2003), 196.
18. Ibid.
19. Gambetta, *Sicilian Mafia*, 7.
20. Ginsborg, *Italy*, 195.
21. Gambetta, *Sicilian Mafia*, 84–85.
22. Ibid.
23. Ibid., 98–99.
24. Gay Talese, *Honor Thy Father* (New York: Ivy Books, 1992), 163.
25. Ibid., 165.
26. Blok, *Mafia of a Sicilian Village*, 199.
27. For detailed accounts of the collaboration between the mafia and Christian Democratic politicians, see Jane C. Schneider and Peter T. Schneider, *Reversible Destiny: Mafia, Anti-Mafia, and the Struggle for Palermo* (Berkeley: University of California Press, 2003); and Stille, *Excellent Cadavers*.
28. Richard Gambino, *Blood of My Blood* (New York: Anchor/Doubleday, 1974), 293.
29. Ibid.
30. Gambetta, *Sicilian Mafia*, 259.
31. George De Stefano, "Family Lies," *Film Comment*, August 1987, 23.
32. Ibid.
33. Gambino, *Blood of My Blood*, 280–281.

34. De Stefano, "Family Lies," 22.
35. Ibid., 24.
36. Ibid.
37. Gambino, *Blood of My Blood*, 286.
38. Ibid., 298.
39. James B. Jacobs with Coleen Friel and Robert Raddick, *Gotham Unbound: How New York City Was Liberated from the Grip of Organized Crime* (New York: New York University Press, 1999), 7.
40. Gary W. Potter, "Organized Crime and the Mafia," http://www.policestudies.eku.edu.
41. Ibid.
42. Gambino, *Blood of My Blood*, 298
43. Donald Cressey, a leading proponent of the "Cosa Nostra" model of organized crime, based his 1969 book, *Theft of the Nation: The Structure and Operations of Organized Crime in America*, primarily on official data collected by federal agencies. His critics, including Dwight Smith (*The Mafia Mystique*, 1990), argue that a focus on Italian American crime groups can yield only a partial picture of organized crime in America, and not even of its most important aspects, which Smith sees as the national drug trade, which is not controlled by Italians, and "the rise in exorbitant white collar crimes," also not an Italian specialty.
44. Francis Ianni, "Organized Crime, an Integral and Indigenous Part of the American Social and Economic System," *Washington Post*, September 29, 1977.
45. Ibid.
46. Megan Sharp, "Romanticizing the Mafia," *Clio's Eye: A Film and Audio Visual Magazine for the Historian* (http://clioseye.sfasu.edu), Spring 2002.
47. Jacobs, *Gotham Unbound*, 131.
48. Ibid.
49. Ibid., 132.
50. Edward Conlon, "Mob Stories; Our Crime Correspondent Gives an Aficionado's Tour of the American Mafia," *American Spectator*, November 1992.
51. Jacobs, *Gotham Unbound*, 1.
52. Ibid., 9.
53. James B. Jacobs, interview by the author, New York City, May 15, 2002.
54. Pete Hamill, "Execs Make Mob Look Legit," New York *Daily News*, August 5, 2002.
55. George De Stefano, "UnGoodfellas," *Nation*, February 7, 2000, 32.
56. William K. Rashbaum, "After Mob Defections, U.S. Indicts Man It Calls a Boss," *New York Times*, January 10, 2003.
57. William Glaberson, "Peter Gotti Is Convicted in Mob Trial," *New York Times*, March 18, 2003.
58. Ibid.
59. Jacobs, *Gotham Unbound*, 1.
60. U.S. Senate Permanent Subcommittee on Investigations, *Organized Crime: 25 Years After Valachi*, 101st Congress, April 11–29, 1988, 206.
61. Tom Fontana, interview by the author, New York City, August 23, 2002.

62. Martin Scorsese, in "TimesTalks" dialogue with Janet Maslin, Museum of the Moving Image, Astoria, N.Y., November 17, 2002.
63. Jack Newfield, "Dumb-Dumb's Bullets," *New York*, April 7–14, 2003.
64. Ibid.
65. Gay Talese, telephone interview by the author, March 11, 2003.

3. A GENRE IS BORN: THE APPEAL OF PURE POWER

1. Carlos Clarens, *Crime Movies: An Illustrated History* (New York: Norton, 1980), 33.
2. Robert Casillo, "Moments in Italian-American Cinema: From *Little Caesar* to Coppola and Scorsese," in A. J. Tamburri, P. A. Giordano, and F. L. Gardaphé, eds., *From the Margin: Writings in Italian Americana* (West Lafayette, Ind.: Purdue University Press, 1991), 375.
3. Ibid., 54.
4. Ibid., 84.
5. Clarens, *Crime Movies*, 85.
6. Casillo, "Moments in Italian-American Cinema," 378.
7. Ibid.
8. Clarens, *Crime Movies*, 93.
9. Ibid., 379.
10. Ibid.
11. Stephen Fox, *Blood and Power: Organized Crime in Twentieth Century America* (New York: Penguin, 1989), 35, 46.
12. George De Stefano, "Family Lies," *Film Comment*, August 1987, 22.
13. Jonathan Munby, *Public Enemies, Public Heroes: Screening the Gangster from "Little Caesar" to "Touch of Evil"* (Chicago: University of Chicago Press, 1999), 54, 55.
14. Clarens, *Crime Movies*, 82.
15. Gay Talese, *Unto the Sons* (New York: Knopf, 1992), 462.
16. Munby, *Public Enemies*, 31.
17. Ibid.
18. Ibid., 32.
19. Robert Warshow, *The Immediate Experience: Movies, Comics, Theatre and Other Aspects of Popular Culture* (New York: Atheneum, 1971), 137.
20. Munby, *Public Enemies*, 58.
21. Ibid., 60.
22. Ibid., 61.
23. Ibid.
24. Fred Gardaphé, "Fresh Garbage: The Gangster as Suburban Trickster," in Regina Barreca, ed., *A Sitdown with "The Sopranos"* (New York: Palgrave Macmillan, 2002), 94.
25. Ibid., 94–95.

26. Ibid., 95.

27. Casillo, "Moments in Italian-American Cinema," 379.

28. Gardaphé, "Fresh Garbage," 97.

29. Clarens, *Crime Movies*, 89.

30. Ibid., 192.

31. Casillo, "Moments in Italian-American Cinema," 380.

32. Ibid. After Victor Mature died in 1999, I was shocked to discover that the dark-complexioned, sleepy-eyed actor was not an Italian American whose real name was Maturo, as I had grown up believing, but instead was the son of immigrants from Austria and Switzerland. My misconception about Mature's ethnicity was the only instance in which my parents, and other Italian Americans I knew, misidentified a non-Italian as an Italian with a changed name. Finding the paisan behind the Anglo surname was a favorite pastime of Italian Americans when I was growing up. Singers Frankie Laine and Bobby Darin, actors John Saxon and Aldo Ray, actresses Anne Bancroft and Paula Prentiss—these and others were pegged as paisans who "passed."

33. Ibid., 381.

34. Richard Gambino, *Blood of My Blood* (New York: Anchor/Doubleday, 1974), 288.

35. Casillo, "Moments in Italian-American Cinema," 380.

36. Ibid., 383.

37. Clarens, *Crime Movies*, 272–273.

38. Ibid., 273.

39. Casillo, "Moments in Italian-American Cinema," 382.

40. Ibid.

41. Clarens, *Crime Movies*, 27.

42. Ibid., 271, 280.

43. David Chase, interview by Peter Bogdanovich, in *The Sopranos: The Complete First Season*, HBO Home Video.

44. Warshow, *Immediate Experience*, 130.

45. Leo Braudy, "Genre: The Conventions of Connection," in Gerald Mast, Marshall Cohen, and Leo Braudy, eds., *Film Theory and Criticism* (New York: Oxford University Press, 1992), 435–452.

46. Ibid., 438.

47. Gambino, *Blood of My Blood*, 354.

48. Ibid., 309.

49. De Stefano, "Family Lies," 26.

50. Matthew Purdy, "Gangstas vs. Gangsters, All Knockoffs," *New York Times*, December 11, 2002.

51. Patrick Goldstein, "Hollywood's Marriage to the Mob; This Fall's Crime Wave Is Just the Latest Round in the Movies' Long-Running Love Affair with Gangsters and Godfathers," *Los Angeles Times*, September 23, 1990.

52. Raymond De Felitta, interview by the author, New York City, June 21, 2002.

53. Ann Patchett, "Scared Senseless," *New York Times Magazine*, October 20, 2002.

54. Lorenzo Carcaterra, "John Gotti's Greatest Hits," *Details*, December 2000, 110–113.

55. Ibid.

56. Susan King, "Hangin' With the Mob; Director Mike Newell Personally Researched His New Film 'Donnie Brasco,' " *Los Angeles Times*, February 27, 1997.

57. Ethel Spector Person, "Knowledge and Authority: The Godfather Fantasy," *Journal of the American Psychoanalytic Association* 49, no. 4 (Fall 2001): 1143.

58. Ibid., 1146.

59. Mario Puzo, *The Godfather* (New York: Signet, 1978), 14.

60. Michael Parenti, *Make-Believe Media* (New York: St. Martin's, 1992), 160–161.

61. Ibid.

62. Goldstein, "Hollywood's Marriage to the Mob."

63. Clarens, *Crime Movies*, 138.

4. DON CORLEONE WAS MY GRANDFATHER

1. Harlan Lebo, *The Godfather Legacy* (New York: Fireside/Simon and Schuster, 1997), 19.

2. Ibid., 23.

3. Ibid.

4. *The Kid Stays in the Picture* (2002), a documentary film directed by Nanette Burstein and Brett Morgen, from Robert Evans's book of the same name.

5. Lebo, *Godfather Legacy*, 23.

6. *A Decade Under the Influence* (2003), a documentary film directed by Jonathan Demme and produced by Independent Film Channel (IFC).

7. Lebo, *Godfather Legacy*, 25.

8. Mario Puzo, *The Godfather Papers . . . and Other Confessions* (New York: Fawcett Crest, 1972), 58.

9. Lebo, *Godfather Legacy*, 58.

10. *The Fortunate Pilgrim* got a second life as a 1988 television miniseries, starring Sophia Loren as Lucia Santa, with John Turturro and Annabella Sciorra, young actors at the start of their careers, as the mob-connected son Lorenzo and the rebellious daughter Octavia.

11. Puzo, *Godfather Papers*, 34.

12. Ibid., 3.

13. Ibid., 4.

14. Ibid.

15. *A Decade Under the Influence*.

16. Puzo, *Godfather Papers*, 64.

17. *A Decade Under the Influence*.

18. Vera Dika, "The Representation of Ethnicity in *The Godfather*," in Nick Browne, ed., *Francis Ford Coppola's "The Godfather" Trilogy* (New York: Cambridge University Press, 2000), 76–108.

19. Ibid., 84.

20. Ibid., 88.

21. Richard Gambino, *Blood of My Blood* (New York: Anchor/Doubleday, 1974), 14.

22. George Guida, "Novel Paesans," *Melus*, Summer 2001, http://www.findarticles
.com/p/articles/mi_m2278/is_2_26/ai_80852620.

23. Dika, "Representation of Ethnicity," 89.

24. Fred Gardaphé, *Italian Signs, American Streets* (Durham, N.C.: Duke University Press, 1996), 89.

25. Ibid.

26. Albert Mobilio, *Salon.com*, July 9, 1999.

27. Allen Barra, "The Schlockfather," *Salon.com*, July 20, 2000.

28. Richard Gambino, "Despair, Italian Style," *Village Voice*, May 23, 1974.

29. Ibid.

30. Bill Tonelli, "The Godmother: The Woman Who Taught Mario Puzo the Value of Secrecy," *Slate.com*, May 9, 2003. Tonelli perhaps didn't realize just how apt was his comparison between two American clans, one real, the other fictional but so vividly brought to life on-screen that we speak of the Corleones as if they really existed. Joseph Kennedy, the Irish American patriarch, was a gangster who made his fortune in bootlegging, doing business with the likes of Frank Costello, Al Capone, and others. "As big a crook as we've got anywhere in this country," said Harry Truman of Kennedy, while Franklin D. Roosevelt, Jr., pronounced him "one of the most evil, disgusting men I have ever known" (Stephen Fox, *Blood and Power: Organized Crime in Twentieth Century America* [New York: Penguin, 1990], 308). But like Vito Corleone, the shady Hibernian had great hopes for his sons, who would redeem the family honor by rising in the "legitimate" world of politics. John F. Kennedy, however, wouldn't have made it to the White House had it not been for the help he got from his father's underworld connections (ibid., 335).

31. Ibid.

32. Ibid.

33. Robert Viscusi, interview by the author, Brooklyn, N.Y., May 3, 2002.

34. Seth Schiesel, "How to Be Your Own Godfather," *New York Times*, July 10, 2005.

35. Mobilio, *Salon.com*, July 9, 1999.

36. Charles McGrath, "Knocked Off," *New York Times*, November 10, 2002.

37. Puzo, *Godfather Papers*, 41.

38. Ibid.

39. Mario Puzo, *The Godfather* (New York: Signet, 1978), 14.

40. Carlos Clarens, *Crime Movies: An Illustrated History* (New York: Norton, 1980), 277.

41. Alessandro Camon, "*The Godfather* and the Mythology of Mafia," in Nick Browne, ed., *Francis Ford Coppola's "The Godfather" Trilogy* (New York: Cambridge University Press, 2000), 57–75.

42. Ibid., 58.

43. Jane C. Schneider and Peter T. Schneider, *Reversible Destiny: Mafia, Antimafia, and the Struggle for Palermo* (Berkeley: University of California Press, 2003).

44. Ibid., 3.
45. Camon, "*Godfather* and the Mythology," 59.
46. Ibid.
47. Ibid.
48. Ibid., 60.
49. Ibid., 59.
50. John Blades, "One Man's Mafia," *Chicago Tribune*, August 9, 1996.
51. Larry McShane, " 'Godfather' Author Mario Puzo Dead at 78," Associated Press, July 3, 1999.
52. Puzo, *Godfather Papers*, 36.
53. Ibid.
54. McShane, " 'Godfather' Author."
55. Joseph D. Pistone, *The Way of the Wiseguy* (Philadelphia: Running Press, 2004), 147.
56. Camon, "*Godfather* and the Mythology," 70–71.
57. Ibid., 71.
58. Ibid., 60.
59. Puzo, *The Godfather*, 291.
60. Ibid., 285.
61. Ibid., 222.
62. Ibid.
63. Alessia Ricciardi, "Toward an Italian-American Sublime: The Case of *The Godfather*," *Voices in Italian Americana* 11 (Spring 2000): 15–27.
64. Ibid., 27.
65. Clarens, *Crime Movies*, 277.
66. Puzo, *The Godfather*, 290.
67. Clarens, *Crime Movies*, 277.
68. Ibid.
69. Vincent Canby, "Review: 'The Godfather,' " *New York Times*, March 16, 1972.
70. Camon, "*Godfather* and the Mythology," 65.
71. Clarens, *Crime Movies*, 289.
72. Ibid., Mike Bygrave, "A Family Business," *The Guardian*, December 31, 1988.
73. Clarens, *Crime Movies*, 285–87.
74. Stephen Fox, "Family History." American Movie Channel, www.amctv.com.
75. Jerry Capeci, *The Complete Idiot's Guide to the Mafia* (New York: Alpha, 2002), 209.
76. Ibid., 209.
77. Puzo, *The Godfather*, 246.
78. Clarens, *Crime Movies*, 278.
79. Ibid.
80. Fox, *Blood and Power*, 371.
81. Puzo, *The Godfather*, 17.
82. Ibid., 133.
83. Lebo, *Godfather Legacy*, 37.

84. Ibid.

85. Ibid.

86. Ibid., 38.

87. John Denvir, "Myth and Meaning: Francis Ford Coppola and Popular Response to the *Godfather* Trilogy," in John Denvir, ed., *Legal Reelism: Movies as Legal Texts* (Urbana: University of Illinois Press, 1996), 1–22.

88. This is no longer true. Sicily has produced many police officials and magistrates. See Gore Vidal's essay on the Sicilian author Leonardo Sciascia, "Sciascia's Italy," in *The Second American Revolution* (New York: Vintage, 1983), 96. Vidal notes that ever since World War II, "Sicilians have been over-represented in the country's police and judiciary in rather the same way that, post Civil War, American Southerners took control of the Congress and the military . . ." Some of these police and magistrates have heroically fought the mafia and have paid with their lives, the best-known being Giovanni Falcone and Paolo Borsellino, whose effectiveness in prosecuting mafiosi resulted in their being assassinated in 1992.

89. Puzo, *The Godfather*, 325.

90. Ibid., 325–326.

91. Barra, "The Schlockfather."

92. Capeci, *Complete Idiot's Guide*, 209.

93. John Hooper, "Calvi Was Murdered by the Mafia, Italian Experts Rule," *Guardian*, July 25, 2003.

94. Ibid.

95. Carlo Calvi, BBC interview, July 24, 2003.

96. Dika, "Representation of Ethnicity," 103.

97. Ibid.

98. Mary Pat Kelly, *Martin Scorsese: A Journey* (New York: Thunder's Mouth Press, 1991), 261.

99. Chris Messenger, *"The Godfather" and American Culture* (Albany: State University of New York Press, 2002), 9.

100. Sandra M. Gilbert, "Life with (God)Father," in Regina Barreca, ed., *A Sitdown with "The Sopranos"* (New York: Palgrave Macmillan, 2002), 11.

101. Dika, "Representation of Ethnicity," 95–96.

102. Messenger, *"Godfather" and American Culture*, 12.

103. "Baseball Writer Picked for Godfather Sequel," *Guardian*, February 10, 2003.

104. Michiko Kakutani, " 'The Godfather Returns': You Think You're Out, but They Try to Pull You Back In," *New York Times*, November 12, 2004.

105. Mark Winegardner, *The Godfather Returns* (New York: Random House, 2004), 258.

5. FROM MEAN STREETS TO SUBURBAN MEADOW: *THE SOPRANOS* REWRITES THE GENRE

1. Stephen Holden, "Sympathetic Brutes in a Pop Masterpiece," *New York Times*, June 6, 1999.

2. Chris Messenger, *"The Godfather" and American Culture: How the Corleones Became "Our Gang"* (Albany: State University of New York Press, 2002), 255.
3. Ibid.
4. David Chase interview, "Times Talks," *New York Times*, January 11, 2002.
5. Harold Bloom, *The Anxiety of Influence* (New York: Oxford University Press, 1973). Bloom describes six stages in the journey of a "new" artist to develop his or her own distinctive voice. *Clinamen* is the first move any artist must make if he or she is to develop a creative voice that is in some way their own. The other five are *tessera* (completion and antithesis), *kenosis* (repetition and discontinuity), *daemonization* (the counter-sublime), *askesis* (purgation and solipsism), and finally *apophrades* (the return of the dead). The five further stages involve varying strategies by which new artists deny, revise, or otherwise modify the influence of the precursor or precursors.
6. Fred Gardaphé, "Fresh Garbage: The Gangster as Suburban Trickster," in Regina Barreca, ed., *A Sitdown with "The Sopranos"* (New York: Palgrave Macmillan, 2002), 90.
7. David Chase interview, *HBO.com*, 2000.
8. Michael Rispoli, interview by the author, New York City, March 20, 2004.
9. Peter Applebome, "A New Home Base and a Fresh Disguise, but the Same Old Corruption," *New York Times*, July 11, 2004.
10. Ibid.
11. Peter Applebome, "Investigations, Indictments, Resignations: New Jersey Is Nothing if Not Consistent," *New York Times*, July 18, 2004.
12. Alison Leigh Cowan, "Connecticut Man Charged in Extortion by Mob," *New York Times*, September 30, 2004.
13. David Chase, interview by Peter Bogdanovich, *The Sopranos: The Complete First Season*, HBO Home Video.
14. Flavia Alaya, interview by the author, New York City, June 14, 2002.
15. Chase interview, by Bogdanovich.
16. Holden, "Sympathetic Brutes in a Pop Masterpiece."
17. Ellen Willis, "Our Mobsters, Ourselves," *Nation*, April 2, 2001.
18. Carlos Clarens, *Crime Movies: An Illustrated History* (New York: Norton, 1980), 138.
19. Chase, interview by Peter Bogdanovich.
20. Ibid.
21. Glen O. Gabbard, *The Psychology of "The Sopranos": Love, Death, Desire and Betrayal in America's Favorite Gangster Family* (New York: Basic Books, 2002), 8.
22. Ibid., 2–3.
23. Ibid., 3.
24. Rebecca Scarpati, telephone interview by the author, September 9, 2004.
25. Gabbard, *Psychology of "The Sopranos,"* 2–3.
26. Ibid., 3.
27. Dominic Chianese, interview by the author, New York City, July 23, 2004.

28. Gabbard, *Psychology of "The Sopranos"*, ch. 1.

29. Joseph D. Pistone, *The Way of the Wiseguy* (Philadelphia: Running Press, 2004), 18.

30. Armond White, *New York Press* 14, no. 24 (2003).

31. Chase, interview by Peter Bogdanovich.

32. Ibid.

33. Gardaphé, "Fresh Garbage," 93.

34. Robert Viscusi, interview by the author, Brooklyn, N.Y., May 3, 2002.

35. Karl Marx, "The Eighteenth Brumaire of Louis Bonaparte," *Karl Marx and Frederick Engels: Selected Works* (New York: International Publishers, 1974), 95–180.

36. Holden, "Sympathetic Brutes in a Pop Masterpiece."

37. "The Real Boss of 'The Sopranos': David Chase Interview," *New York Times*, February 29, 2004.

38. Ellen Willis notes the series's connection to earlier mob movies, but she also sees literary antecedents in nineteenth-century English novels: "While the sheer entertainment and suspense of the plot twists are reminiscent of Dickens and his early serials, the underlying themes evoke George Eliot: The world of Tony Soprano is a kind of postmodern *Middlemarch*, whose inhabitants' moral and spiritual development (or devolution) unfolds within and against the norms of a parochial social milieu." Willis, "Our Mobsters, Ourselves."

39. David Bianculli, "Emmy Err Time: Too Many Nominations Are Wide of the Mark," New York *Daily News*, July 16, 2004.

40. Bernard Weintraub, "HBO Is Big Winner at Emmy Awards," *New York Times*, September 20, 2004.

41. *The New York Times on "The Sopranos*," introduction by Stephen Holden (New York: iBooks, 2000), xi.

42. Letizia Airos, "The Sopranos: Here We Are Again," www.usitalia.info/archivio/dettaglio.asp?Art_id-806&data-03/14/2004.com, March 14, 2004.

43. Chase, interview by Peter Bogdanovich.

44. David Chase, quoted at *www.tvtome.com*.

45. Pistone, *Way of the Wiseguy*, 182.

46. Ibid., 64.

47. "Interview with Joseph D. Pistone aka Donnie Brasco," *Varsity.co.nz*, June 24, 2004.

48. Pistone, *Way of the Wiseguy*, 28–30.

49. Ibid.

50. Ibid, 40.

51. Ibid., 107.

52. Ibid., 188.

53. William Glaberson, "An Archetypal Mob Trial: It's Just Like in the Movies," *New York Times*, May 23, 2004.

54. Ibid.

55. Pistone, *Way of the Wiseguy*, 140.

56. Ibid., 164.
57. Gabbard, *Psychology of "The Sopranos,"* 36–37.
58. Alessandro Camon, *"The Godfather* and the Mythology of Mafia," in Nick Browne, ed., *Francis Ford Coppola's "The Godfather" Trilogy* (New York: Cambridge University Press, 2000), 59.
59. Pistone, *Way of the Wiseguy,* 193.
60. Ibid., 18.
61. Catherine Don Diego, "Hits, Whacks, and Smokes: The Celluloid Gangster as Horror Icon," *Postscript* 31 (2002): 87–98.
62. Pistone, *Way of the Wiseguy,* 134.
63. Ibid., 53.
64. Ibid.
65. Ibid., 182.
66. Ibid., 53.
67. David Chase, interview by Caryn James, *New York Times,* January 11, 2002.
68. Raymond De Felitta, interview by the author, New York City, June 21, 2002.
69. Greg B. Smith, "Junior: I Wanted to Go Legit," New York *Daily News,* September 30, 2004.
70. Sandra M. Gilbert, "Life With (God)Father," in Barreca, ed., *A Sitdown with "The Sopranos,"* 15.
71. Annabella Sciorra, interview by the author, New York City, September 9, 2002.
72. Chianese, interview by the author.
73. Sciorra, interview by the author.
74. Rispoli, interview by the author.
75. Viscusi, interview by the author.
76. Allen Rucker, *The Sopranos: A Family History* (New York: New American Library, 2000).

6. Act Like a Man: Sex and Gender in the Mafia Myth

1. Robert Aldrich, *The Seduction of the Mediterranean: Writing, Art and Homosexual Fantasy* (London: Routledge, 1993). See in particular ch. 5, "Mediterranean Men in Art and Photography," for its account of Von Gloeden's life in Sicily.
2. Richard Gambino, *Blood of My Blood* (New York: Anchor/Doubleday, 1974), 183–211.
3. Mario Puzo, *The Godfather* (New York: Signet, 1978), 442.
4. Carlos Clarens, *Crime Movies: An Illustrated History* (New York: Norton, 1980), 82.
5. Ibid., 61.
6. Cindy Donatelli and Sharon Alward, "'I Dread You': Married to the Mob in *The Godfather, Goodfellas,* and *The Sopranos,*" in David Lavery, ed., *This Thing of Ours* (New York: Columbia University Press, 2002), 67.
7. Ibid., 63.

8. Clarens, *Crime Movies*, 287.
9. Ibid.
10. Ibid.
11. Ibid.
12. Donatelli and Alward, "I Dread You," 62.
13. Puzo, *The Godfather*, 438.
14. Vera Dika, "The Representation of Ethnicity in *The Godfather*," in Nick Browne, ed., *Francis Ford Coppola's "The Godfather" Trilogy* (New York: Cambridge University Press, 2000), 76–108.
15. Donatelli and Alward, "I Dread You," 63.
16. Ibid., 60.
17. Ibid.
18. Rebecca Traister, "Is *The Sopranos* a Chick Show? Why an Ultraviolent Drama About a New Jersey Mafioso Paints a More Nuanced Portrait of Women Than Anything You'll Find on Lifetime," *Salon.com*, March 6, 2004.
19. Regina Barreca, "Why I Like the Women in *The Sopranos* Even Though I'm Not Supposed To," in Regina Barreca, ed., *A Sitdown with "The Sopranos"* (New York: Palgrave Macmillan, 2002), 30–31.
20. Ibid., 29.
21. Ibid., 29–30.
22. Ibid., 36.
23. Ibid., 30.
24. Ibid., 35.
25. Kenneth Ciongoli, telephone interview by the author, March 29, 2002.
26. Leonardo Sciascia, quoted in Gore Vidal, "Sciascia's Italy," in *The Second American Revolution and Other Essays, 1976–1982* (New York: Vintage, 1983), 96–97.
27. Barreca, "Why I Like the Women," 44.
28. Traister, "Is *The Sopranos* a Chick Show?"
29. Jane C. Schneider and Peter T. Schneider, *Reversible Destiny: Mafia, Antimafia, and the Struggle for Palermo* (Berkeley: University of California Press, 2003), 93.
30. Annabella Sciorra, interview by the author, New York City, September 9, 2002.
31. Robert Viscusi, "Breaking the Silence: Strategic Imperatives for Italian American Culture," *Voices in Italian Americana* 1, no. 1 (Spring 1990): 1–13.
32. Puzo, *The Godfather*, 15.
33. Ibid., 27.
34. Curzio Malaparte, quoted in Aldrich, *Seduction of the Mediterranean*, 180.
35. Frank Bruni, "Encounter With Girolamo Lo Verso: Dons Don't Have More Fun," *New York Times*, August 24, 2003.
36. Glen O. Gabbard, *The Psychology of "The Sopranos": Love, Death, Desire and Betrayal in America's Favorite Gangster Family* (New York: Basic Books, 2002), 158–159.
37. Paul Ginsborg, *Italy and Its Discontents* (New York: Palgrave Macmillan, 2003), 198–199.

38. Ibid.
39. Schneider and Schneider, *Reversible Destiny*, 94.
40. "Sicily Police Arrest Women 'Bosses' in Mafia Swoop," Reuters, July 13, 2004.
41. Schneider and Schneider, *Reversible Destiny*, 94.
42. Ibid., 96.
43. Ibid.
44. Ibid.
45. Ibid., 92.
46. Gabbard, *Psychology of "The Sopranos,"* 166.
47. Nick Tosches, *Dino: Living High in the Dirty Business of Dreams* (New York: Dell, 1992), 154.
48. David Carter, *Stonewall: The Riots That Sparked the Gay Revolution* (New York: St. Martin's, 2004).
49. Greg B. Smith, "Gotti Shown Giving Smooch to Gay Mobster," New York *Daily News*, May 1, 2003.
50. John Marzulli, "First Sonny, Now 'Cher,'" New York *Daily News*, June 9, 2004.
51. Anthony M. De Stefano, "'Gay Hitman' Shot Dead in Texas," *Newsday*, March 7, 1991.
52. George Chauncey, *Gay New York: Gender, Urban Culture, and the Making of the Gay Male World, 1890–1940* (New York: Basic Books, 1994), 72.
53. Ibid.
54. Ibid., 74, 75.
55. Ibid., 76.
56. Joyce Millman, "A Romance Between Mobsters and Their Mole," *New York Times*, August 17, 2003.

7. MOULANYANS, MEDIGAHNS, AND WONDER BREAD WOPS: RACE AND RACISM ON-SCREEN AND OFF

1. Mario Puzo, *The Godfather* (New York: Signet, 1978), 288.
2. Robert Coles, *The Moral Intelligence of Children* (New York: Plume, 1998), 18.
3. Chazz Palmintieri, interview by the author, New York City, July 1, 2002.
4. The Howard Beach attackers actually were an ethnically mixed bunch, and the acknowledged ringleader was a white South African named Jon Lester. But because the incident occurred in a largely Italian enclave in Queens, New York, it was generally portrayed as an instance of Italian-on-black crime.
5. Pasquale Verdicchio, "Spike Lee's Guineas," *Diferentia* 6–7 (Spring/Autumn 1994): 178.
6. Ibid.
7. Ibid., 181.
8. Bill Adler, "Will the Little Girls Understand?," *Rolling Stone*, February 19, 1981.
9. Verdicchio, "Spike Lee's Guineas," 185.
10. "'Do the Right Thing': Issues and Images," *New York Times*, July 9, 1989.
11. Ibid.

12. Michael Parenti, *Make-Believe Media* (New York: St. Martin's, 1992), 144.

13. Verdicchio, "Spike Lee's Guineas," 177–178.

14. Giorgio Bertellini, "New York City and the Representation of Italian Americans in the Cinema," in Philip V. Cannistraro, ed., *The Italians of New York* (New York: New-York Historical Society, 2000), 122.

15. Interview with Spike Lee, *Newsweek*, June 10, 1991.

16. Angelo Mazzocco, "Of Spike Lee's *Jungle Fever*," *Voices in Italian Americana* 6, no. 2 (Fall 1995): 188.

17. Ibid., 187.

18. Ibid., 188.

19. Annabella Sciorra, interview by the author, New York City, September 9, 2002.

20. John Gennari, "Giancarlo Giuseppe Alessandro Esposito: Life in the Borderlands," in Jennifer Guglielmo and Salvatore Salerno, eds., *Are Italians White?: How Race Is Made in America* (New York: Routledge, 2003), 244.

21. "Spike Lee on *Summer of Sam*," interview by Nasser Metcalfe, *Blackfilm.com*, July 1999.

22. Clyde Haberman, "A Stereotype Hollywood Can't Refuse," *New York Times*, July 30, 1999.

23. Michael Rispoli, interview by the author, New York City, March 20, 2004.

24. Raymond De Felitta, interview by the author, New York City, June 21, 2002.

25. Alessandro Camon, "*The Godfather* and the Mythology of Mafia," in Nick Browne, ed., *Francis Ford Coppola's "The Godfather" Trilogy* (New York: Cambridge University Press, 2000), 58.

26. Robert Viscusi, interview by the author, Brooklyn, N.Y., May 3, 2002.

27. Robert Viscusi, "A Literature Considering Itself: The Allegory of Italian America," in A. J. Tamburri, P. A. Giordano, and F. Gardaphé, eds., *From the Margin: Writings in Italian Americana* (West Lafayette, Ind.: Purdue University Press, 1991), 270.

28. Robert Orsi, "The Religious Boundaries of an Inbetween People: Street *Feste* and the Problem of the Dark-Skinned Other in Italian Harlem, 1920–1990," *American Quarterly* 44, no. 3 (September 1992): 313.

29. Verdicchio, "Spike Lee's Guineas," 179.

30. Orsi, "Religious Boundaries of an Inbetween People," 115.

31. Ibid.

32. Ibid., 314.

33. Matthew Frye Jacobson, *Whiteness of a Different Color: European Immigrants and the Alchemy of Race* (Cambridge, Mass.: Harvard University Press, 1998), 57.

34. Rudolph Vecoli, "Are Italian Americans Just White Folks?," *Italian Americana* 13, no. 2 (Summer 1995): 156.

35. Jacobson, *Whiteness of a Different Color*, 4.

36. Ibid.

37. Orsi, "Religious Boundaries of an Inbetween People," 317.

38. Ibid.

39. Vecoli, "Are Italian Americans Just White Folks?," 156.

40. Jacobson, *Whiteness of a Different Color*, 4.
41. Garry Boulard, "Blacks, Italians, and the Making of New Orleans Jazz," *Journal of Ethnic Studies* 16, no. 1 (Spring 1988): 54.
42. Ibid., 55.
43. Ibid., 56.
44. Ibid., 63.
45. Nick Tosches, *Dino: Living High in the Dirty Business of Dreams* (New York: Dell, 1992), 153.
46. Ronald L. Morris, *Wait Until Dark: Jazz and the Underworld, 1880–1940* (Bowling Green, Ohio: Bowling Green State University Press, 1980).
47. Tosches, *Dino*, 153.
48. Morris, *Wait Until Dark*, 134.
49. Ibid., 12.
50. Ibid., 171, 165.
51. Jon Pareles, "For This Super Sunday, It's All About Mardi Gras Revelry," *New York Times*, March 22, 2004.
52. "George Wallington, Jazz Musician, 69," Obituary, *New York Times*, February 16, 1993.
53. George De Stefano, "Bread, Wine, and Soul: Jazzman Joe Lovano," *Voices in Italian Americana* 6, no. 1 (1995): 15.
54. Ibid., 20.
55. David Witter, "The Italian Roots of Jazz," *Fra Noi*, March 1996, 49.
56. Richard M. Sudhalter, *Lost Chords: White Musicians and Their Contribution to Jazz* (New York: Oxford University Press, 2001).
57. Vecoli, "Are Italian Americans Just White Folks?," 156.
58. Orsi, "Religious Boundaries of an Inbetween People," 317.
59. Richard Gambino, *Blood of My Blood* (New York: Anchor/Doubleday, 1974), 346.
60. Gil Fagiani, interview by the author, New York City, December 10, 2004.
61. Gerald Meyer, *Vito Marcantonio: Radical Politician, 1902–1954* (Albany: State University of New York Press, 1989), 124, 125.
62. Ibid., 119, 127.
63. Ibid., 129.
64. George De Stefano, "Family Lies," *Film Comment*, August 1987, 26.
65. Thomas A. Guglielmo, *White on Arrival: Italians, Race, Color, and Power in Chicago, 1890–1945* (New York: Oxford University Press, 2003), 8–9.
66. Ibid., 9, 93.
67. Ibid., 85, 86.
68. Ibid., 176, 174, 175.
69. Robert Casillo, "Moments in Italian-American Cinema: From Little Caesar to Coppola and Scorsese," in Tamburri, Giordano, and Gardaphé, eds., *From the Margin*, 383.
70. Iron Eyes Cody, *Iron Eyes: My Life as a Hollywood Indian* (New York: Everest House, 1982).
71. Angela Aleiss, "Native Son," *Times-Picayune*, May 26, 1996.

72. Micaela di Leonardo, *The Varieties of Ethnic Experience: Kinship, Class, and Gender Among California Italian-Americans* (Ithaca, N.Y.: Cornell University Press, 1984), 175.

73. Orsi, "Religious Boundaries of an Inbetween People," 335.

74. Robert Gearty, "Stoolie: I Sparked Hawkins Race Slay," New York *Daily News*, August 19, 2005; Julia Preston, "Gotti Witness Tells of Role in Bias Attack in Brooklyn," *New York Times*, August 19, 2005.

75. George De Stefano, "La Dolce Bensonhurst," *Outweek*, October 8, 1989, 34–37.

76. Nelson George, "Brothers in Arms: The Borough's Warring Tribes Are Closer than We Think," *Village Voice*, May 29, 1990, 27–28.

77. Mark Bauman and Samme Chittum, "Married to the Mob: The Wiseguy Wannabees," *Village Voice*, May 29, 1990, 40–43.

78. Jerome Krase, "Bensonhurst, Brooklyn: Italian American Victimizers and Victims," *Voices in Italian Americana* 5, no. 2 (1994): 48, 49.

79. Ibid., 44, 45.

80. Fagiani, interview by the author.

81. Krase, "Bensonhurst, Brooklyn," 45.

82. Joseph Sciorra, "Italians Against Racism: The Murder of Yusuf Hawkins (RIP) and My March on Bensonhurst," in Jennifer Guglielmo and Salvatore Salerno, eds., *Are Italians White?: How Race Is Made in America* (New York: Routledge, 2003), 192–209.

83. Ibid., 194, 193, 204–205.

84. Robert Viscusi, "Breaking the Silence: Strategic Imperatives for Italian American Culture," *Voices in Italian Americana* 1, no. 1 (Spring 1990): 1.

85. Ibid.

86. Vera Dika, "The Representation of Ethnicity in *The Godfather*," in Nick Browne, ed., *Francis Ford Coppola's "The Godfather" Trilogy* (New York: Cambridge University Press, 2000), 96.

87. John Marzulli and Patrice O'Shaughnessy, "Profitable Record Label Under the Microscope in Federal Drug Probe," New York *Daily News*, December 6, 2004.

88. Ibid.

89. Jeff Giles, "And Justice for Al," *Newsweek*, June 3, 2002, 54.

90. Chris Messenger, *"The Godfather" and American Culture: How the Corleones Became "Our Gang"* (Albany: State University of New York Press, 2002), 12.

91. Todd Boyd, "Is Stagolee's Stetson Like a Rapper's Baggy Pants?," *New York Times*, June 7, 2003.

92. Frankie Hi NRG, "Fight da Faida," translation by Virginia Carlsten and Joe Sciorra, *www.italianrap.com*.

8. CULTURAL HOLOCAUST OR NATIONAL MYTH?: THE POLITICS OF ANTIDEFAMATION

1. Jennifer Steinhauer with Robert Worth, " 'Sopranos' Uninvited, Mayor Finds a Parade He Can Refuse," *New York Times*, October 12, 2002.

2. Tara Bahrampour, "New Roles, Old Stereotypes," *New York Times*, October 13, 2002.

3. Dominic Chianese, interview by the author, New York City, July 23, 2004.

4. Sophie Arie, "Don't Honour Wise Guy De Niro, Say US Italians," *Guardian*, August 13, 2004.

5. Associated Press, September 11, 2004.

6. Arie, "Don't Honour Wise Guy De Niro."

7. Ibid.

8. Rosario A. Iaconis, " 'Sopranos' Stereotypes Must Be Wiped Out," *Newsday*, October 14, 2002.

9. Bahrampour, "New Roles, Old Stereotypes."

10. Paul Basile, "Anti-Bias Position Paper," *Fra Noi*, January 2002.

11. "Heard on Campus: Camille Paglia Gets in Tony Soprano's Face," *Pennsylvania Gazette*, January 2, 2002.

12. Isaac Guzman, "Reviving Old Mob Scores," New York *Daily News*, October 7, 2002.

13. Marie Cocco, "Italian-Americans Can Shed 'Sopranos' Image," *Newsday*, September 17, 2002.

14. Frank Pagliese, interview by the author, New York City, July 12, 2002.

15. Harvey Wasserman, "Was Willie Horton Gay? Will George W. Bush Be the Hate-Homosexuals Candidate?," *Free Press* (Columbus, Ohio), December 23, 2003.

16. Jim Dwyer, "A Legacy of Giuliani Years: Damage Suits Against City," *New York Times*, December 24, 2004.

17. *Imus in the Morning*, WABC Radio, September 13, 1991.

18. *New Republic*, March 10, 1986.

19. Kevin Sack, "Budget Foes' Common Ground: Cherry Garcia," *New York Times*, April 12, 1995.

20. WABC Radio, January 6, 1992.

21. Doug Ireland, "Gloves Off in the Garden State," *Nation*, August 5, 1999.

22. William Donohue, president of the Catholic League, on *Scarborough Country*, MSNBC, December 8, 2004.

23. Libero della Piana, "Are Italians the New Anti-Racist Front?," *RaceWire* (free wire service for the ethnic press), RaceWire, c/o Applied Research Center, 11 Park Place, Ste. 914, New York, NY 10007.

24. Chris Messenger, *"The Godfather" and American Culture: How the Corleones Became "Our Gang"* (Albany: State University of New York Press, 2002), 9.

25. William Connell, "PBS, the Mafia, and the Medici," *USItalia.info*, March 7, 2004.

26. George Anastasia, "If Shakespeare Were Alive Today, He'd Be Writing for *The Sopranos*," in Regina Barreca, ed., *A Sitdown with "The Sopranos"* (New York: Palgrave Macmillan, 2002), 161.

27. Fred Gardaphé, "Fresh Garbage: The Gangster as Suburban Trickster," in Barreca, ed., *A Sitdown with "The Sopranos*," 105.

28. George Anastasia, *Blood and Honor* (New York: Morrow, 1991).
29. Anastasia, "If Shakespeare Were Alive Today," 162.
30. Ibid., 163.
31. Robert Viscusi, interview by the author, Brooklyn, N.Y., May 3, 2002.
32. Kenneth Ciongoli, telephone interview by the author, March 29, 2002.
33. Michael Bronski, *Pulp Friction* (New York: St. Martin's Griffin, 2003), 10.
34. Ariel Levy, "Dying Is Easy, Comedy Is Hard," *New York*, September 13, 2004, 80–81.
35. Chianese, interview by the author.
36. Anastasia, "If Shakespeare Were Alive Today," 152.
37. Chianese, interview by the author.
38. Annabella Sciorra, interview by the author, New York City, September 9, 2002.
39. Chianese, interview by the author.
40. Ian Rothkerch, "Actors Have a Sit-Down: On Working with James Gandolfini, Their Favorite Lines and Where to Find The Best Braciola," *Salon.com*, May 17, 2001.
41. Ibid.
42. Michael Rispoli, interview by the author, New York City, March 20, 2004.
43. Anastasia, "If Shakespeare Were Alive Today," 151.
44. Ibid., 160–161.
45. Ibid., 152.
46. Ciongoli, interview by the author.
47. Micaela di Leonardo, telephone interview by the author, July 25, 2002.
48. James B. Jacobs with Christopher Panarella and Jay Worthington, *Busting the Mob: United States v. Cosa Nostra* (New York: New York University Press, 1994).
49. James B. Jacobs, interview by the author, New York City, May 15, 2002.
50. Rebecca Scarpeti, telephone interview by the author, September 3, 2004.
51. Bill Tonelli, "A 'Sopranos' Secret: Given the Choice, We'd All Be Mobsters," *New York Times*, March 4, 2001.
52. Bill Tonelli, interview by the author, New York City, March 22, 2002.
53. Ibid.
54. Frank De Caro, "Italian-American Characters of Greater Complexity: *The Sopranos* Aren't Negative Stereotypes," *USA Weekend*, September 15, 2002.
55. Viscusi, interview by the author.
56. Ibid.
57. Maria Laurino, "From the Fonz to 'The Sopranos,' Not Much Evolution," *New York Times*, December 24, 2001.
58. Ibid.
59. Viscusi, interview by the author.
60. All quotes are taken from the interview with David Chase conducted by Peter Bogdanovich, *The Sopranos: The Complete First Season*, HBO Home Video.
61. Leonard Covello, *The Heart Is the Teacher*, quoted in Fred L. Gardaphé, *Leaving Little Italy* (Albany: State University of New York Press, 2004), 5.

62. Steven R. Schirripa, *A Goomba's Guide to Life* (New York: Clarkson Potter, 2002), 3–4.

9. CONCLUSION: *ADDIO*, GODFATHER?

1. Another popular sobriquet for Italian American organized crime has been extended to gays and lesbians. Armstrong Williams, a prominent black conservative who was paid nearly a quarter million dollars by the Bush White House to promote the president's agenda in his columns and syndicated talk show, has decried "the rhetoric of the homosexual Cosa Nostra." Doreen Brandt, "White House Pays Off Anti-Gay Commentator," *365Gay.com*, January 7, 2005.

2. Gay Talese, telephone interview by the author, March 11, 2003.

3. Mackenzie Dawson Parks, "Revise Guys: Bada Bing! Italian men not so macho after all," *New York Post*, June 22, 2005.

4. Ivan Chrysler, "Enzo Avitabile and Bottari," *bbc.co.uk.*, December 2004.

5. Robert Bianco, "*Family* Sinks ABC to Yet Another Low," *USA Today*, March 3, 2003.

6. Alessandra Stanley, "John Gotti's Daughter Glares at Reality," *New York Times*, August 2, 2004.

7. Tom Fontana, interview by the author, New York City, August 23, 2002.

8. Frank Pugliese, interview by the author, New York City, July 12, 2002.

9. Stephen Holden, "Review: 'Mail Order Bride,' " *New York Times*, November 21, 2003.

10. Stephen Holden, "A Familiar Group of Wiseguys," *New York Times*, January 25, 2002.

11. Dave Kehr, "Review: 'This Thing of Ours,' " *New York Times*, July 18, 2003.

12. Robert Bianco, "*Line of Fire* Aims High, Friggin' Misses," *USA Today*, December 1, 2003.

13. James B. Jacobs with Coleen Friel and Robert Raddick, *Gotham Unbound: How New York Was Liberated from the Grip of Organized Crime* (New York: New York University Press, 1999), 1.

14. Corey Kilgannon, "Phone Executive Admits Conspiracy in Mob Fraud," *New York Times*, January 9, 2005.

15. Charles Bagli, "MTA Project Rocked Anew by Mafia Link," *New York Times*, September 16, 2004.

16. Tom Robbins, "The Mob's Latest Maritime Maneuvers: They Cover the Waterfront," *Village Voice*, February 27–March 5, 2002.

17. William Glaberson, "Old Mobs Never Die, and Cliché but Brutal Methods Refuse to Fade," *New York Times*, January 26, 2003.

18. Ibid.

19. Joseph D. Pistone, *The Way of the Wiseguy* (Philadelphia: Running Press, 2004), 11.

20. Ibid.

21. He instead was rewarded for his cooperation, when, in June 2005, Judge Nicholas Garaufis gave him two life sentences.
22. William K. Rashbaum, " 'Last Don' Reported to Be First One to Betray Mob," *New York Times*, January 28, 2005.
23. Paul Harris, "Mafia Crumbles as the Last Don Is First to Sing: Mob Bosses Are Fleeing as a Godfather Squeals," *Observer*, February 13, 2005.
24. Ibid.
25. "Two Cops Who Killed for Mafia," John Marzulli. New York *Daily News*, March 10, 2005.
26. Ibid.
27. Ibid.
28. Pat Milton and Larry McShane, "Mafia Madness: NYPD Detectives as Hitmen, FBI Agent as Mobster?," New York *Daily News*, March 14, 2005.
29. Ibid.
30. Paul Ginsborg, *Italy and Its Discontents* (New York: Palgrave Macmillan, 2003), 195.
31. David Willey, " 'Cancer' of Italian Mafia Slated," *BBC News*, January 4, 2005.
32. "Ecco i rapporti tra Cosa nostra instituzioni e società civile," *La Repubblica*, October 2, 2004.
33. Peter Popham, "Secrets of Who Pays What to Sicilian Mafia Revealed for First Time," *Independent*, January 20, 2005.
34. Diego Gambetta, *The Sicilian Mafia: The Business of Private Protection* (Cambridge, Mass: Harvard University Press, 1993).
35. Nick Vivarelli, "Italy Gives Film $1 Million, Then Bans It," *Denver Rocky Mountain News*, March 6, 1998.
36. Clare Longrigg, "Smartfellas," *The Guardian*, May 9, 2005.
37. Mary Pat Kelly, *Martin Scorsese: A Journey* (New York: Thunder's Mouth Press, 1991), 261.
38. Chris Messenger, *"The Godfather" and American Culture: How the Corleones Became "Our Gang"* (Albany: State University of New York Press, 2002), 12.
39. Robert Viscusi, interview by the author, Brooklyn, N.Y., May 3, 2002.
40. Gay Talese, "Where Are the Italian American Novelists?," *New York Times Book Review*, March 14, 1993.
41. Kelly, *Martin Scorsese*, 262.
42. Viscusi, interview by the author.
43. Josephine Gattuso Hendin, "Social Constructions and Aesthetic Achievements: Italian American Writing as Ethnic Art," *Melus*, September 22, 2003.
44. Anthony Julian Tamburri, "Beyond 'Pizza' and 'Nonna!' or, What's Bad About Italian/American Criticism?: Further Directions for Italian/American Cultural Studies," *Melus*, September 22, 2003.
45. Fred Misurella, "Truth Behind the Fiction of Italian-Americans," *Christian Science Monitor*, April 15, 2002.
46. Dan Barry, "Take Gleason, Then Add a Little Italy," *New York Times*, June 5, 2004.

47. Anita Gates, "Yo! Queens Goombahs," *New York Times*, August 28, 2004.
48. David Blaylock, "Review: *Chooch*," *Village Voice*, August 23, 2004.
49. George Guida, "Novel Paesans: The Reconstruction of Italian-American Male Identity in Anthony Valerio's *Conversation with Johnny* and Robert Viscusi's *Astoria*," *Melus*, Summer 2001.
50. Fontana, interview by the author.
51. Maria Russo, "Fuhgeddaboudit: 'The Sopranos' Have Made Being Italian-American Seem Cool Again, But Maybe It's Time to Say Arrivederci to All That," *Salon.com*, August 24, 2000.
52. Paolo Pontoniere, "European-Americans Dropping Ancestral Roots—Except Italian-Americans," *Pacific News Service*, June 19, 2002.
53. Richard D. Alba, *Italian Americans: Into the Twilight of Ethnicity* (Englewood Cliffs, N.J.: Prentice-Hall, 1985).
54. Donald Tricarico, "Contemporary Italian American Ethnicity: Into the Mainstream," in Richard N. Juliani and Philip V. Cannistraro, eds., *Italian Americans: The Search for a Usable Past* (American Italian Historical Association, 1986), 260.
55. Stuart Hall, "Cultural Identity and Cinematic Representation," *Framework* 36 (1989): 69.
56. Rudolph Vecoli, "Are Italian Americans Just White Folks?," *Italian Americana* 13, no. 2 (Summer 1995): 158, 159.
57. Robert Viscusi, "Breaking the Silence: Strategic Imperatives for Italian American Culture," *Voices in Italian Americana* 1, no. 1 (1990): 8.
58. Gattuso Hendin, "Social Constructions and Aesthetic Achievements."
59. Nicholas Montemarano, *A Fine Place* (New York: Context Books, 2002).
60. Jake Mooney, "The House That Sal Built," *New York Times*, December 26, 2004.
61. Corey Kilgannon, "Beating of Queens Satanist Prompts Hate Crime Charges," *New York Times*, January 12, 2005.

Acknowledgments

Organized crime, its reality and the pop-culture mythology of the Mafia; southern Italian immigration to the United States; the politics of race, ethnicity, class, and sexuality; cultural archetypes and ethnic stereotypes; assimilation and cultural pluralism—*mamma mia*, how to make sense of all this? The artists and intellectuals, activists and educators who generously gave of their time to talk to me, and those whose works influenced my thinking, and those who provided invaluable support and assistance—this book wouldn't exist without you.

Grazie mille to: Flavia Alaya; Robert Casillo; Dominic Chianese; the late Carlos Clarens; John D'Appolito; Johnny De Carlo; Ray De Felitta; Libero della Piana; Jeffrey Escoffier; Gil Fagiani; Fondazione Falcone, Palermo, Sicily; Tom Fontana; Giovanni Gallo, in Catania, Sicily; Diego Gambetta; Richard Gambino; Fred Gardaphé, State University of New York, Stony Brook; Thomas Guglielmo; Clyde Haberman, *The New York Times*; Professor James B. Jacobs, New York University; Maria Laurino; Micaela di Leonardo; Joe Lovano, Enzo Avitabile, Almamegretta, and Daniele Sepe, for the great and inspiring sounds; Chris Messenger; Jonathan Munby; Katherine Narducci; Robert Orsi; Chazz Palmintieri; Frank Pugliese; David A. J. Richards, New York University; Michael Rispoli; the late Edward W. Said; Rebecca Scarpati; Jane C. Schneider and Peter T. Schneider; Annabella Sciorra; Joseph Sciorra; Gay Talese; Bill Tonelli; and Robert Viscusi, Brooklyn College.

And *grazie tane* to my editor, Denise Oswald, and to Sarah Almond, Sarah Russo, and everybody at Faber and Faber and Farrar, Straus and Giroux, whose professionalism, support, and great ideas made the writing and editing of this, my first book, such a rewarding experience.

Index

Abbott, Diahnne, 240
ABC, 349, 352, 357
Abshire, Alton, 278
Abshire, May, 278–79
Adler, Jerry, 235
Adonis, Joe, 40
African Americans, 245, 276, 326, 328, 330, 343, 352, 379, 381, 387; civil rights and, 107; Italian American attacks on, 35, 238–39, 243, 280–86, 390, 410*n*4; Italian American relations with, 259, 261, 262–72, 309–12; as Mardi Gras Indians, 265–66; police brutality against, 309–10; racism and, 90, 231–52, 255, 257–58, 259, 268, 313, 317, 325; rap music and mafia fascination of, 8, 87, 132, 288–92, 293–94; segregation and, 28; *Sopranos'* view of, 144, 154, 233–35, 237, 292; stereotypes of, 12, 104, 307–308, 392; in urban neighborhoods, 90, 169; vs. Italians in non-mafia films, 243–52, 255
Agnelli family, 115
Agnello, Frank, 350
Aiello, Danny, 244
Aiello, Michele, 366
Alaya, Flavia, 87, 145
Alba, Richard, 382, 386
alcohol, 58, 60, 61, 75–76, 328
Aleiss, Angela, 277–79

Allen, Woody, 107, 322
Alley, Charles, 279
Alter, Jonathan, 38
Alward, Sharon, 180, 187, 188, 191, 204, 205
American Italian Historical Association, 314, 388
Analyze That, 6, 91, 299
Analyze This, 4, 6, 85, 91, 139, 147, 220, 299, 322, 356
Anastasia, George, 313, 315–16, 320, 324, 348
Andreotti, Giulio, 128, 365
Anello, Calogero (char.), 237–41
Anello, Lorenzo (char.), 237–39
Anti-Defamation League, 81, 312
anxiety of influence, 141, 406*n*5
Apalachin, N.Y., 42–43, 83
Apollonia (char.), 134, 187–88, 293
Aprile, Jackie (char.), 142, 175, 208, 220
Aprile, Jackie, Jr. (char.), 185, 229–30, 233
Arab Americans, 307, 312
Arabs, Italian Americans cast as, 277
Arkin, Alan, 147
Armstrong, Louis, 263–64, 267
Arts and Entertainment network, 349–50
Asians, stereotypes of, 12, 392
assimilation, 29, 112, 175, 237, 325, 345, 382, 384

Buttiglione, Rocco, 184
Bygrave, Mike, 119

Caan, James, 110, 220
Cagney, James, 10, 138, 185–86, 220
Calabria, 9, 25, 53, 305–306, 384
Calderone, Salvatore, 390
Calvi, Carlo, 130
Calvi, Roberto, 129–30
Camon, Alessandro, 95, 112–15, 118,
  166–67, 258
Camonte, Tony ("Scarface") (char.), 5,
  72–73, 75–76, 78, 80, 83, 104, 344
Campania, 144, 171, 384
Canby, Vincent, 118
Capeci, Jerry, 119–20, 124
capitalism, 24, 60, 178, 237; *Godfather*
  as metaphor for, 93, 103, 105, 115,
  117, 126, 138, 353; mafia and, 49
Capone, 73, 344
Capone, Albert Francis, 74
Capone, Alphonse, 29, 55, 71, 73, 74,
  76, 124, 264, 289–90, 403n30
Capone, Mae Coughlin, 74
Capone n' Noreaga, 8, 290
Cappa, Charlie (char.), 186, 221, 228,
  232–33, 292, 305
Caracappa, Steven, 363–64
Carcaterra, Lorenzo, 89–90
Carr, Sam, 253
Carter, Jonathan, 39
Casillo, Nick, 79
Casillo, Robert, 72–73, 82, 276
Casino, 6, 93, 318
Castallamare del Golfo, 56, 65
Castellano, Paul, 223
Catholic church, 14, 92, 96, 184, 197–
  98, 216, 218, 225, 231, 272, 328,
  369, 391; in *Godfather III*, 126–29,
  190; land appropriated from, 20, 46;
  and Sicilian disenfranchisement, 19,
  31, 123; in *Sopranos*, 152, 178, 210,
  211, 337
Catholic League for Religious and Civil
  Rights, 312

CBS, 160, 227
Census, U.S., 27, 382
cento passi, I ("The Hundred Steps"),
  367–68
Chase, David, 4, 16, 83, 137–38, 142,
  145, 152–53, 160, 166, 168, 174–
  75, 181, 205, 227, 308, 316, 321–
  25, 328, 338, 339, 345, 349, 354,
  357, 365, 372; criticisms of, 13, 206,
  291, 301–302, 311, 314–15, 320,
  336, 340; on *Sopranos*, 10, 136, 139,
  140–41, 143, 146–47, 154–55, 158,
  161, 171, 178, 337, 340–41
Chauncey, George, 224–25
Chayefsky, Paddy, 82
Chianese, Dominic, 140, 148, 152, 174,
  319–21, 335; Columbus Day Parade
  and, 13, 296–97
Chicago, 43, 64, 266, 268; Little Italy in,
  55
Chiklis, Michael, 154
Christian Democrats, 50–51, 128, 365
Christ in Concrete (Di Donato), 373,
  374–75
Cifaretto, Ralphie (char.), 208, 213, 216,
  229, 280
Ciongoli, Kenneth, 206, 309, 311, 312,
  314, 316–18, 324–25, 341
City University of New York (CUNY),
  285, 300, 351; Italian American In-
  stitute of, 13, 386, 388
Civello, Johnny Boy (char.), 221, 227–
  28, 297
Clarens, Carlos, 72, 79, 80, 94, 118–19,
  146, 185–86, 188–90
Clarke, Mae, 186, 220
Clinton, Bill, 38
Cobb, Lee J., 73, 360
Cocco, Marie, 306, 348
Cody, Frank (DeCorti), 277–78
Cody, Iron Eyes (Espera DeCorti), 277–
  80
Cohen, Mickey, 94
Colicchio, Victor, 253, 256
Colombian crime syndicates, 9
Colombo, Joe, 101

Sopranos, The (cont.)
 ther in, 125, 138–41, 147, 154–57;
 domestic lives in, 143–44, 145,
 150–51, 160–61, 339–40; food in,
 177, 218, 338–39; gumads in, 137,
 144, 187; "A Hit Is a Hit," episode
 of, 176, 234–37; homosexuality in,
 229–30; Italian American experience
 and, 173–79, 306; Italian American
 fans of, 302, 303, 306, 331–32, 342,
 348, 380–81; Italian Americans' criticism of, 13, 109, 174–75, 206, 245,
 296–97, 300–308, 311, 314–17,
 319–21, 327–31, 335, 348–49,
 351–52; "The Legend of Tennessee
 Moltisanti" episode of, 357; mafia
 decline in, 16–17, 137, 141, 144–
 46, 157–58, 164–65, 381; mafia and
 societal corruption in, 138, 169, 237,
 353, 372; Mafia myth in, 139, 156;
 mafiosi as suburbanites in, 15, 74,
 138, 141–43, 145, 160, 175–76,
 331; merchandising of, 5; misogyny
 and homophobia as intertwined in,
 220; open call auditions for, 14,
 330–31; popularity and success of,
 4–5, 86, 88, 158–60, 287, 313,
 325, 377; psychiatrists on, 5, 91,
 147–51; publishing spin-offs of, 7,
 158–59; quality of writing on, 322–
 23; racial attitudes in, 144, 154,
 233–37, 292; RICO Mafia Class of
 2003 in, 161; "Unidentified Black
 Males" episode of, 233; "The
 Weight," episode of, 140, 174;
 women in, 204–15, 216; world as
 corrupt as mob in, 147
Sorrentino, Paolo, 370–71
Sorvino, Mira, 254
Sorvino, Paul, 201, 364
Spatafore, Vito (char.), 163, 229–30,
 233
Spielberg, Steven, 6, 298
Stanley, Alessandra, 349
Steiger, Rod, 73
Stella, Frank, 373

St. John, Nicholas, 197
St. Joseph's Day, 265–66
stock market scams, 143, 163
Stockwell, Dean, 197
Stompanato, Johnny, 94
Stonewall Inn, 222
Stonewall riot, 222, 227
strip clubs, 163
Studio Dante, 388–89
St. Valentine's Day Massacre, 73, 77,
 346
Sud Side Stori, 369–70
Summa, Joey, 377–78
Summer of Sam, 253–57, 347, 391
Sundance Film Festival, 88
syndicalism, 24

Talese, Gay, 7, 38, 50, 55, 68–69, 75,
 346, 361, 373, 374, 375, 376,
 377
Tamburri, Anthony Julian, 376, 388
Tano da Morire, 369–70
Tarantino, Quentin, 275
Task Force on Organized Crime, 45, 57
taxes, 20, 40, 260
Teamsters, 356
television, news reporters on, 38
This Thing of Ours, 6, 355, 356–57, 372
Thorpe, Richard, 79, 80
Tonelli, Bill, 108–109, 118, 295, 328–
 31, 380, 403n30
Tonti's Social Club, 263
"Tony Soprano, the Media and Popular
 Culture" (Paglia), 304–305
Tormey, John, 241
Tornando a casa, 368–69
Torre, Roberta, 369–70
Torricelli, Robert, 38–39, 302
Torrio, Johnny, 71, 73
Tosches, Nick, 44, 222, 264
Traister, Rebecca, 210
Trapani, 218
Travolta, John, 220
Tresca, Carlo, 24, 199
Triebwasser, Joseph, 227